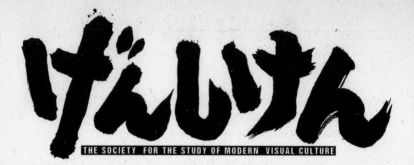

THE SOCIETY FOR THE STUDY OF MODERN VISUAL CULTURE

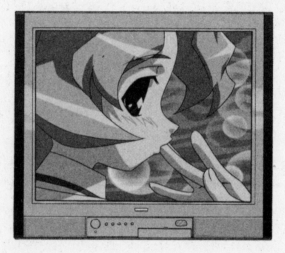

KIO SHIMOKU

Contents

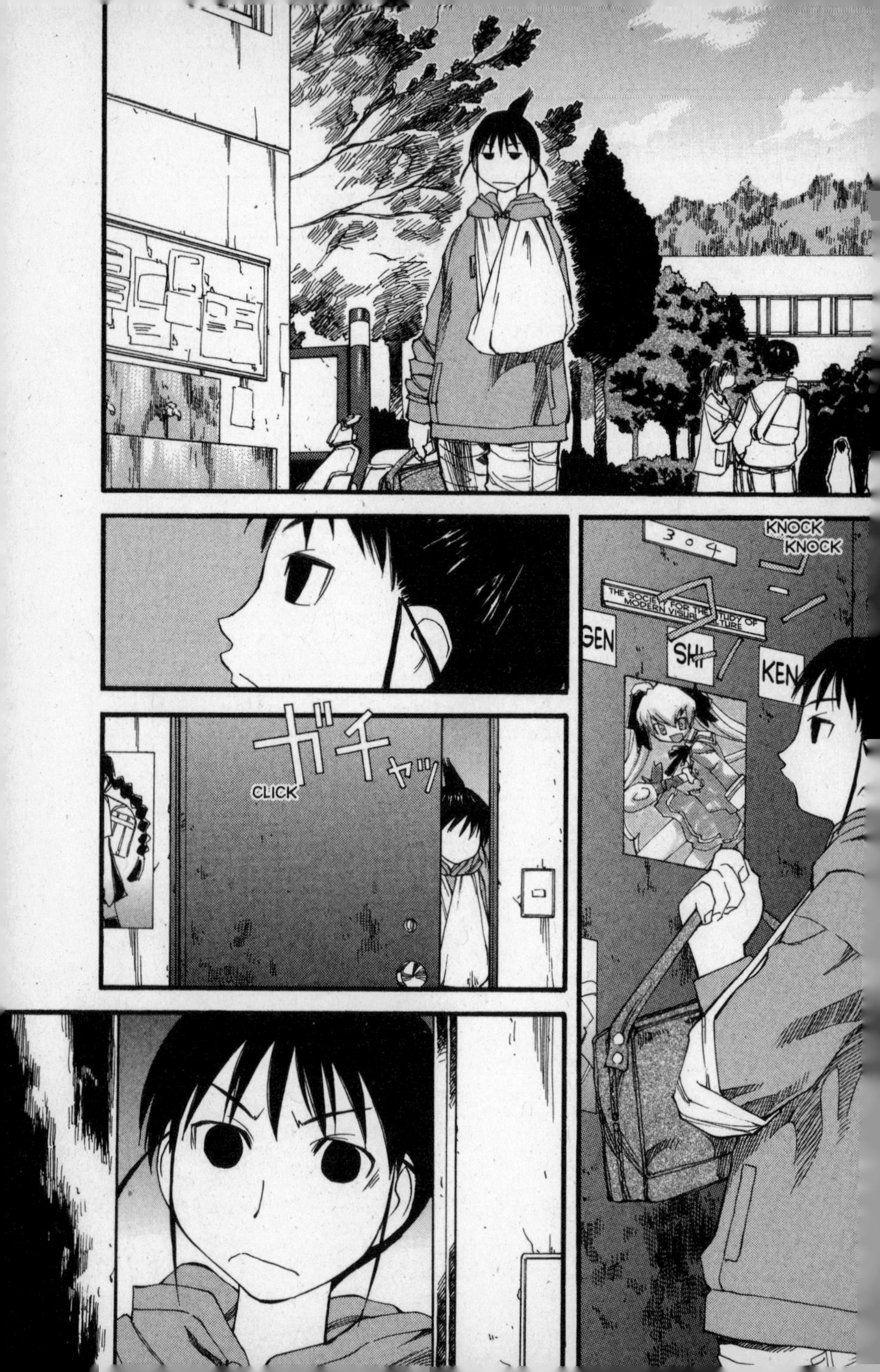
KNOCK KNOCK
304
THE SOCIETY FOR THE STUDY OF MODERN VISUAL CULTURE
GEN
SHI
KEN
ガチャッ
CLICK

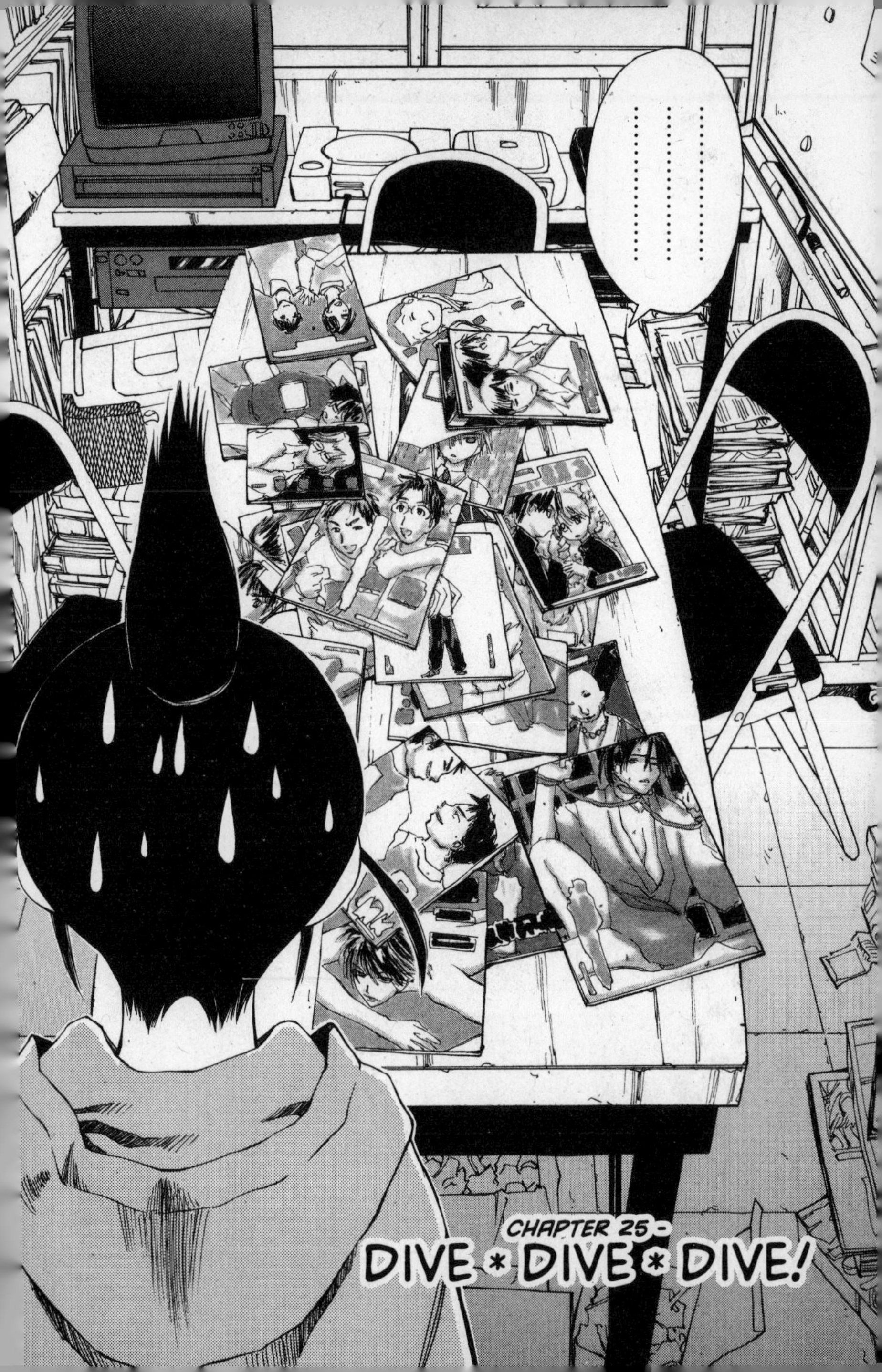
......
......
......
CHAPTER 25 -
DIVE * DIVE * DIVE!

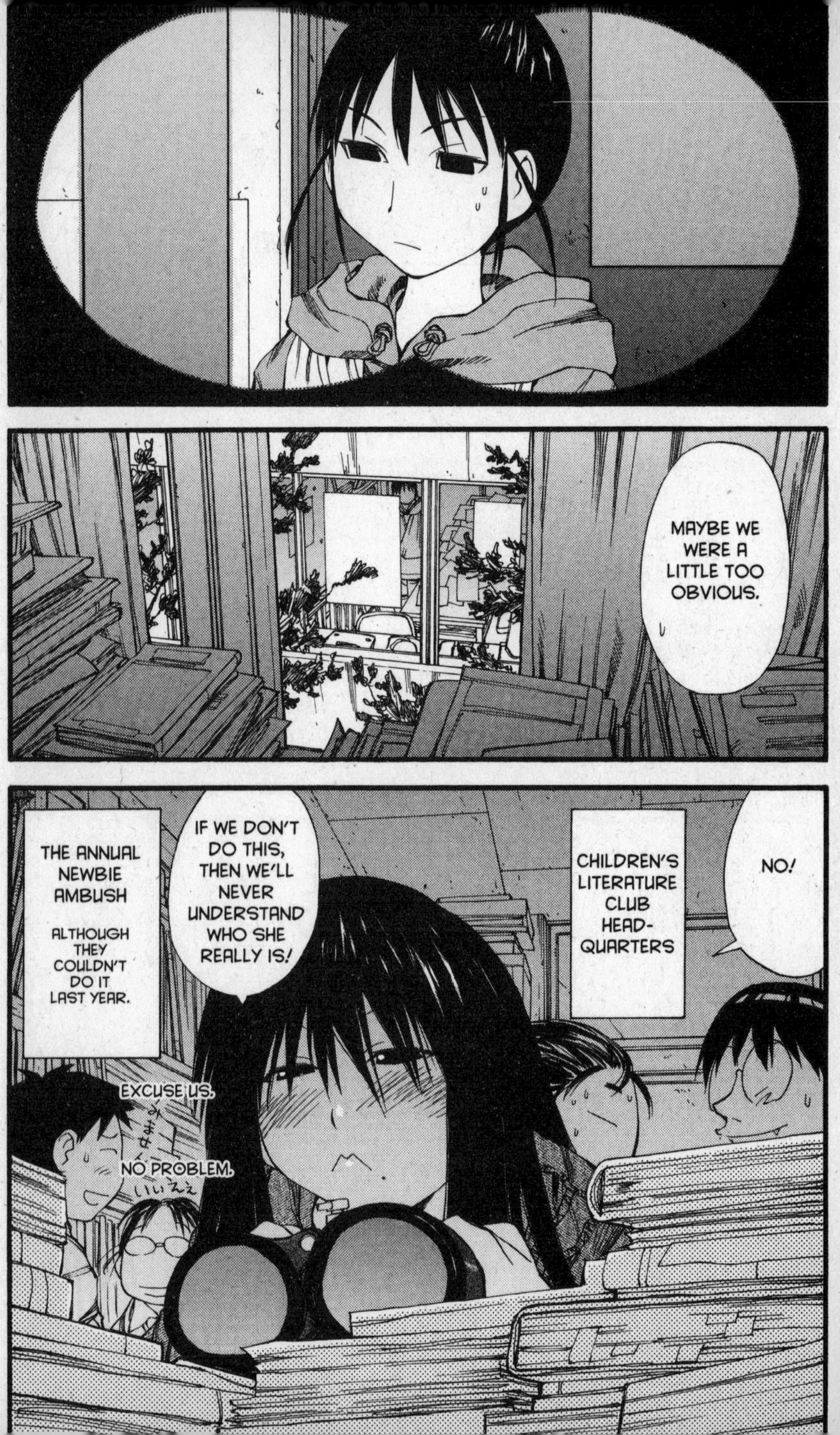

MAYBE WE WERE A LITTLE TOO OBVIOUS.
NO!
CHILDREN'S LITERATURE CLUB HEAD-QUARTERS
IF WE DON'T DO THIS, THEN WE'LL NEVER UNDERSTAND WHO SHE REALLY IS!
THE ANNUAL NEWBIE AMBUSH
ALTHOUGH THEY COULDN'T DO IT LAST YEAR.
EXCUSE US.
NO PROBLEM.

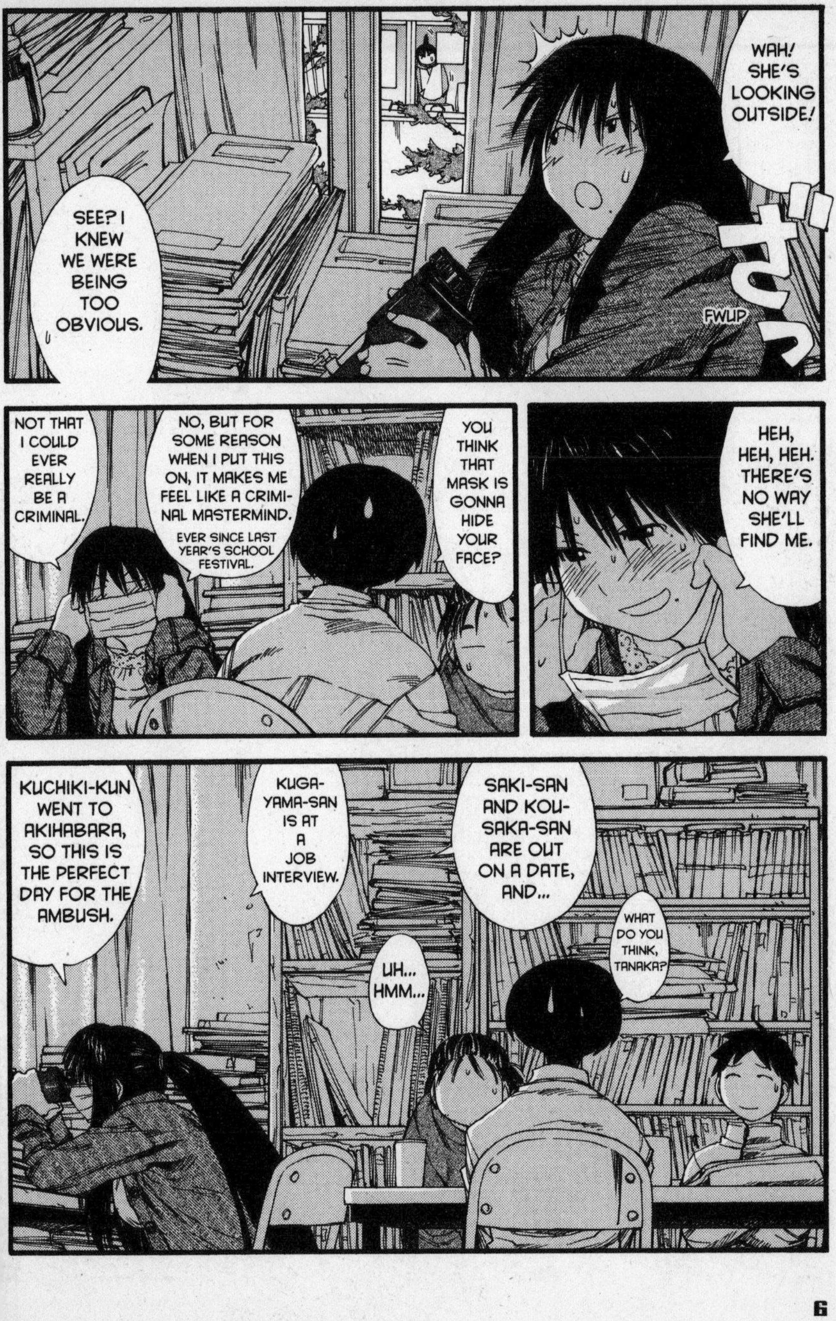
WAH! SHE'S LOOKING OUTSIDE!
ざっ
FWUP
SEE? I KNEW WE WERE BEING TOO OBVIOUS.
HEH, HEH, HEH. THERE'S NO WAY SHE'LL FIND ME.
YOU THINK THAT MASK IS GONNA HIDE YOUR FACE?
NO, BUT FOR SOME REASON WHEN I PUT THIS ON, IT MAKES ME FEEL LIKE A CRIMINAL MASTERMIND.
EVER SINCE LAST YEAR'S SCHOOL FESTIVAL.
NOT THAT I COULD EVER REALLY BE A CRIMINAL.
SAKI-SAN AND KOUSAKA-SAN ARE OUT ON A DATE, AND...
KUGAYAMA-SAN IS AT A JOB INTERVIEW.
KUCHIKI-KUN WENT TO AKIHABARA, SO THIS IS THE PERFECT DAY FOR THE AMBUSH.
WHAT DO YOU THINK, TANAKA?
UH... HMM...

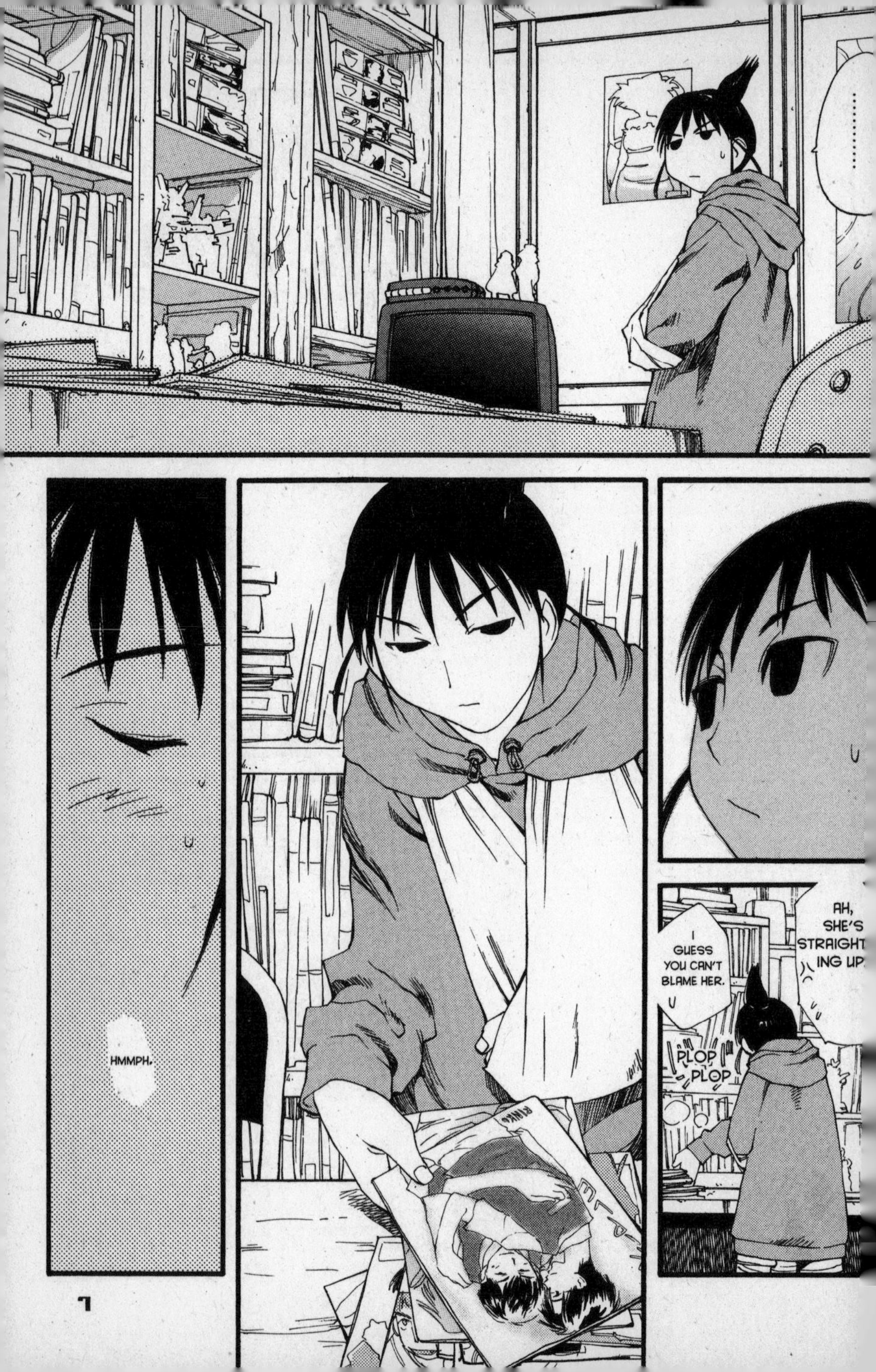
......
AH, SHE'S STRAIGHTENING UP.
I GUESS YOU CAN'T BLAME HER.
PLOP PLOP
HMMPH.

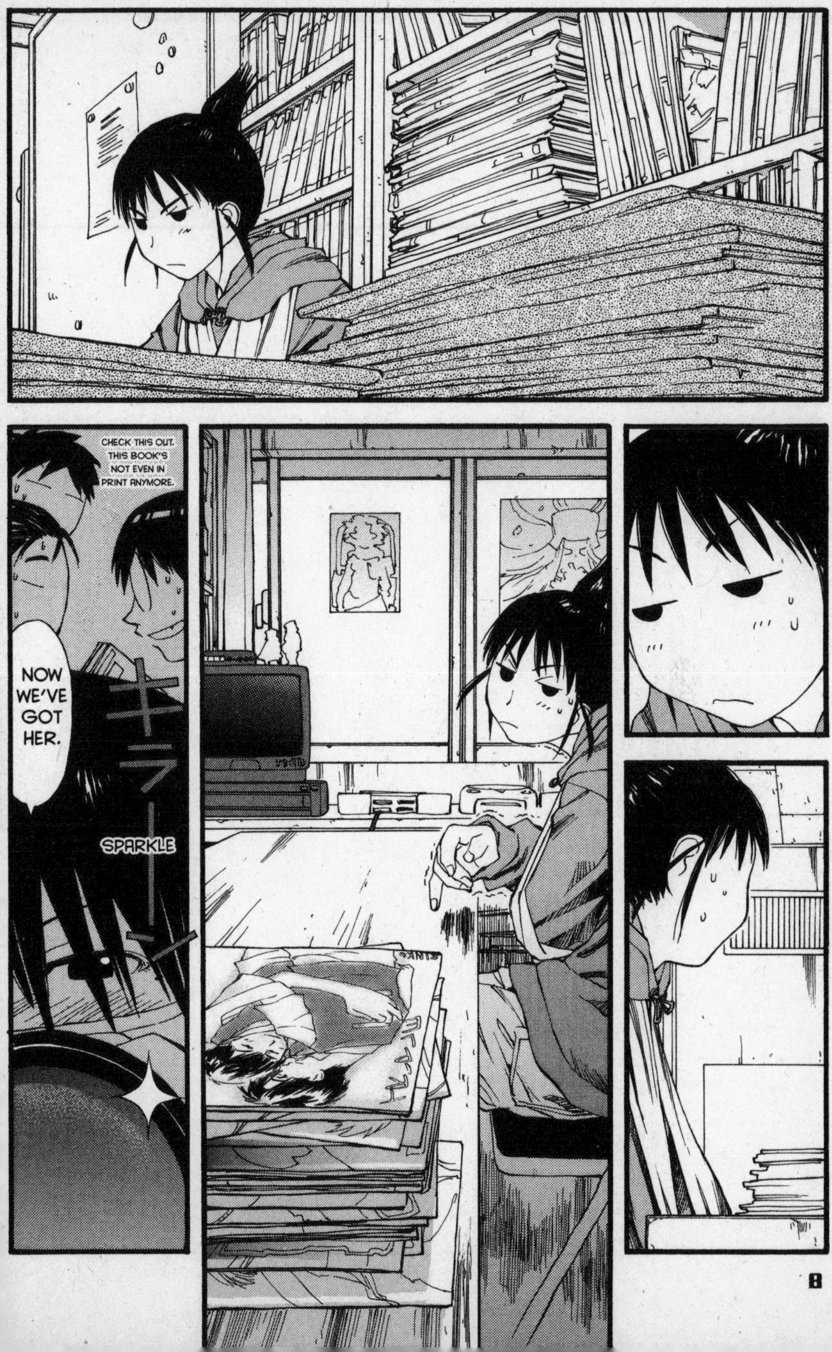
CHECK THIS OUT. THIS BOOK'S NOT EVEN IN PRINT ANYMORE.
NOW WE'VE GOT HER.
SPARKLE

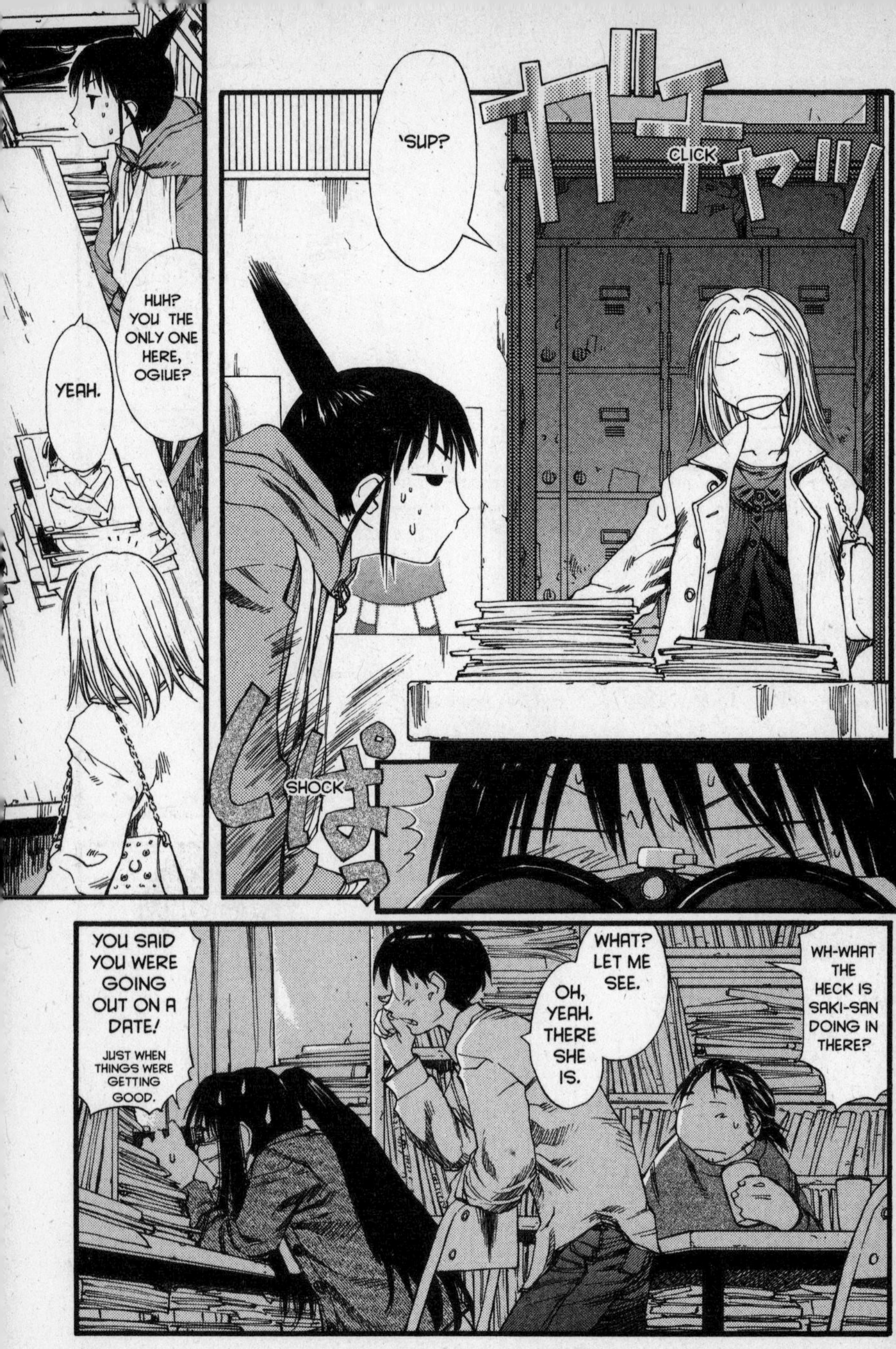
CLICK
'SUP?
SHOCK
HUH? YOU THE ONLY ONE HERE, OGIUE?
YEAH.
WH-WHAT THE HECK IS SAKI-SAN DOING IN THERE?
WHAT? LET ME SEE.
OH, YEAH. THERE SHE IS.
YOU SAID YOU WERE GOING OUT ON A DATE!
JUST WHEN THINGS WERE GETTING GOOD.

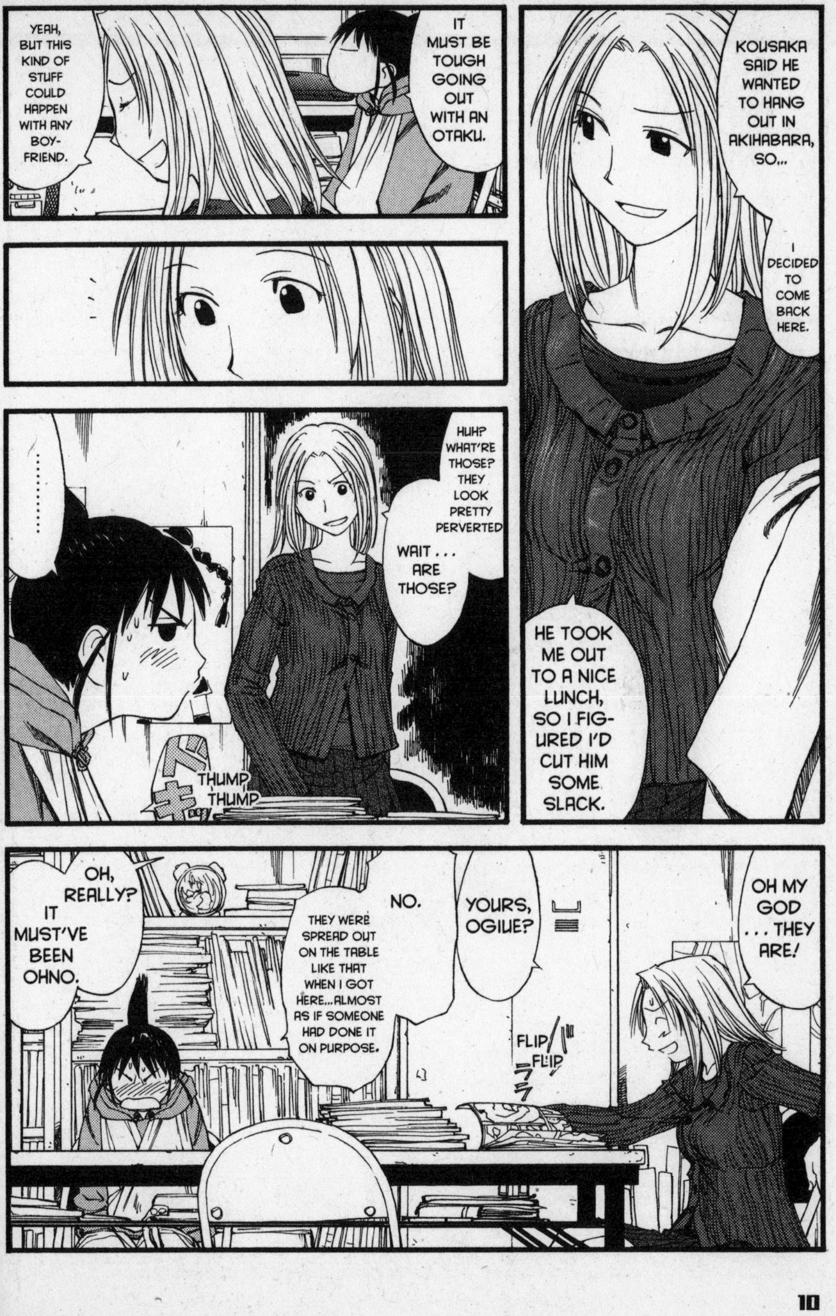
KOUSAKA SAID HE WANTED TO HANG OUT IN AKIHABARA, SO...
I DECIDED TO COME BACK HERE.
HE TOOK ME OUT TO A NICE LUNCH, SO I FIG-URED I'D CUT HIM SOME SLACK.
IT MUST BE TOUGH GOING OUT WITH AN OTAKU.
YEAH, BUT THIS KIND OF STUFF COULD HAPPEN WITH ANY BOY-FRIEND.
HUH? WHAT'RE THOSE? THEY LOOK PRETTY PERVERTED
WAIT . . . ARE THOSE?
....
THUMP THUMP
OH MY GOD . . . THEY ARE!
FLIP FLIP
YOURS, OGIUE?
NO.
THEY WERE SPREAD OUT ON THE TABLE LIKE THAT WHEN I GOT HERE...ALMOST AS IF SOMEONE HAD DONE IT ON PURPOSE.
OH, REALLY? IT MUST'VE BEEN OHNO.

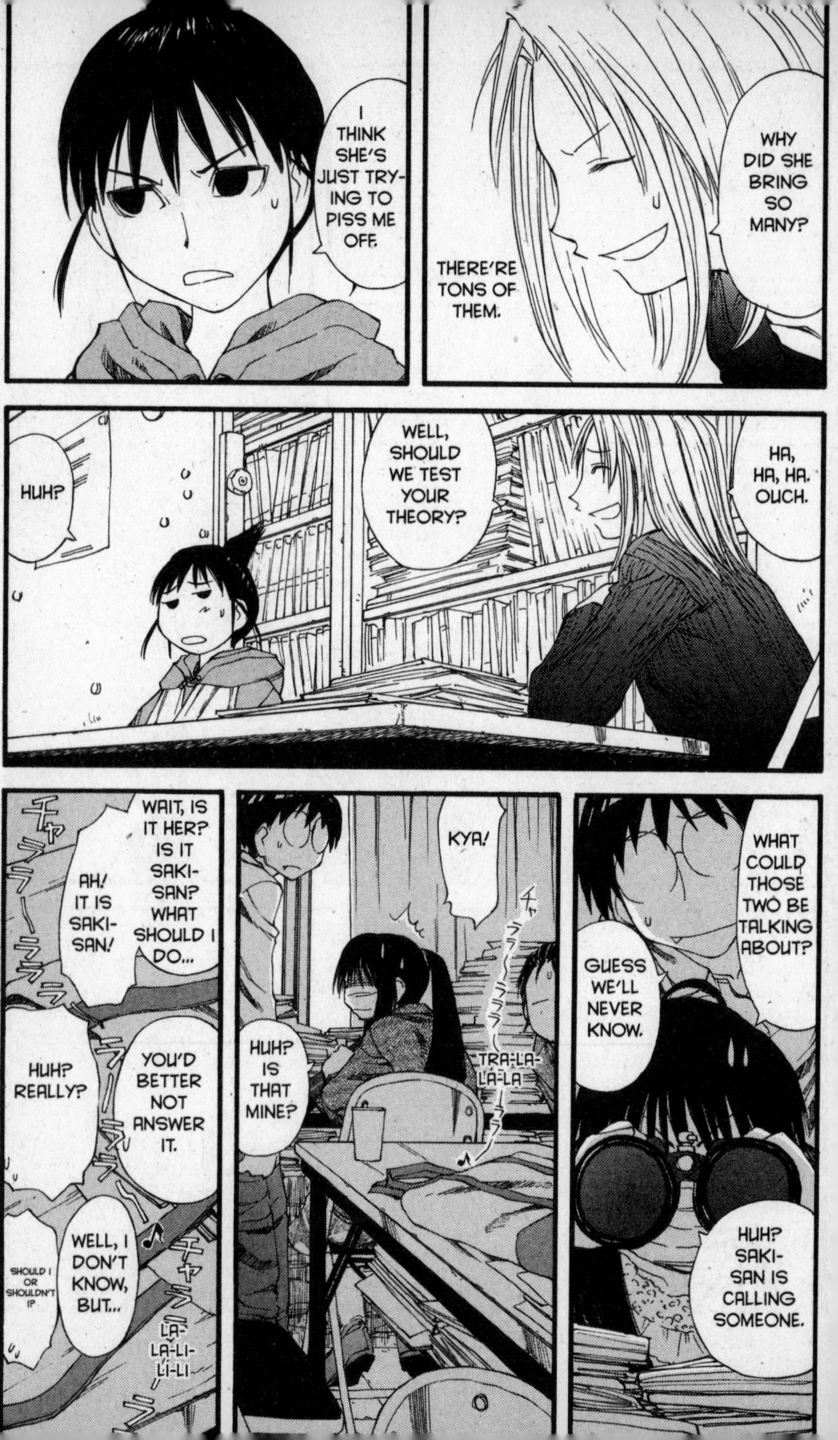
WHY DID SHE BRING SO MANY?
THERE'RE TONS OF THEM.
I THINK SHE'S JUST TRYING TO PISS ME OFF.
HA, HA, HA. OUCH.
WELL, SHOULD WE TEST YOUR THEORY?
HUH?
WHAT COULD THOSE TWO BE TALKING ABOUT?
GUESS WE'LL NEVER KNOW.
HUH? SAKI-SAN IS CALLING SOMEONE.
KYA!
TRA-LA-LA-LA
HUH? IS THAT MINE?
WAIT, IS IT HER? IS IT SAKI-SAN? WHAT SHOULD I DO...
AH! IT IS SAKI-SAN!
YOU'D BETTER NOT ANSWER IT.
HUH? REALLY?
WELL, I DON'T KNOW, BUT...
SHOULD I OR SHOULDN'T I?
LA-LA-LI-LI-LI

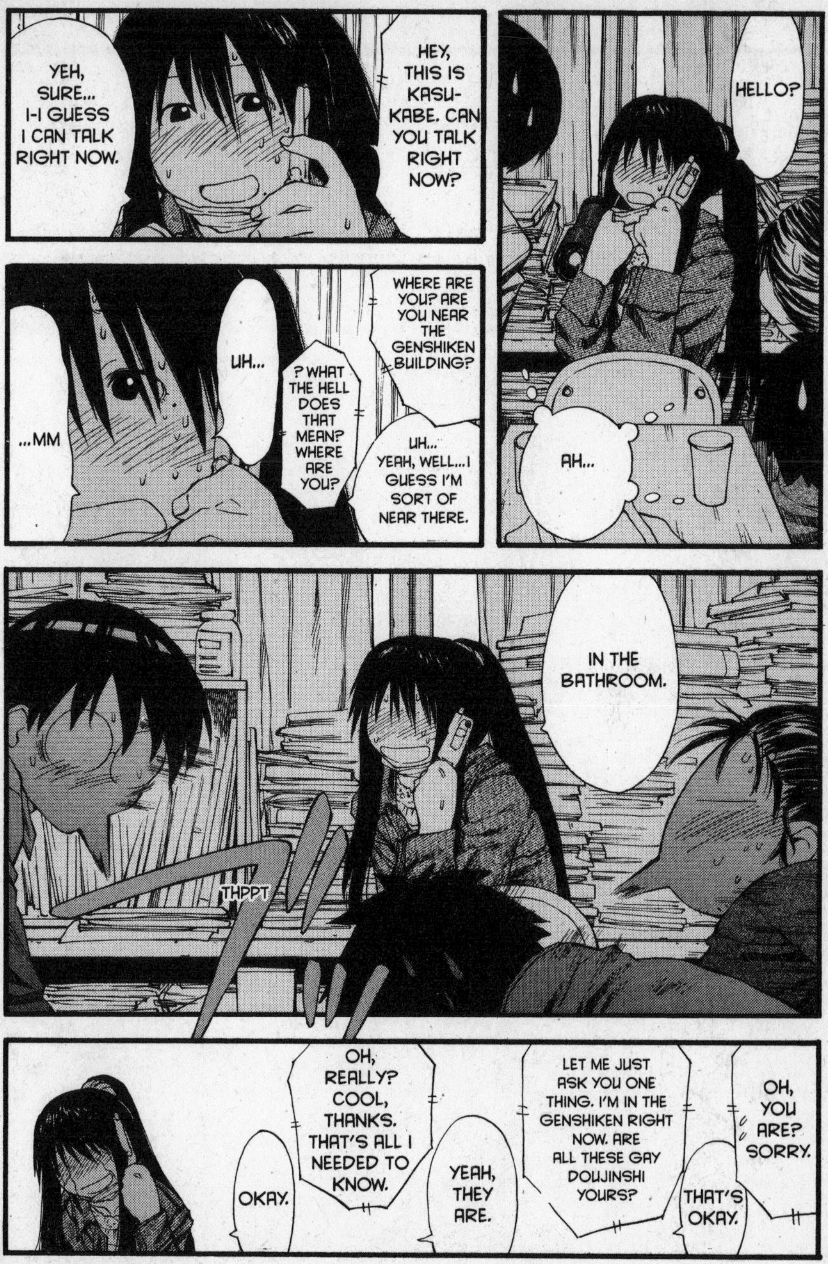
HELLO?
AH...
HEY, THIS IS KASU-KABE. CAN YOU TALK RIGHT NOW?
YEH, SURE... I-I GUESS I CAN TALK RIGHT NOW.
WHERE ARE YOU? ARE YOU NEAR THE GENSHIKEN BUILDING?
UH... YEAH, WELL...I GUESS I'M SORT OF NEAR THERE.
? WHAT THE HELL DOES THAT MEAN? WHERE ARE YOU?
UH...
...MM
IN THE BATHROOM.
THPPT
OH, YOU ARE? SORRY.
THAT'S OKAY.
LET ME JUST ASK YOU ONE THING. I'M IN THE GENSHIKEN RIGHT NOW. ARE ALL THESE GAY DOUJINSHI YOURS?
YEAH, THEY ARE.
OH, REALLY? COOL, THANKS. THAT'S ALL I NEEDED TO KNOW.
OKAY.

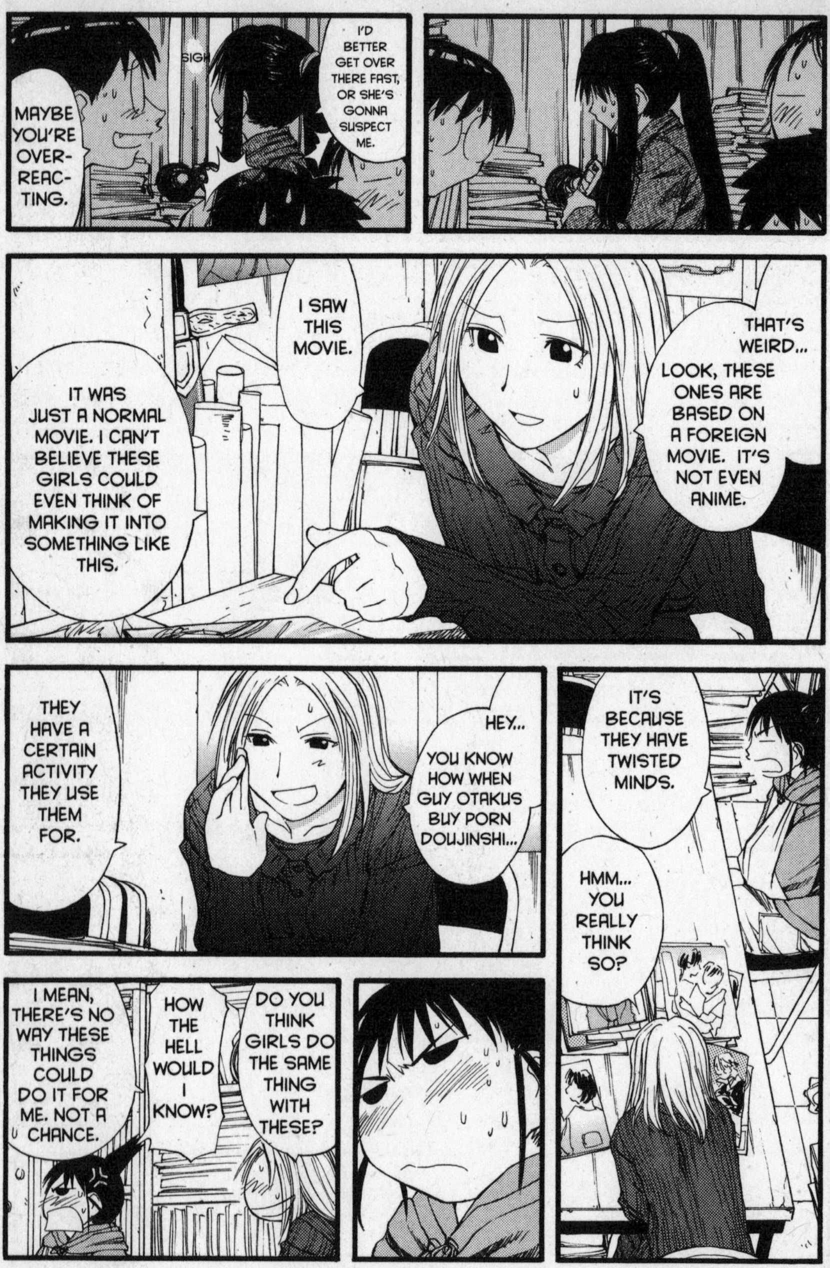

I'D BETTER GET OVER THERE FAST, OR SHE'S GONNA SUSPECT ME.
SIGH
MAYBE YOU'RE OVER-REACTING.
THAT'S WEIRD...
LOOK, THESE ONES ARE BASED ON A FOREIGN MOVIE. IT'S NOT EVEN ANIME.
I SAW THIS MOVIE.
IT WAS JUST A NORMAL MOVIE. I CAN'T BELIEVE THESE GIRLS COULD EVEN THINK OF MAKING IT INTO SOMETHING LIKE THIS.
IT'S BECAUSE THEY HAVE TWISTED MINDS.
HMM... YOU REALLY THINK SO?
HEY...
YOU KNOW HOW WHEN GUY OTAKUS BUY PORN DOUJINSHI...
THEY HAVE A CERTAIN ACTIVITY THEY USE THEM FOR.
DO YOU THINK GIRLS DO THE SAME THING WITH THESE?
HOW THE HELL WOULD I KNOW?
I MEAN, THERE'S NO WAY THESE THINGS COULD DO IT FOR ME. NOT A CHANCE.

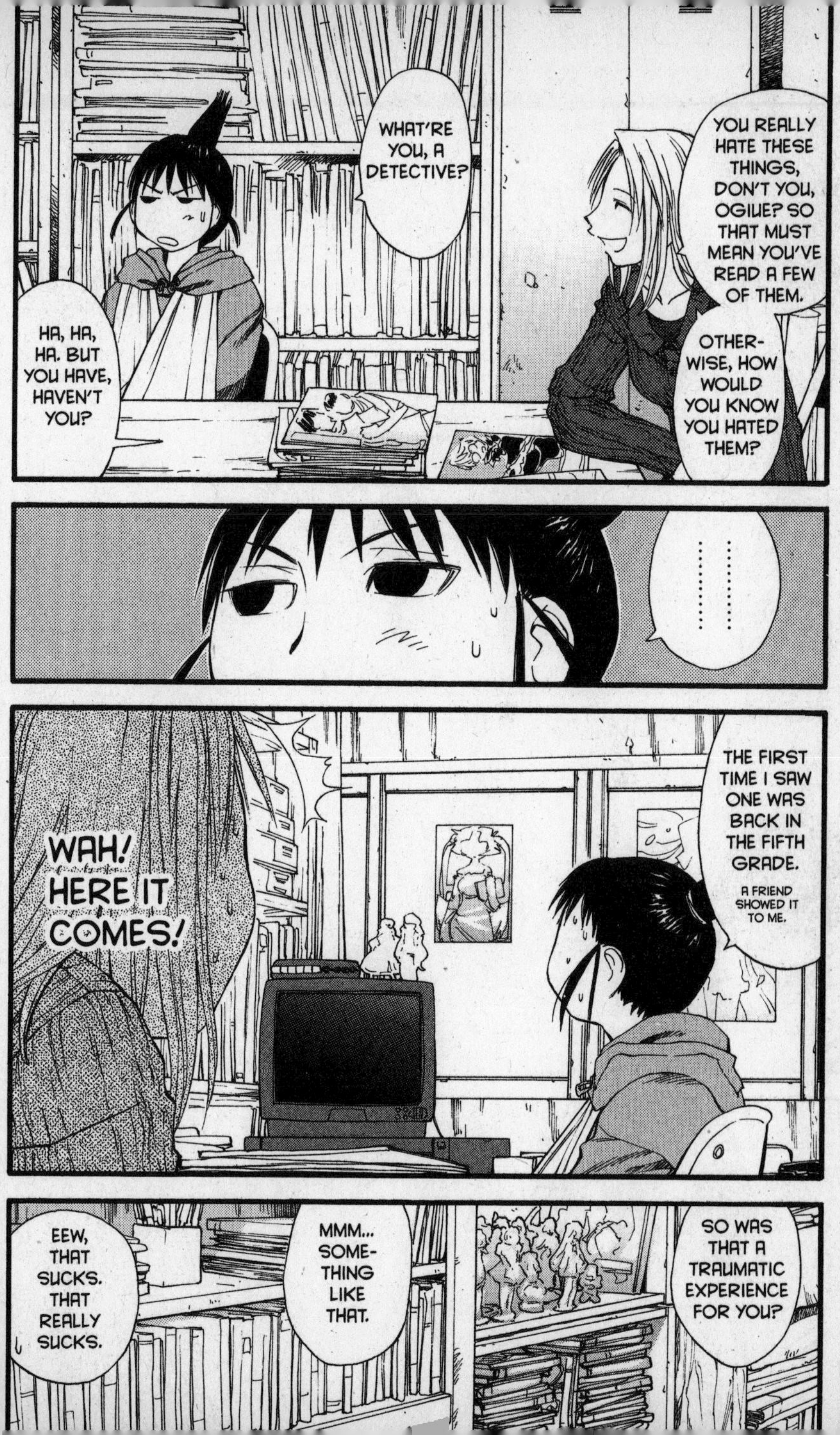
YOU REALLY HATE THESE THINGS, DON'T YOU, OGIUE? SO THAT MUST MEAN YOU'VE READ A FEW OF THEM.
OTHER-WISE, HOW WOULD YOU KNOW YOU HATED THEM?
WHAT'RE YOU, A DETECTIVE?
HA, HA, HA. BUT YOU HAVE, HAVEN'T YOU?
......
THE FIRST TIME I SAW ONE WAS BACK IN THE FIFTH GRADE.
A FRIEND SHOWED IT TO ME.
WAH! HERE IT COMES!
SO WAS THAT A TRAUMATIC EXPERIENCE FOR YOU?
MMM... SOME-THING LIKE THAT.
EEW, THAT SUCKS. THAT REALLY SUCKS.

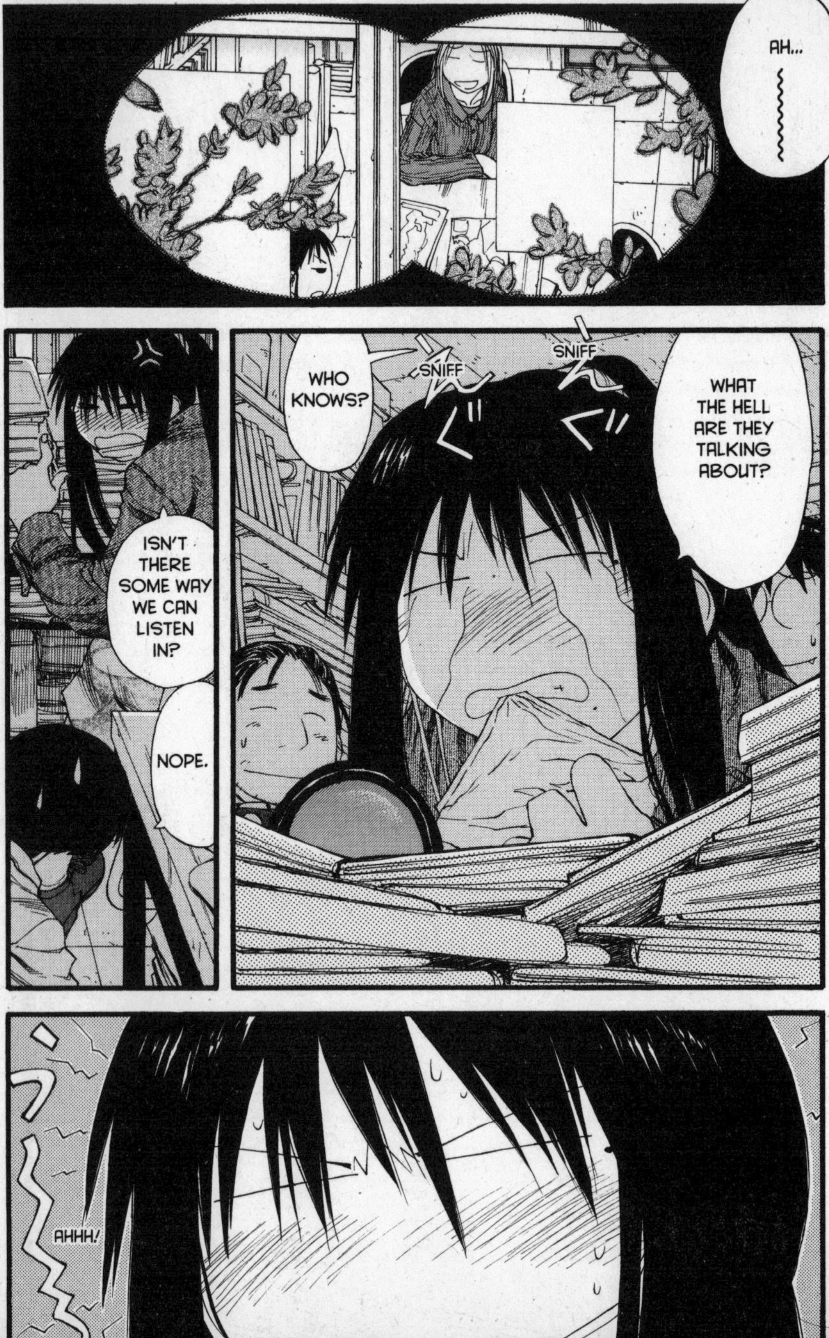
AH...
WHAT THE HELL ARE THEY TALKING ABOUT?
SNIFF
SNIFF
WHO KNOWS?
ISN'T THERE SOME WAY WE CAN LISTEN IN?
NOPE.
AHHH!

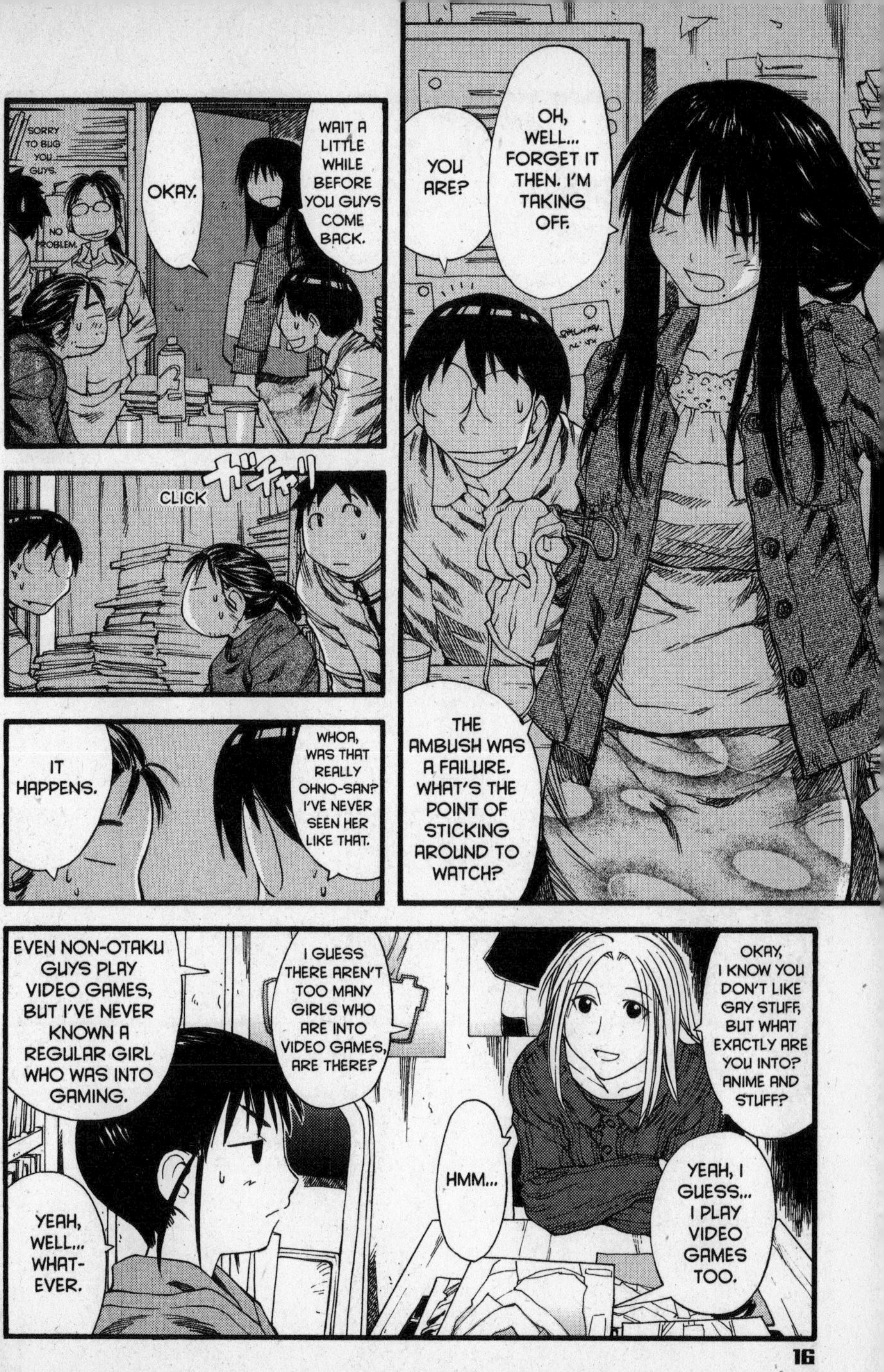
OH, WELL... FORGET IT THEN. I'M TAKING OFF.
YOU ARE?
THE AMBUSH WAS A FAILURE. WHAT'S THE POINT OF STICKING AROUND TO WATCH?
WAIT A LITTLE WHILE BEFORE YOU GUYS COME BACK.
OKAY.
SORRY TO BUG YOU GUYS.
NO PROBLEM.
ガチャリ
CLICK
WHOA, WAS THAT REALLY OHNO-SAN? I'VE NEVER SEEN HER LIKE THAT.
IT HAPPENS.
OKAY, I KNOW YOU DON'T LIKE GAY STUFF, BUT WHAT EXACTLY ARE YOU INTO? ANIME AND STUFF?
I GUESS THERE AREN'T TOO MANY GIRLS WHO ARE INTO VIDEO GAMES, ARE THERE?
EVEN NON-OTAKU GUYS PLAY VIDEO GAMES, BUT I'VE NEVER KNOWN A REGULAR GIRL WHO WAS INTO GAMING.
YEAH, I GUESS... I PLAY VIDEO GAMES TOO.
HMM...
YEAH, WELL... WHAT-EVER.

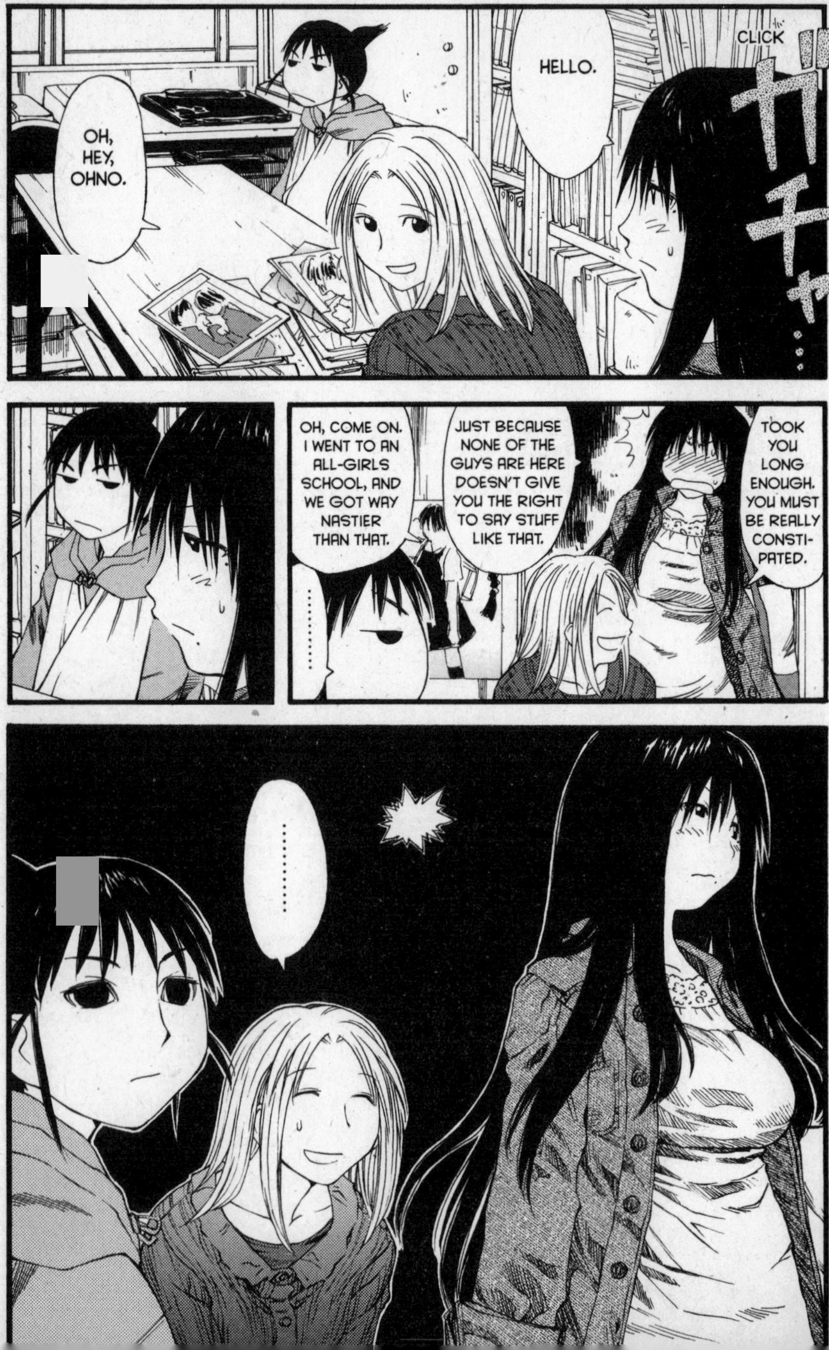
CLICK
ガチャ...
HELLO.
OH, HEY, OHNO.
TOOK YOU LONG ENOUGH. YOU MUST BE REALLY CONSTIPATED.
JUST BECAUSE NONE OF THE GUYS ARE HERE DOESN'T GIVE YOU THE RIGHT TO SAY STUFF LIKE THAT.
OH, COME ON. I WENT TO AN ALL-GIRLS SCHOOL, AND WE GOT WAY NASTIER THAN THAT.
......
......

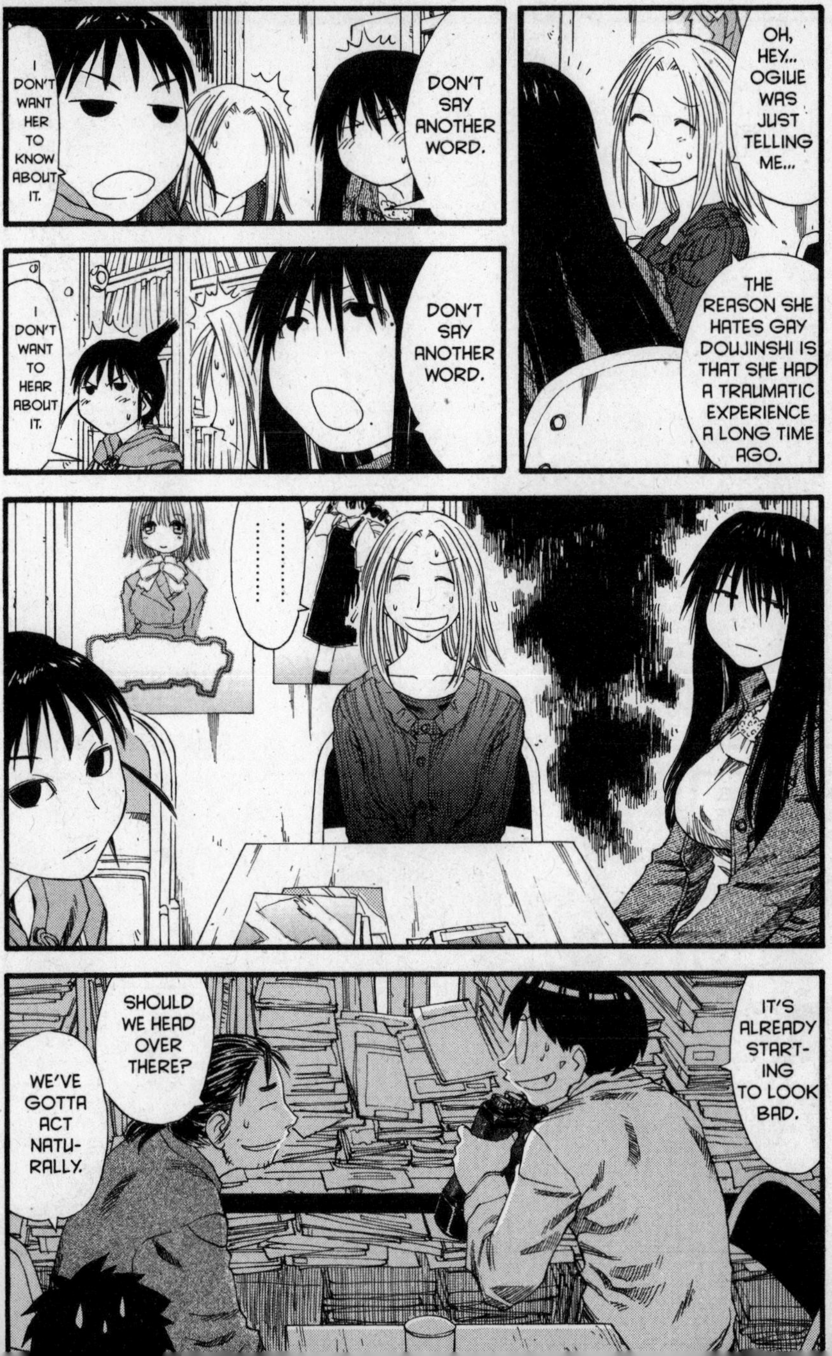
OH, HEY... OGIUE WAS JUST TELLING ME...
THE REASON SHE HATES GAY DOUJINSHI IS THAT SHE HAD A TRAUMATIC EXPERIENCE A LONG TIME AGO.
DON'T SAY ANOTHER WORD.
I DON'T WANT HER TO KNOW ABOUT IT.
DON'T SAY ANOTHER WORD.
I DON'T WANT TO HEAR ABOUT IT.
......
IT'S ALREADY START-ING TO LOOK BAD.
SHOULD WE HEAD OVER THERE?
WE'VE GOTTA ACT NATU-RALLY.

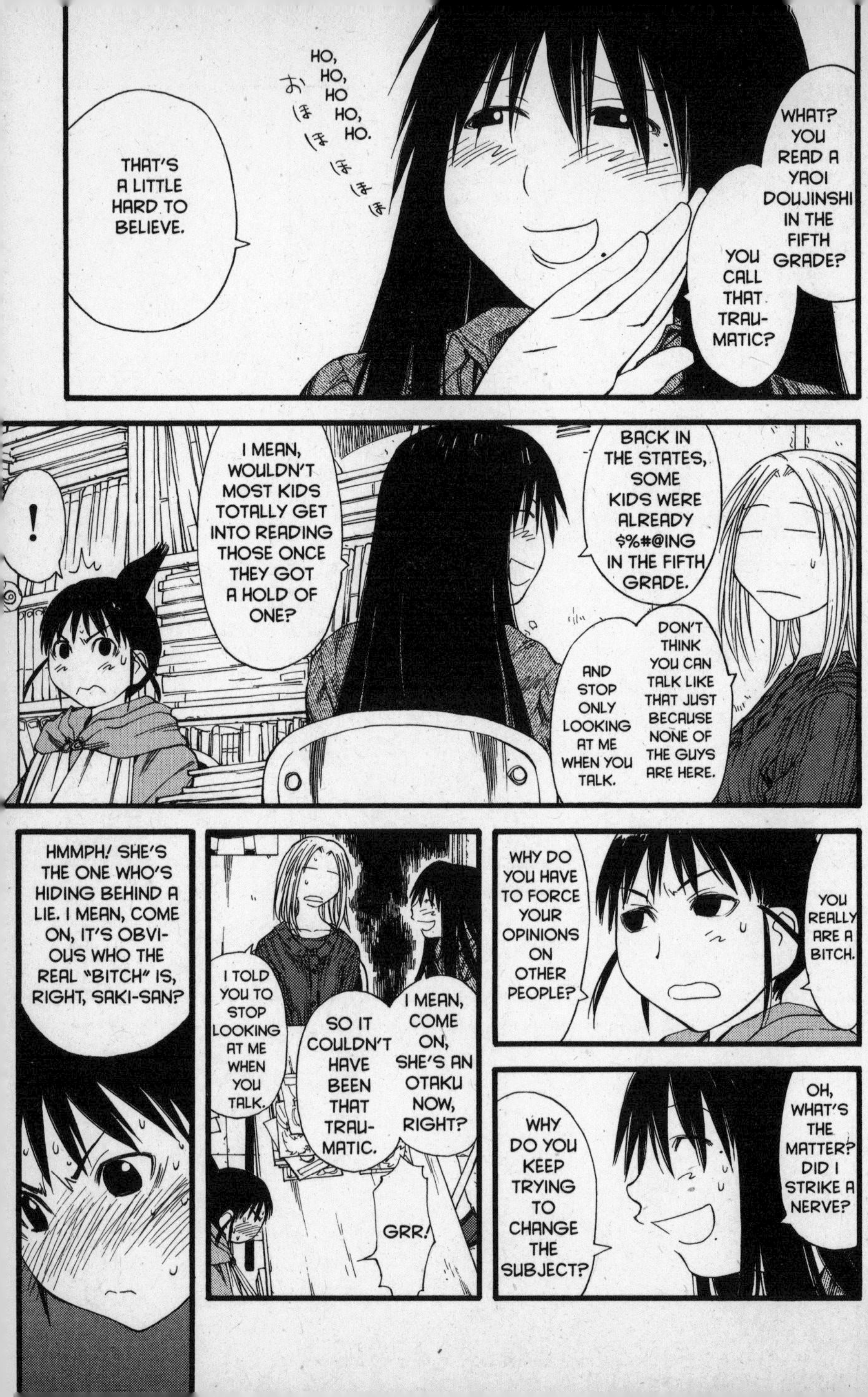
WHAT? YOU READ A YAOI DOUJINSHI IN THE FIFTH GRADE?
YOU CALL THAT TRAU-MATIC?
HO, HO, HO HO, HO.
おほほほほほ
THAT'S A LITTLE HARD TO BELIEVE.
BACK IN THE STATES, SOME KIDS WERE ALREADY $%#@ING IN THE FIFTH GRADE.
DON'T THINK YOU CAN TALK LIKE THAT JUST BECAUSE NONE OF THE GUYS ARE HERE.
AND STOP ONLY LOOKING AT ME WHEN YOU TALK.
I MEAN, WOULDN'T MOST KIDS TOTALLY GET INTO READING THOSE ONCE THEY GOT A HOLD OF ONE?
!
YOU REALLY ARE A BITCH.
WHY DO YOU HAVE TO FORCE YOUR OPINIONS ON OTHER PEOPLE?
OH, WHAT'S THE MATTER? DID I STRIKE A NERVE?
WHY DO YOU KEEP TRYING TO CHANGE THE SUBJECT?
I MEAN, COME ON, SHE'S AN OTAKU NOW, RIGHT?
SO IT COULDN'T HAVE BEEN THAT TRAU-MATIC.
I TOLD YOU TO STOP LOOKING AT ME WHEN YOU TALK.
GRR!
HMMPH! SHE'S THE ONE WHO'S HIDING BEHIND A LIE. I MEAN, COME ON, IT'S OBVIOUS WHO THE REAL "BITCH" IS, RIGHT, SAKI-SAN?

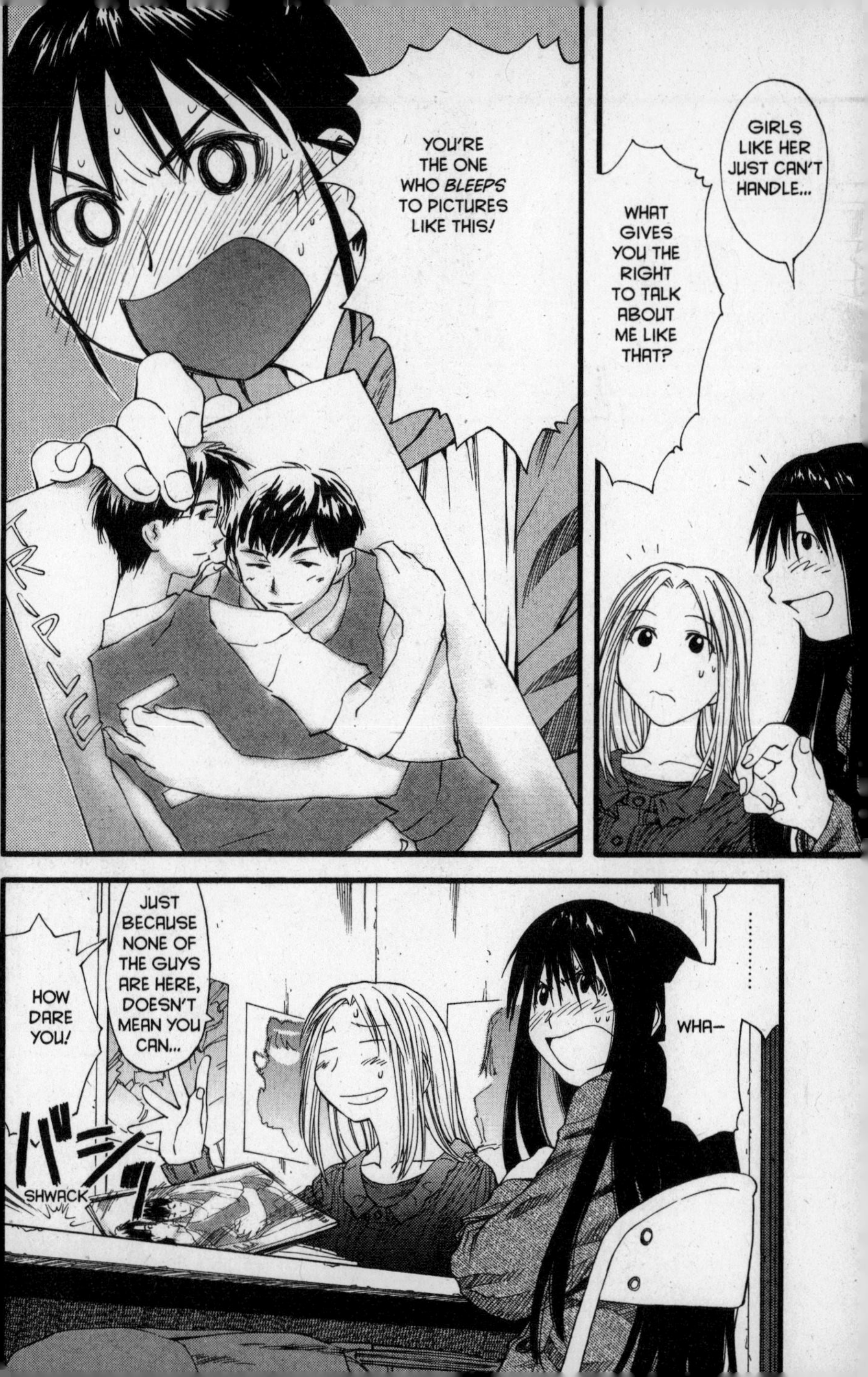
GIRLS LIKE HER JUST CAN'T HANDLE...
WHAT GIVES YOU THE RIGHT TO TALK ABOUT ME LIKE THAT?
YOU'RE THE ONE WHO *BLEEPS* TO PICTURES LIKE THIS!
TRI-PLE
......
WHA-
JUST BECAUSE NONE OF THE GUYS ARE HERE, DOESN'T MEAN YOU CAN...
HOW DARE YOU!
SHWACK

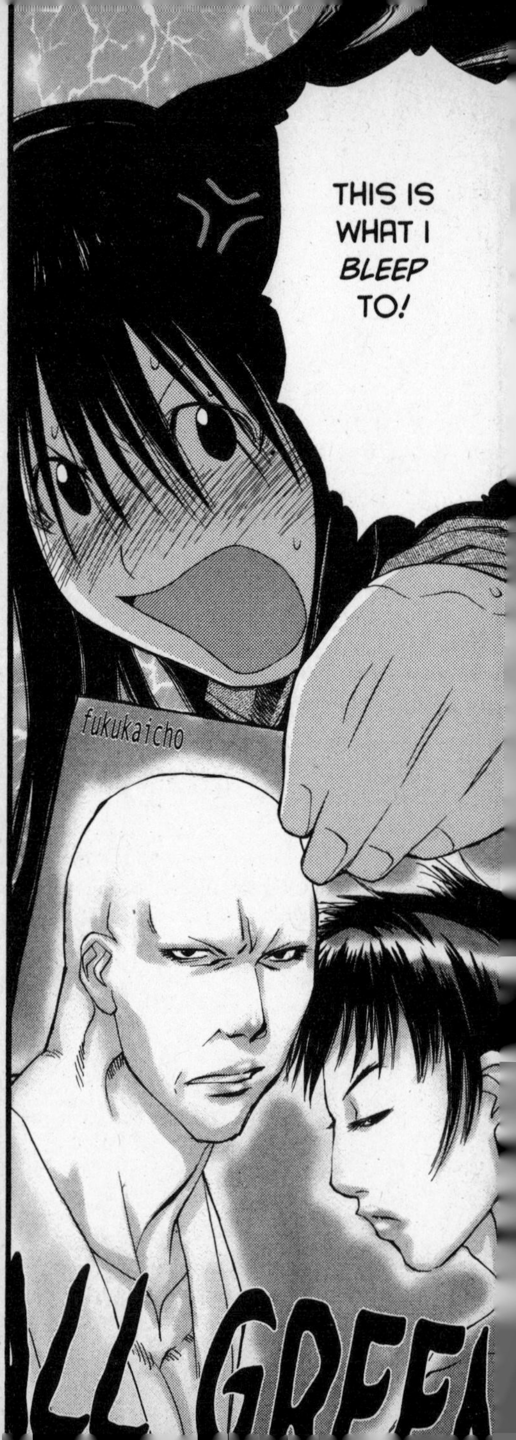
THIS IS WHAT I *BLEEP* TO!
fukukaicho
LL GREE

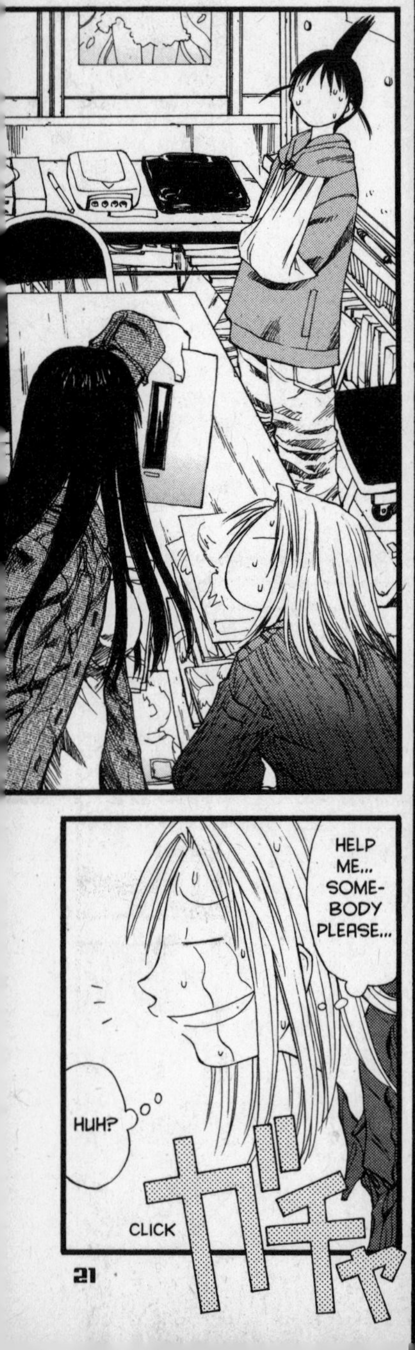
HELP ME... SOME-BODY PLEASE...
HUH?
CLICK
ガチャ

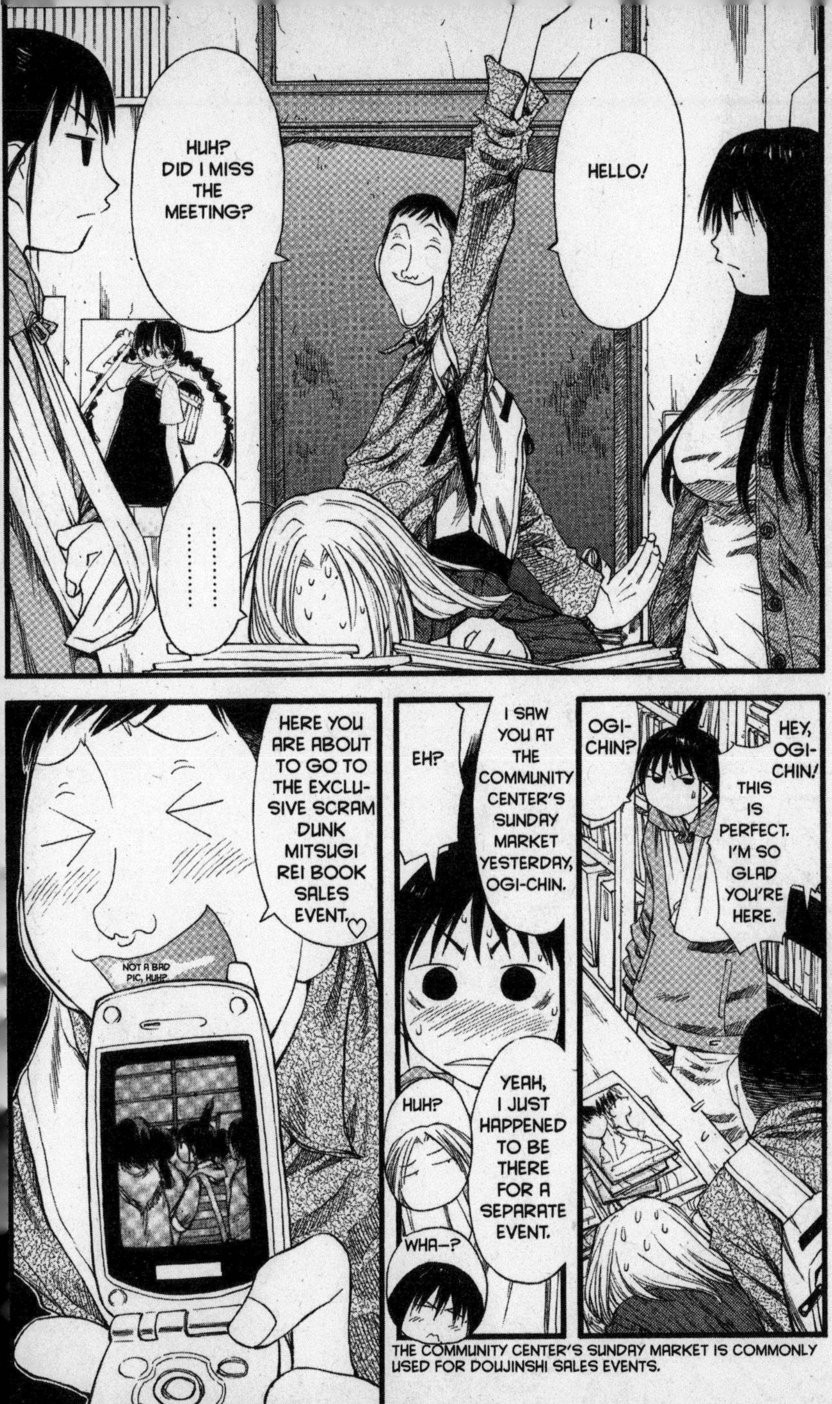
HELLO!
HUH? DID I MISS THE MEETING?
......
HEY, OGI-CHIN! THIS IS PERFECT. I'M SO GLAD YOU'RE HERE.
OGI-CHIN?
I SAW YOU AT THE COMMUNITY CENTER'S SUNDAY MARKET YESTERDAY, OGI-CHIN.
EH?
YEAH, I JUST HAPPENED TO BE THERE FOR A SEPARATE EVENT.
HUH?
WHA-?
HERE YOU ARE ABOUT TO GO TO THE EXCLUSIVE SCRAM DUNK MITSUGI REI BOOK SALES EVENT.♡
NOT A BAD PIC, HUH?

THE COMMUNITY CENTER'S SUNDAY MARKET IS COMMONLY USED FOR DOUJINSHI SALES EVENTS.

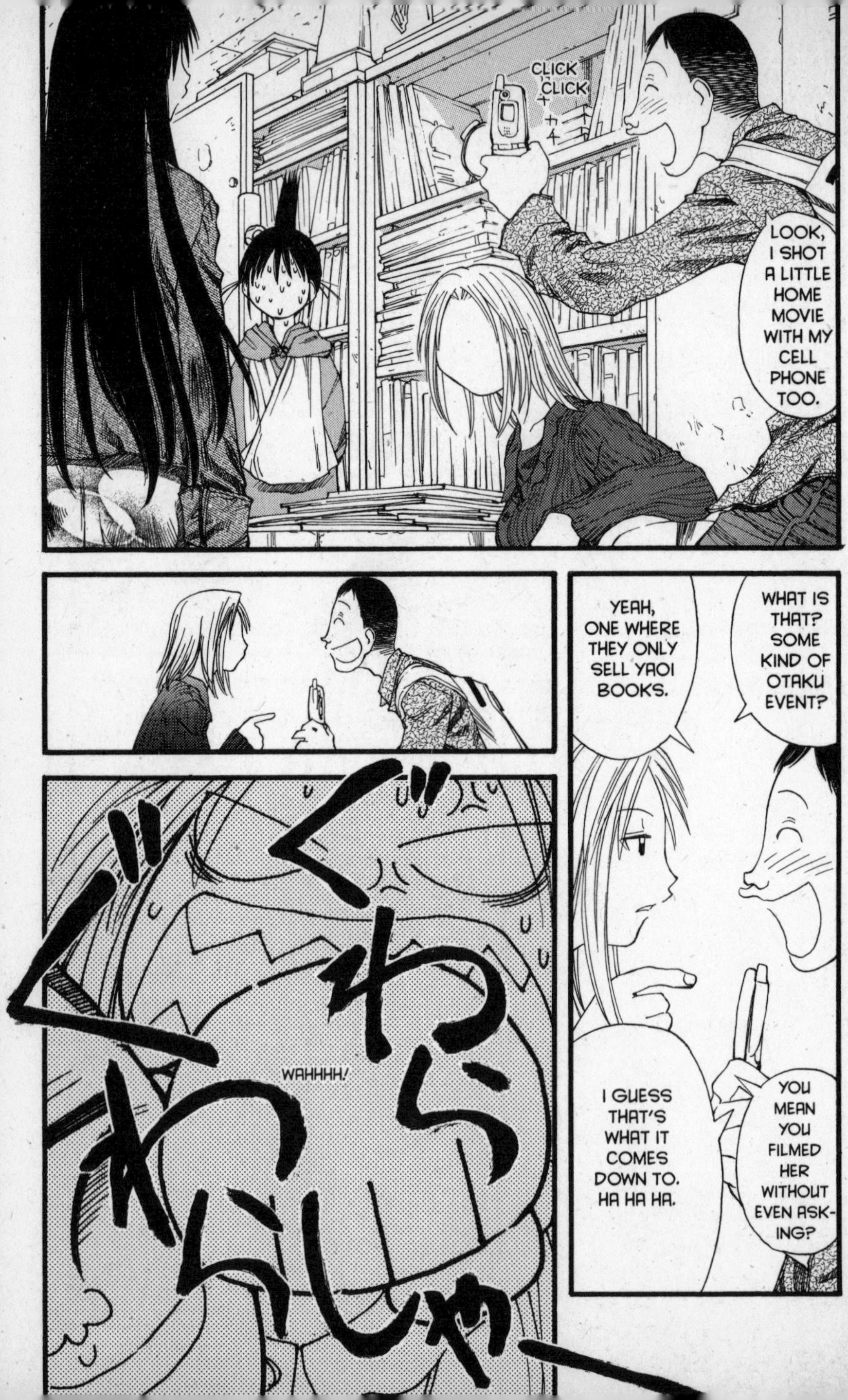
CLICK
CLICK
LOOK, I SHOT A LITTLE HOME MOVIE WITH MY CELL PHONE TOO.
WHAT IS THAT? SOME KIND OF OTAKU EVENT?
YEAH, ONE WHERE THEY ONLY SELL YAOI BOOKS.
YOU MEAN YOU FILMED HER WITHOUT EVEN ASKING?
I GUESS THAT'S WHAT IT COMES DOWN TO. HA HA HA.
WAHHHH!

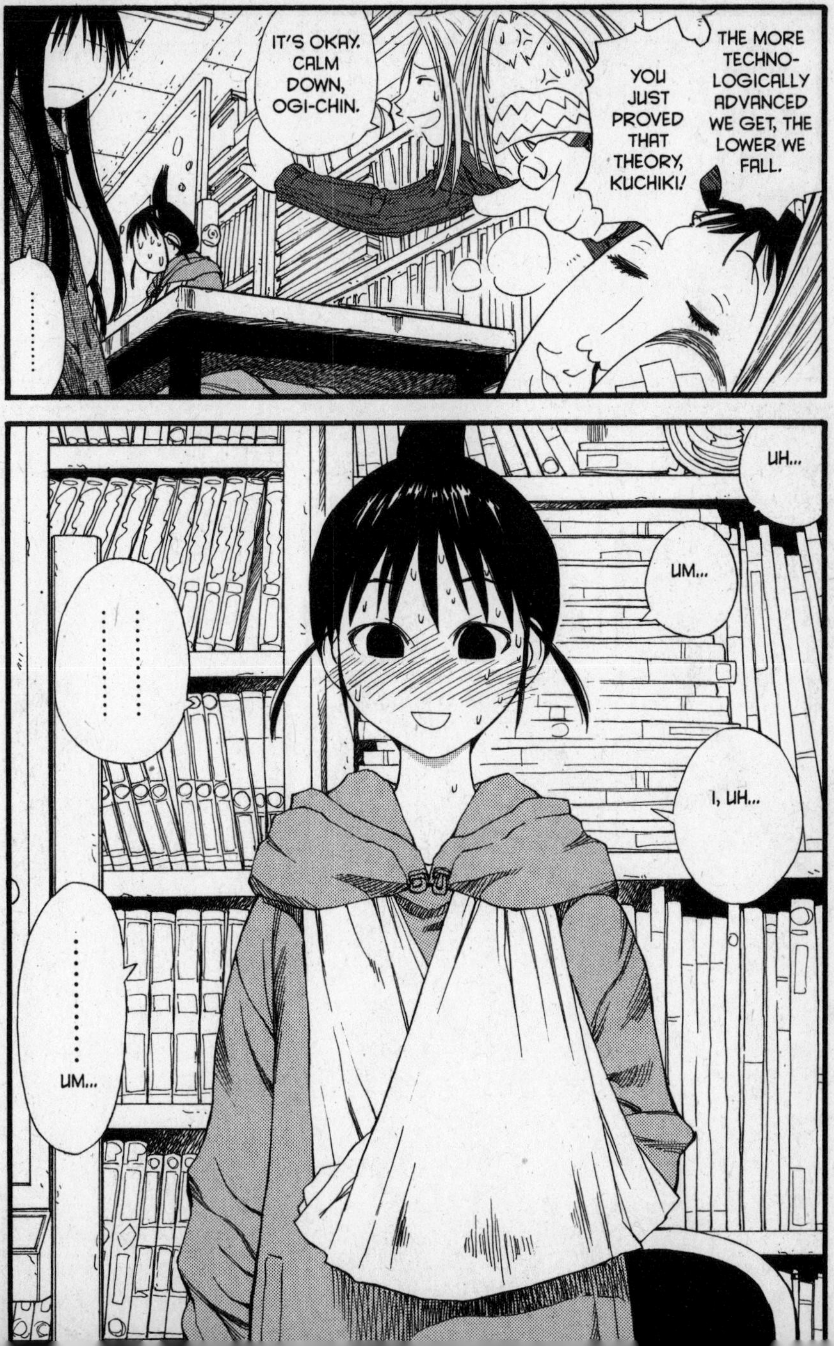
THE MORE TECHNO-LOGICALLY ADVANCED WE GET, THE LOWER WE FALL.
YOU JUST PROVED THAT THEORY, KUCHIKI!
IT'S OKAY. CALM DOWN, OGI-CHIN.
......
UH...
UM...
I, UH...
......
......UM...

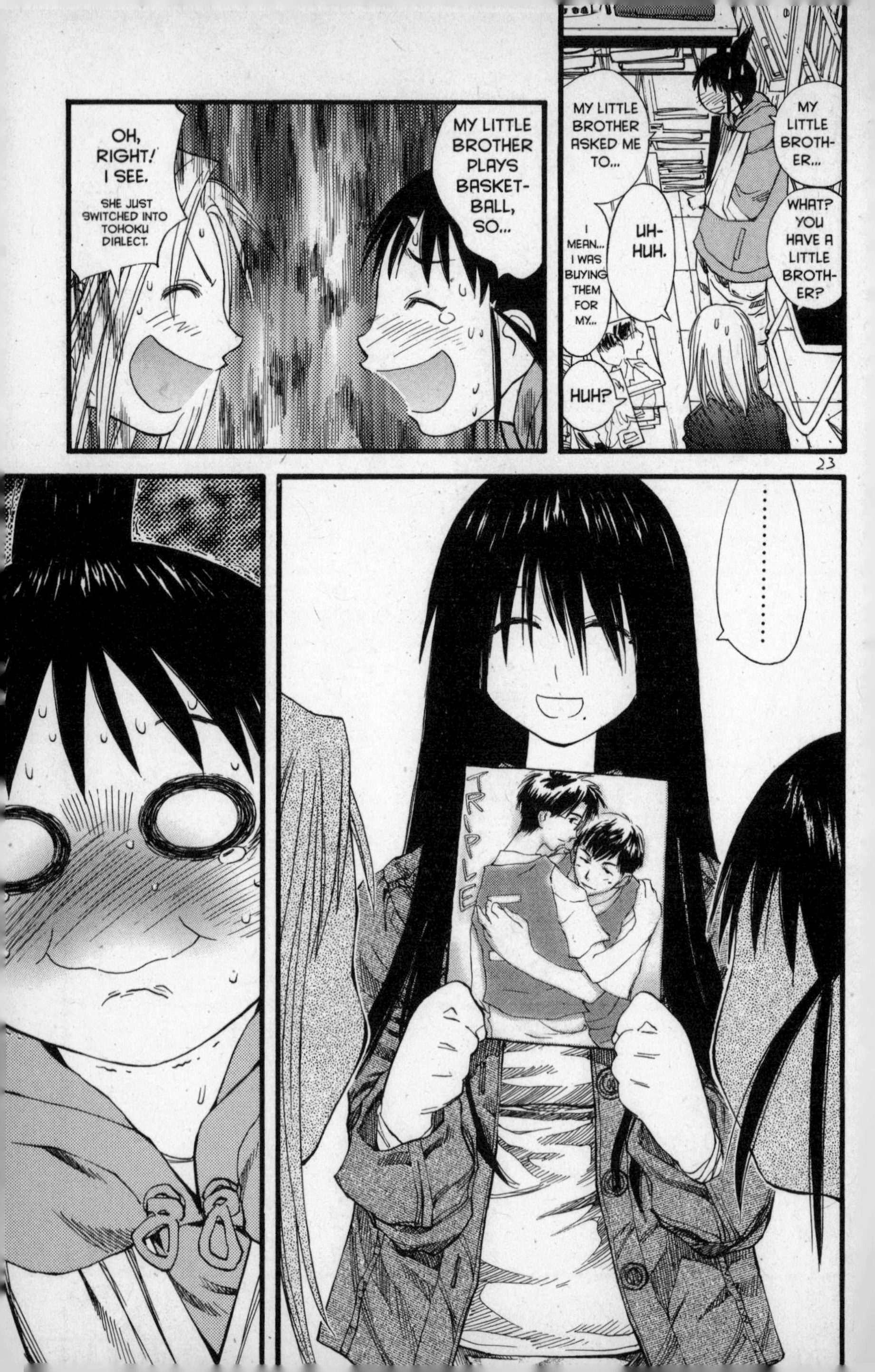
MY LITTLE BROTHER...
MY LITTLE BROTHER ASKED ME TO...
WHAT? YOU HAVE A LITTLE BROTHER?
UH-HUH.
I MEAN... I WAS BUYING THEM FOR MY...
HUH?
MY LITTLE BROTHER PLAYS BASKETBALL, SO...
OH, RIGHT! I SEE.
SHE JUST SWITCHED INTO TOHOKU DIALECT.
......
TRIPLE

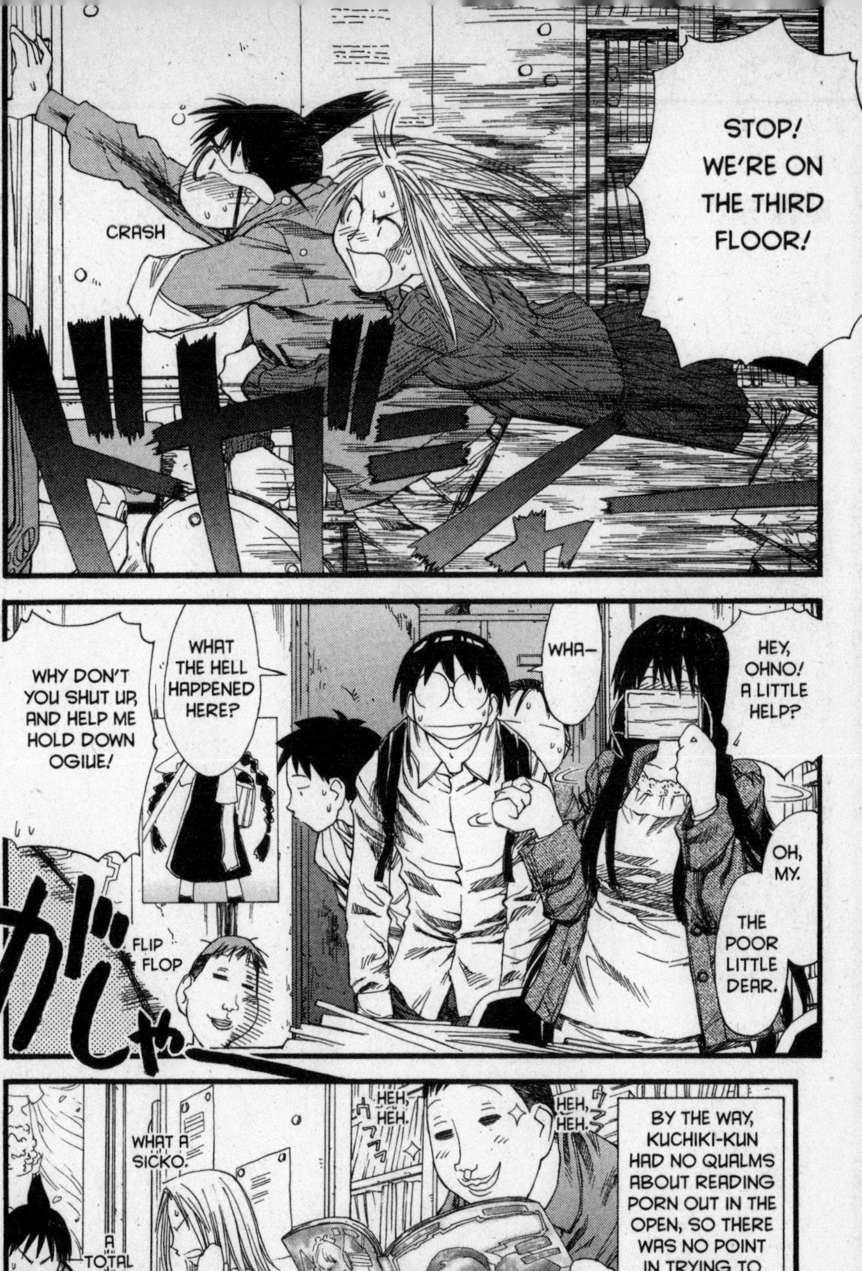
STOP! WE'RE ON THE THIRD FLOOR!
CRASH
HEY, OHNO! A LITTLE HELP?
OH, MY.
THE POOR LITTLE DEAR.
WHA—
WHAT THE HELL HAPPENED HERE?
WHY DON'T YOU SHUT UP, AND HELP ME HOLD DOWN OGIUE!
FLIP FLOP
BY THE WAY, KUCHIKI-KUN HAD NO QUALMS ABOUT READING PORN OUT IN THE OPEN, SO THERE WAS NO POINT IN TRYING TO AMBUSH HIM.
HEH, HEH.
HEH, HEH.
WHAT A SICKO.
A TOTAL SICKO.

END OF CHAPTER 25

THE RETURN OF MY FAVORITE SCENES FROM KUJI-UN - PART 1

BY 72-YEAR-OLD PIT VIPER

EPISODE 1 "AN UNBALANCED ENCOUNTER"

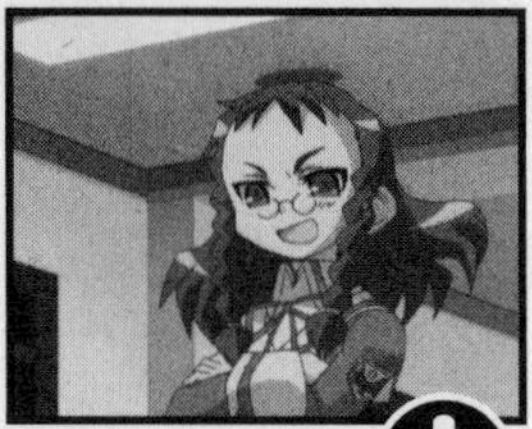

▲ HER HEAD IS TOUCHING THE CEILING. "HA, HA, HA."

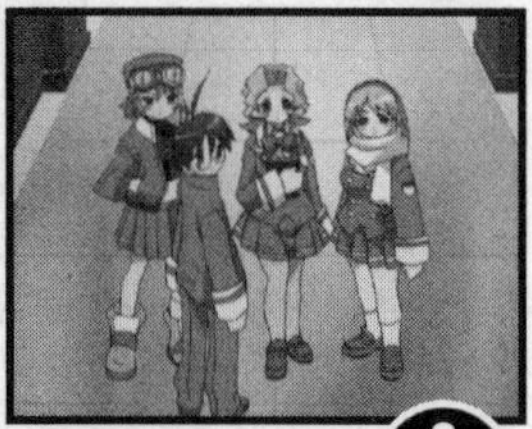

▲ WHAT'S GOING ON HERE...

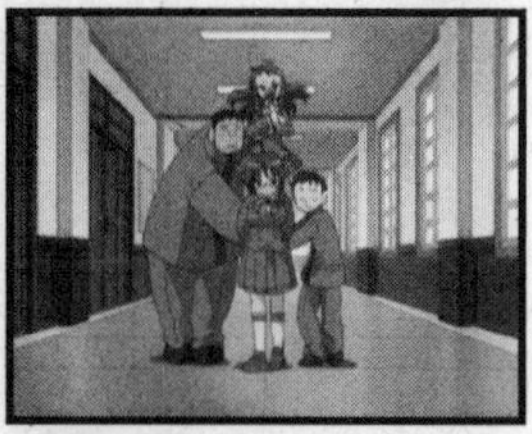

▲ RIGHT AFTER THIS, SHE KICKS YAMADA ON HER WAY DOWN. THAT GUY IS SO TALL.

HELLO. IT'S ME, PIT VIPER. HAVE YOU ALL BEEN GOOD LITTLE BOYS AND GIRLS? I'VE BEEN VERY BAD. THE LAST DVD IN THE SERIES FINALLY... FINALLY CAME OUT. SO, I FIGURED THAT THIS WAS THE PERFECT TIME TO HAVE EVERYBODY CHOOSE THEIR FAVORITE SCENES AGAIN.

I THOUGHT ABOUT CHOOSING KOYUKI FOR ABOUT TWO OR THREE SECONDS, BUT THEN I DECIDED ON RENKO-CHAN. I LOVE KAMISHAKUJII. I JUST LOVE KAMISHAKUJII. IKUE OONITA'S VOICE IS A PERFECT MATCH. EVERY TIME I HEAR HER DOING THE VOICES OF OTHER CHARACTERS, I CAN ONLY THINK OF RENKO-CHAN. WOULDN'T IT BE COOL IF SOMEBODY DID COSPLAY OF IKUE OONITA? [LAUGHS]

WELL FIRST, I'D BETTER GET THIS OUT OF THE WAY. I'M TALKING ABOUT HER FIRST SCENE IN EPISODE 1. YOU KNOW EXACTLY WHAT TYPE OF CHARACTER SHE IS FROM THE MOMENT YOU LAY EYES ON HER, AND THE FACT THAT THE CEILING ACTUALLY MOVES WAS REALLY COOL. THAT COULD ONLY HAPPEN IN ANIME. THERE'S THAT SCENE, AND THEN OF COURSE THERE'S THE ONE FROM EPISODE 25. I'M TALKING ABOUT THE SCENE WHERE RENKO SHOWS UP IN TEARS, AND TRIES TO CONVINCE TOKINO NOT TO DROP OUT OF THE STUDENT BODY TOURNAMENT. IT REALLY MAKES YOU THINK ABOUT THEIR RELATIONSHIP. REMEMBER THE STORY ABOUT THEIR PAST IN EPISODE 11? TOKINO TRANSFERS OUT OF HER SECOND-GRADE CLASS, AND MOVES TO ANOTHER SCHOOL, LEAVING A VOID IN RENKO'S LIFE. RENKO, TRAUMATIZED BY TOKINO'S DISAPPEARANCE, BEGINS TO DRIVE HER ENTIRE CLASS (INCLUDING THE TEACHER) CRAZY. SHE ENDS UP TRYING TO DESTROY HER CLASS, AND FINALLY HER PARENTS ARE CALLED IN. ONCE SHE SEES HER PARENTS STANDING BEFORE HER, SHE DECIDES TO BECOME A GOOD GIRL, AND RESTRAINS HERSELF ALL THE WAY THROUGH JUNIOR HIGH. RENKO IS ACTUALLY THE DAUGHTER OF A WEALTHY FAMILY. HER CAT IS THE ONLY MEMBER OF HER FAMILY WHO SHE CAN TALK TO. AT SCHOOL, SHE TRIES TO PLAY THE ROLE OF THE QUIET RICH GIRL, BUT THAT ENDS WHEN SHE'S REUNITED WITH TOKINO. OF COURSE SHE HATES TOKINO, AND THINKS OF HER ONLY AS AN ENEMY, BUT IN A WAY, SHE HAS COME TO DEPEND ON HER ENEMY. THAT REALLY COMES THROUGH IN THIS SCENE. BESIDES, WHO WOULDN'T WANNA HUG RENKO? HA, HA, HA. [BLUSH] WELL, IT SEEMS THAT RENKO'S PARENTS ARE AWARE THAT SHE'S OVERDOING IT. HOPEFULLY, SOMEDAY, HER PARENTS WILL BE ABLE TO SEE THE REAL RENKO. OF COURSE, IT MUST BE TOKINO WHO HOLDS THE KEY TO THAT MOMENT. IF THIS EVER HAPPENS IN THE MANGA, THEY'D BETTER MAKE IT INTO ANIME.

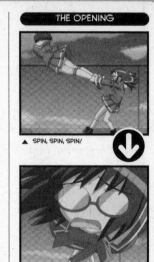

THE OPENING

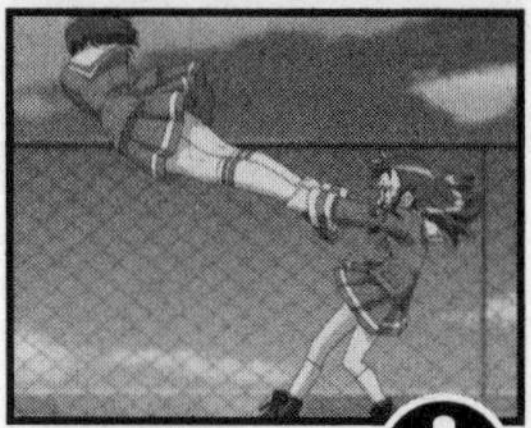

▲ SPIN, SPIN, SPIN!

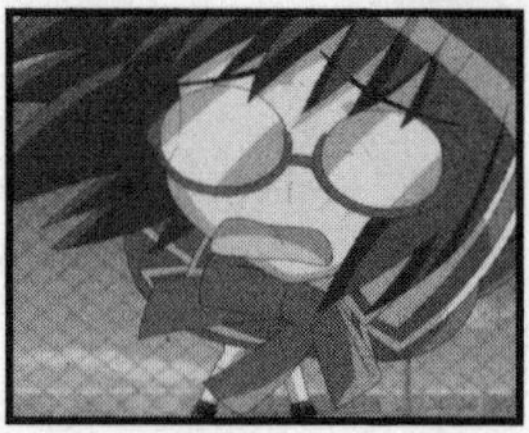

▲ SPIN, SPIN, SPIN!

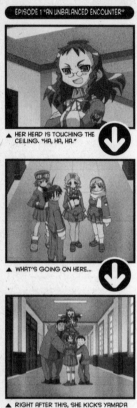

EPISODE 25 "KUJIBIKI FOREVER"

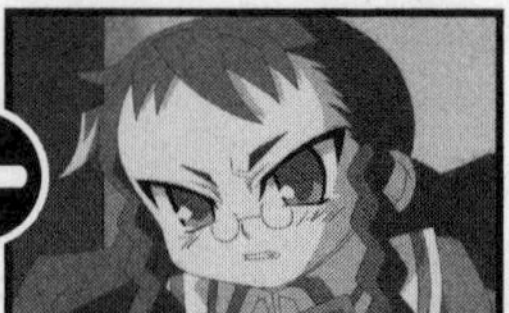

▲ RENKO: "YOU'VE GOT TO FACE THE CHALLENGE! IS THERE ANYTHING IN THIS WORLD MORE IMPORTANT THAN A CHALLENGE? THERE ISN'T, AND YOU KNOW THAT." SHE CRIES WHILE DELIVERING THIS SPEECH.

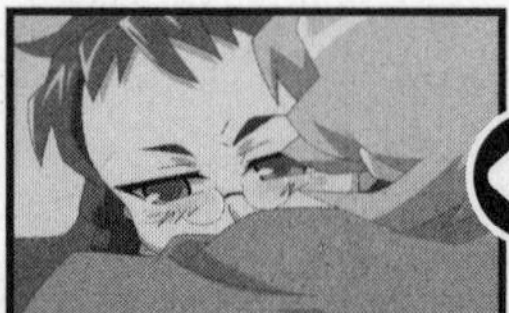

▲ TOKINO: "THANK YOU." RENKO REALLY LETS GO HERE. I HEARD THAT DURING THE REHEARSALS FOR THIS SCENE, IKUE OONITA WHISPERED "IS THIS A LESBIAN SCENE?"

PREPARATION

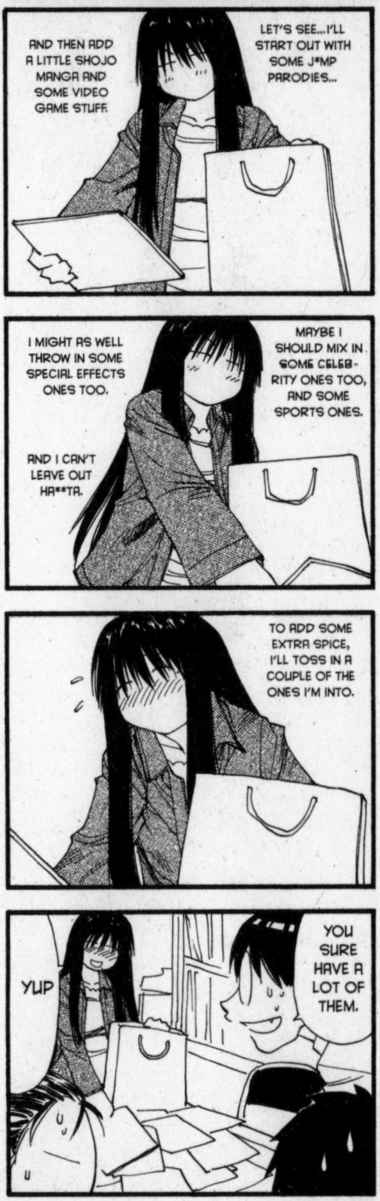
LET'S SEE...I'LL START OUT WITH SOME J*MP PARODIES...
AND THEN ADD A LITTLE SHOJO MANGA AND SOME VIDEO GAME STUFF.
MAYBE I SHOULD MIX IN SOME CELEBRITY ONES TOO, AND SOME SPORTS ONES.
I MIGHT AS WELL THROW IN SOME SPECIAL EFFECTS ONES TOO.
AND I CAN'T LEAVE OUT HA**TA.
TO ADD SOME EXTRA SPICE, I'LL TOSS IN A COUPLE OF THE ONES I'M INTO.
YOU SURE HAVE A LOT OF THEM.
YUP

ORTEGA?

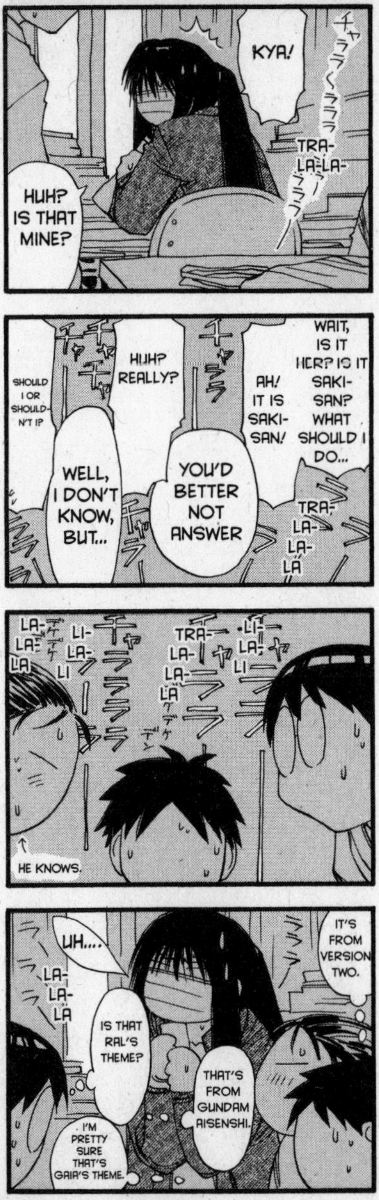
TRA-LA-LA-
KYA!
HUH? IS THAT MINE?
WAIT, IS IT HER? IS IT SAKI-SAN? WHAT SHOULD I DO...
AH! IT IS SAKI-SAN!
HUH? REALLY?
SHOULD I OR SHOULDN'T I?
YOU'D BETTER NOT ANSWER
TRA-LA-LA-LA
WELL, I DON'T KNOW, BUT...
LI-LA-LI
TRA-LA-LA-LA
LI-LA-LI
LA-LA-LA
HE KNOWS.
IT'S FROM VERSION TWO.
UH....
LA-LA-LA
IS THAT RAL'S THEME?
THAT'S FROM GUNDAM AISENSHI.
I'M PRETTY SURE THAT'S GAIA'S THEME.

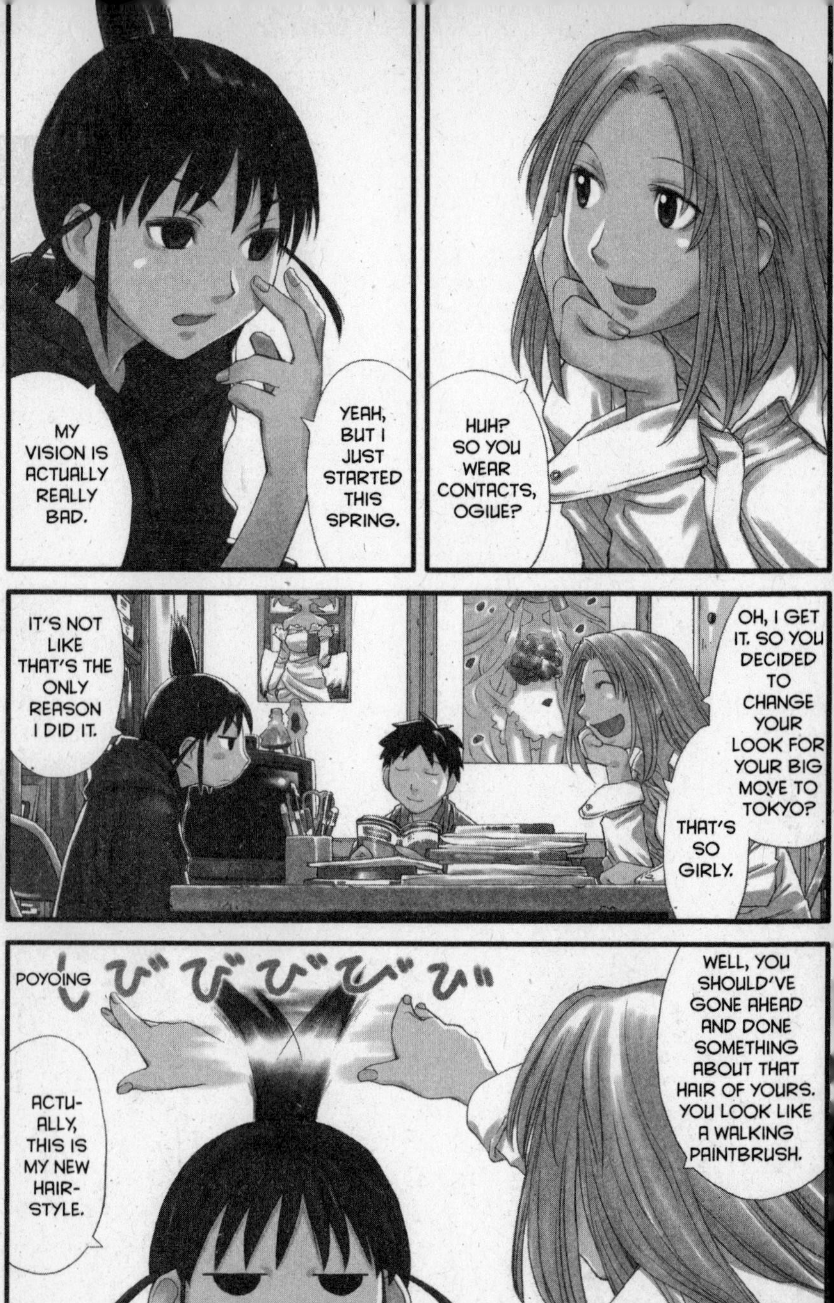
HUH? SO YOU WEAR CONTACTS, OGIUE?
YEAH, BUT I JUST STARTED THIS SPRING.
MY VISION IS ACTUALLY REALLY BAD.
OH, I GET IT. SO YOU DECIDED TO CHANGE YOUR LOOK FOR YOUR BIG MOVE TO TOKYO?
THAT'S SO GIRLY.
IT'S NOT LIKE THAT'S THE ONLY REASON I DID IT.
WELL, YOU SHOULD'VE GONE AHEAD AND DONE SOMETHING ABOUT THAT HAIR OF YOURS. YOU LOOK LIKE A WALKING PAINTBRUSH.
POYOING
ACTU-ALLY, THIS IS MY NEW HAIR-STYLE.

Chapter 26 - Applied Theory of Madarame's Shopping Method

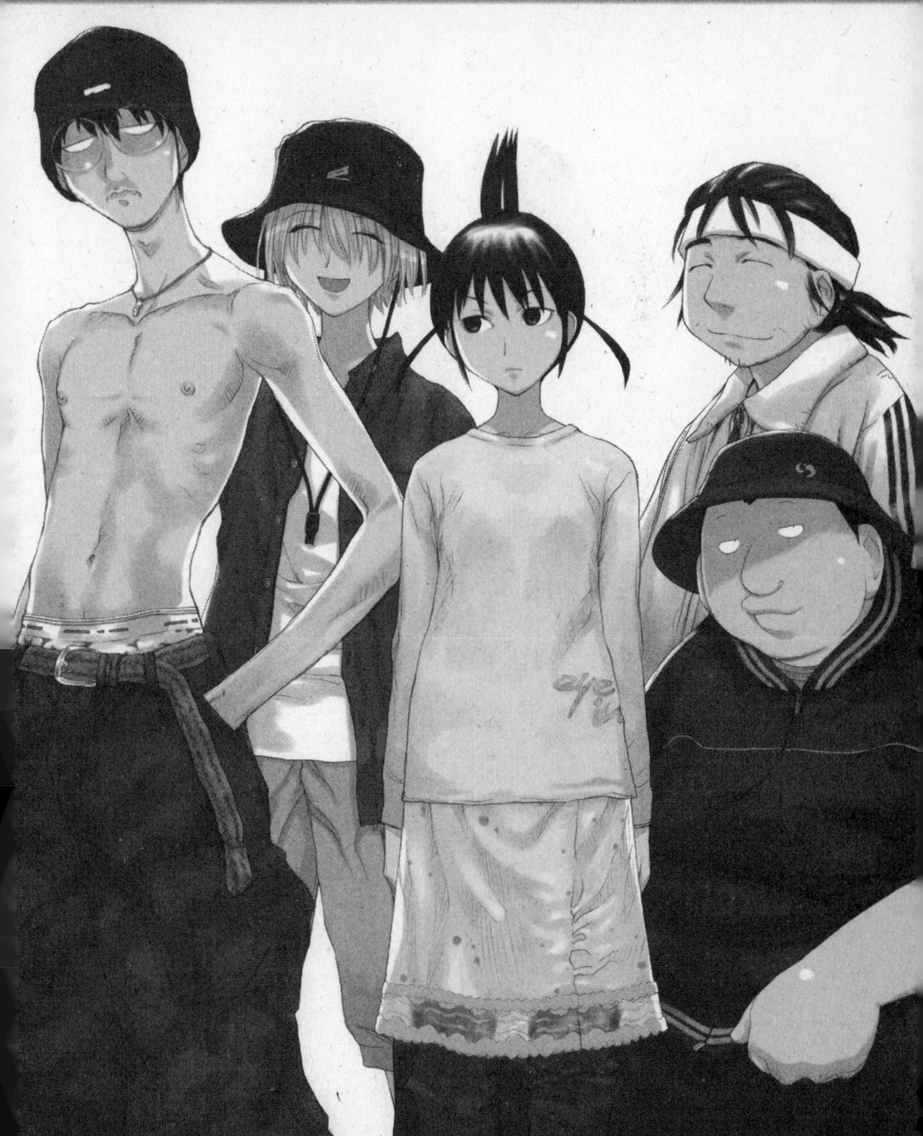

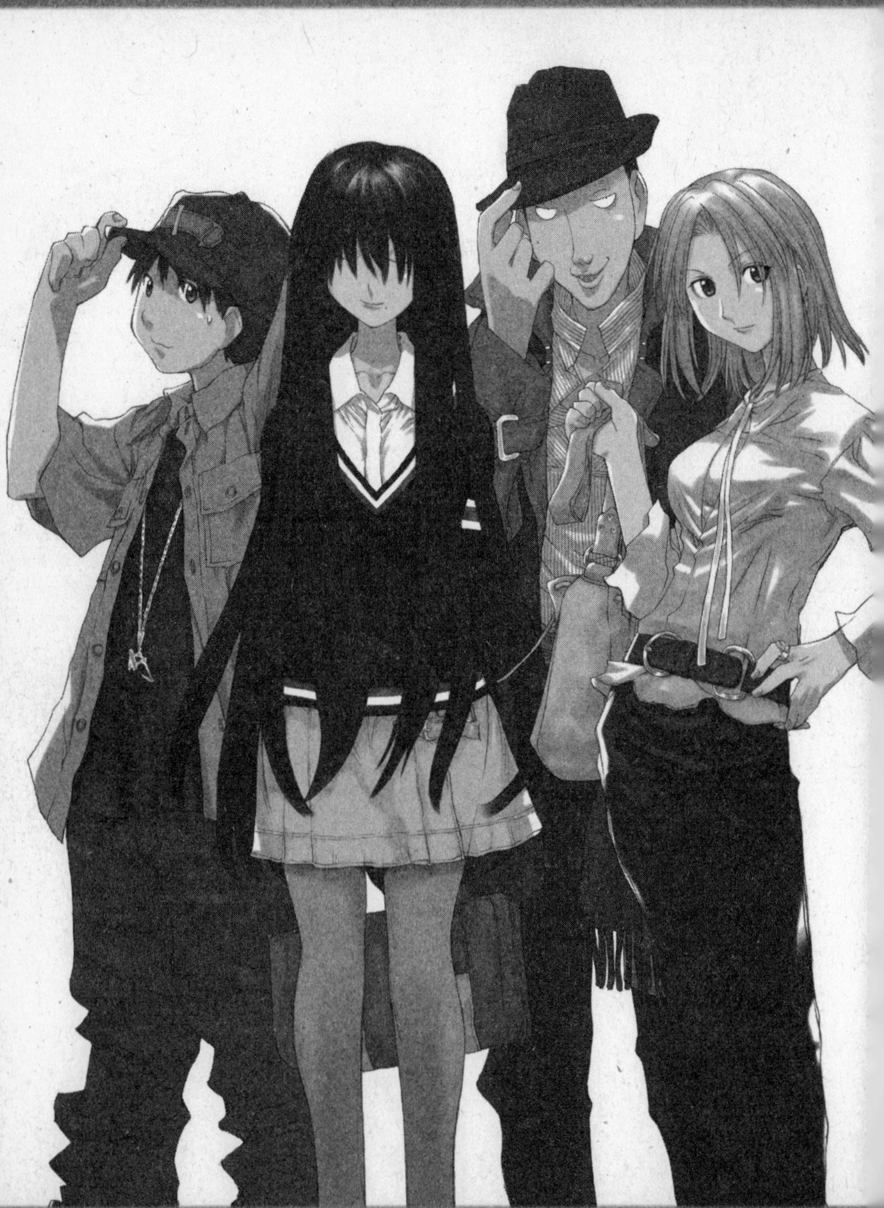

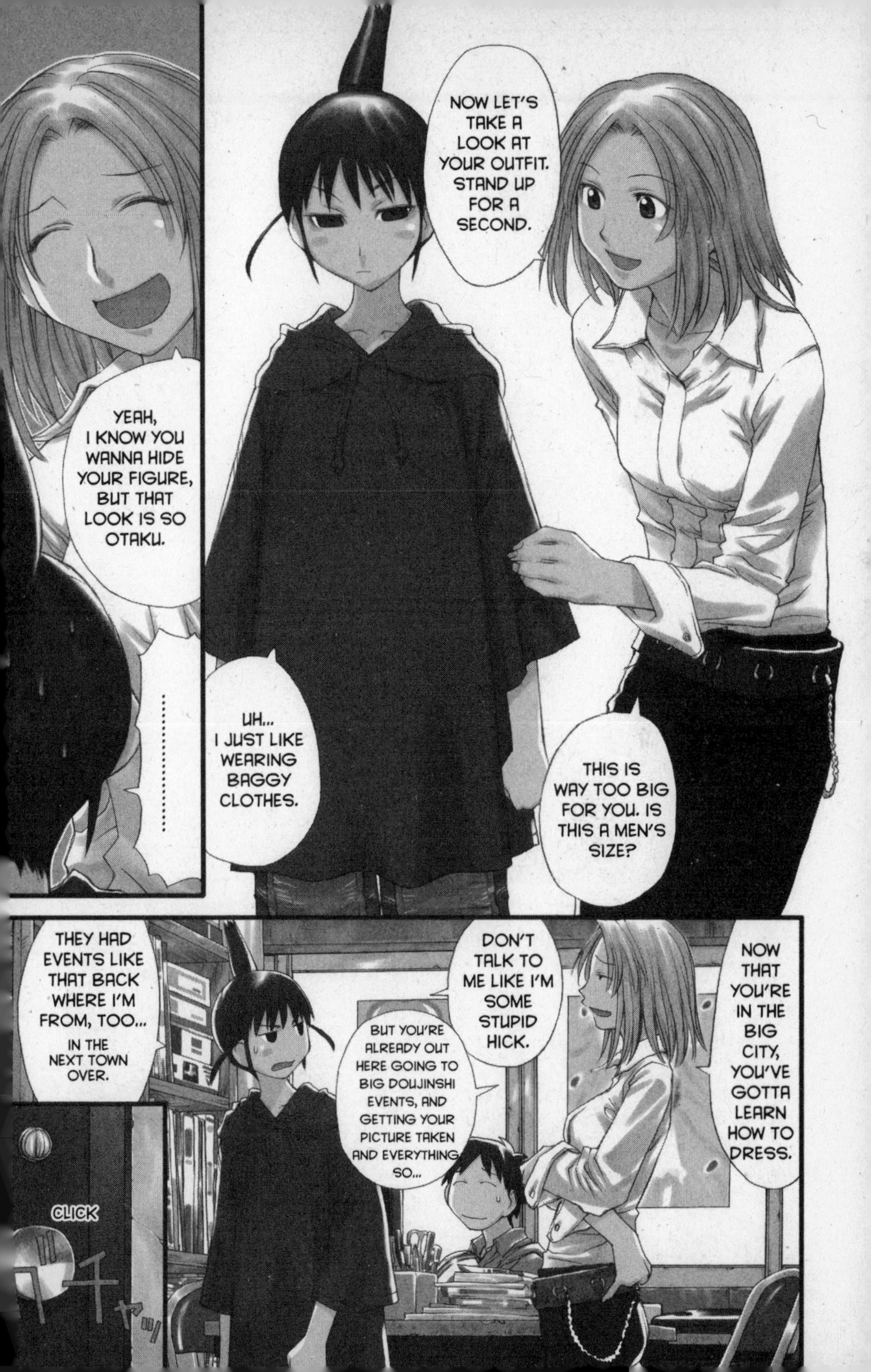
NOW LET'S TAKE A LOOK AT YOUR OUTFIT. STAND UP FOR A SECOND.
THIS IS WAY TOO BIG FOR YOU. IS THIS A MEN'S SIZE?
UH... I JUST LIKE WEARING BAGGY CLOTHES.
YEAH, I KNOW YOU WANNA HIDE YOUR FIGURE, BUT THAT LOOK IS SO OTAKU.
......
NOW THAT YOU'RE IN THE BIG CITY, YOU'VE GOTTA LEARN HOW TO DRESS.
DON'T TALK TO ME LIKE I'M SOME STUPID HICK.
BUT YOU'RE ALREADY OUT HERE GOING TO BIG DOUJINSHI EVENTS, AND GETTING YOUR PICTURE TAKEN AND EVERYTHING SO...
THEY HAD EVENTS LIKE THAT BACK WHERE I'M FROM, TOO... IN THE NEXT TOWN OVER.
CLICK

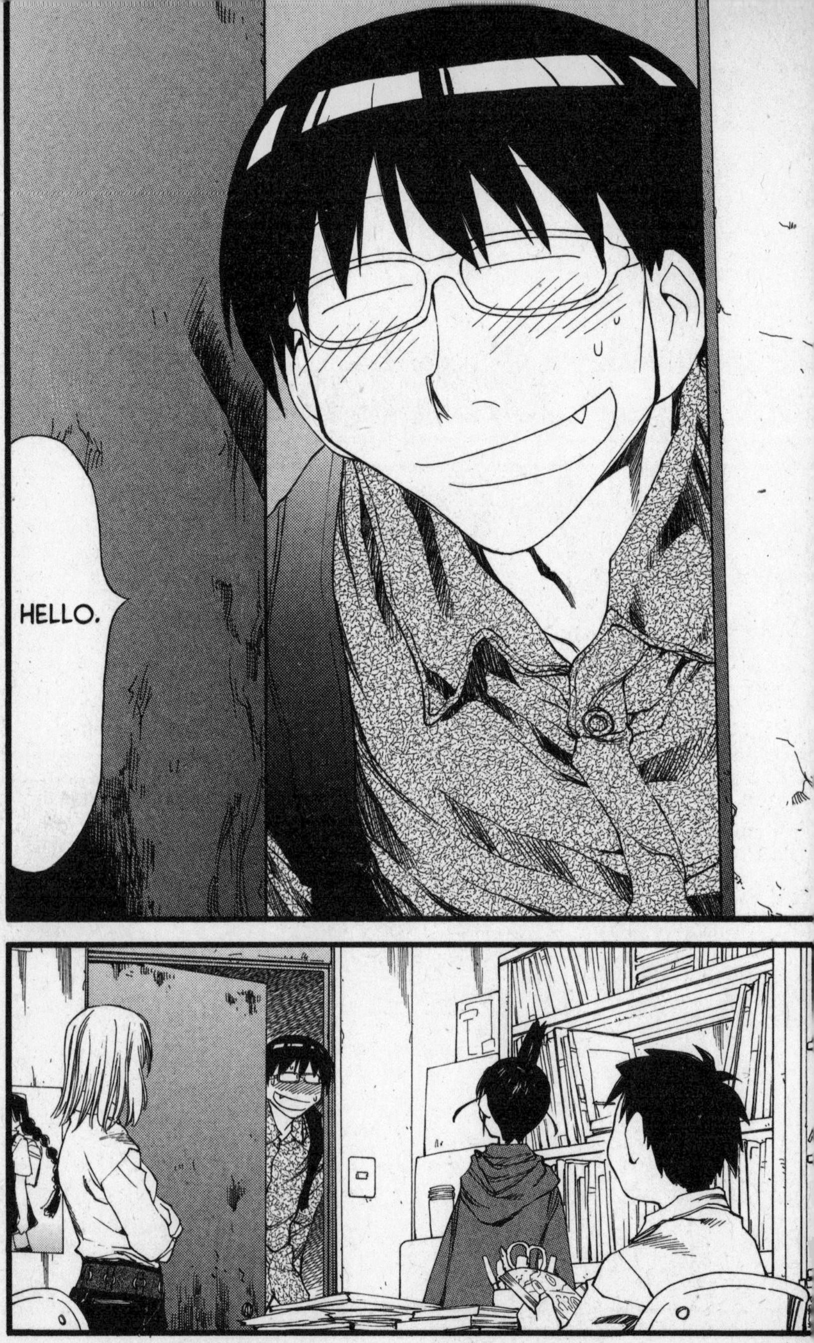
HELLO.

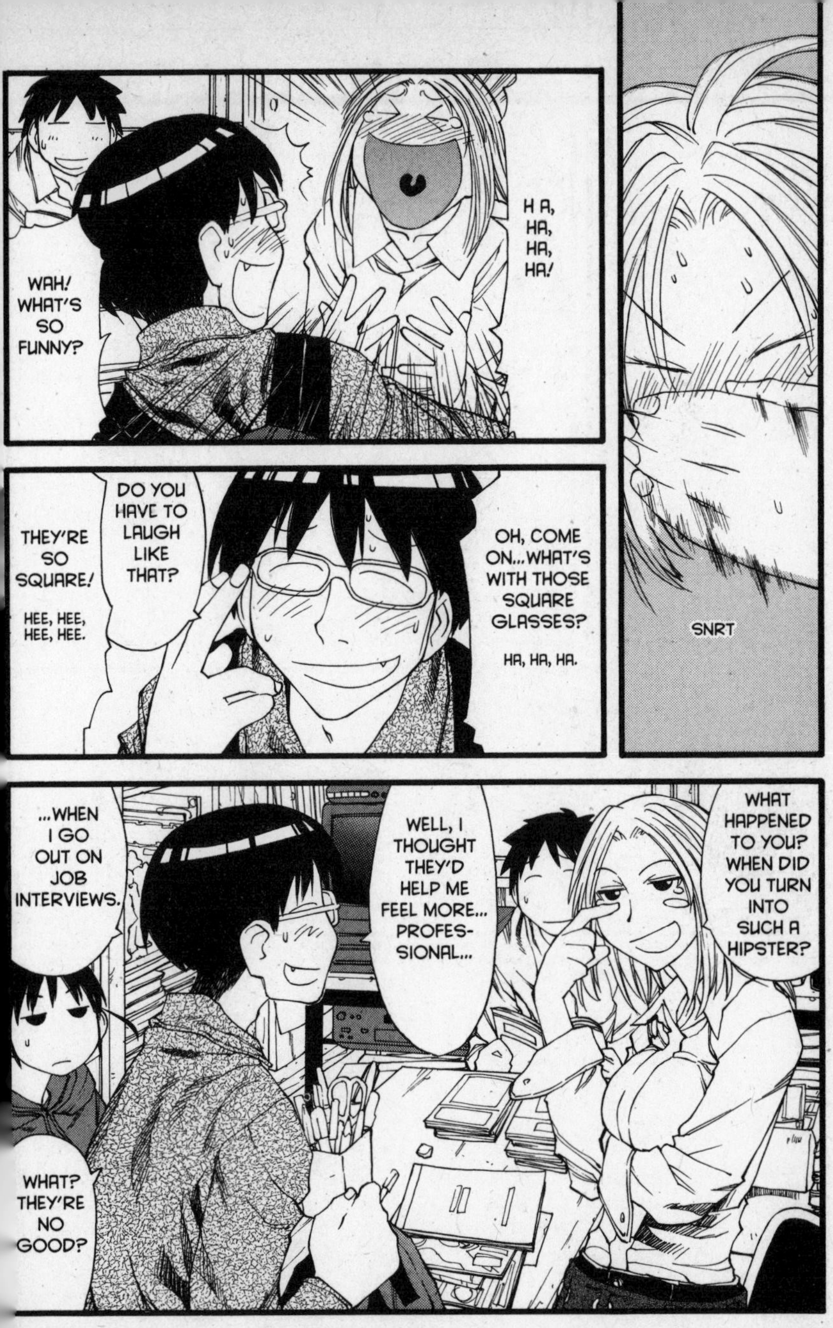
SNRT
HA, HA, HA, HA!
WAH! WHAT'S SO FUNNY?
OH, COME ON...WHAT'S WITH THOSE SQUARE GLASSES?
HA, HA, HA.
DO YOU HAVE TO LAUGH LIKE THAT?
THEY'RE SO SQUARE!
HEE, HEE, HEE, HEE.
WHAT HAPPENED TO YOU? WHEN DID YOU TURN INTO SUCH A HIPSTER?
WELL, I THOUGHT THEY'D HELP ME FEEL MORE... PROFESSIONAL...
...WHEN I GO OUT ON JOB INTERVIEWS.
WHAT? THEY'RE NO GOOD?

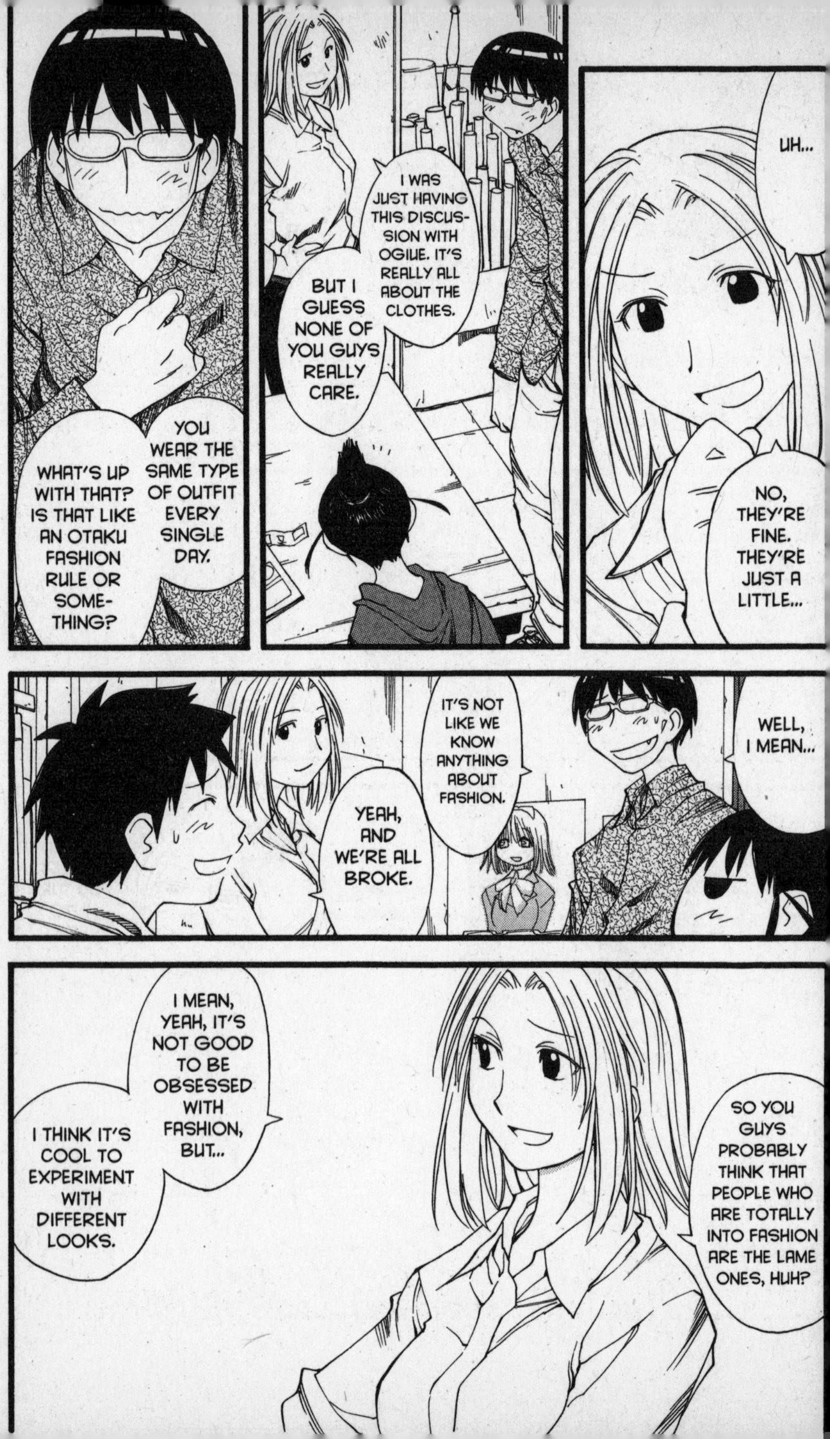
UH...
NO, THEY'RE FINE. THEY'RE JUST A LITTLE...
I WAS JUST HAVING THIS DISCUSSION WITH OGIUE. IT'S REALLY ALL ABOUT THE CLOTHES.
BUT I GUESS NONE OF YOU GUYS REALLY CARE.
YOU WEAR THE SAME TYPE OF OUTFIT EVERY SINGLE DAY.
WHAT'S UP WITH THAT? IS THAT LIKE AN OTAKU FASHION RULE OR SOMETHING?
WELL, I MEAN...
IT'S NOT LIKE WE KNOW ANYTHING ABOUT FASHION.
YEAH, AND WE'RE ALL BROKE.
SO YOU GUYS PROBABLY THINK THAT PEOPLE WHO ARE TOTALLY INTO FASHION ARE THE LAME ONES, HUH?
I MEAN, YEAH, IT'S NOT GOOD TO BE OBSESSED WITH FASHION, BUT...
I THINK IT'S COOL TO EXPERIMENT WITH DIFFERENT LOOKS.

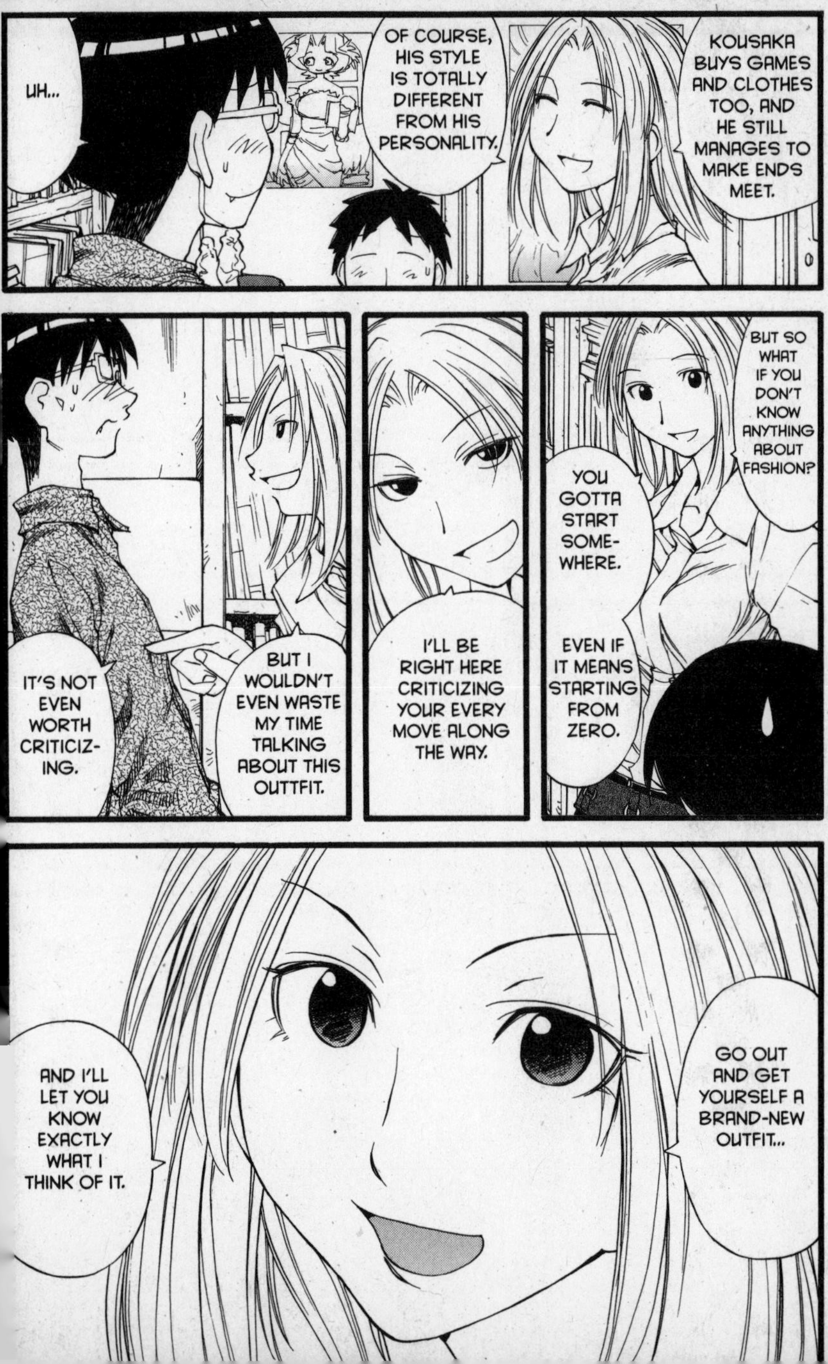
KOUSAKA BUYS GAMES AND CLOTHES TOO, AND HE STILL MANAGES TO MAKE ENDS MEET.
OF COURSE, HIS STYLE IS TOTALLY DIFFERENT FROM HIS PERSONALITY.
UH...
BUT SO WHAT IF YOU DON'T KNOW ANYTHING ABOUT FASHION?
YOU GOTTA START SOME-WHERE.
EVEN IF IT MEANS STARTING FROM ZERO.
I'LL BE RIGHT HERE CRITICIZING YOUR EVERY MOVE ALONG THE WAY.
BUT I WOULDN'T EVEN WASTE MY TIME TALKING ABOUT THIS OUTFIT.
IT'S NOT EVEN WORTH CRITICIZ-ING.
GO OUT AND GET YOURSELF A BRAND-NEW OUTFIT...
AND I'LL LET YOU KNOW EXACTLY WHAT I THINK OF IT.

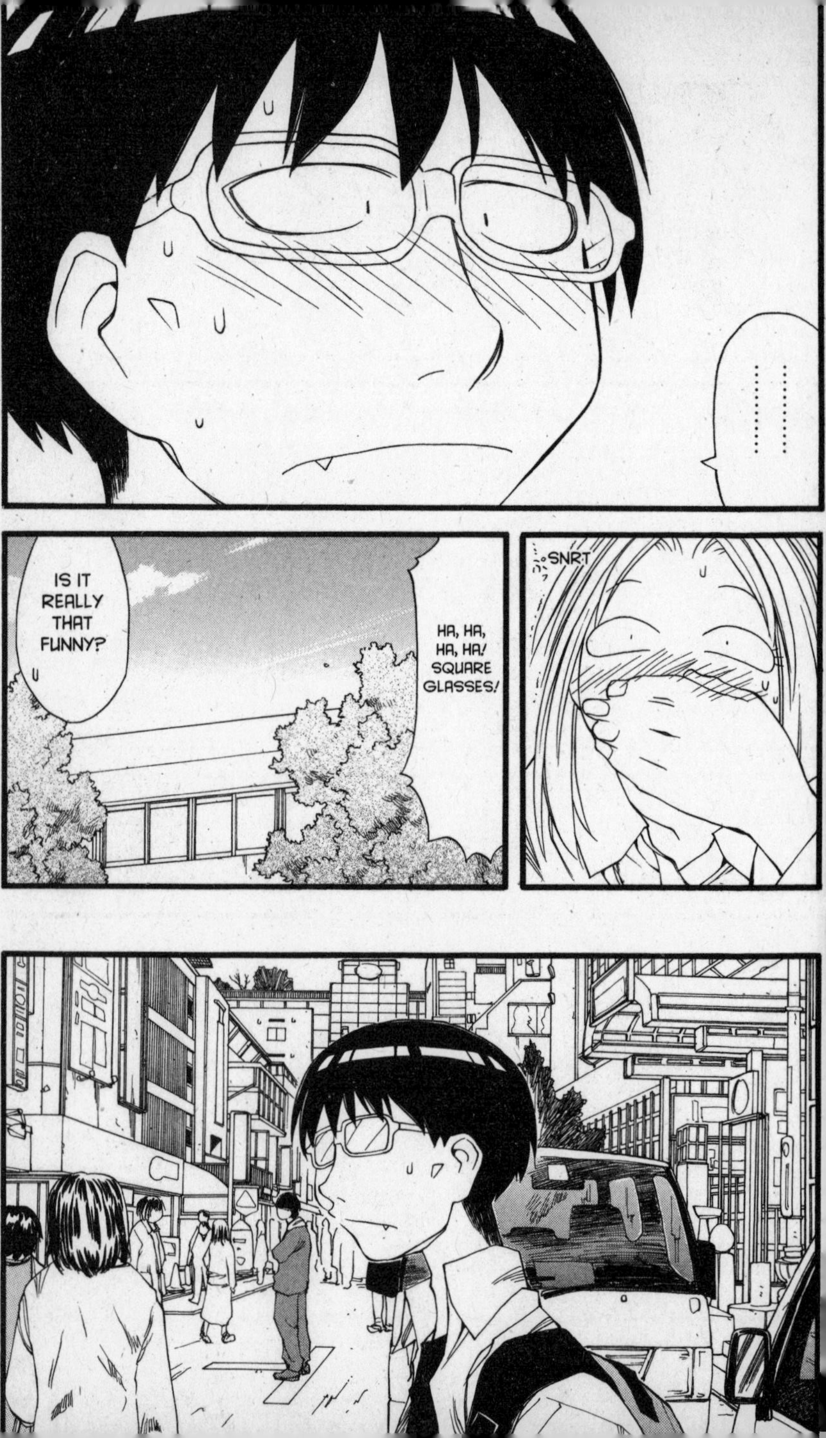
……
SNRT
HA, HA, HA, HA! SQUARE GLASSES!
IS IT REALLY THAT FUNNY?

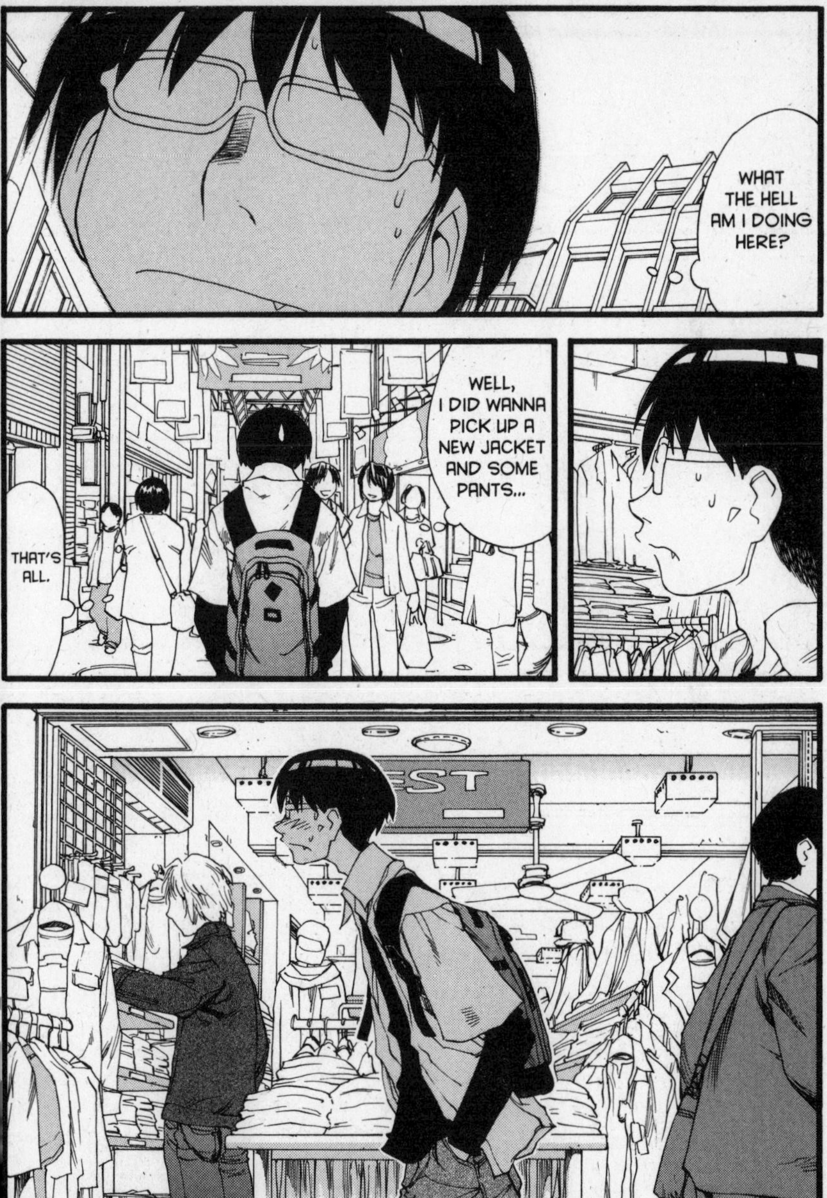
WHAT THE HELL AM I DOING HERE?
WELL, I DID WANNA PICK UP A NEW JACKET AND SOME PANTS...
THAT'S ALL.

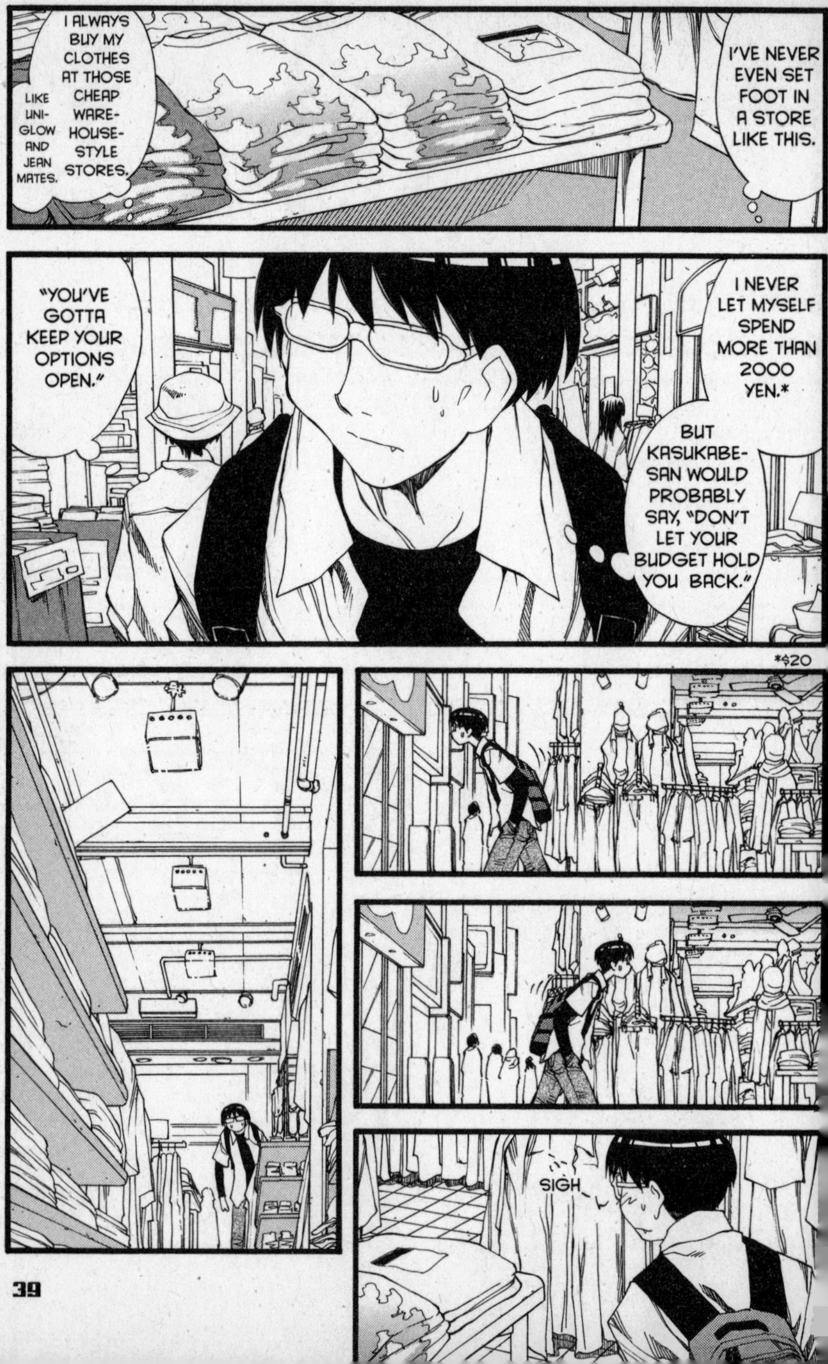
I'VE NEVER EVEN SET FOOT IN A STORE LIKE THIS.
I ALWAYS BUY MY CLOTHES AT THOSE CHEAP WARE-HOUSE-STYLE STORES.
LIKE UNI-GLOW AND JEAN MATES.
I NEVER LET MYSELF SPEND MORE THAN 2000 YEN.*
BUT KASUKABE-SAN WOULD PROBABLY SAY, "DON'T LET YOUR BUDGET HOLD YOU BACK."
"YOU'VE GOTTA KEEP YOUR OPTIONS OPEN."
SIGH

*$20

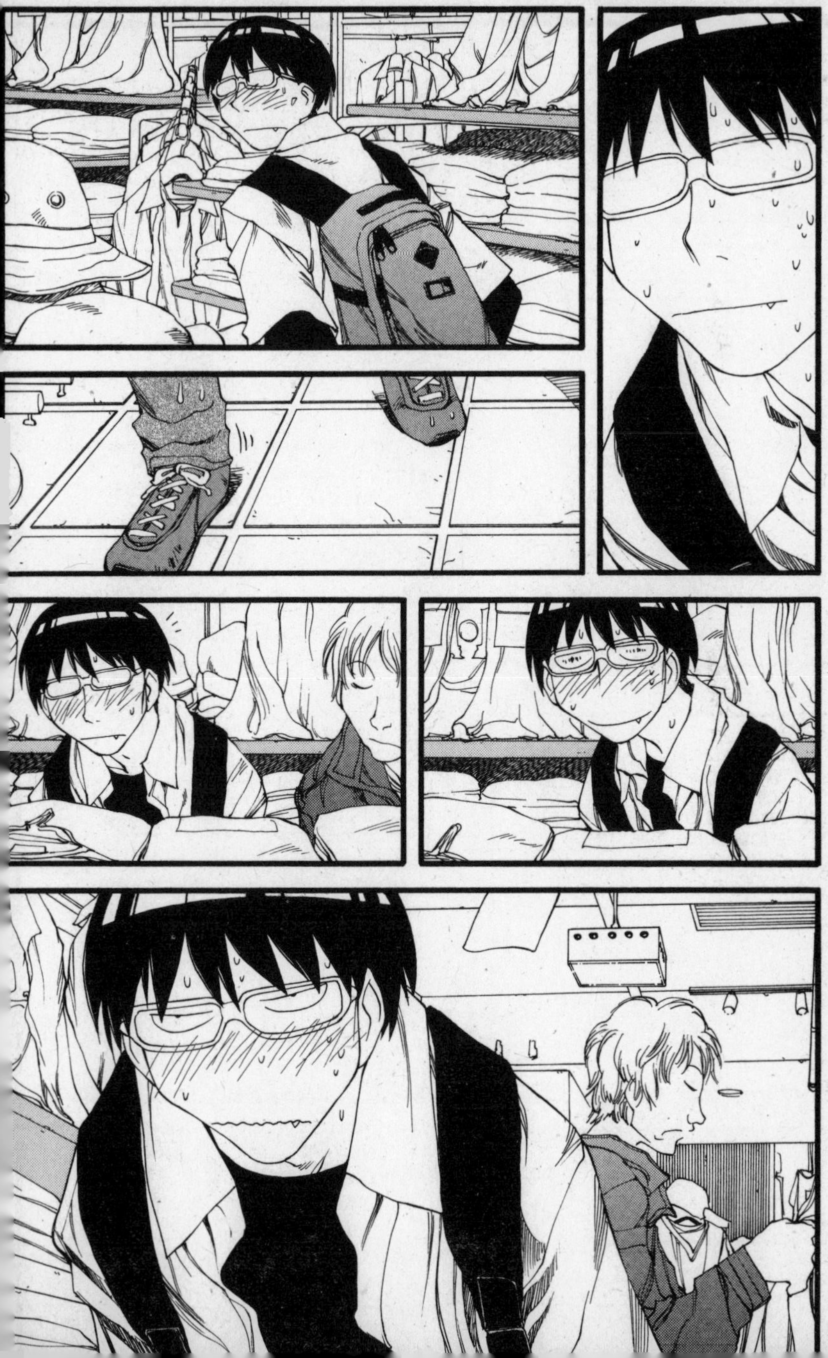

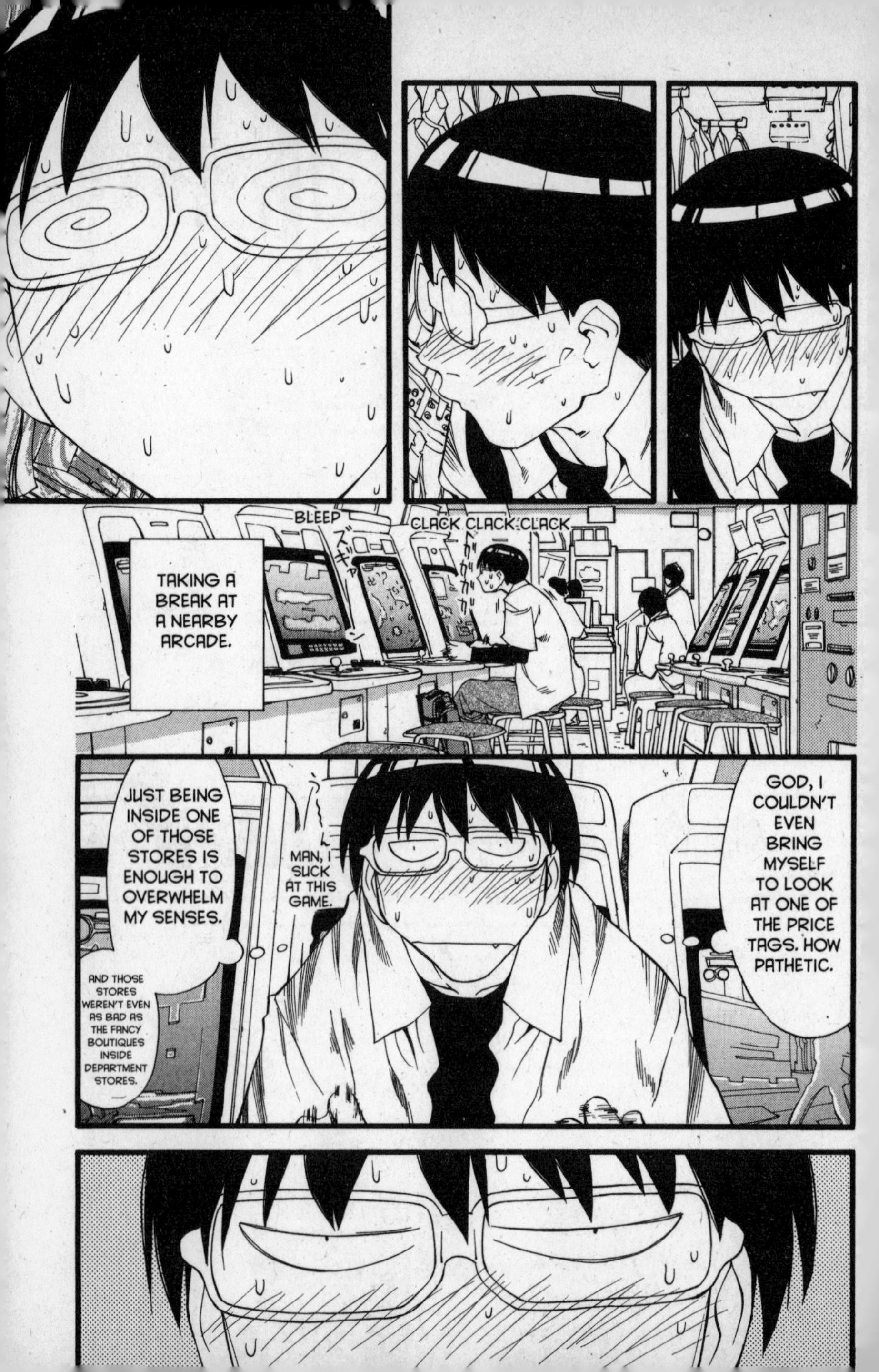
CLACK CLACK CLACK
BLEEP
TAKING A BREAK AT A NEARBY ARCADE.
GOD, I COULDN'T EVEN BRING MYSELF TO LOOK AT ONE OF THE PRICE TAGS. HOW PATHETIC.
MAN, I SUCK AT THIS GAME.
JUST BEING INSIDE ONE OF THOSE STORES IS ENOUGH TO OVERWHELM MY SENSES.
AND THOSE STORES WEREN'T EVEN AS BAD AS THE FANCY BOUTIQUES INSIDE DEPARTMENT STORES.

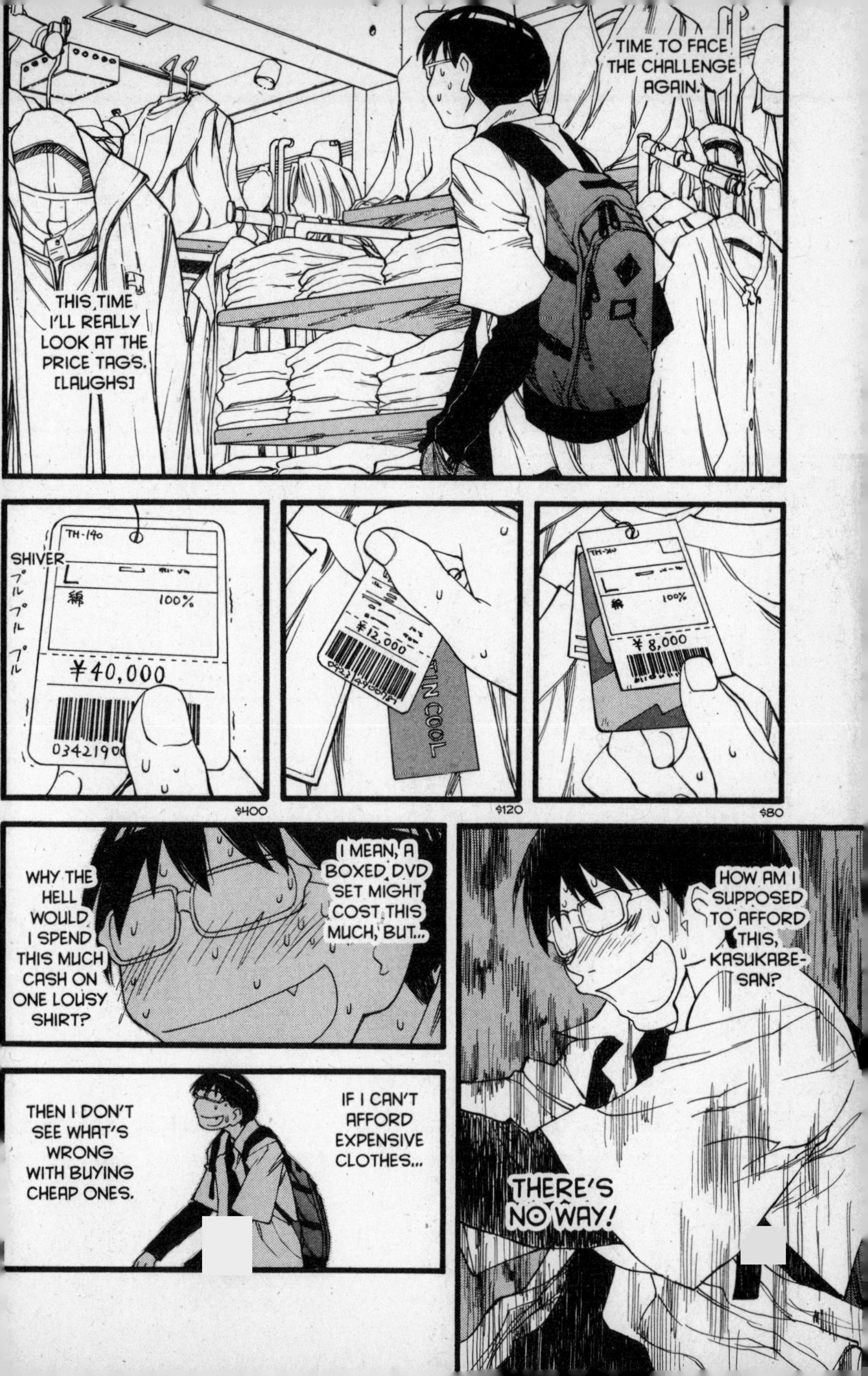
TIME TO FACE THE CHALLENGE AGAIN.
THIS TIME I'LL REALLY LOOK AT THE PRICE TAGS. [LAUGHS]
L
100%
¥8,000
$80
¥12,000
TIN COOL
$120
SHIVER
プル
プル
プル
L
綿 100%
¥40,000
$400
HOW AM I SUPPOSED TO AFFORD THIS, KASUKABE-SAN?
THERE'S NO WAY!
I MEAN, A BOXED DVD SET MIGHT COST THIS MUCH, BUT...
WHY THE HELL WOULD I SPEND THIS MUCH CASH ON ONE LOUSY SHIRT?
IF I CAN'T AFFORD EXPENSIVE CLOTHES...
THEN I DON'T SEE WHAT'S WRONG WITH BUYING CHEAP ONES.

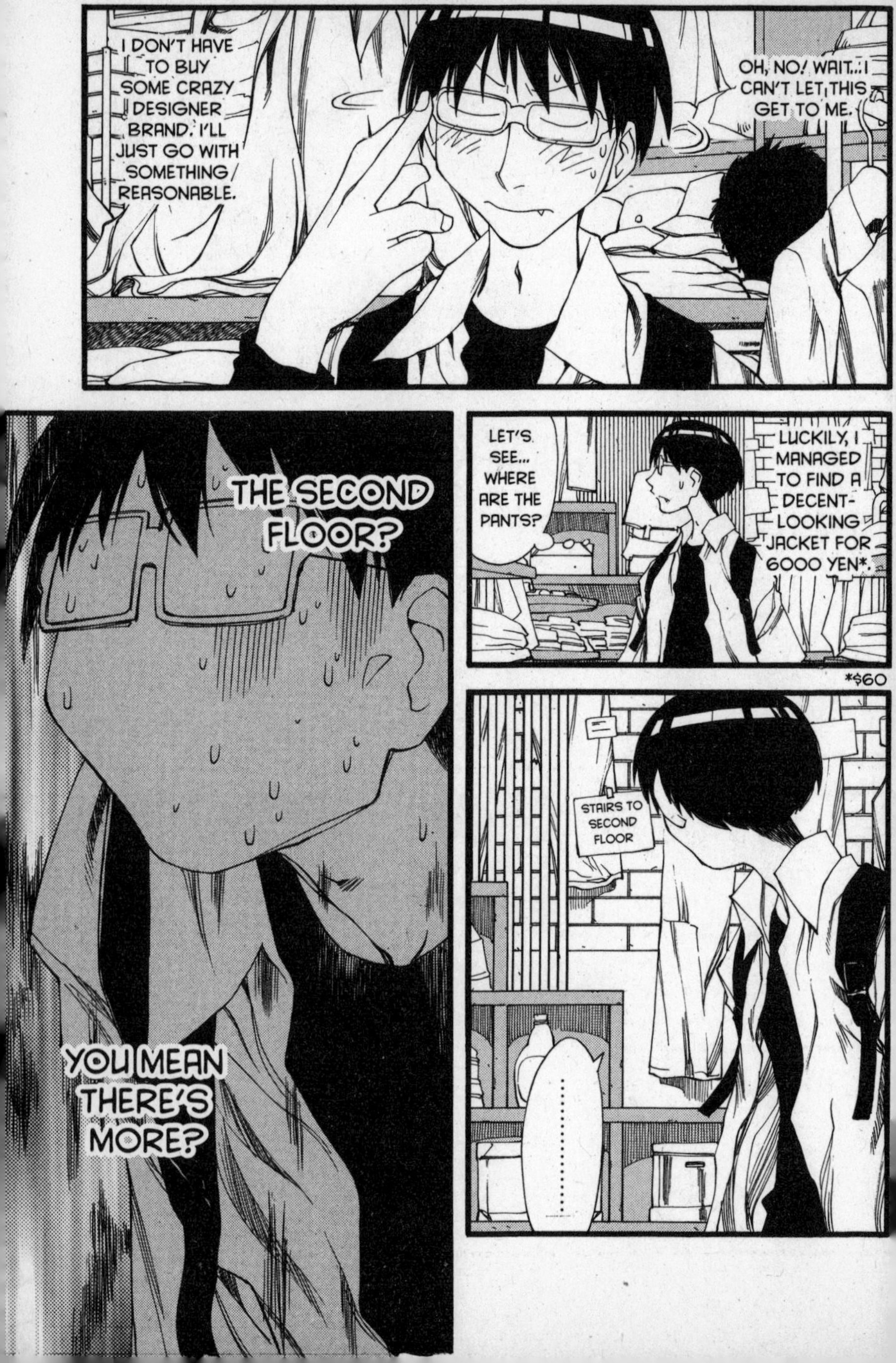
OH, NO! WAIT...I CAN'T LET THIS GET TO ME.
I DON'T HAVE TO BUY SOME CRAZY DESIGNER BRAND. I'LL JUST GO WITH SOMETHING REASONABLE.
LUCKILY, I MANAGED TO FIND A DECENT-LOOKING JACKET FOR 6000 YEN*.
LET'S SEE... WHERE ARE THE PANTS?
*$60
STAIRS TO SECOND FLOOR
......
THE SECOND FLOOR?
YOU MEAN THERE'S MORE?

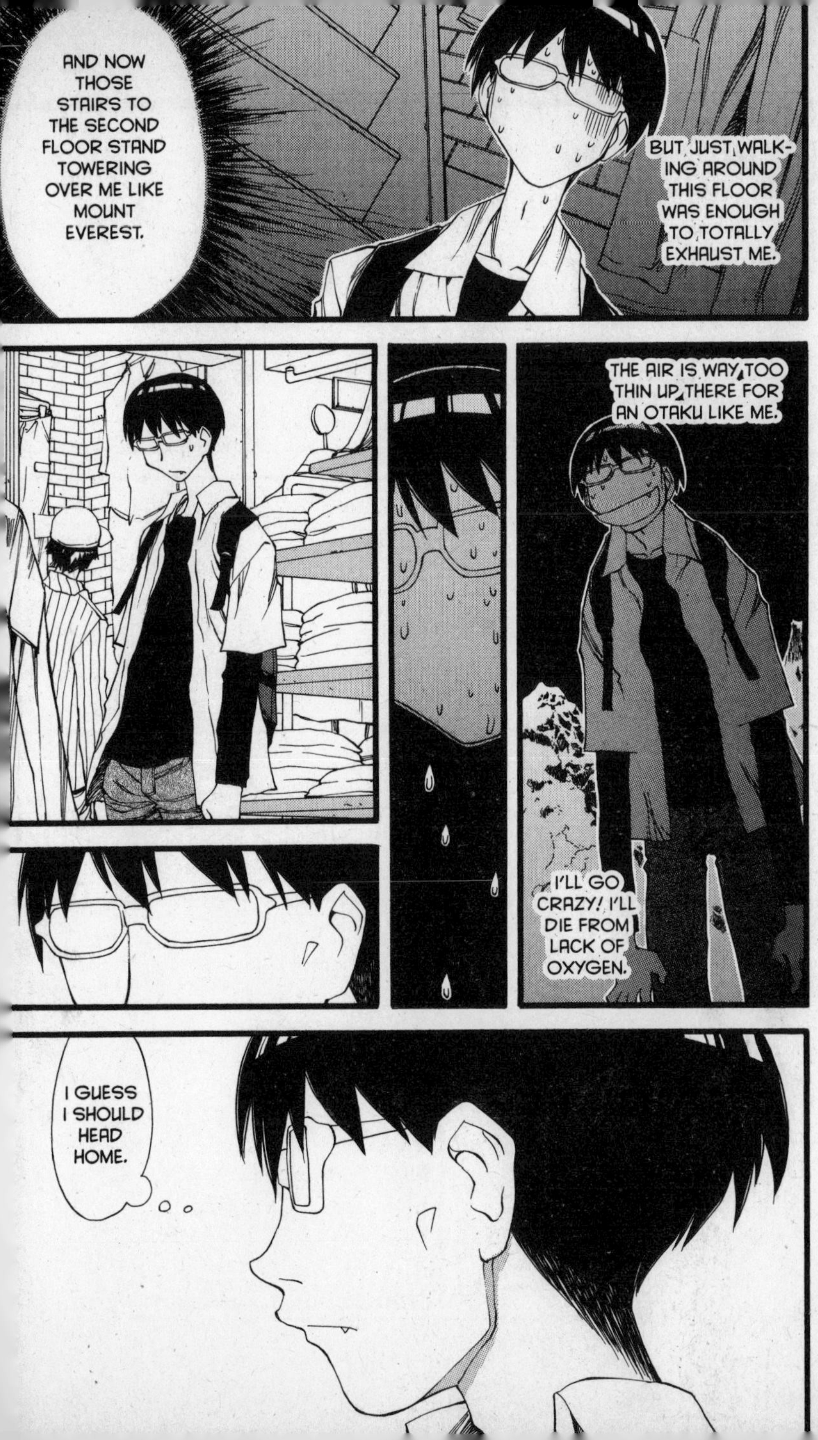
BUT JUST WALKING AROUND THIS FLOOR WAS ENOUGH TO TOTALLY EXHAUST ME.
AND NOW THOSE STAIRS TO THE SECOND FLOOR STAND TOWERING OVER ME LIKE MOUNT EVEREST.
THE AIR IS WAY TOO THIN UP THERE FOR AN OTAKU LIKE ME.
I'LL GO CRAZY! I'LL DIE FROM LACK OF OXYGEN.
I GUESS I SHOULD HEAD HOME.

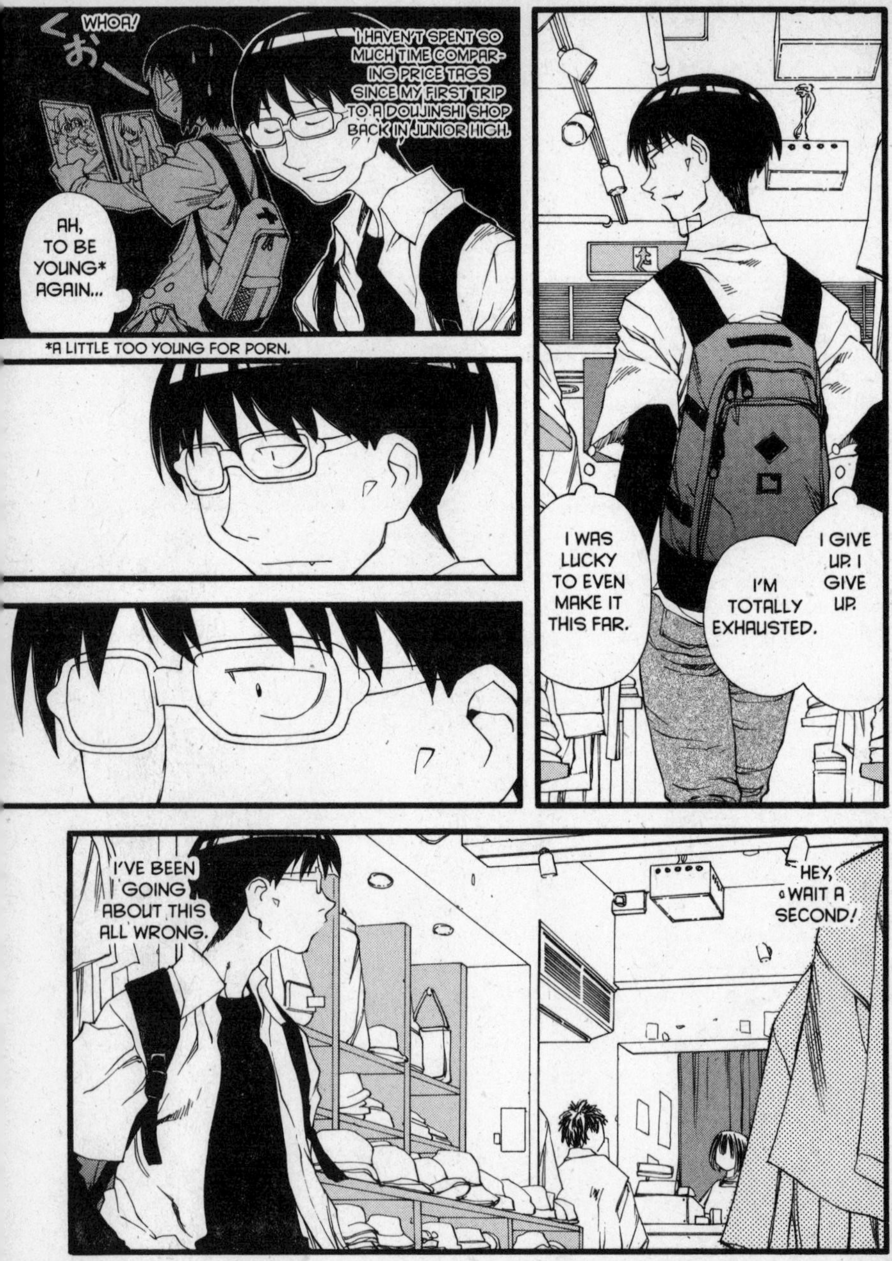
I GIVE UP. I GIVE UP.
I'M TOTALLY EXHAUSTED.
I WAS LUCKY TO EVEN MAKE IT THIS FAR.
I HAVEN'T SPENT SO MUCH TIME COMPARING PRICE TAGS SINCE MY FIRST TRIP TO A DOUJINSHI SHOP BACK IN JUNIOR HIGH.
WHOA!
くお〜
AH, TO BE YOUNG* AGAIN...
*A LITTLE TOO YOUNG FOR PORN.
HEY, WAIT A SECOND!
I'VE BEEN GOING ABOUT THIS ALL WRONG.

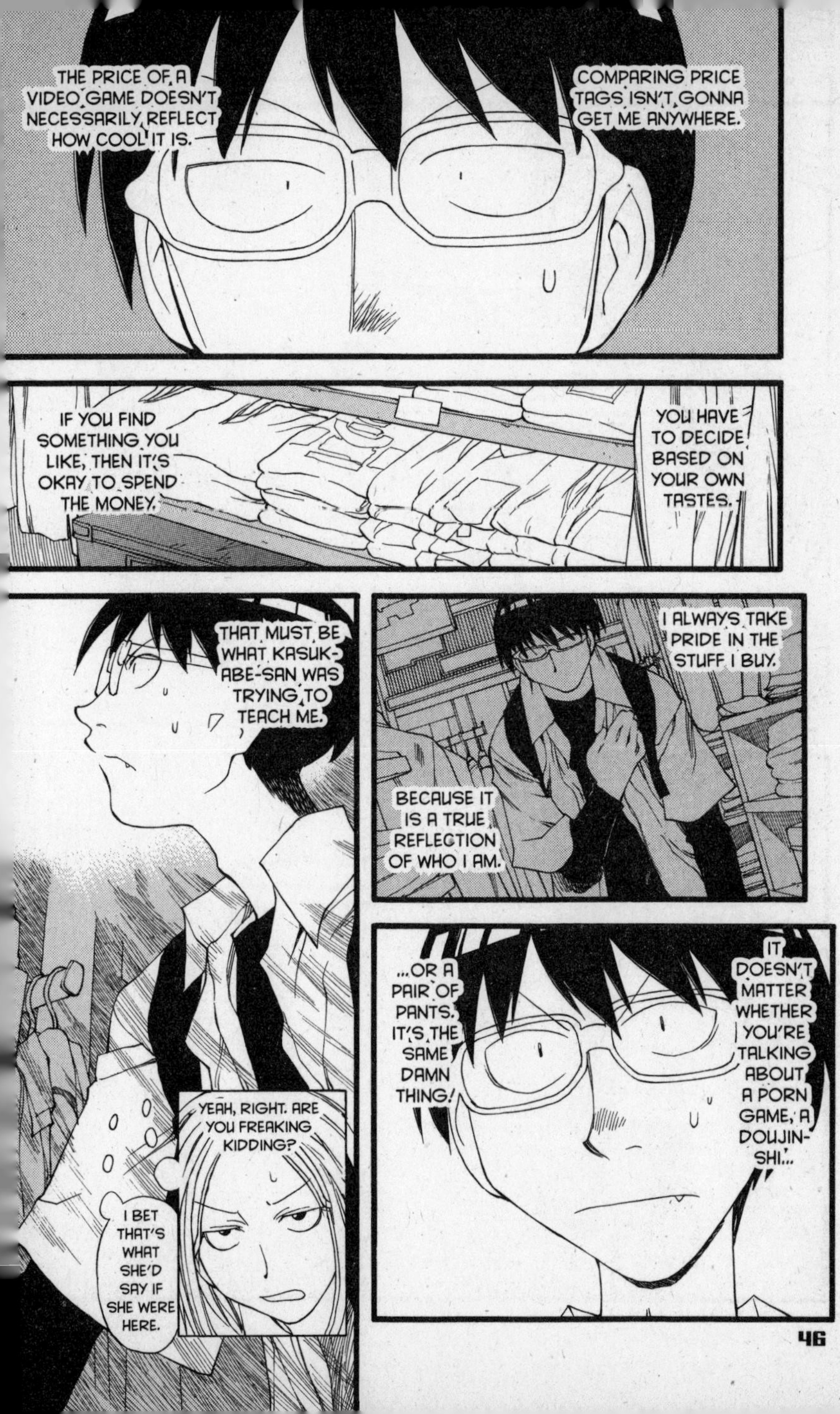
COMPARING PRICE TAGS ISN'T GONNA GET ME ANYWHERE.
THE PRICE OF A VIDEO GAME DOESN'T NECESSARILY REFLECT HOW COOL IT IS.
YOU HAVE TO DECIDE BASED ON YOUR OWN TASTES.
IF YOU FIND SOMETHING YOU LIKE, THEN IT'S OKAY TO SPEND THE MONEY.
I ALWAYS TAKE PRIDE IN THE STUFF I BUY.
BECAUSE IT IS A TRUE REFLECTION OF WHO I AM.
IT DOESN'T MATTER WHETHER YOU'RE TALKING ABOUT A PORN GAME, A DOUJINSHI...
...OR A PAIR OF PANTS. IT'S THE SAME DAMN THING!
THAT MUST BE WHAT KASUKABE-SAN WAS TRYING TO TEACH ME.
YEAH, RIGHT. ARE YOU FREAKING KIDDING?
I BET THAT'S WHAT SHE'D SAY IF SHE WERE HERE.

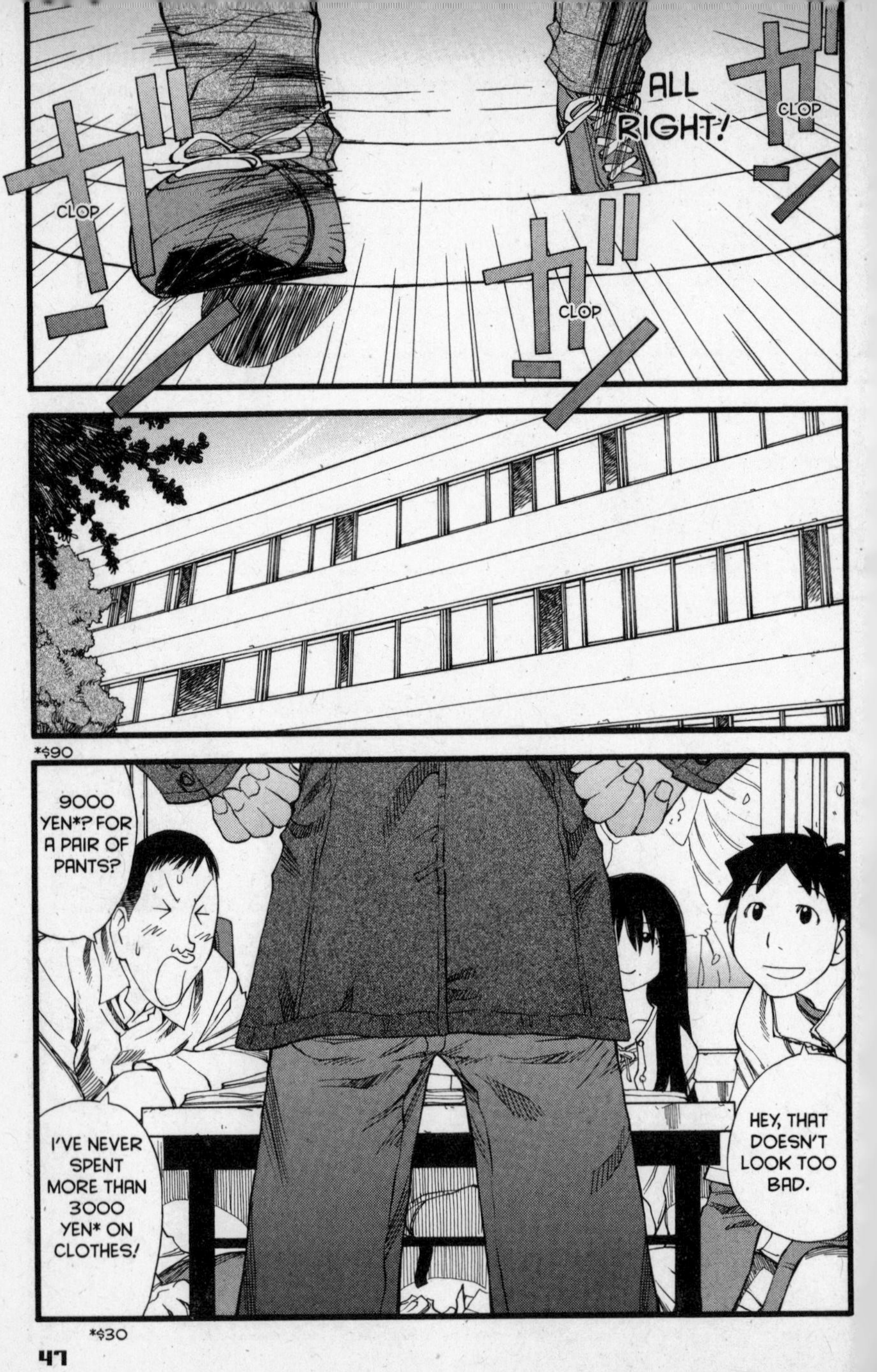
CLOP
ALL RIGHT!
CLOP
CLOP
HEY, THAT DOESN'T LOOK TOO BAD.
9000 YEN*? FOR A PAIR OF PANTS?
I'VE NEVER SPENT MORE THAN 3000 YEN* ON CLOTHES!

*$90

*$30

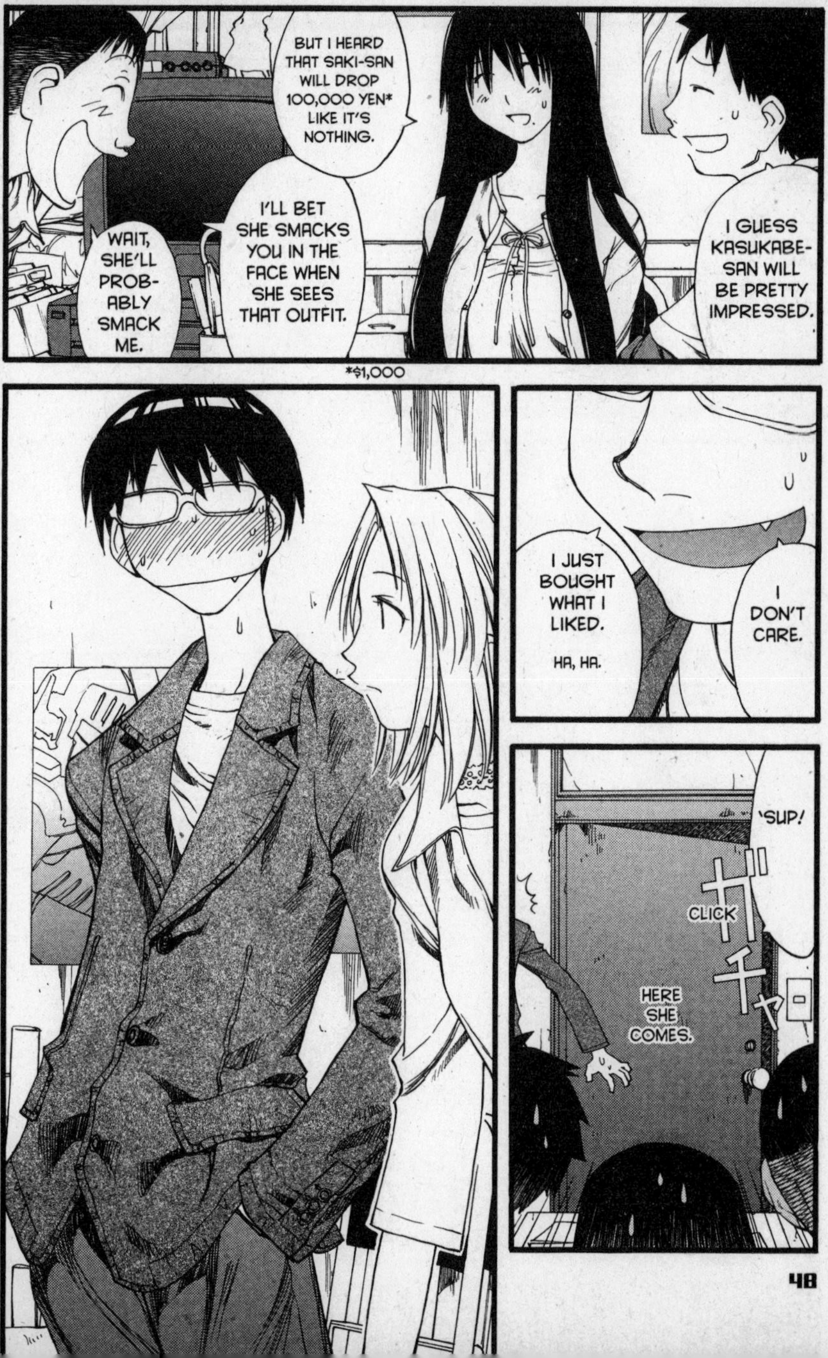
I GUESS KASUKABE-SAN WILL BE PRETTY IMPRESSED.
BUT I HEARD THAT SAKI-SAN WILL DROP 100,000 YEN* LIKE IT'S NOTHING.
I'LL BET SHE SMACKS YOU IN THE FACE WHEN SHE SEES THAT OUTFIT.
WAIT, SHE'LL PROBABLY SMACK ME.
I DON'T CARE.
I JUST BOUGHT WHAT I LIKED.
HA, HA.
'SUP!
ガチャー
CLICK
HERE SHE COMES.

*$1,000

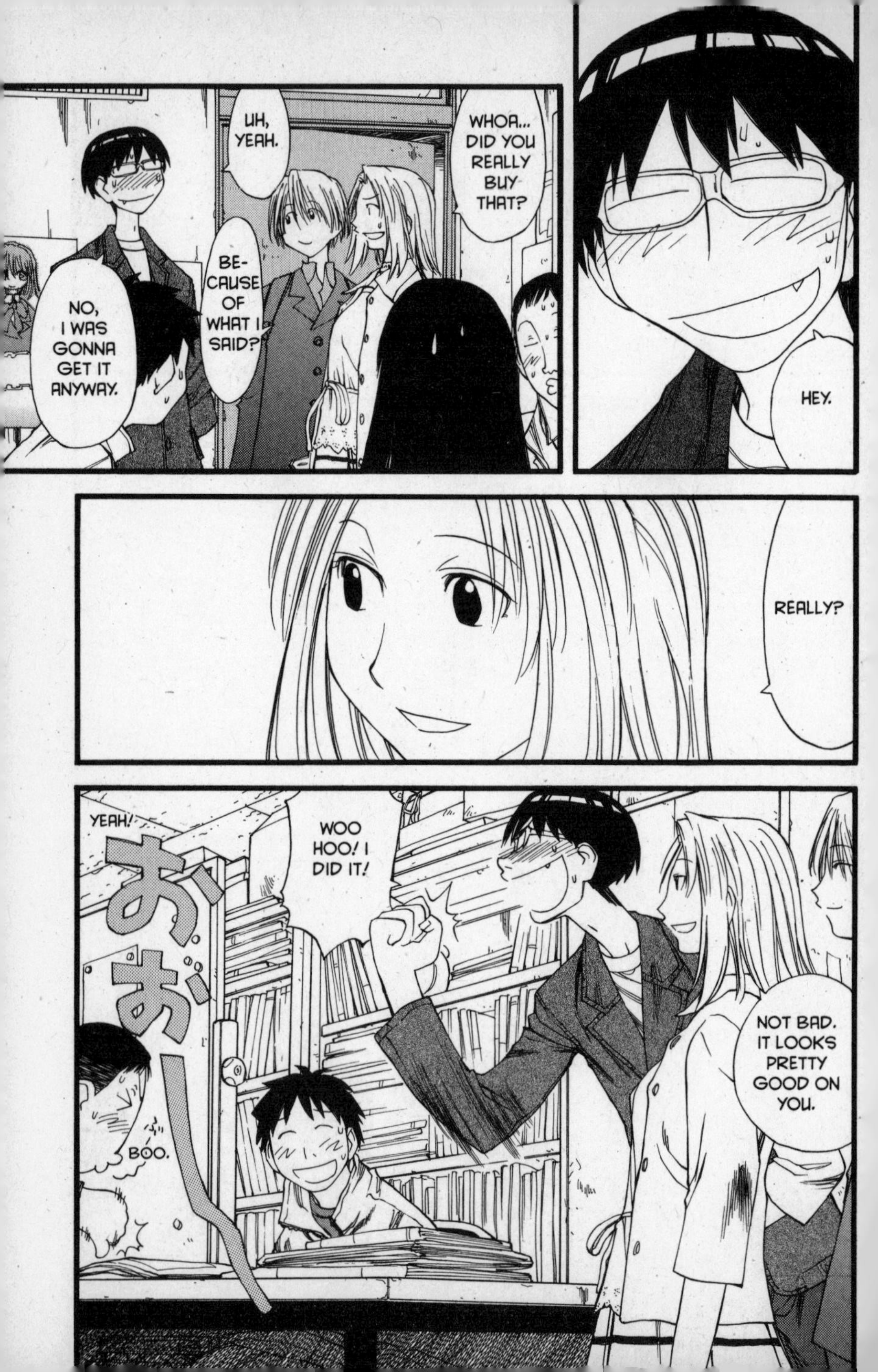
HEY.
WHOA... DID YOU REALLY BUY THAT?
UH, YEAH.
BE-CAUSE OF WHAT I SAID?
NO, I WAS GONNA GET IT ANYWAY.
REALLY?
NOT BAD. IT LOOKS PRETTY GOOD ON YOU.
WOO HOO! I DID IT!
YEAH!
おぉし
BOO.

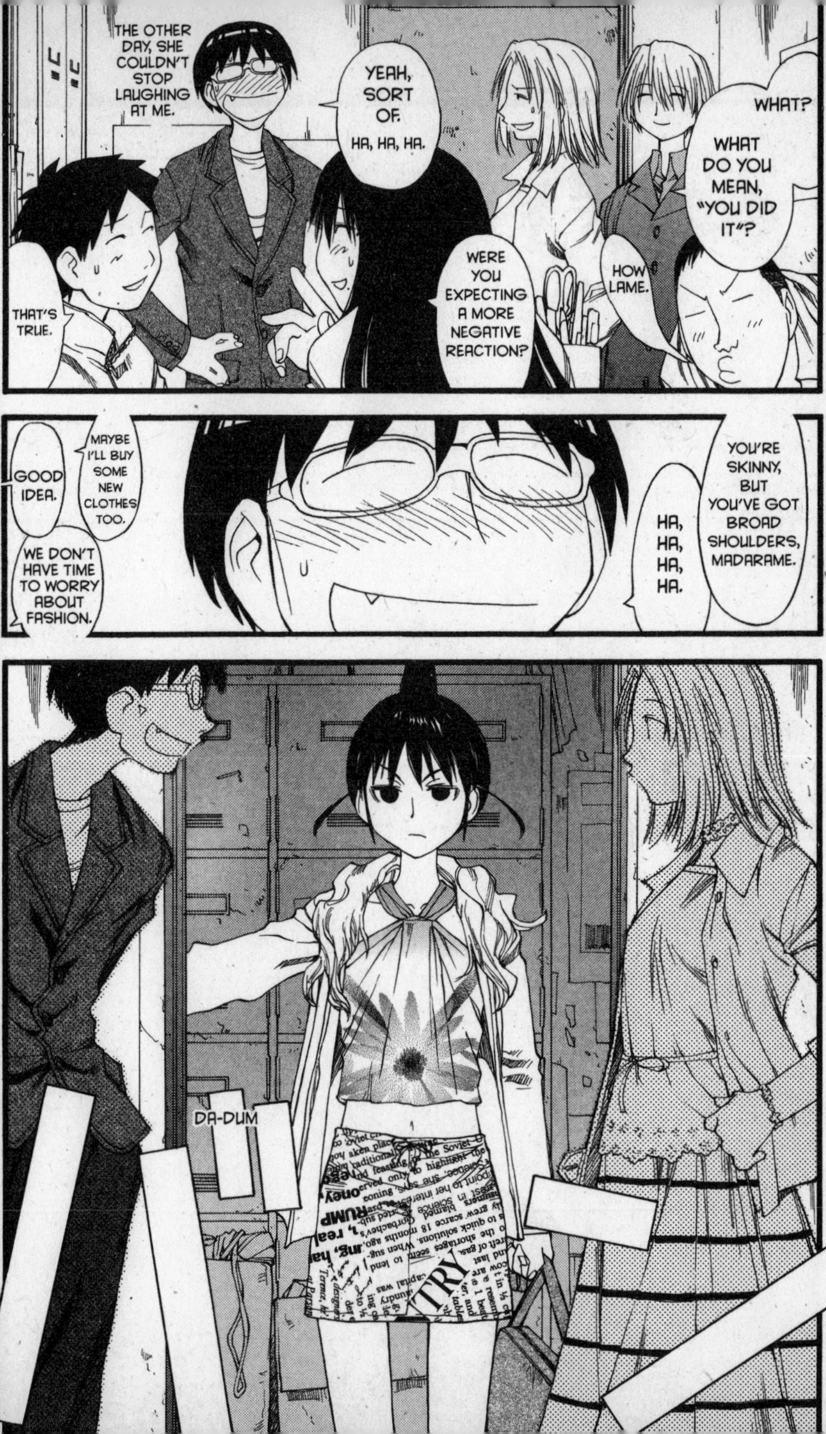
WHAT?
WHAT DO YOU MEAN, "YOU DID IT"?
HOW LAME.
WERE YOU EXPECTING A MORE NEGATIVE REACTION?
YEAH, SORT OF.
HA, HA, HA.
THE OTHER DAY, SHE COULDN'T STOP LAUGHING AT ME.
THAT'S TRUE.
YOU'RE SKINNY, BUT YOU'VE GOT BROAD SHOULDERS, MADARAME.
HA, HA, HA, HA.
MAYBE I'LL BUY SOME NEW CLOTHES TOO.
GOOD IDEA.
WE DON'T HAVE TIME TO WORRY ABOUT FASHION.
DA-DUM

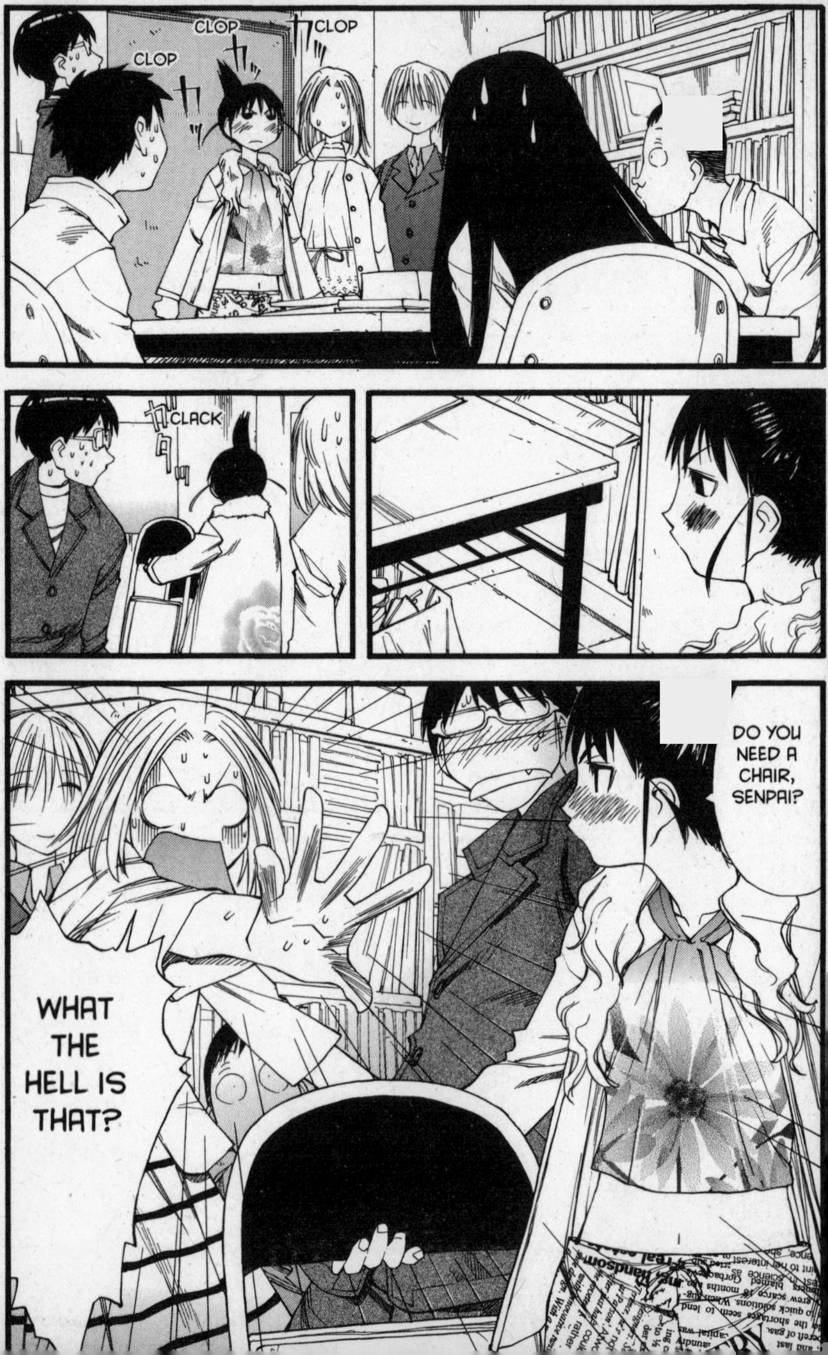
CLOP
CLOP
CLOP
CLACK
DO YOU NEED A CHAIR, SENPAI?
WHAT THE HELL IS THAT?

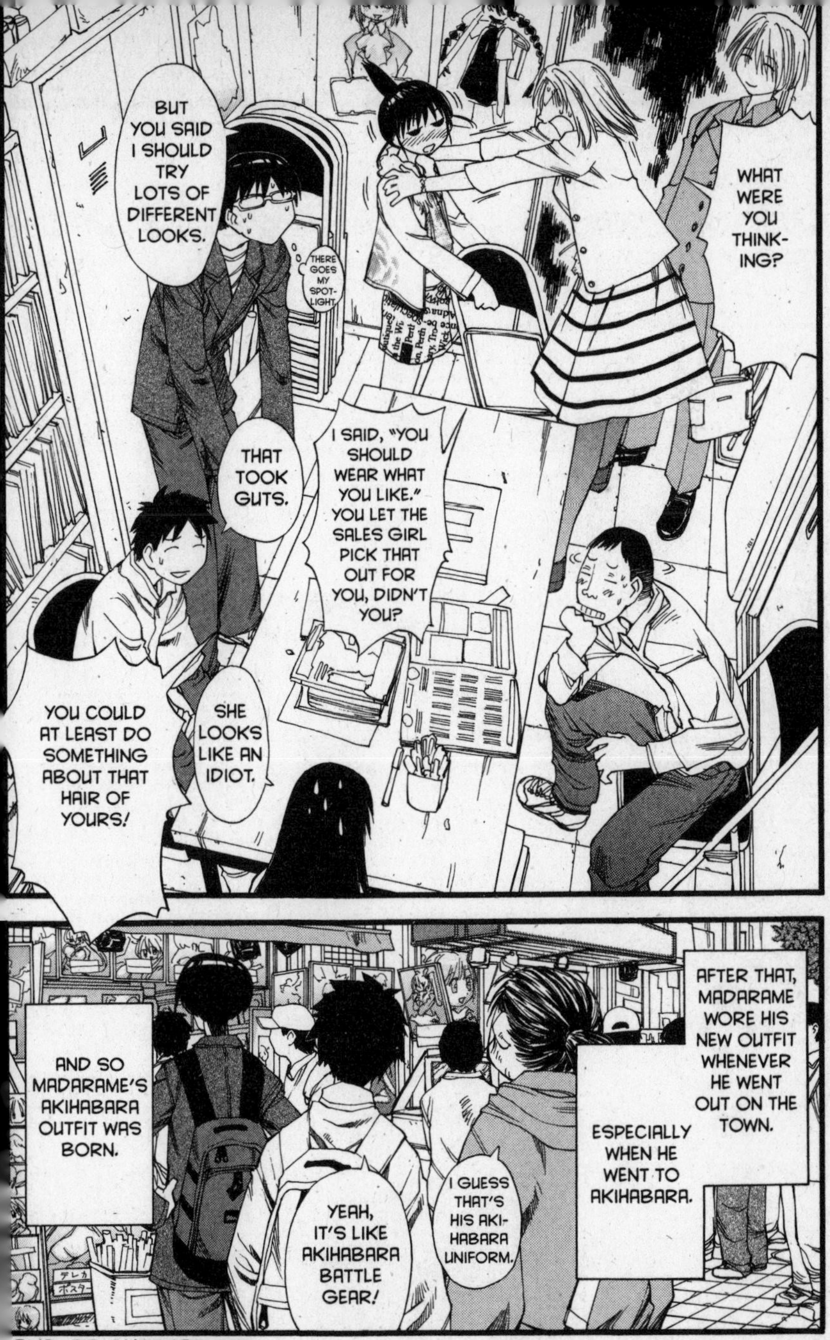
WHAT WERE YOU THINKING?
BUT YOU SAID I SHOULD TRY LOTS OF DIFFERENT LOOKS.
THERE GOES MY SPOTLIGHT.
I SAID, "YOU SHOULD WEAR WHAT YOU LIKE." YOU LET THE SALES GIRL PICK THAT OUT FOR YOU, DIDN'T YOU?
THAT TOOK GUTS.
SHE LOOKS LIKE AN IDIOT.
YOU COULD AT LEAST DO SOMETHING ABOUT THAT HAIR OF YOURS!
AFTER THAT, MADARAME WORE HIS NEW OUTFIT WHENEVER HE WENT OUT ON THE TOWN.
ESPECIALLY WHEN HE WENT TO AKIHABARA.
I GUESS THAT'S HIS AKI-HABARA UNIFORM.
YEAH, IT'S LIKE AKIHABARA BATTLE GEAR!
AND SO MADARAME'S AKIHABARA OUTFIT WAS BORN.

END OF CHAPTER 26

THE RETURN OF MY FAVORITE SCENES FROM KUJI-UN - PART 2

BY BENJAMIN TAKEYO

EPISODE 25 "KUJIBIKI FOREVER"

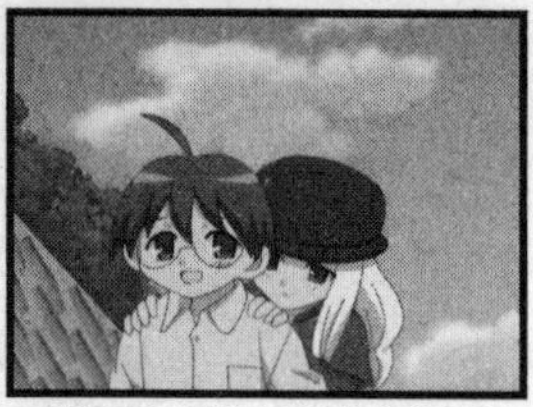

▲ "LET ME DOWN." I LOVE WHEN THEY GET CLOSE LIKE THAT.

I ALWAYS CHOOSE THE PRESIDENT...NO MATTER WHAT. SORRY. I'M JUST GONNA APOLOGIZE RIGHT NOW, AND GET IT OUT OF THE WAY. I'M TRULY SORRY. HUH? WHY? UH...WELL, I CHOSE THREE DIFFERENT PRESIDENT SCENES, COUGH, COUGH. I'LL START WITH THE MOST BASIC.

IN EPISODE 25, THE PRESIDENT GOES TO VISIT THE GRAVE OF CHIHIRO'S PARENTS. SHE PASSES OUT, AND CHIHIRO CARRIES HER AWAY ON HIS BACK. SHE COMES TO WHILE STILL RIDING HIM PIGGYBACK. INSTEAD OF SAYING, "I'M GETTING DOWN," SHE SAYS, "LET ME DOWN." IT SOUNDS SO CUTE.

EPISODE ONE "AN UNBALANCED ENCOUNTER"

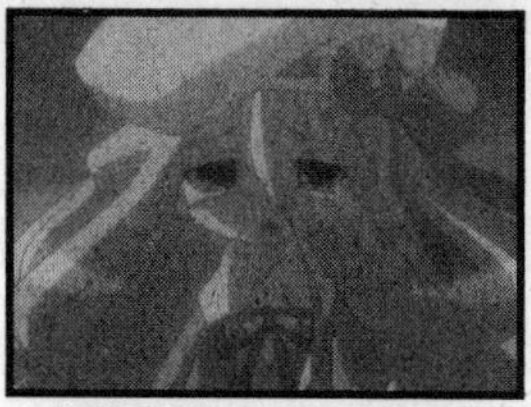

▲ I'M SORRY. I'M SORRY. I'M SORRY. I'M REALLY, TRULY SORRY.

EPISODE 21 "THE COMPLETE KUJI-UN"

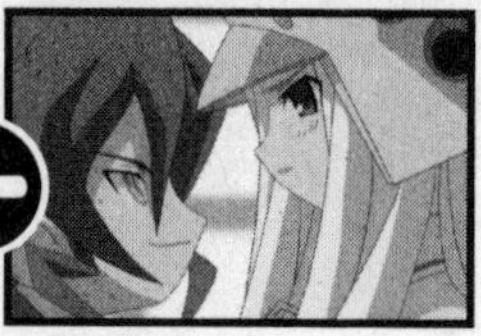

▲ ALEX APPROACHES.

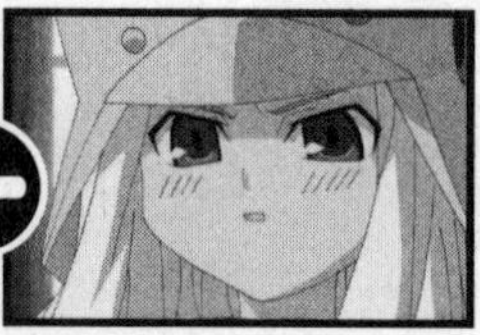

▲ "I'M GONNA DIE." AH, JUST LOOK AT HER.

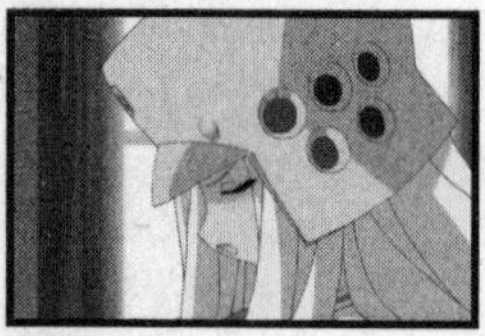

▲ "I'M OKAY."

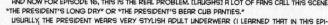

BONUS

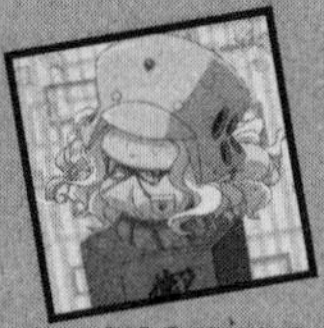

▲ AN EYE-CATCHING MOMENT. HOLD ON...

NEXT IS EPISODE 21, "THE COMPLETE KUJI-UN." THERE'S A NEW SCENE THAT WAS ADDED TO THE DVD. IT MOSTLY SHOWS THE VICE PRESIDENT VS ALICE. WE ALSO GET TO SEE THE PRESIDENT AS SHE...AH, IT'S JUST TOO MUCH FOR ME. I CAN'T EVEN WRITE ABOUT IT. [LAUGHS] WHAT A TENSE MOMENT.

AND NOW FOR EPISODE 16, THIS IS THE REAL PROBLEM. [LAUGHS] A LOT OF FANS CALL THIS SCENE "THE PRESIDENT'S LONG DAY" OR "THE PRESIDENT'S BEAR CUB PANTIES."

USUALLY, THE PRESIDENT WEARS VERY STYLISH ADULT UNDERWEAR (I LEARNED THAT IN THIS EPISODE), BUT ON THIS DAY, HER MOTHER ACCIDENTALLY PUTS ALL OF HER PANTIES IN THE WASH. WHAT A PINCH FOR OUR POOR LITTLE PRESIDENT. BUT IT TURNS OUT THAT SHE HAD HER OWN TOP-SECRET COLLECTION. SHE HAS TONS OF CUTE PANTIES THAT SHE'S COLLECTED OVER THE YEARS. SHE HAD LOTS OF STUFFED ANIMALS AS A KID, BUT NOW SHE'S TRYING HER BEST TO ACT LIKE A GROWNUP. WHAT A GREAT STORY!

OF COURSE, THEY SHOW US THOSE CUTE BEAR PANTIES WHEN THEY'RE ALL FOLDED UP, BUT THEY NEVER EVER SHOW HER WEARING THEM. THEY JUST KEEP LEADING US ON. THEY WERE REALLY CAREFUL IN THIS EPISODE. I WATCHED THE WHOLE THING FRAME BY FRAME, BUT I STILL COULDN'T SEE THEM. THE RUMOR THAT YOU GET TO SEE IT IN THE DVD VERSION IS A BUNCH OF BULL. WHAT A RIP OFF. CHIHIRO GETS TO SEE HER WEARING THEM IN THE END, SO WHY THE HELL DON'T WE? AAHHH! [BENJAMIN]

EPISODE 16 "CHRISTINE OF THE HARBOR"

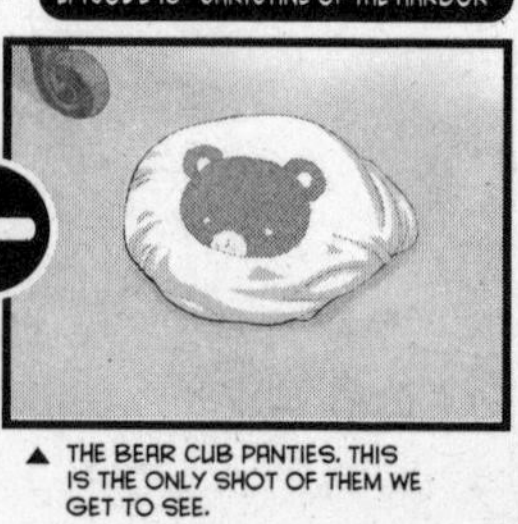

▲ THE BEAR CUB PANTIES. THIS IS THE ONLY SHOT OF THEM WE GET TO SEE.

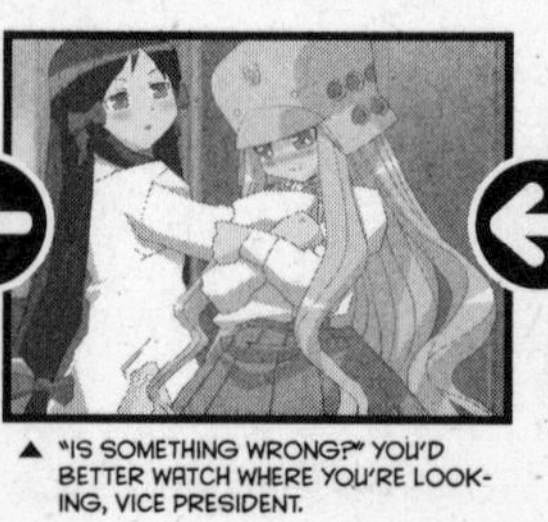

▲ "IS SOMETHING WRONG?" YOU'D BETTER WATCH WHERE YOU'RE LOOKING, VICE PRESIDENT.

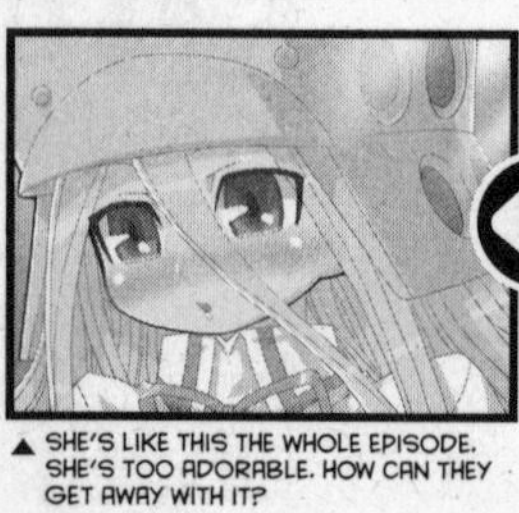

▲ SHE'S LIKE THIS THE WHOLE EPISODE. SHE'S TOO ADORABLE. HOW CAN THEY GET AWAY WITH IT?

IN THE DRESSING ROOM PART 1

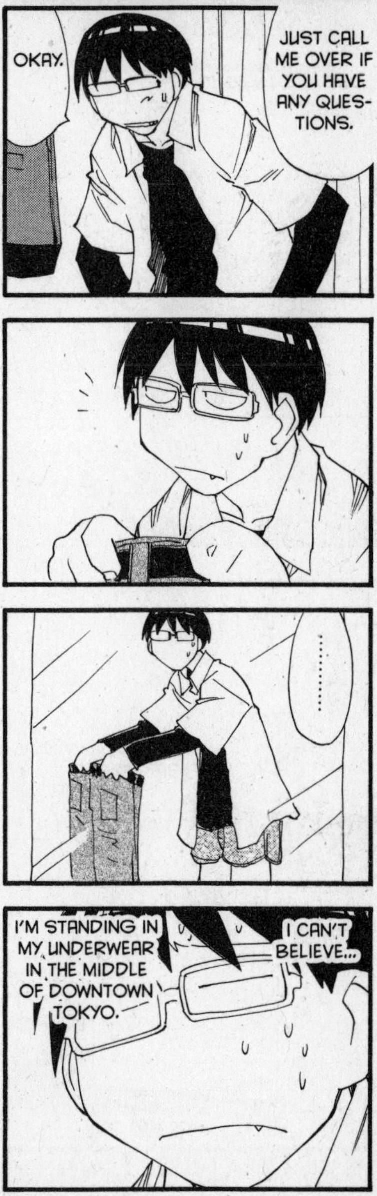
JUST CALL ME OVER IF YOU HAVE ANY QUES-TIONS.
OKAY.
......
I CAN'T BELIEVE...
I'M STANDING IN MY UNDERWEAR IN THE MIDDLE OF DOWNTOWN TOKYO.

IN THE DRESSING ROOM PART 2

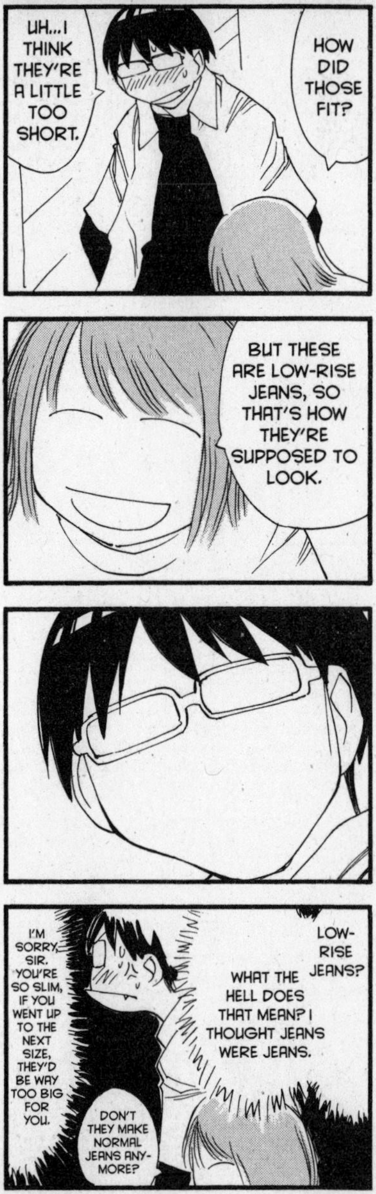
HOW DID THOSE FIT?
UH...I THINK THEY'RE A LITTLE TOO SHORT.
BUT THESE ARE LOW-RISE JEANS, SO THAT'S HOW THEY'RE SUPPOSED TO LOOK.
LOW-RISE JEANS?
WHAT THE HELL DOES THAT MEAN? I THOUGHT JEANS WERE JEANS.
I'M SORRY, SIR. YOU'RE SO SLIM, IF YOU WENT UP TO THE NEXT SIZE, THEY'D BE WAY TOO BIG FOR YOU.
DON'T THEY MAKE NORMAL JEANS ANYMORE?

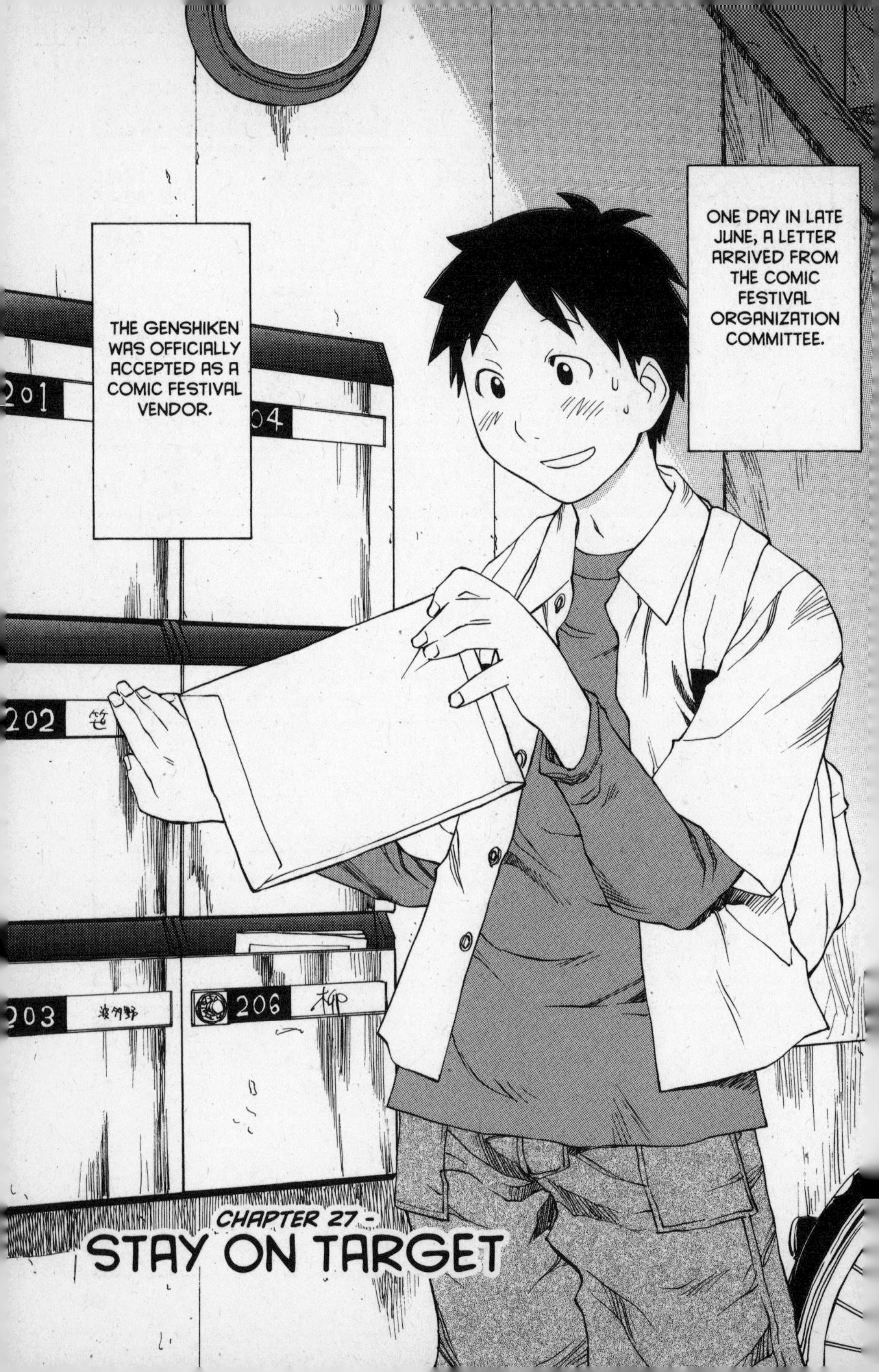
ONE DAY IN LATE JUNE, A LETTER ARRIVED FROM THE COMIC FESTIVAL ORGANIZATION COMMITTEE.
THE GENSHIKEN WAS OFFICIALLY ACCEPTED AS A COMIC FESTIVAL VENDOR.
201
202
203
206
CHAPTER 27 -
STAY ON TARGET

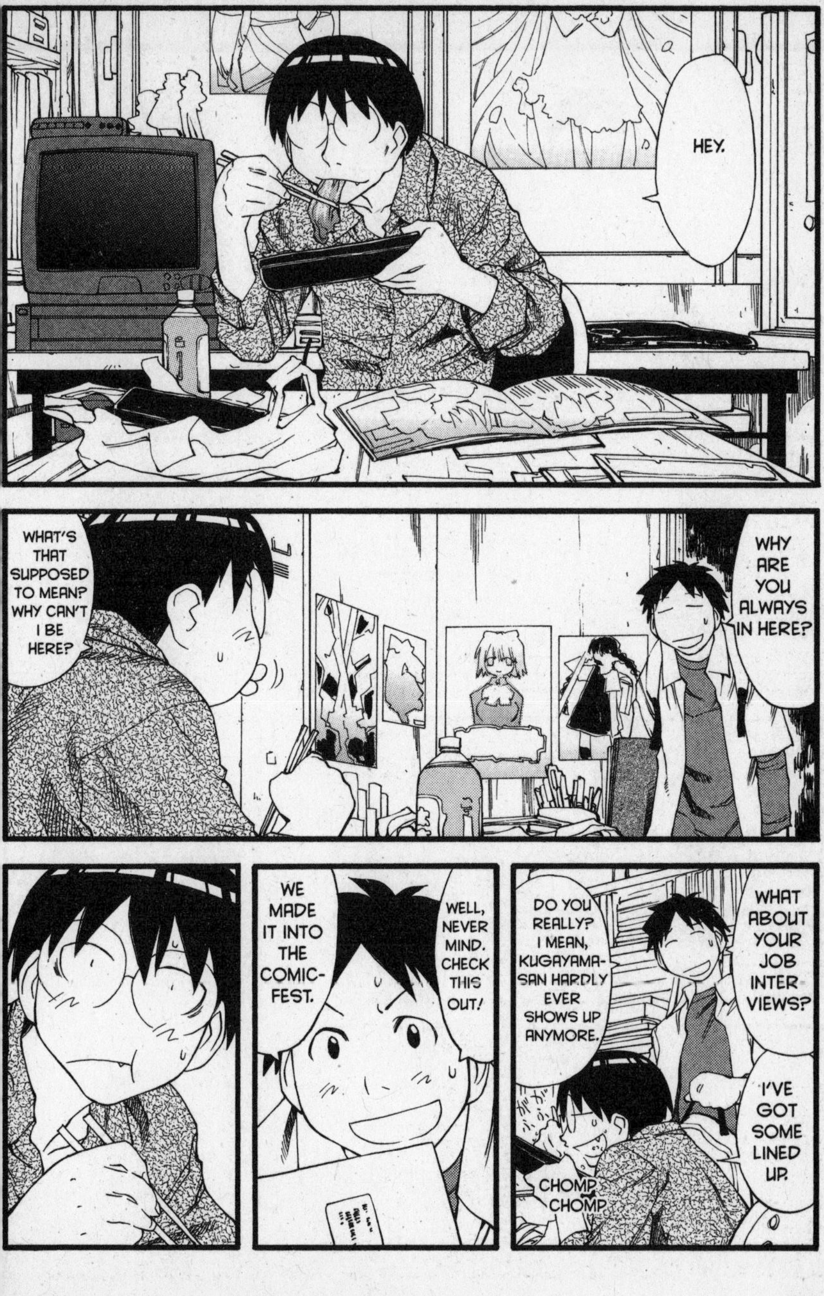
HEY.
WHY ARE YOU ALWAYS IN HERE?
WHAT'S THAT SUPPOSED TO MEAN? WHY CAN'T I BE HERE?
WHAT ABOUT YOUR JOB INTERVIEWS?
I'VE GOT SOME LINED UP.
DO YOU REALLY? I MEAN, KUGAYAMA-SAN HARDLY EVER SHOWS UP ANYMORE.
CHOMP CHOMP
WELL, NEVER MIND. CHECK THIS OUT!
WE MADE IT INTO THE COMIC-FEST.

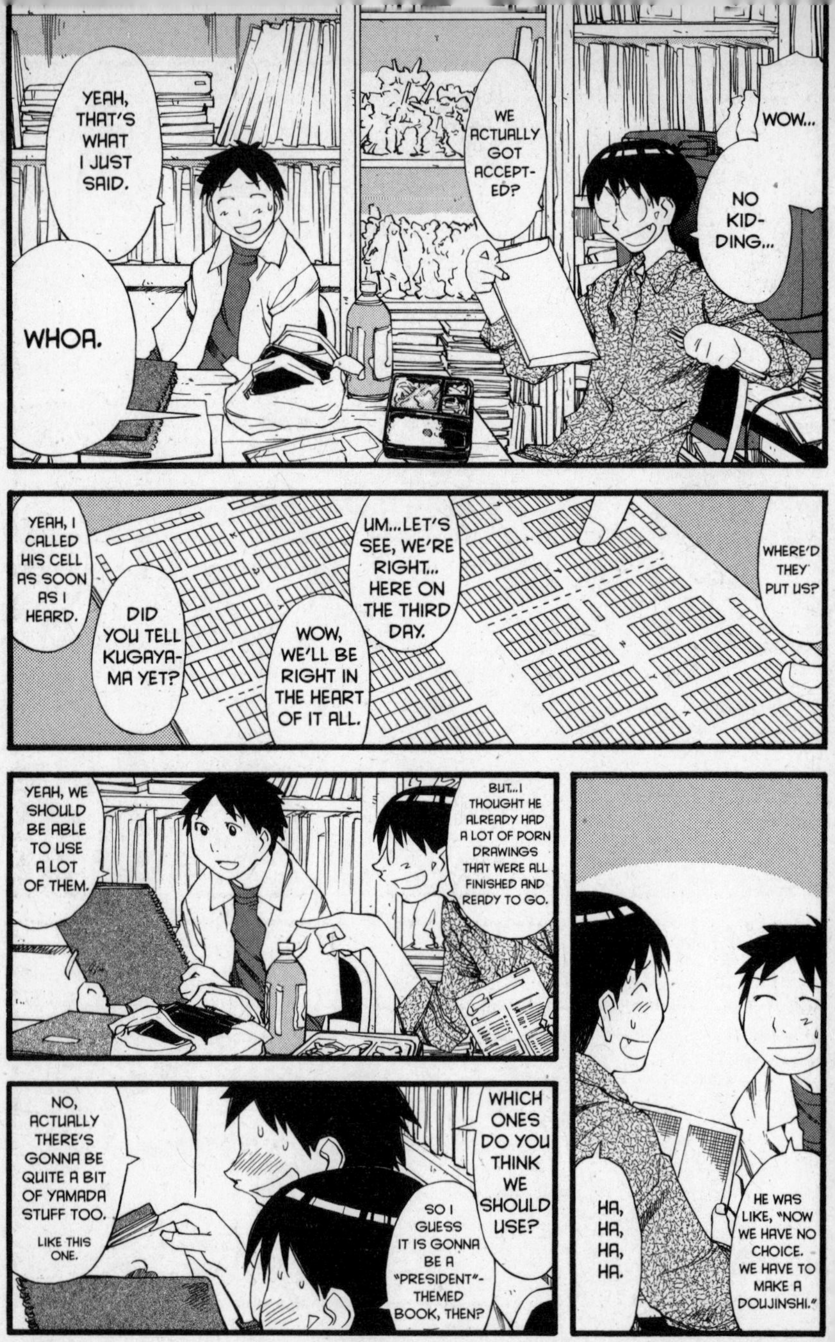
WOW... NO KIDDING...
WE ACTUALLY GOT ACCEPTED?
YEAH, THAT'S WHAT I JUST SAID.
WHOA.
WHERE'D THEY PUT US?
UM...LET'S SEE, WE'RE RIGHT... HERE ON THE THIRD DAY.
WOW, WE'LL BE RIGHT IN THE HEART OF IT ALL.
DID YOU TELL KUGAYAMA YET?
YEAH, I CALLED HIS CELL AS SOON AS I HEARD.
HE WAS LIKE, "NOW WE HAVE NO CHOICE. WE HAVE TO MAKE A DOUJINSHI."
HA, HA, HA, HA.
BUT...I THOUGHT HE ALREADY HAD A LOT OF PORN DRAWINGS THAT WERE ALL FINISHED AND READY TO GO.
YEAH, WE SHOULD BE ABLE TO USE A LOT OF THEM.
...
WHICH ONES DO YOU THINK WE SHOULD USE?
SO I GUESS IT IS GONNA BE A "PRESIDENT"-THEMED BOOK, THEN?
NO, ACTUALLY THERE'S GONNA BE QUITE A BIT OF YAMADA STUFF TOO.
LIKE THIS ONE.

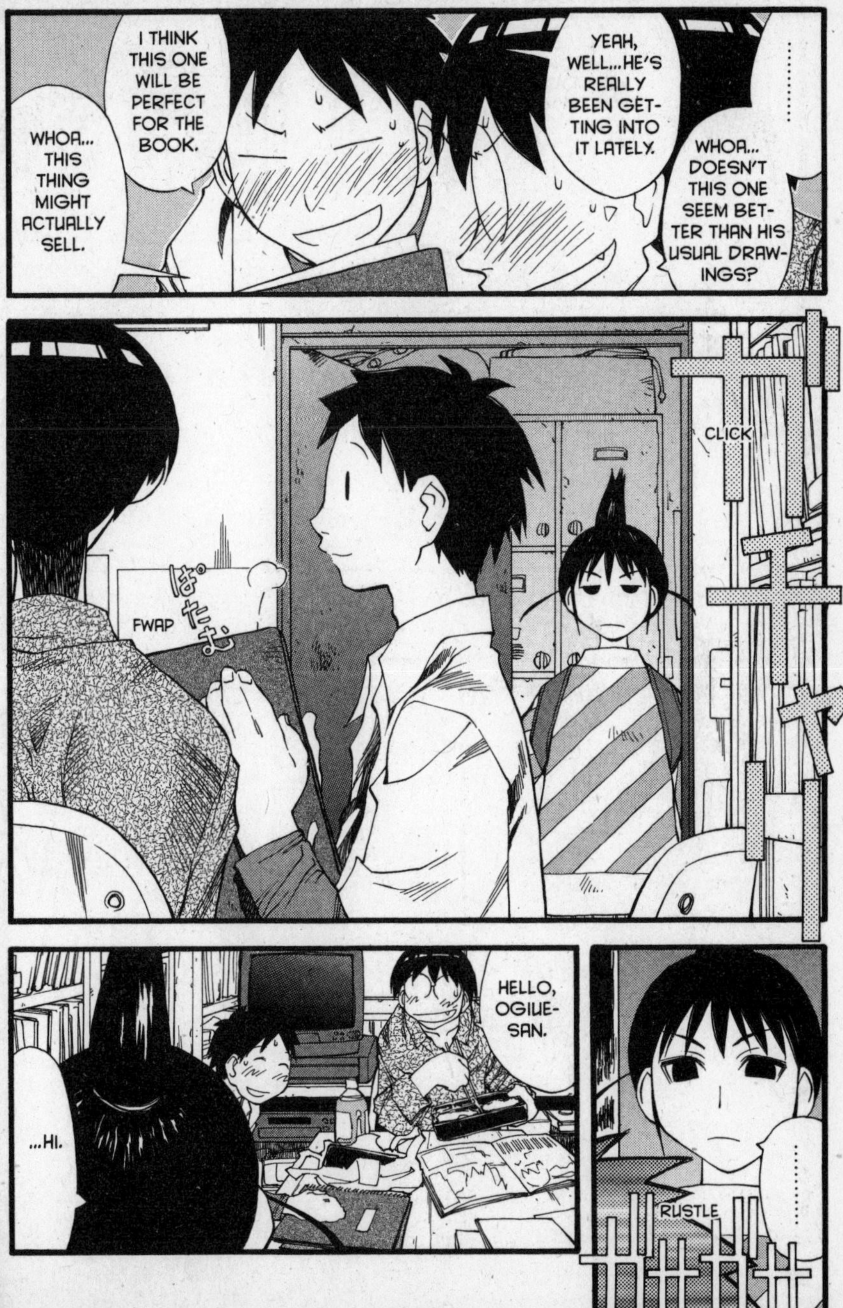
......
YEAH, WELL...HE'S REALLY BEEN GETTING INTO IT LATELY.
WHOA... DOESN'T THIS ONE SEEM BETTER THAN HIS USUAL DRAWINGS?
I THINK THIS ONE WILL BE PERFECT FOR THE BOOK.
WHOA... THIS THING MIGHT ACTUALLY SELL.
ガチャ
CLICK
ぱたむ
FWAP
RUSTLE
HELLO, OGIUE-SAN.
...HI.

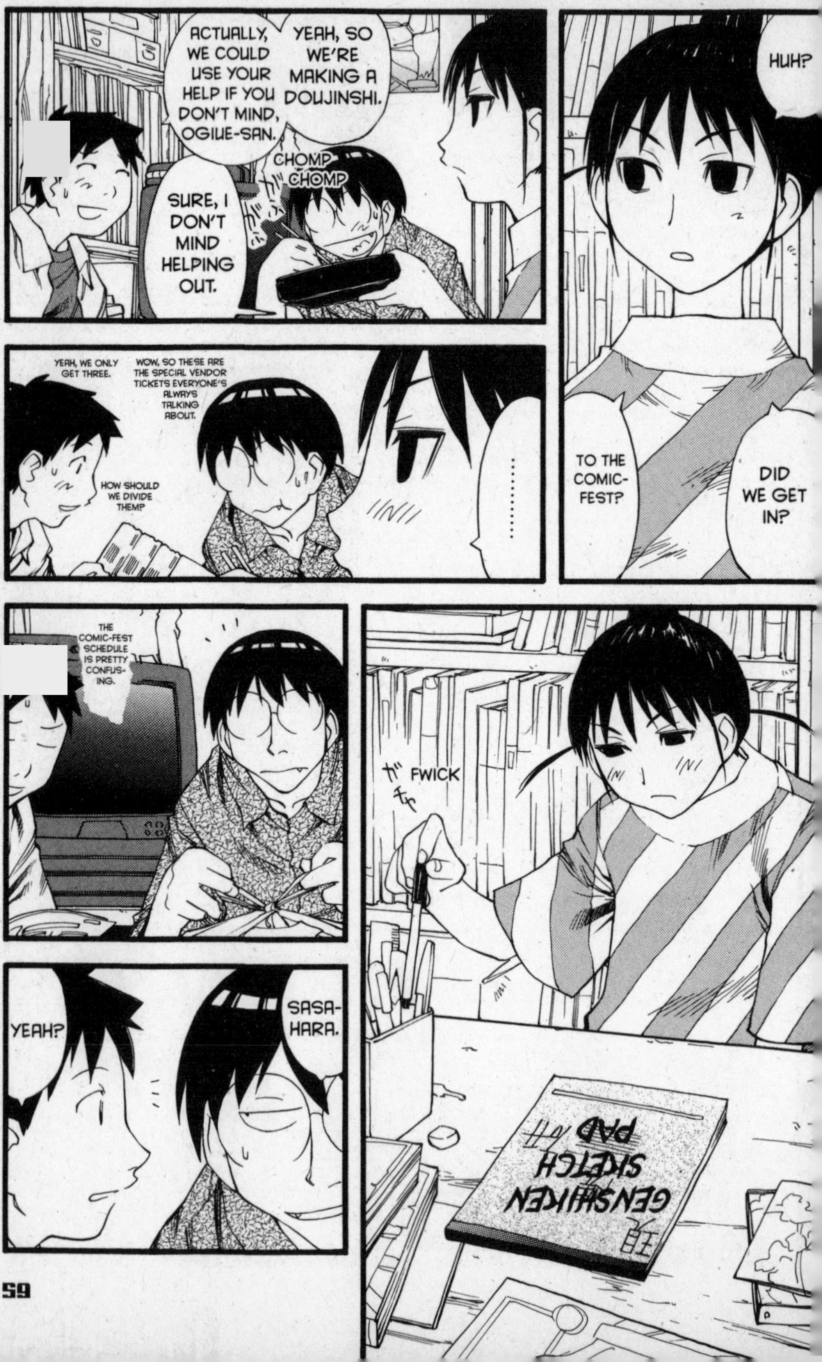
HUH?
DID WE GET IN?
TO THE COMIC-FEST?
YEAH, SO WE'RE MAKING A DOUJINSHI.
ACTUALLY, WE COULD USE YOUR HELP IF YOU DON'T MIND, OGIUE-SAN.
CHOMP CHOMP
SURE, I DON'T MIND HELPING OUT.
......
WOW, SO THESE ARE THE SPECIAL VENDOR TICKETS EVERYONE'S ALWAYS TALKING ABOUT.
YEAH, WE ONLY GET THREE.
HOW SHOULD WE DIVIDE THEM?
FWICK
GENSHIKEN SKETCH PAD
THE COMIC-FEST SCHEDULE IS PRETTY CONFUSING.
SASA-HARA.
YEAH?

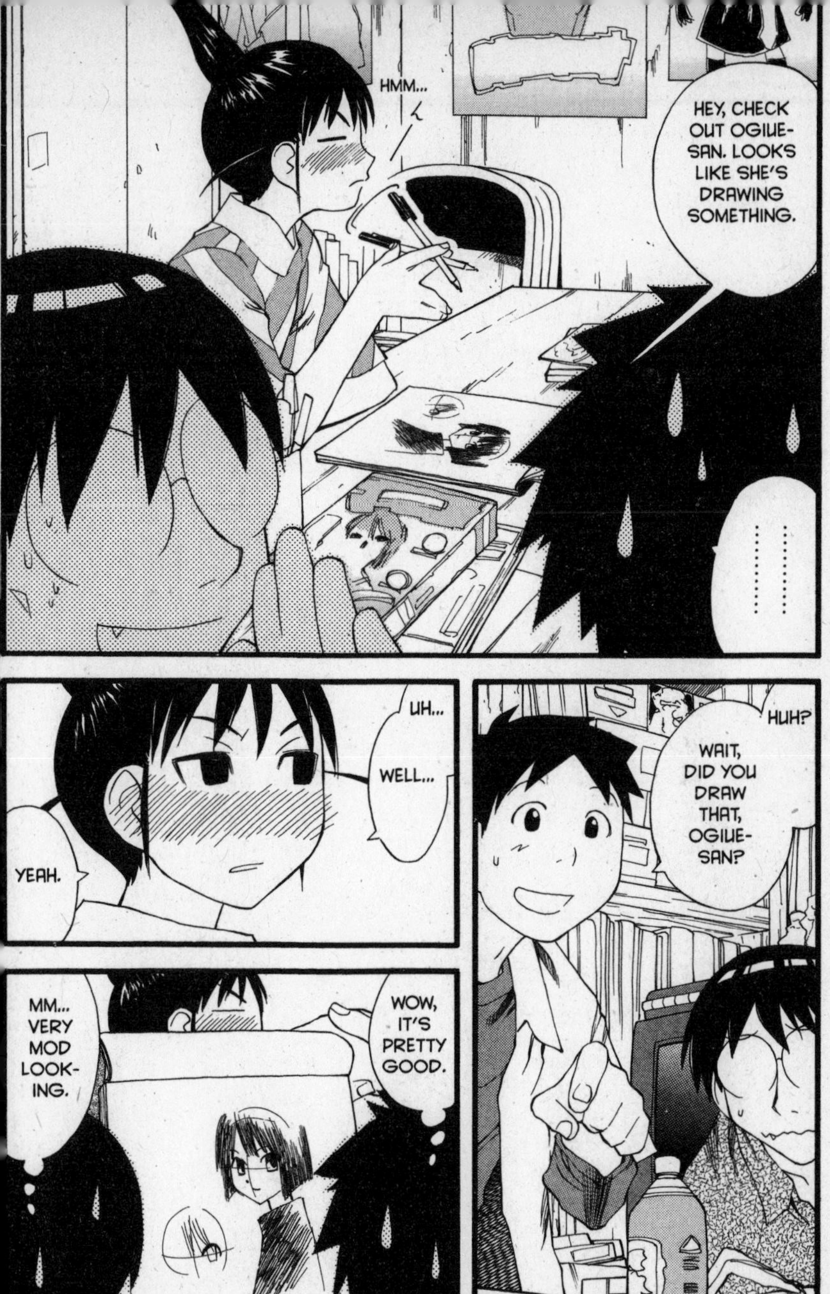
HEY, CHECK OUT OGIUE-SAN. LOOKS LIKE SHE'S DRAWING SOMETHING.
HMM...
......
HUH?
WAIT, DID YOU DRAW THAT, OGIUE-SAN?
UH...
WELL...
YEAH.
WOW, IT'S PRETTY GOOD.
MM... VERY MOD LOOKING.

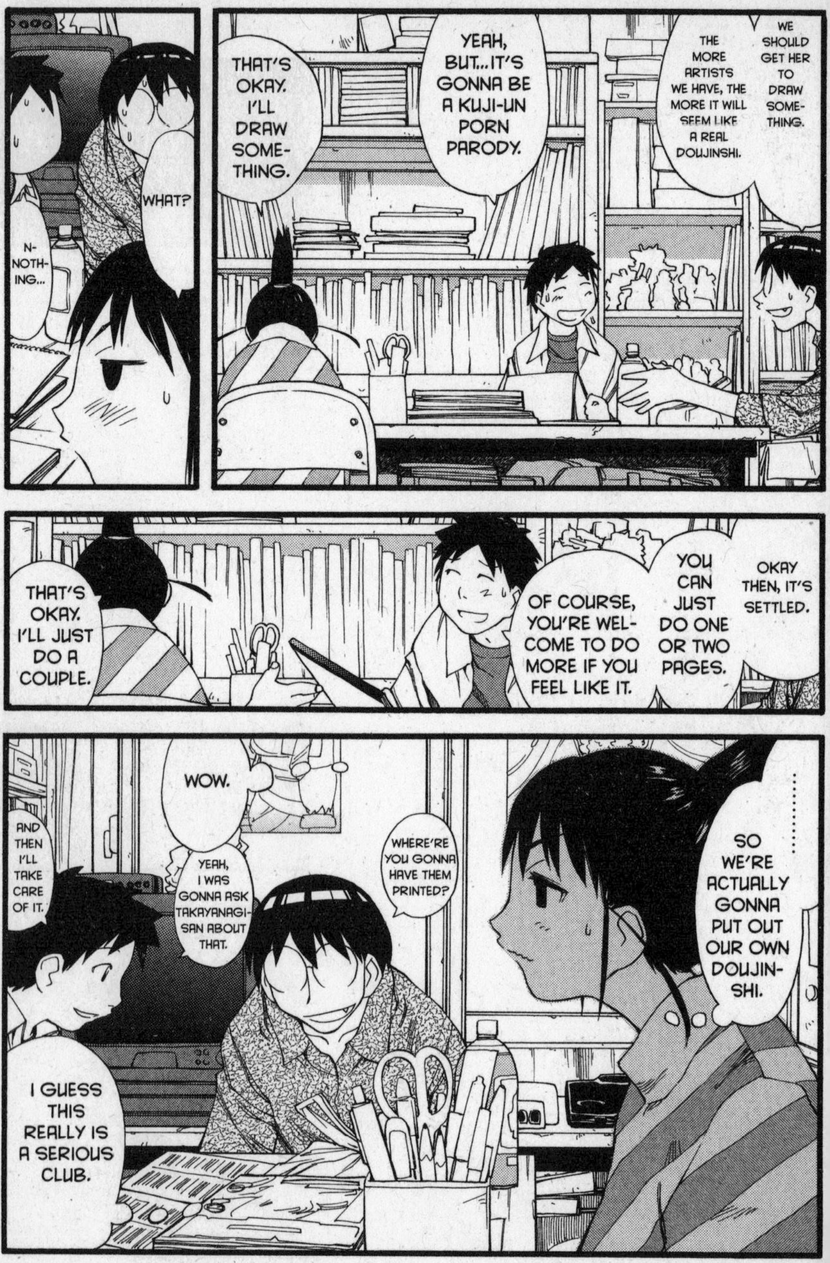
WE SHOULD GET HER TO DRAW SOMETHING.
THE MORE ARTISTS WE HAVE, THE MORE IT WILL SEEM LIKE A REAL DOUJINSHI.
YEAH, BUT...IT'S GONNA BE A KUJI-UN PORN PARODY.
THAT'S OKAY. I'LL DRAW SOMETHING.
WHAT?
N-NOTHING...
OKAY THEN, IT'S SETTLED.
YOU CAN JUST DO ONE OR TWO PAGES.
OF COURSE, YOU'RE WELCOME TO DO MORE IF YOU FEEL LIKE IT.
THAT'S OKAY. I'LL JUST DO A COUPLE.
......
SO WE'RE ACTUALLY GONNA PUT OUT OUR OWN DOUJINSHI.
WHERE'RE YOU GONNA HAVE THEM PRINTED?
WOW.
YEAH, I WAS GONNA ASK TAKAYANAGI-SAN ABOUT THAT.
AND THEN I'LL TAKE CARE OF IT.
I GUESS THIS REALLY IS A SERIOUS CLUB.

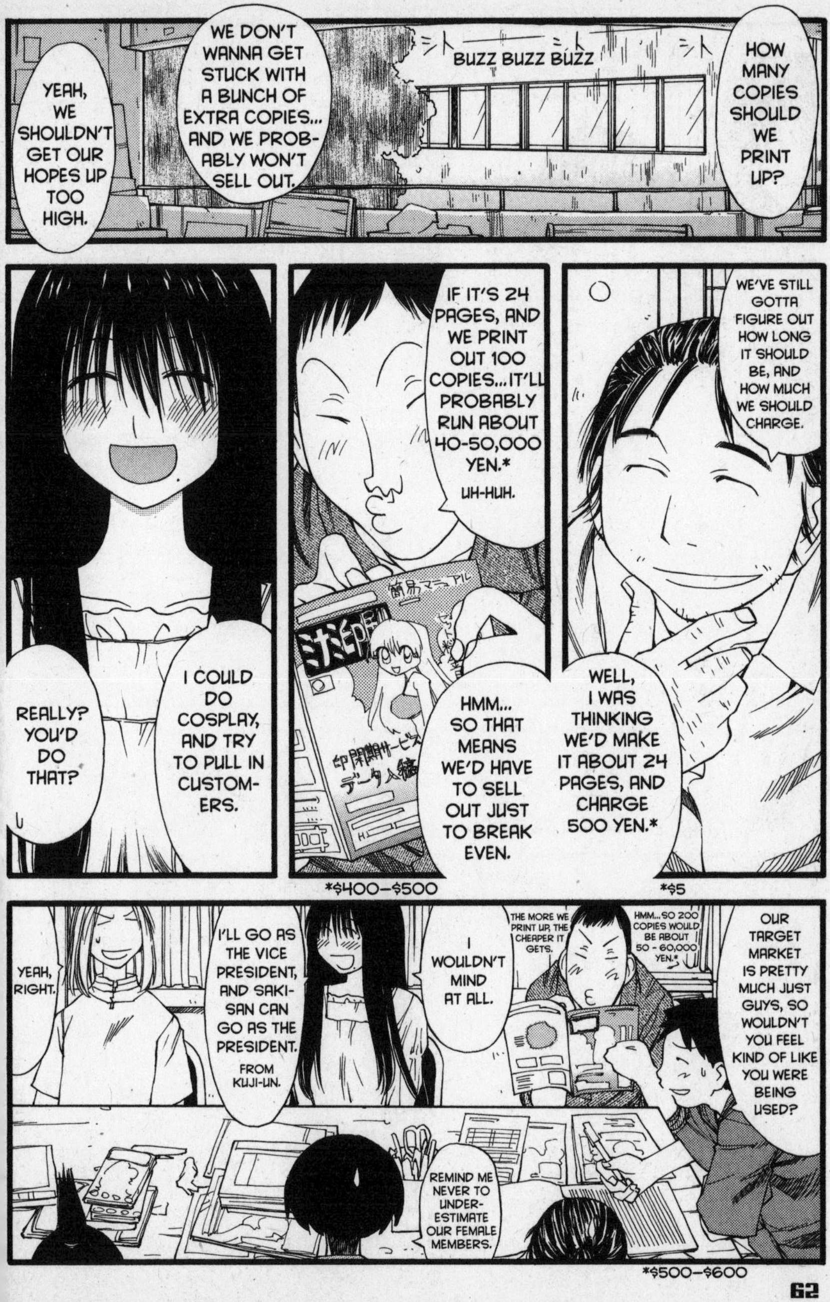

HOW MANY COPIES SHOULD WE PRINT UP?
シト シト シト BUZZ BUZZ BUZZ
WE DON'T WANNA GET STUCK WITH A BUNCH OF EXTRA COPIES... AND WE PROBABLY WON'T SELL OUT.
YEAH, WE SHOULDN'T GET OUR HOPES UP TOO HIGH.
WE'VE STILL GOTTA FIGURE OUT HOW LONG IT SHOULD BE, AND HOW MUCH WE SHOULD CHARGE.
WELL, I WAS THINKING WE'D MAKE IT ABOUT 24 PAGES, AND CHARGE 500 YEN.*
IF IT'S 24 PAGES, AND WE PRINT OUT 100 COPIES...IT'LL PROBABLY RUN ABOUT 40-50,000 YEN.*
UH-HUH.
HMM... SO THAT MEANS WE'D HAVE TO SELL OUT JUST TO BREAK EVEN.
I COULD DO COSPLAY, AND TRY TO PULL IN CUSTOMERS.
REALLY? YOU'D DO THAT?
*$5
*$400—$500
OUR TARGET MARKET IS PRETTY MUCH JUST GUYS, SO WOULDN'T YOU FEEL KIND OF LIKE YOU WERE BEING USED?
HMM...SO 200 COPIES WOULD BE ABOUT 50 - 60,000 YEN.*
THE MORE WE PRINT UP, THE CHEAPER IT GETS.
I WOULDN'T MIND AT ALL.
I'LL GO AS THE VICE PRESIDENT, AND SAKI-SAN CAN GO AS THE PRESIDENT.
FROM KUJI-UN.
YEAH, RIGHT.
REMIND ME NEVER TO UNDER-ESTIMATE OUR FEMALE MEMBERS.
*$500—$600

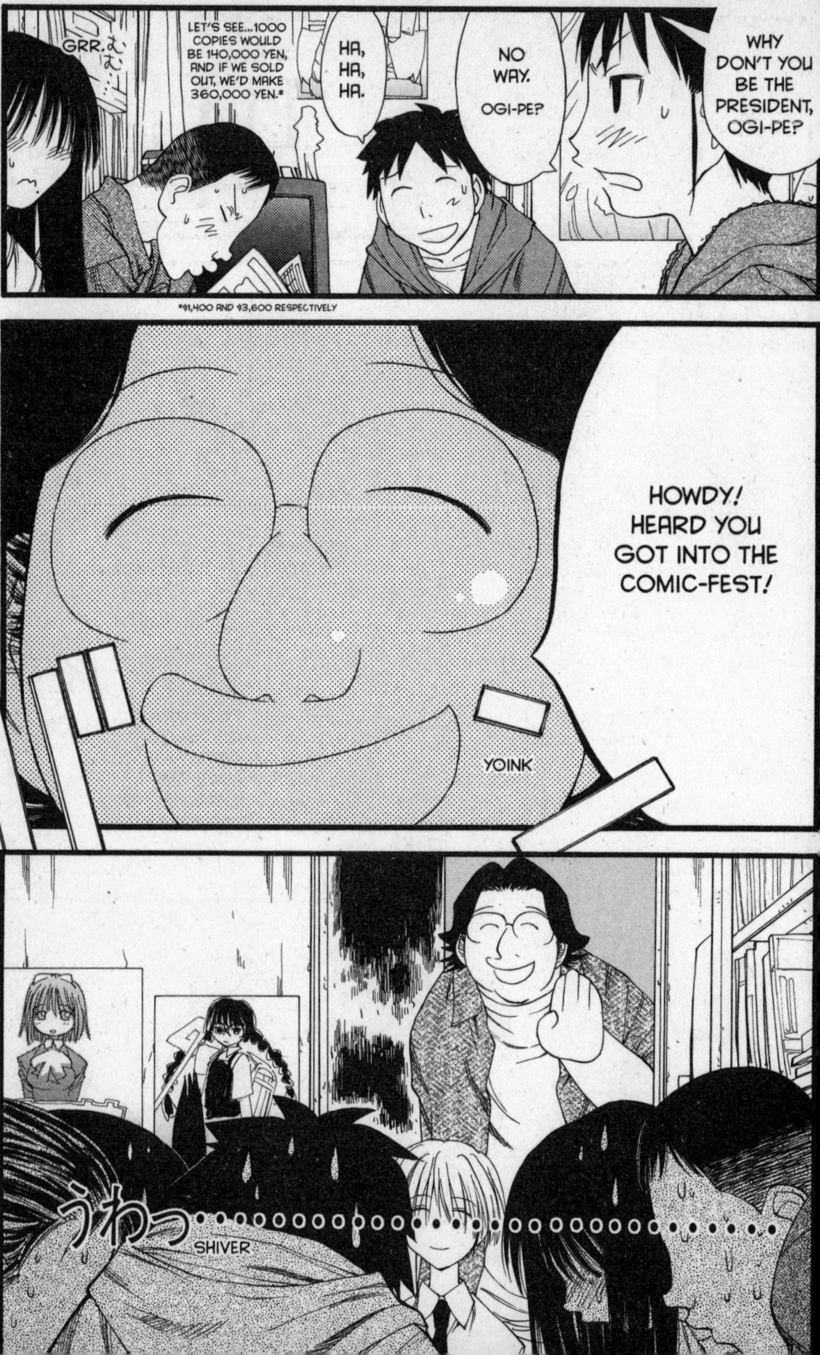
WHY DON'T YOU BE THE PRESIDENT, OGI-PE?
NO WAY.
OGI-PE?
HA, HA, HA.
LET'S SEE...1000 COPIES WOULD BE 140,000 YEN, AND IF WE SOLD OUT, WE'D MAKE 360,000 YEN.*
GRR. むむ
*$1,400 AND $3,600 RESPECTIVELY
HOWDY! HEARD YOU GOT INTO THE COMIC-FEST!
YOINK
うわっ
SHIVER

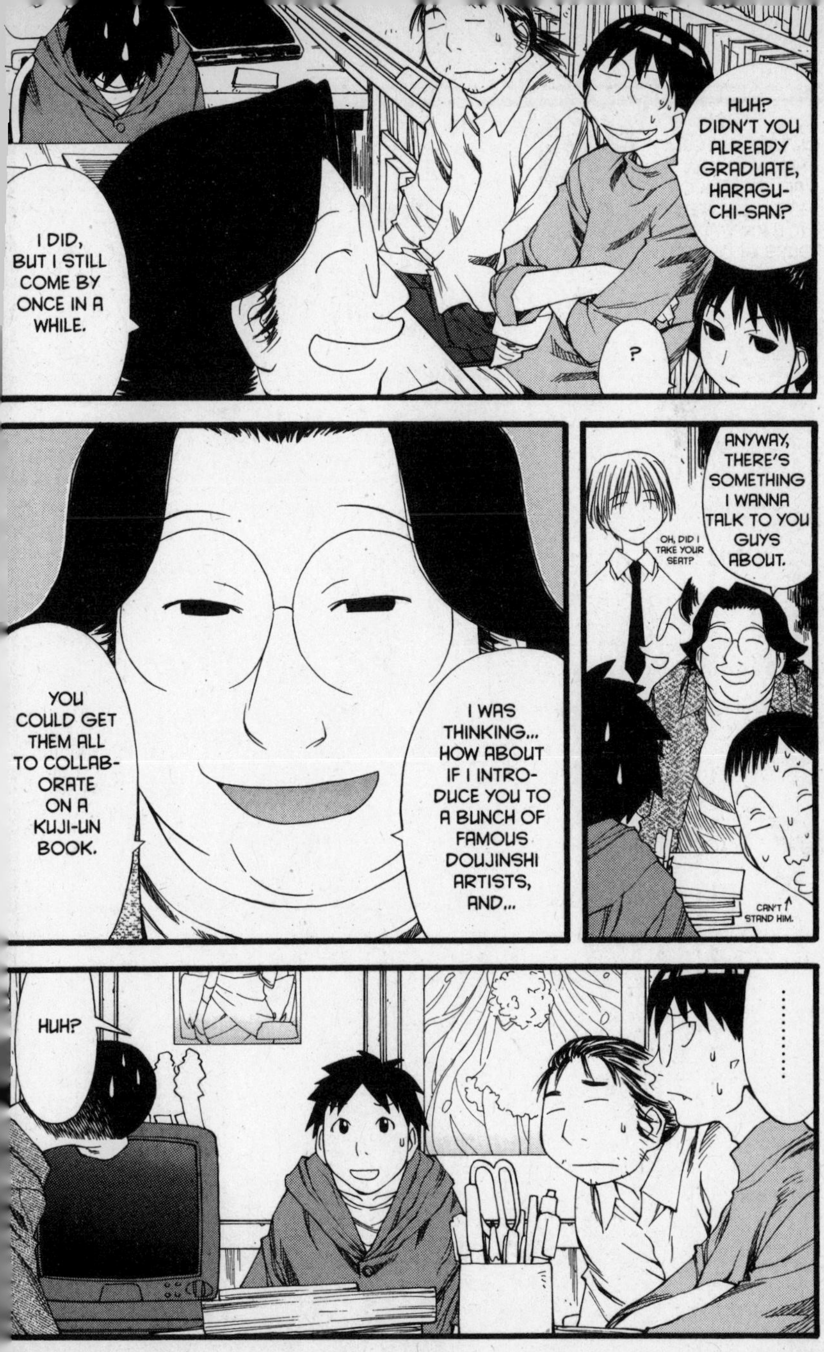
HUH? DIDN'T YOU ALREADY GRADUATE, HARAGUCHI-SAN?
I DID, BUT I STILL COME BY ONCE IN A WHILE.
?
ANYWAY, THERE'S SOMETHING I WANNA TALK TO YOU GUYS ABOUT.
OH, DID I TAKE YOUR SEAT?
CAN'T STAND HIM.
I WAS THINKING... HOW ABOUT IF I INTRODUCE YOU TO A BUNCH OF FAMOUS DOUJINSHI ARTISTS, AND...
YOU COULD GET THEM ALL TO COLLABORATE ON A KUJI-UN BOOK.
....
HUH?

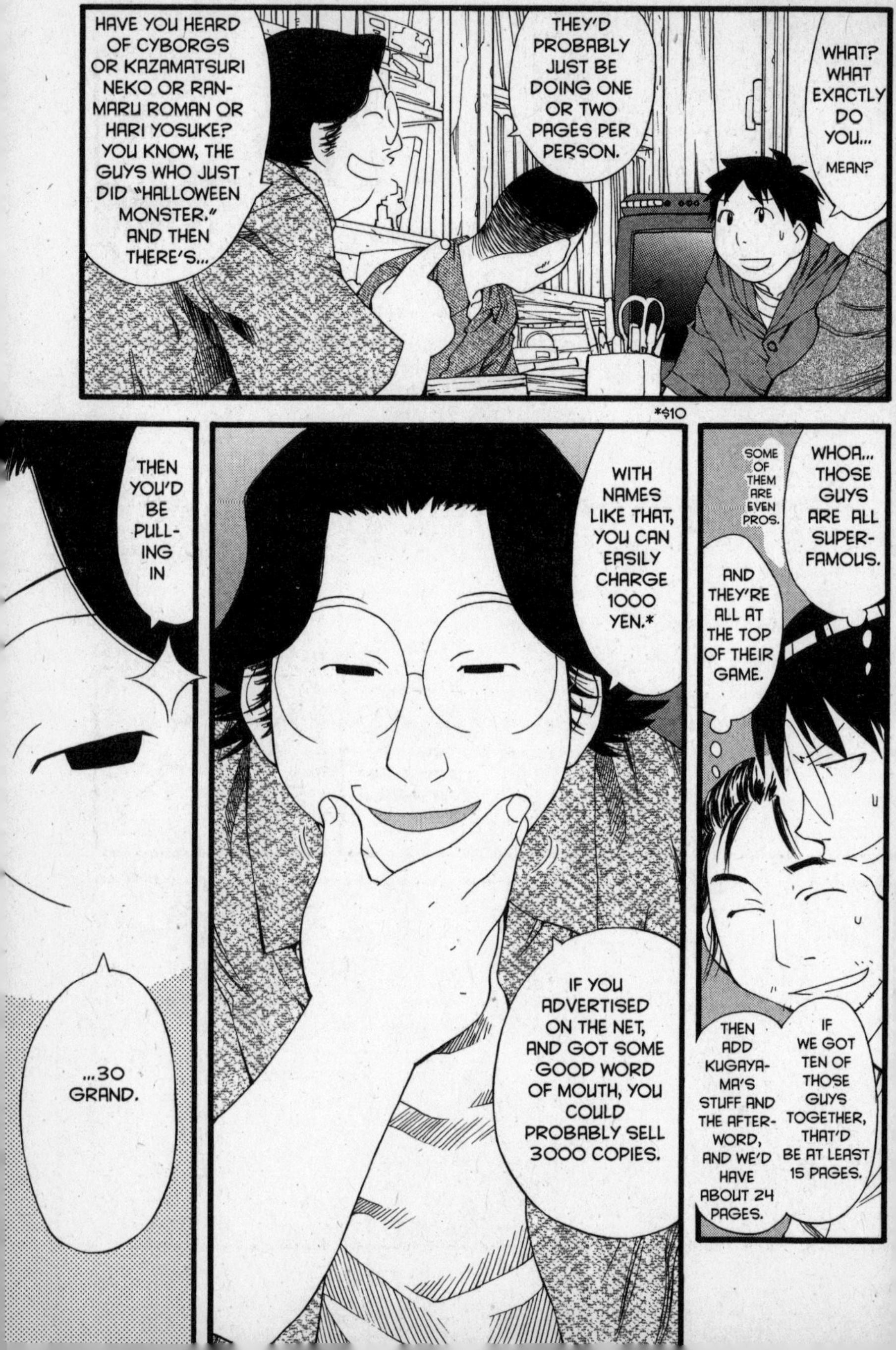
WHAT? WHAT EXACTLY DO YOU...
MEAN?
THEY'D PROBABLY JUST BE DOING ONE OR TWO PAGES PER PERSON.
HAVE YOU HEARD OF CYBORGS OR KAZAMATSURI NEKO OR RAN-MARU ROMAN OR HARI YOSUKE? YOU KNOW, THE GUYS WHO JUST DID "HALLOWEEN MONSTER." AND THEN THERE'S...
*$10
WHOA... THOSE GUYS ARE ALL SUPER-FAMOUS.
SOME OF THEM ARE EVEN PROS.
AND THEY'RE ALL AT THE TOP OF THEIR GAME.
IF WE GOT TEN OF THOSE GUYS TOGETHER, THAT'D BE AT LEAST 15 PAGES.
THEN ADD KUGAYAMA'S STUFF AND THE AFTER-WORD, AND WE'D HAVE ABOUT 24 PAGES.
WITH NAMES LIKE THAT, YOU CAN EASILY CHARGE 1000 YEN.*
IF YOU ADVERTISED ON THE NET, AND GOT SOME GOOD WORD OF MOUTH, YOU COULD PROBABLY SELL 3000 COPIES.
THEN YOU'D BE PULL-ING IN
...30 GRAND.

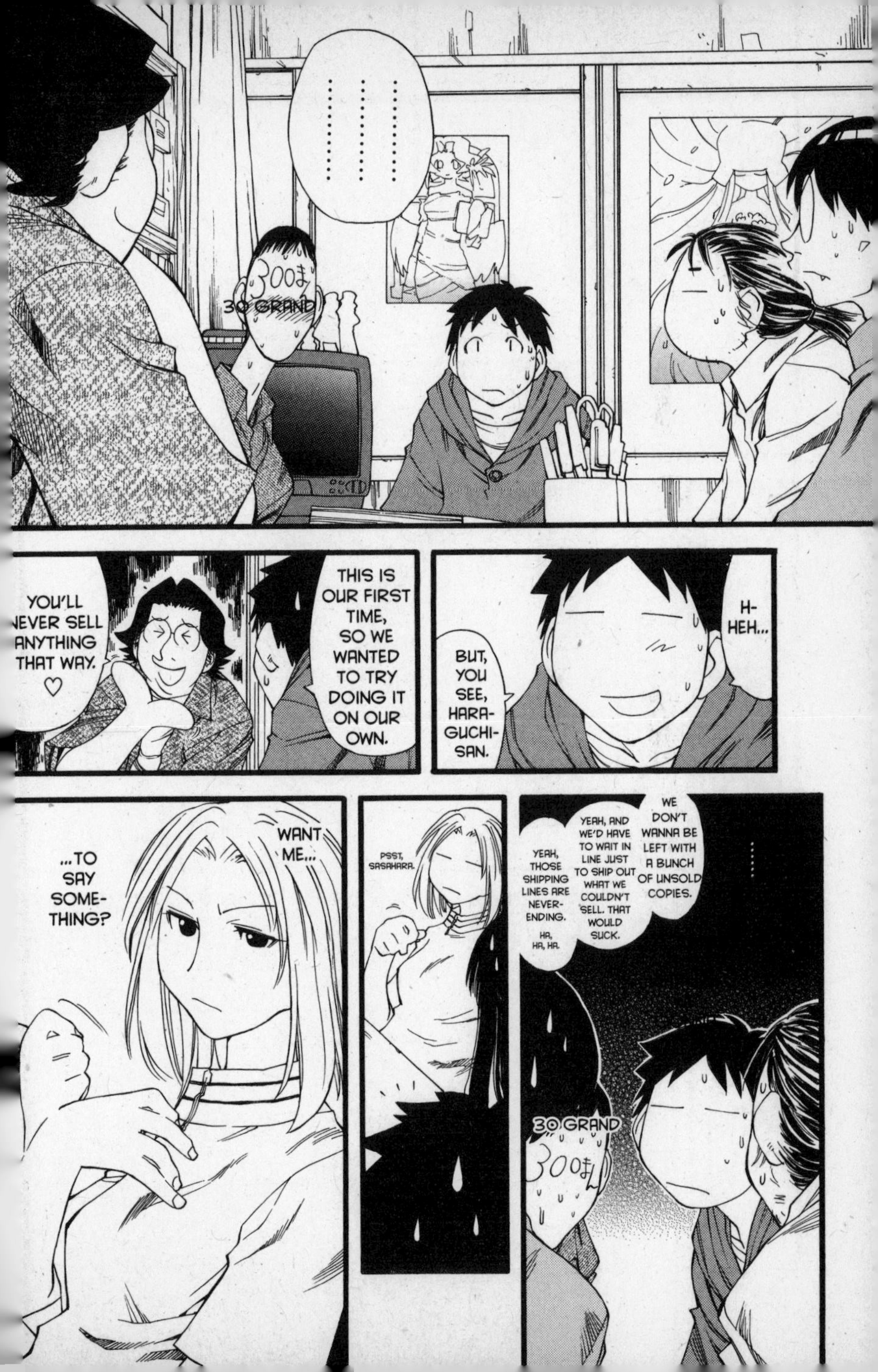
......
30 GRAND
H-HEH...
BUT, YOU SEE, HARAGUCHI-SAN.
THIS IS OUR FIRST TIME, SO WE WANTED TO TRY DOING IT ON OUR OWN.
YOU'LL NEVER SELL ANYTHING THAT WAY. ♡
......
WE DON'T WANNA BE LEFT WITH A BUNCH OF UNSOLD COPIES.
YEAH, AND WE'D HAVE TO WAIT IN LINE JUST TO SHIP OUT WHAT WE COULDN'T SELL. THAT WOULD SUCK.
YEAH, THOSE SHIPPING LINES ARE NEVER-ENDING.
HA, HA, HA.
30 GRAND
PSST, SASAHARA.
WANT ME...
...TO SAY SOMETHING?

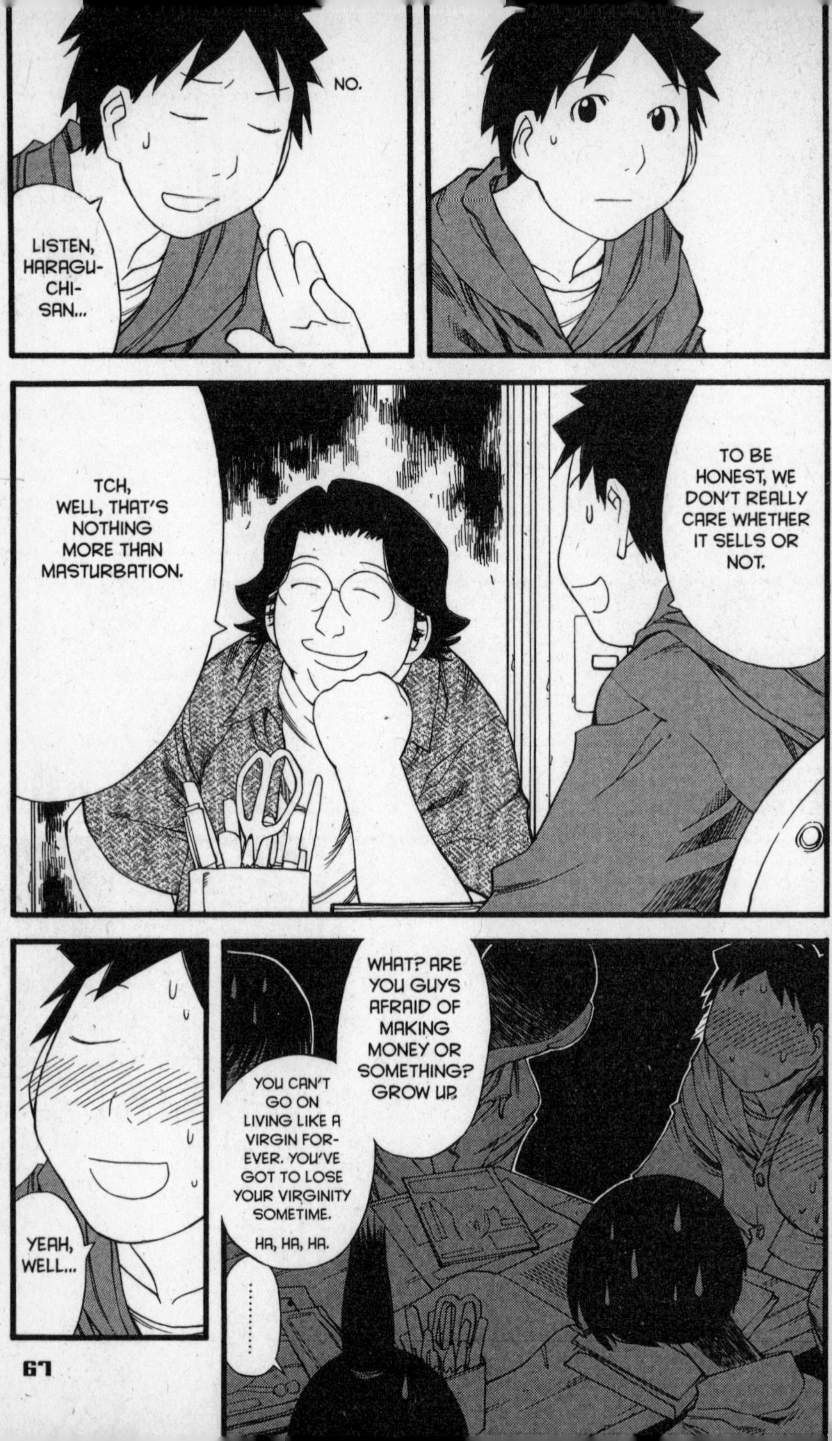
NO.
LISTEN, HARAGUCHI-SAN...
TO BE HONEST, WE DON'T REALLY CARE WHETHER IT SELLS OR NOT.
TCH, WELL, THAT'S NOTHING MORE THAN MASTURBATION.
WHAT? ARE YOU GUYS AFRAID OF MAKING MONEY OR SOMETHING? GROW UP.
YOU CAN'T GO ON LIVING LIKE A VIRGIN FOREVER. YOU'VE GOT TO LOSE YOUR VIRGINITY SOMETIME.
HA, HA, HA.
......
YEAH, WELL...

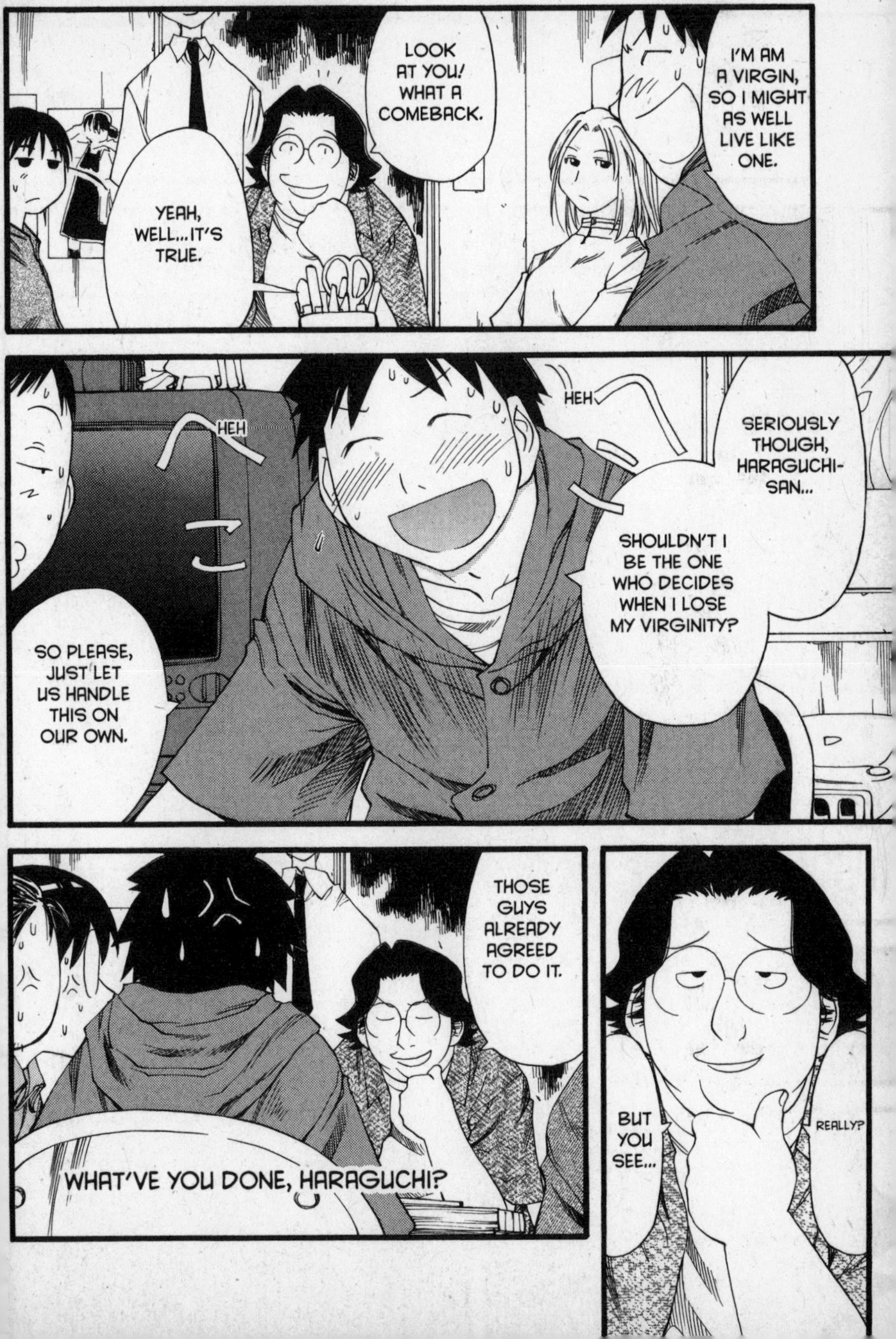
I'M AM A VIRGIN, SO I MIGHT AS WELL LIVE LIKE ONE.
LOOK AT YOU! WHAT A COMEBACK.
YEAH, WELL...IT'S TRUE.
SERIOUSLY THOUGH, HARAGUCHI-SAN...
SHOULDN'T I BE THE ONE WHO DECIDES WHEN I LOSE MY VIRGINITY?
HEH
HEH
SO PLEASE, JUST LET US HANDLE THIS ON OUR OWN.
REALLY?
BUT YOU SEE...
THOSE GUYS ALREADY AGREED TO DO IT.
WHAT'VE YOU DONE, HARAGUCHI?

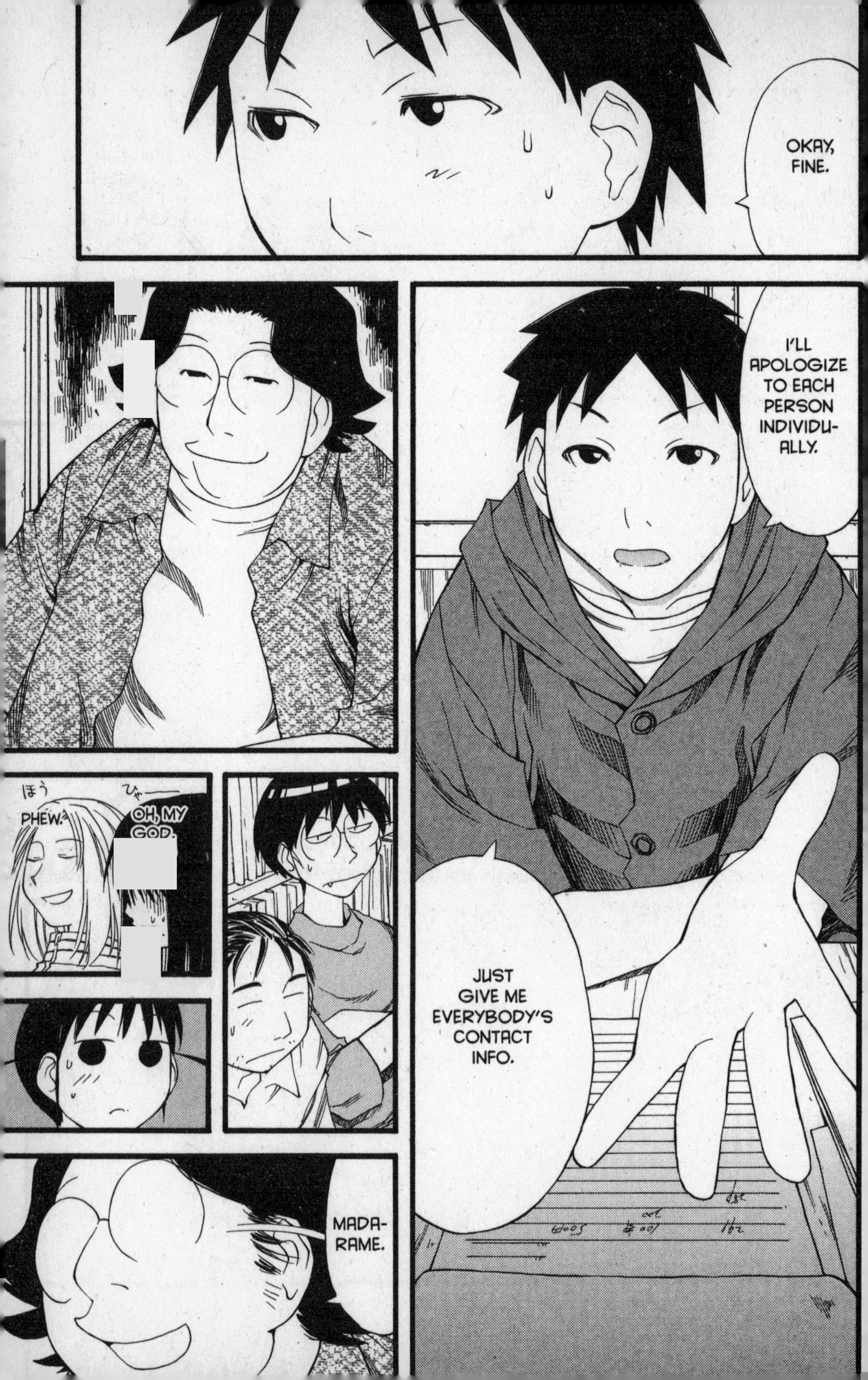
OKAY, FINE.
I'LL APOLOGIZE TO EACH PERSON INDIVIDUALLY.
JUST GIVE ME EVERYBODY'S CONTACT INFO.
ぴゃー
OH, MY GOD.
ほう
PHEW.
MADA-RAME.

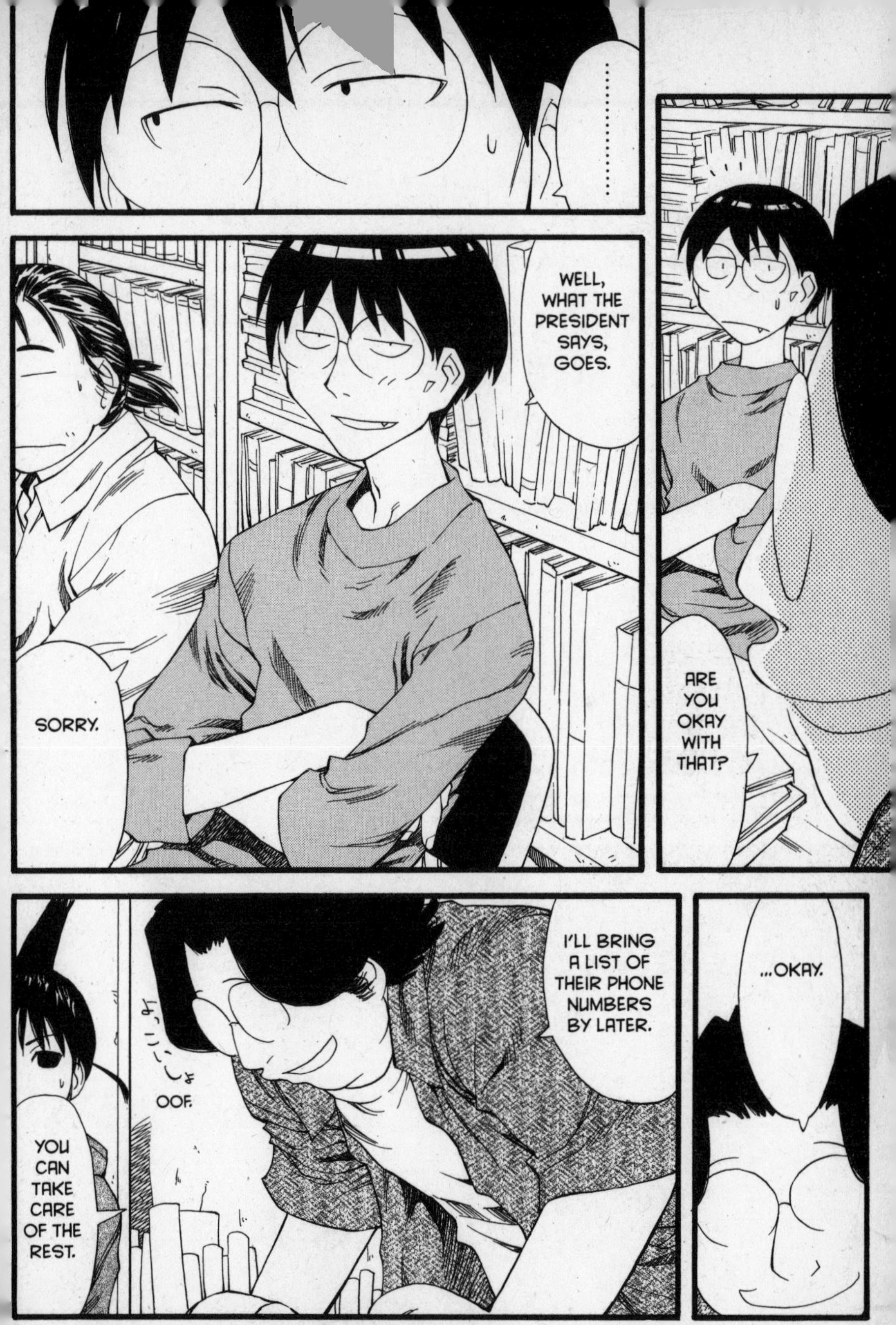
ARE YOU OKAY WITH THAT?
……
WELL, WHAT THE PRESIDENT SAYS, GOES.
SORRY.
...OKAY.
I'LL BRING A LIST OF THEIR PHONE NUMBERS BY LATER.
よっこいしょ
OOF.
YOU CAN TAKE CARE OF THE REST.

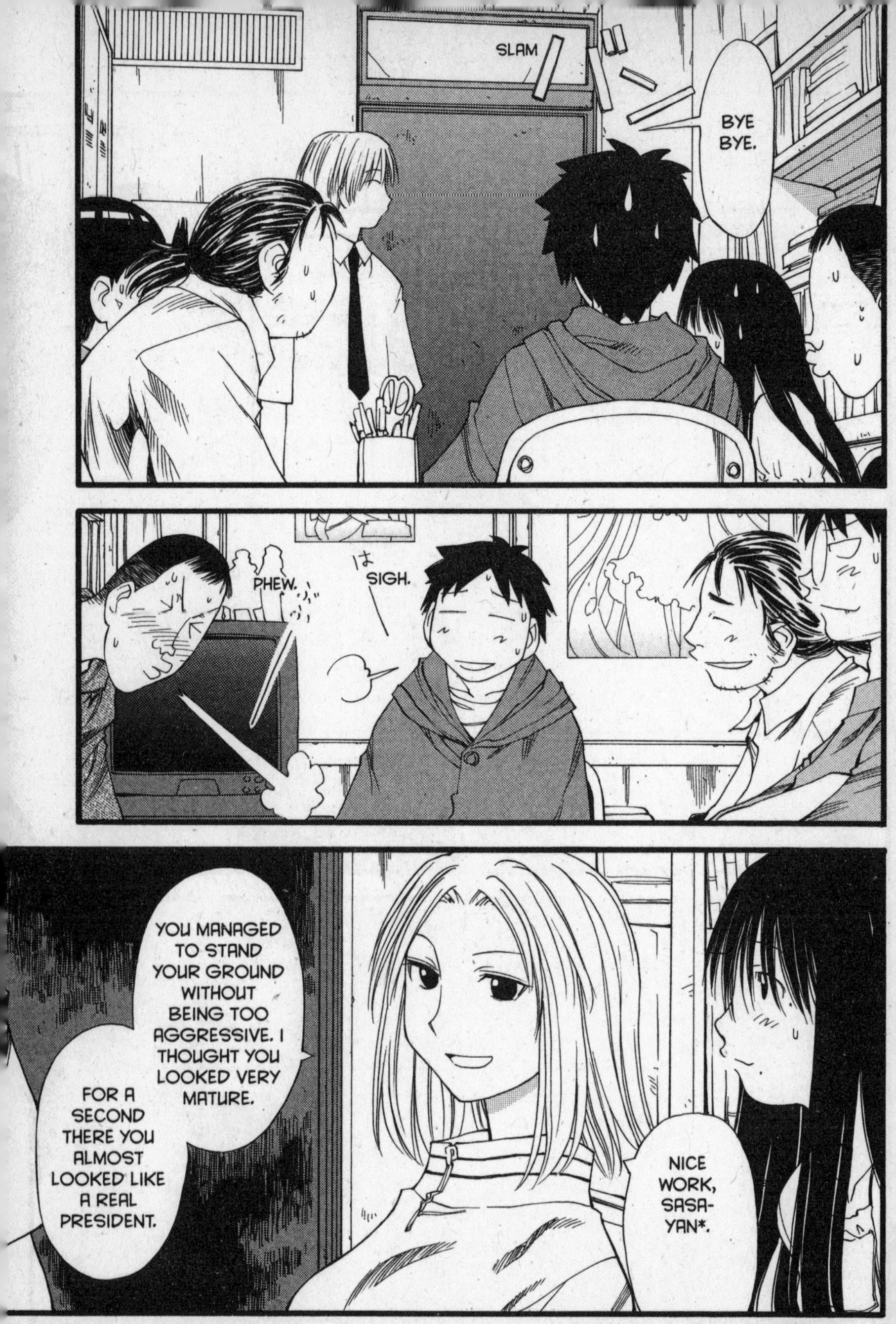
BYE BYE.
SLAM
は SIGH.
PHEW.
NICE WORK, SASA-YAN*.
YOU MANAGED TO STAND YOUR GROUND WITHOUT BEING TOO AGGRESSIVE. I THOUGHT YOU LOOKED VERY MATURE.
FOR A SECOND THERE YOU ALMOST LOOKED LIKE A REAL PRESIDENT.

*SAKI'S NICKNAME FOR SASAHARA

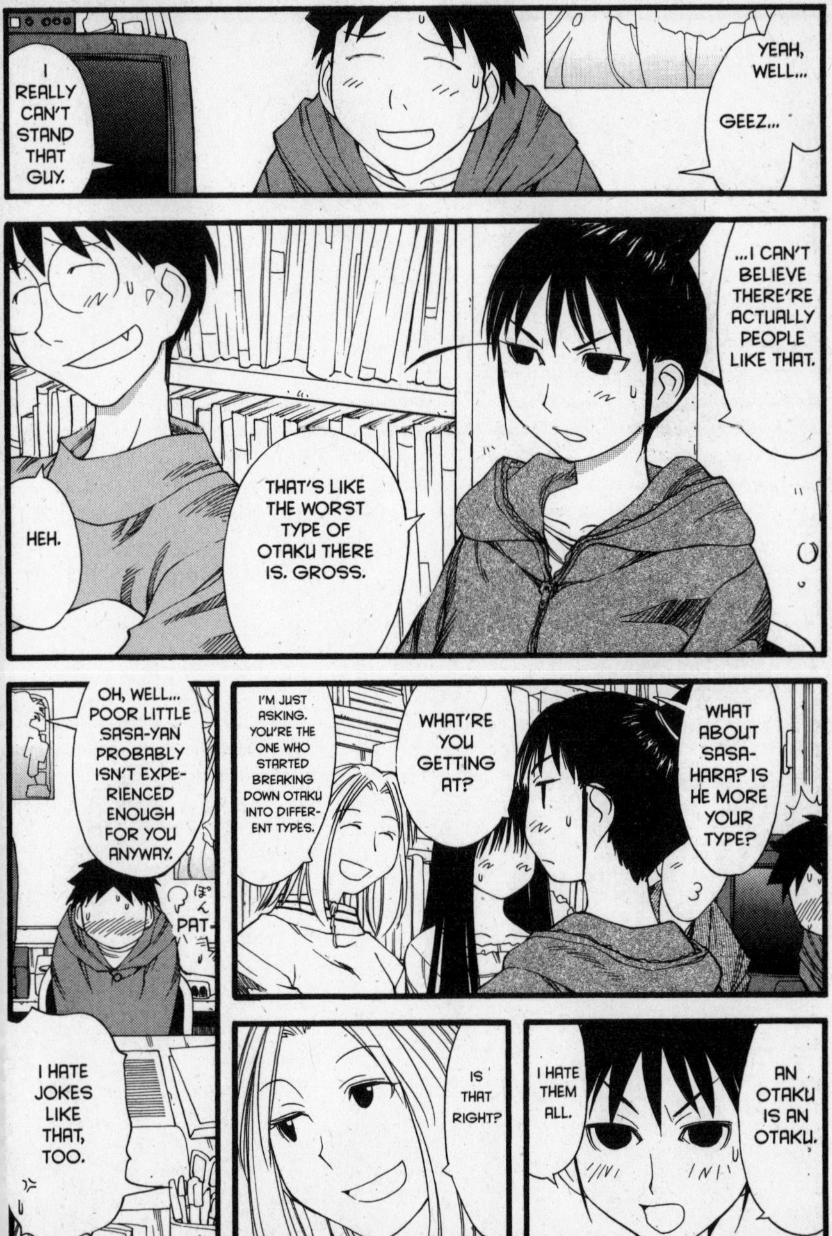
YEAH, WELL... GEEZ...
I REALLY CAN'T STAND THAT GUY.
...I CAN'T BELIEVE THERE'RE ACTUALLY PEOPLE LIKE THAT.
THAT'S LIKE THE WORST TYPE OF OTAKU THERE IS. GROSS.
HEH.
WHAT ABOUT SASAHARA? IS HE MORE YOUR TYPE?
WHAT'RE YOU GETTING AT?
I'M JUST ASKING. YOU'RE THE ONE WHO STARTED BREAKING DOWN OTAKU INTO DIFFERENT TYPES.
AN OTAKU IS AN OTAKU.
I HATE THEM ALL.
IS THAT RIGHT?
OH, WELL... POOR LITTLE SASA-YAN PROBABLY ISN'T EXPERIENCED ENOUGH FOR YOU ANYWAY.
ぽん PAT
I HATE JOKES LIKE THAT, TOO.

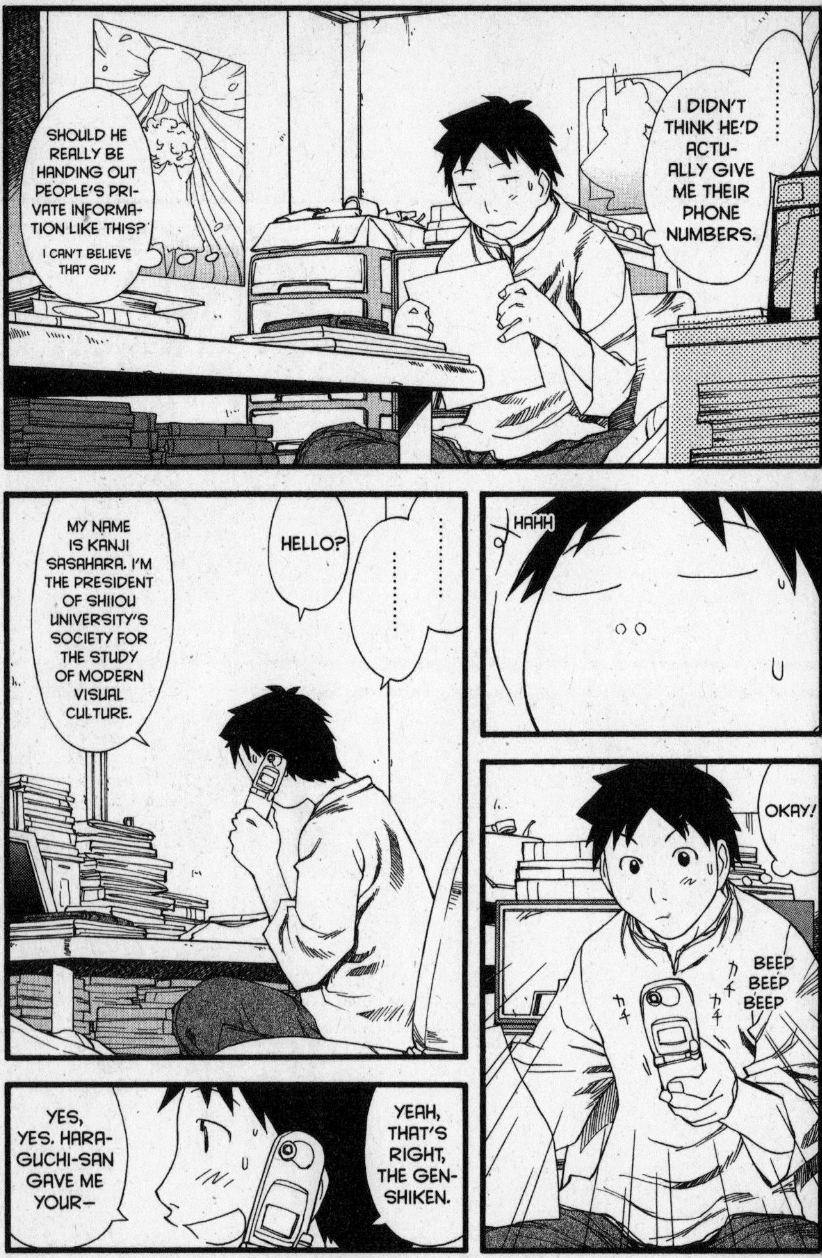
......
I DIDN'T THINK HE'D ACTU-ALLY GIVE ME THEIR PHONE NUMBERS.
SHOULD HE REALLY BE HANDING OUT PEOPLE'S PRI-VATE INFORMA-TION LIKE THIS?
I CAN'T BELIEVE THAT GUY.
HAHH
OKAY!
BEEP BEEP BEEP
カチ カチ カチ
......
......
HELLO?
MY NAME IS KANJI SASAHARA. I'M THE PRESIDENT OF SHIIOU UNIVERSITY'S SOCIETY FOR THE STUDY OF MODERN VISUAL CULTURE.
YEAH, THAT'S RIGHT, THE GEN-SHIKEN.
YES, YES. HARA-GUCHI-SAN GAVE ME YOUR—

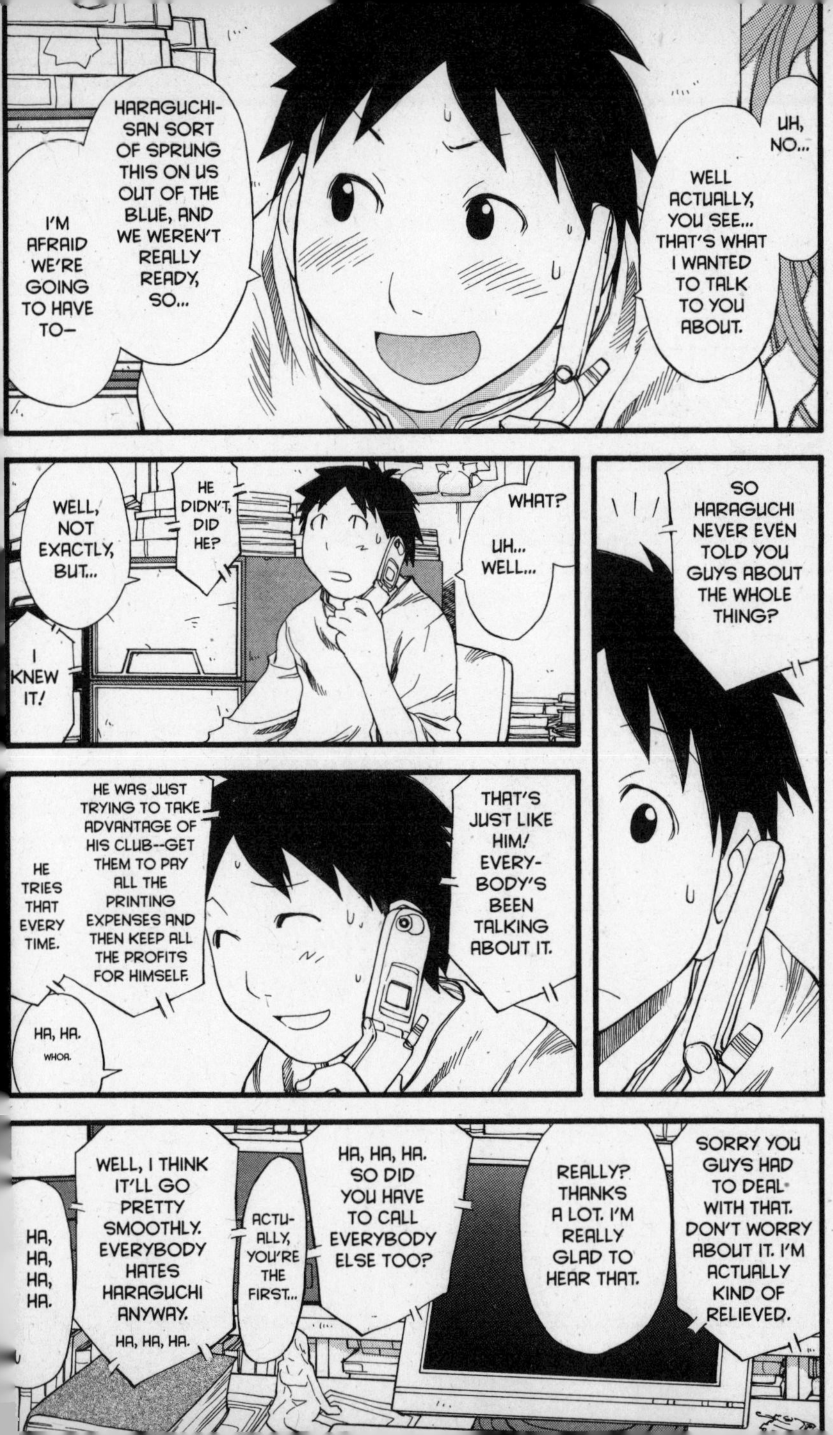
UH, NO...
WELL ACTUALLY, YOU SEE... THAT'S WHAT I WANTED TO TALK TO YOU ABOUT.
HARAGUCHI-SAN SORT OF SPRUNG THIS ON US OUT OF THE BLUE, AND WE WEREN'T REALLY READY, SO...
I'M AFRAID WE'RE GOING TO HAVE TO—
SO HARAGUCHI NEVER EVEN TOLD YOU GUYS ABOUT THE WHOLE THING?
WHAT?
UH... WELL...
HE DIDN'T, DID HE?
WELL, NOT EXACTLY, BUT...
I KNEW IT!
THAT'S JUST LIKE HIM! EVERY-BODY'S BEEN TALKING ABOUT IT.
HE WAS JUST TRYING TO TAKE ADVANTAGE OF HIS CLUB--GET THEM TO PAY ALL THE PRINTING EXPENSES AND THEN KEEP ALL THE PROFITS FOR HIMSELF.
HE TRIES THAT EVERY TIME.
HA, HA.
WHOA.
SORRY YOU GUYS HAD TO DEAL WITH THAT. DON'T WORRY ABOUT IT. I'M ACTUALLY KIND OF RELIEVED.
REALLY? THANKS A LOT. I'M REALLY GLAD TO HEAR THAT.
HA, HA, HA. SO DID YOU HAVE TO CALL EVERYBODY ELSE TOO?
ACTU-ALLY, YOU'RE THE FIRST...
WELL, I THINK IT'LL GO PRETTY SMOOTHLY. EVERYBODY HATES HARAGUCHI ANYWAY.
HA, HA, HA.
HA, HA, HA, HA.

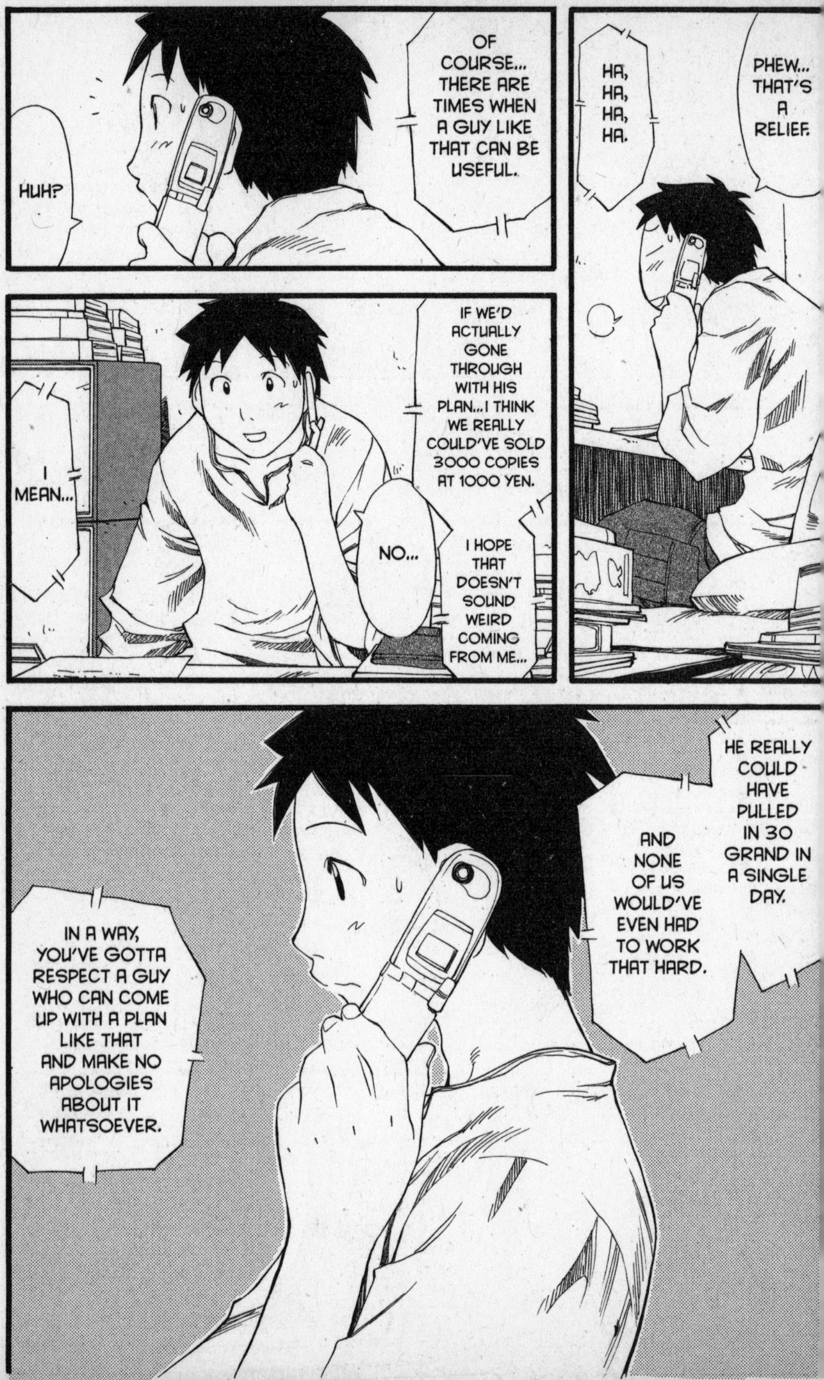
PHEW... THAT'S A RELIEF.
HA, HA, HA, HA.
OF COURSE... THERE ARE TIMES WHEN A GUY LIKE THAT CAN BE USEFUL.
HUH?
IF WE'D ACTUALLY GONE THROUGH WITH HIS PLAN...I THINK WE REALLY COULD'VE SOLD 3000 COPIES AT 1000 YEN.
I HOPE THAT DOESN'T SOUND WEIRD COMING FROM ME...
NO...
I MEAN...
HE REALLY COULD HAVE PULLED IN 30 GRAND IN A SINGLE DAY.
AND NONE OF US WOULD'VE EVEN HAD TO WORK THAT HARD.
IN A WAY, YOU'VE GOTTA RESPECT A GUY WHO CAN COME UP WITH A PLAN LIKE THAT AND MAKE NO APOLOGIES ABOUT IT WHATSOEVER.

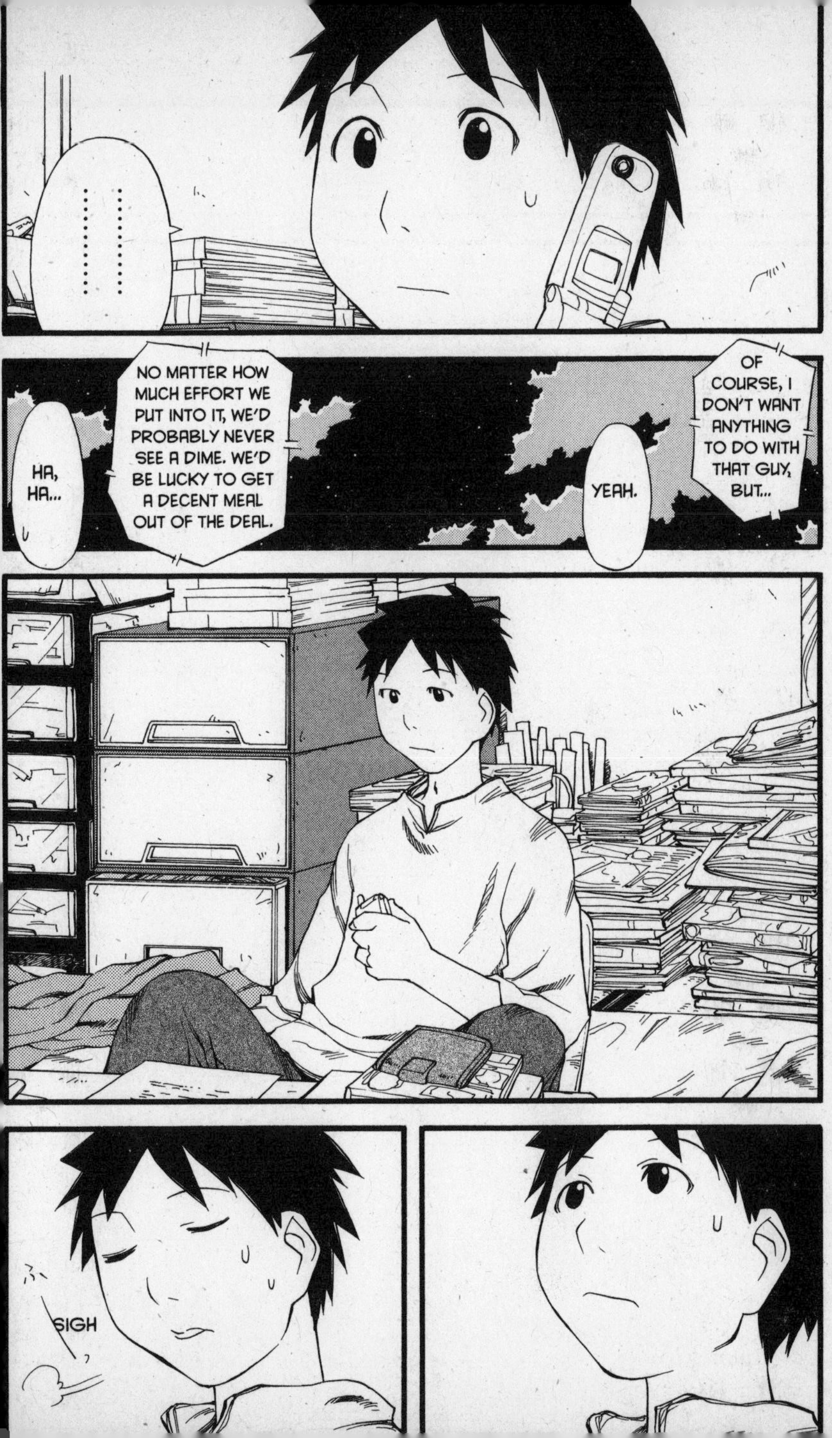
......
OF COURSE, I DON'T WANT ANYTHING TO DO WITH THAT GUY, BUT...
YEAH.
NO MATTER HOW MUCH EFFORT WE PUT INTO IT, WE'D PROBABLY NEVER SEE A DIME. WE'D BE LUCKY TO GET A DECENT MEAL OUT OF THE DEAL.
HA, HA...
SIGH

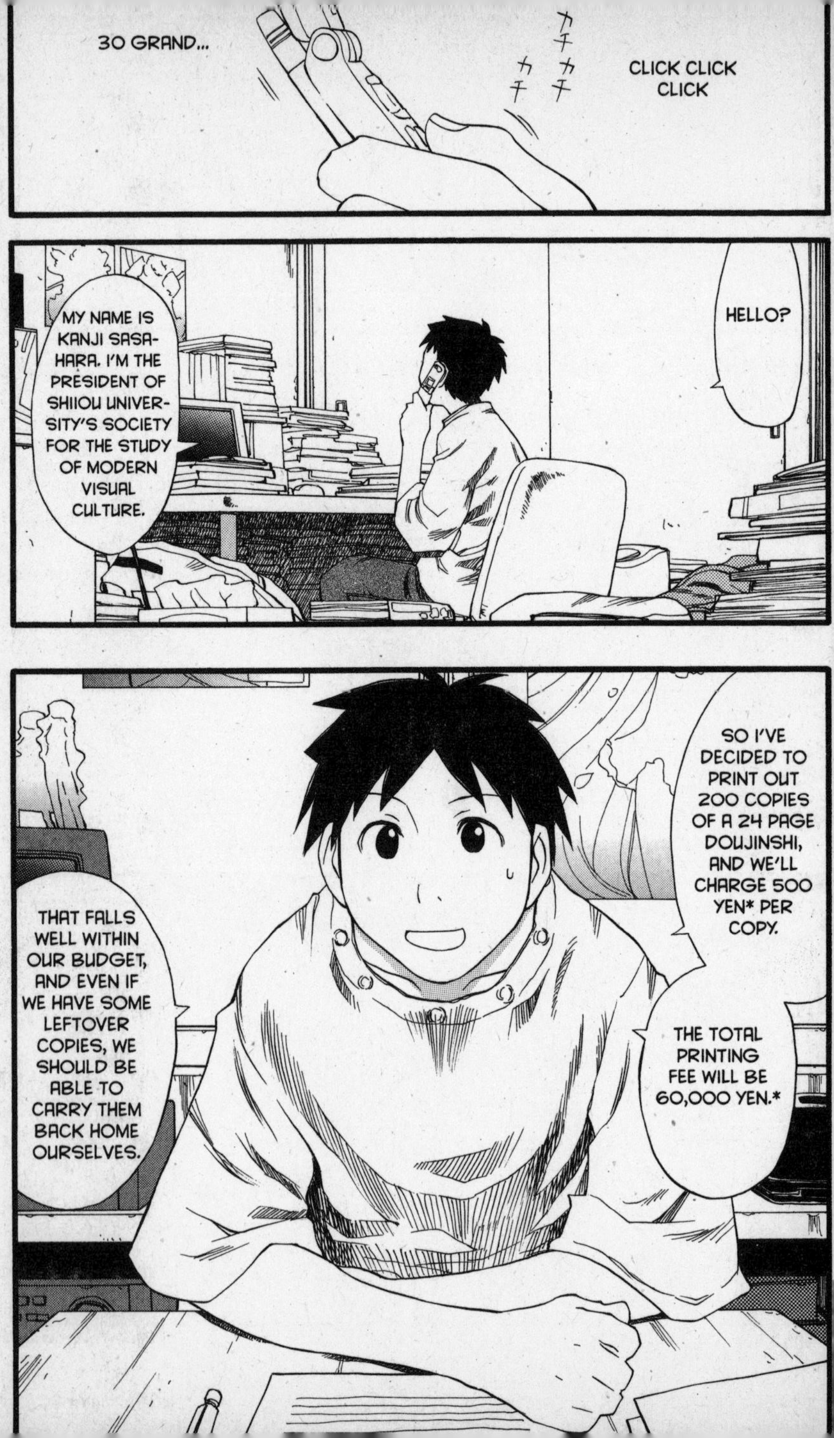
CLICK CLICK CLICK
カチカチカチ
30 GRAND...
HELLO?
MY NAME IS KANJI SASA-HARA. I'M THE PRESIDENT OF SHIIOU UNIVER-SITY'S SOCIETY FOR THE STUDY OF MODERN VISUAL CULTURE.
SO I'VE DECIDED TO PRINT OUT 200 COPIES OF A 24 PAGE DOUJINSHI, AND WE'LL CHARGE 500 YEN* PER COPY.
THE TOTAL PRINTING FEE WILL BE 60,000 YEN.*
THAT FALLS WELL WITHIN OUR BUDGET, AND EVEN IF WE HAVE SOME LEFTOVER COPIES, WE SHOULD BE ABLE TO CARRY THEM BACK HOME OURSELVES.

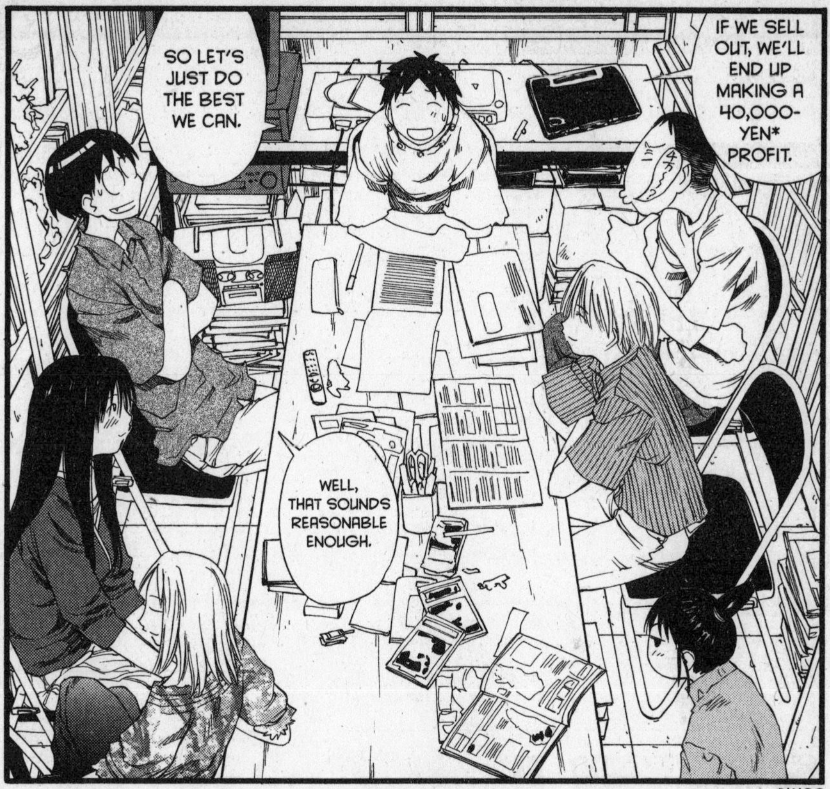
IF WE SELL OUT, WE'LL END UP MAKING A 40,000-YEN* PROFIT.
SO LET'S JUST DO THE BEST WE CAN.
WELL, THAT SOUNDS REASONABLE ENOUGH.

*$400

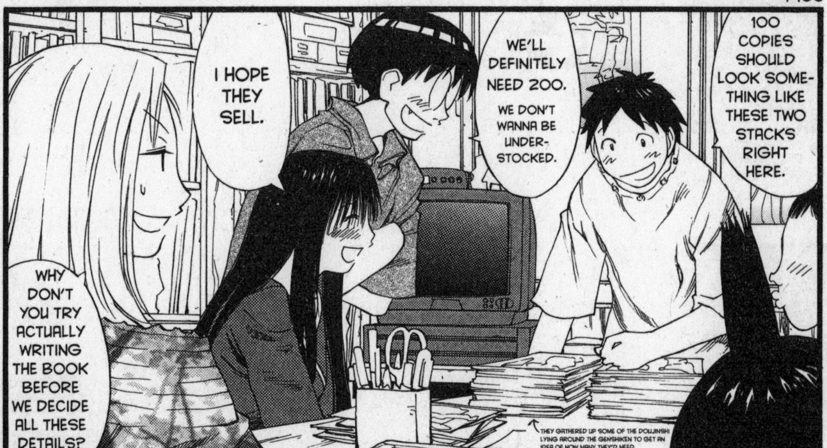
100 COPIES SHOULD LOOK SOME-THING LIKE THESE TWO STACKS RIGHT HERE.
WE'LL DEFINITELY NEED 200.
WE DON'T WANNA BE UNDER-STOCKED.
I HOPE THEY SELL.
WHY DON'T YOU TRY ACTUALLY WRITING THE BOOK BEFORE WE DECIDE ALL THESE DETAILS?
THEY GATHERED UP SOME OF THE DOUJINSHI LYING AROUND THE GENSHIKEN TO GET AN IDEA OF HOW MANY THEY'D NEED.

END OF CHAPTER 27

THE RETURN OF MY FAVORITE SCENES FROM KUJI-UN - PART 3

BY THE OWL

EPISODE 3 "WITH KNOW-HOW COMES LUCK"

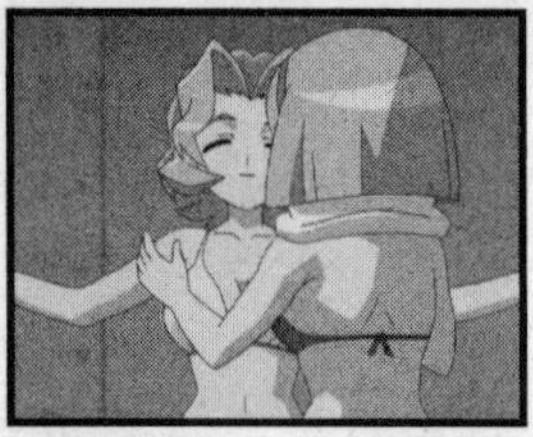

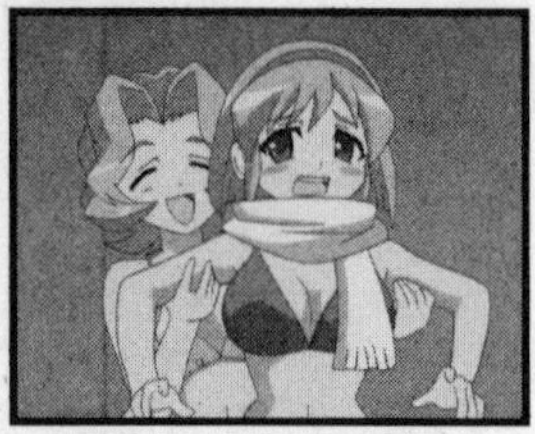

▲ "STOP IT! HAVE YOU NO SHAME?" "THAT GOES DOUBLE FOR YOU, KOMAKI. [HEART]" "QUIT IT." I REALLY WANTED TO SEE THEM JIGGLE AROUND LIKE JELLO.

YOU KNOW...LATELY I'VE BEEN GETTING INTO KOMAKI. [LAUGHS] KOMAKI'S CHARACTER REALLY STARTED TO DEVELOP IN THE ANIME. EARLY ON IN THE MANGA SERIES, SHE WAS KIND OF NEITHER HERE NOR THERE. SHE STARTED OUT AS SORT OF A COLD, DEVILISH CHARACTER, BUT NOW SHE'S TURNED INTO A LAID-BACK MATERNAL TYPE. IN THE ANIME, HOWEVER, SHE'S BEEN PORTRAYED AS A MATERNAL CHARACTER SINCE THE VERY BEGINNING. WHEN YUKARI TAMURA DOES HER VOICE, YOU CAN ALMOST HEAR THAT TRANSFORMATION. IT'S AMAZING. OF COURSE, I DON'T KNOW IF SHE'S ACTUALLY DOING IT THAT WAY ON PURPOSE. [LAUGHS] ANYWAY, EVER SINCE THE ANIME CAME OUT, I'VE REALLY STARTED TO LIKE KOMAKI.

SO HERE ARE A COUPLE OF SCENES JUST OFF THE TOP OF MY HEAD. I WANTED A LITTLE MORE FOCUS PUT ON THE JIGGLING BOOB SCENE IN EPISODE THREE. AND IN EPISODE 25, I WANTED TO SEE MORE SCENES WITH KOYUKI, BUT I GUESS I'M NEVER SATISFIED. KOMAKI WAS ALL OVER EPISODE 25, SO I LOVED IT...BUT MAYBE MOST PEOPLE HAD THEIR EYES ON KOYUKI. [LAUGHS] [THE OWL]

I WANTED TO TALK ABOUT THE KOYUKI SCENE IN EPISODE 25 TOO. EVERYBODY KNOWS ABOUT HOW ONE OF THE ARTISTS SCRIBBLED, "KOYUKI IS A PURE AND INNOCENT GIRL" ON ONE OF THE CELLS IN THIS EPISODE. IN THE DVD, ALL THE ART HAS BEEN CLEANED UP. EVERYONE SHOULD CHECK IT OUT. EPISODE 25 WRAPS UP THE WHOLE STORY WAY BETTER THAN THE FINAL EPISODE DID (EPISODE 26). PIT VIPER

EPISODE 6 "THERE ARE SEVEN PEOPLE?"

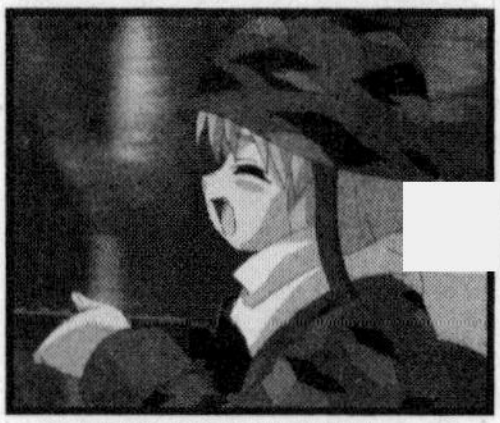

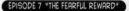

▲ "I'M TIRED OF PLAYING WAR."

EPISODE 7 "THE FEARFUL REWARD"

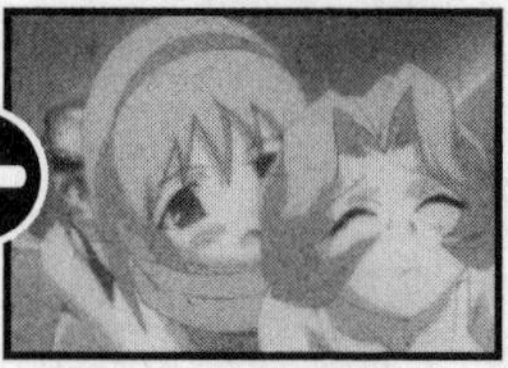

▲ BATTLE IN THE SAUNA. KOMAKI STARTS TELLING GHOST STORIES IN AN ATTEMPT TO TAKE HER MIND OFF THE HEAT.

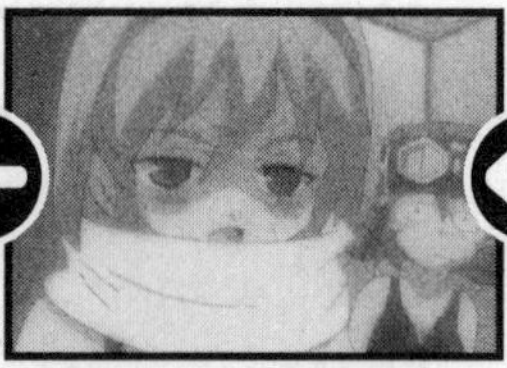

▲ "HEY, WE CAN'T PLAY THIS GAME UNLESS WE HAVE AT LEAST FIVE PEOPLE, RIGHT?" HER VOICE EVEN CHANGES FOR A MOMENT. AMAZING.

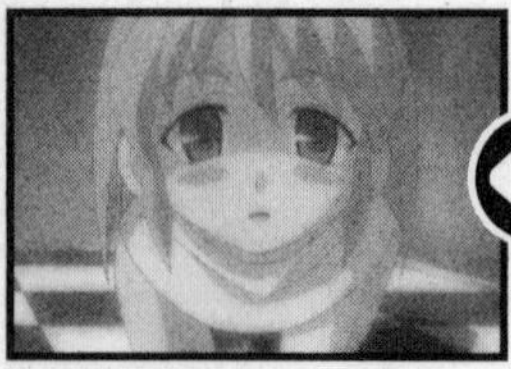

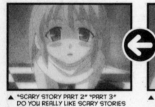

▲ "SCARY STORY PART 2" "PART 3" DO YOU REALLY LIKE SCARY STORIES THAT MUCH?

EPISODE 25 "KUJIBIKI FOREVER"

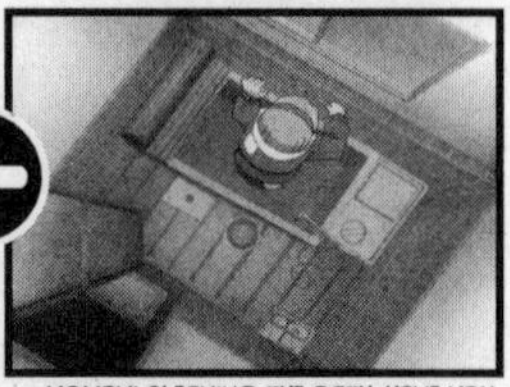

▲ KOMAKI CLEANING THE BATH. HAVE YOU EVER SEEN SUCH DEEP CHARACTER EXPLORATION IN AN ANIME?

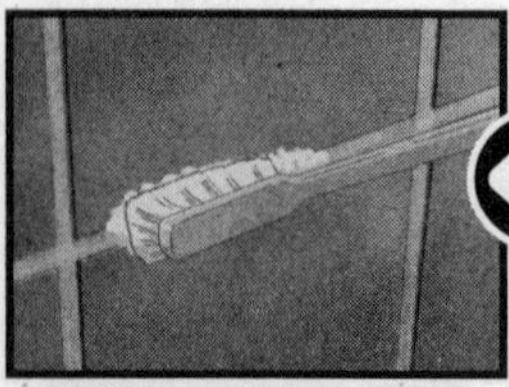

▲ THE BRISTLES ON HER TOOTHBRUSH ARE STICKING OUT.

EPISODE 12 "LET'S DANCE! IT'S THE KUJIBIKI SINGING CONTEST"

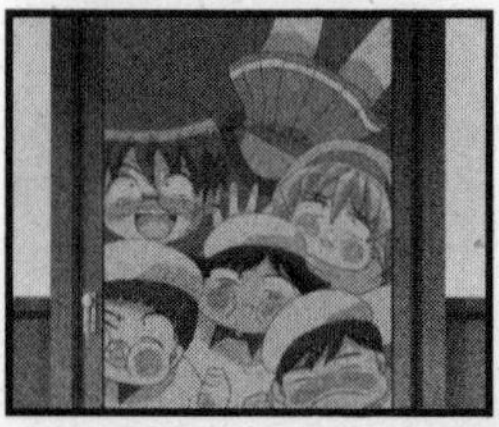

▲ EVERYBODY'S BLOWN AWAY BY TOKINO'S PECULIAR SINGING VOICE.

MASTER OF THE DOUJINSHI

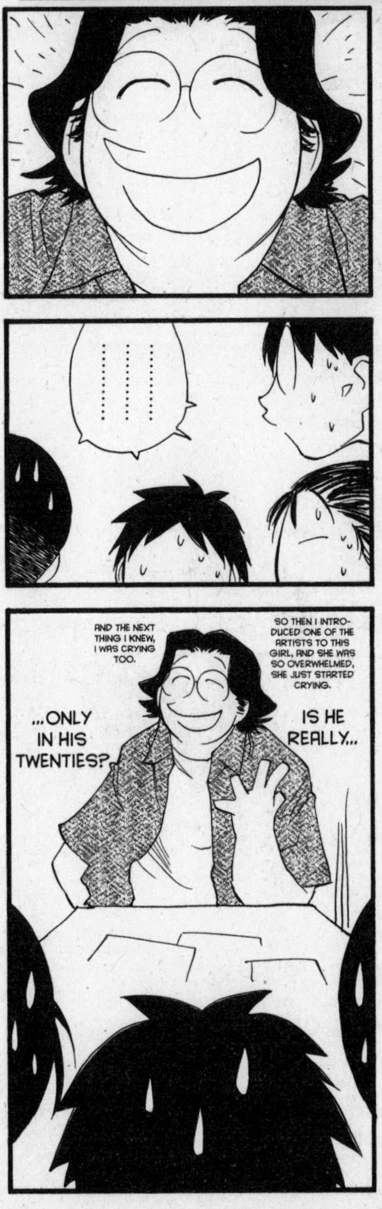
......
SO THEN I INTRODUCED ONE OF THE ARTISTS TO THIS GIRL, AND SHE WAS SO OVERWHELMED, SHE JUST STARTED CRYING.
AND THE NEXT THING I KNEW, I WAS CRYING TOO.
IS HE REALLY...
...ONLY IN HIS TWENTIES?

SO THEY'VE ALREADY...?

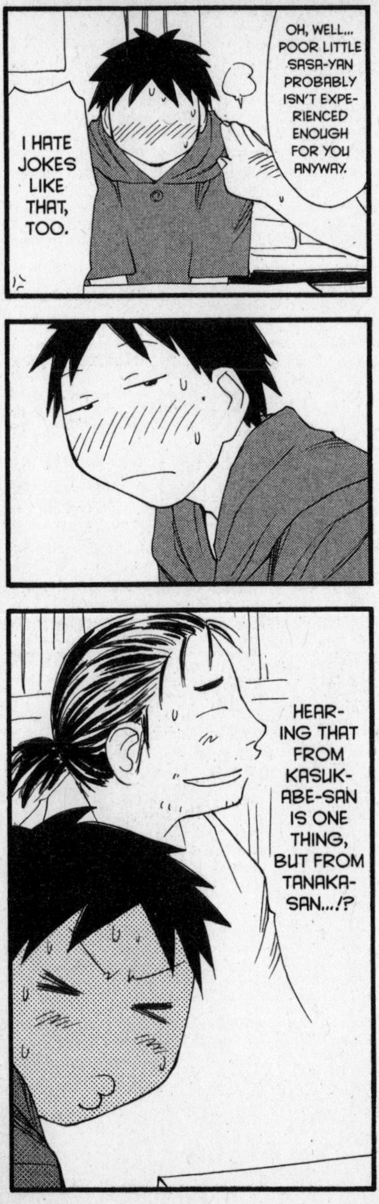
OH, WELL... POOR LITTLE SASA-YAN PROBABLY ISN'T EXPERIENCED ENOUGH FOR YOU ANYWAY.
I HATE JOKES LIKE THAT, TOO.
HEARING THAT FROM KASUKABE-SAN IS ONE THING, BUT FROM TANAKA-SAN...!?

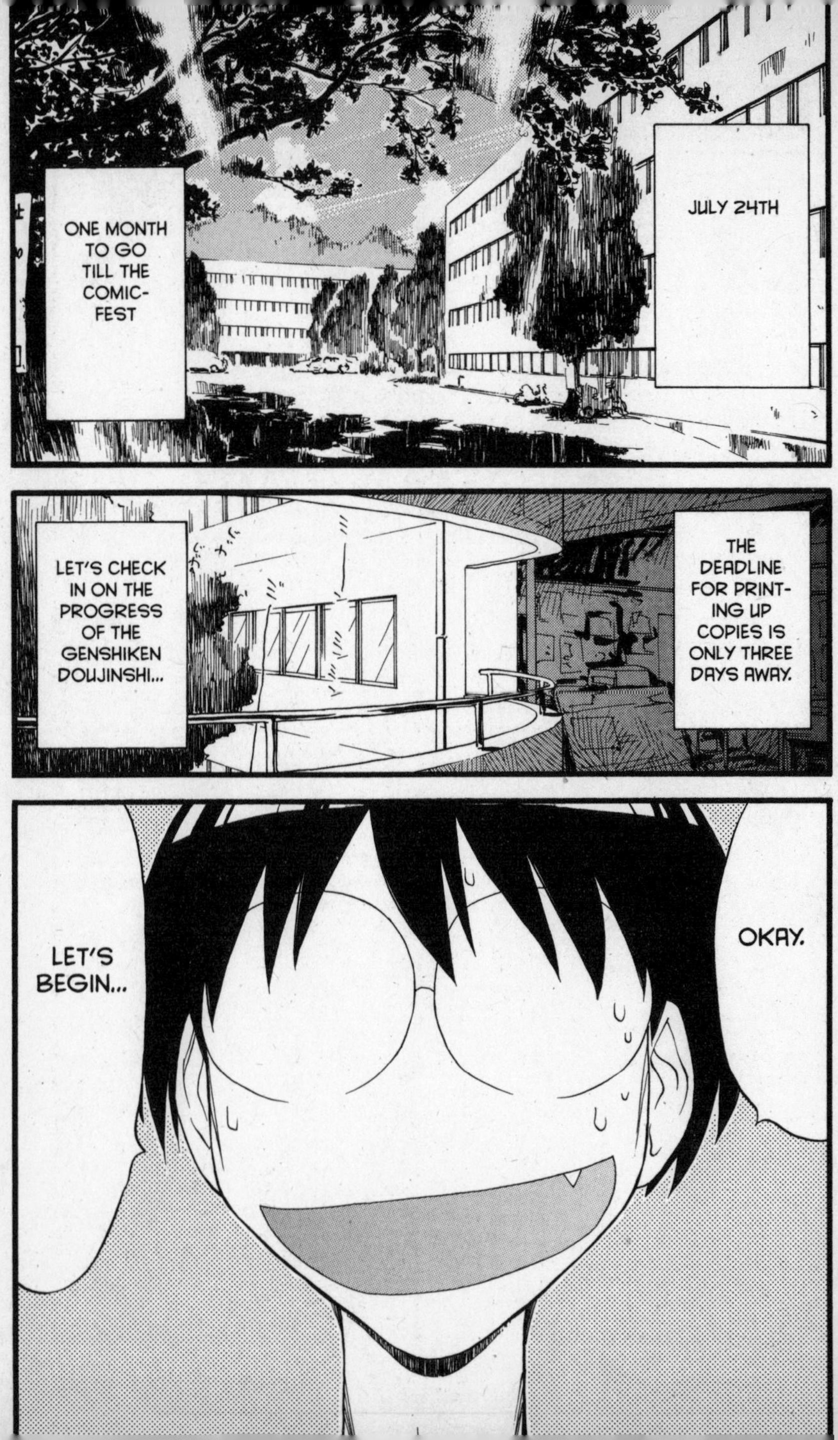
JULY 24TH
ONE MONTH TO GO TILL THE COMIC-FEST
THE DEADLINE FOR PRINTING UP COPIES IS ONLY THREE DAYS AWAY.
LET'S CHECK IN ON THE PROGRESS OF THE GENSHIKEN DOUJINSHI...
OKAY.
LET'S BEGIN...

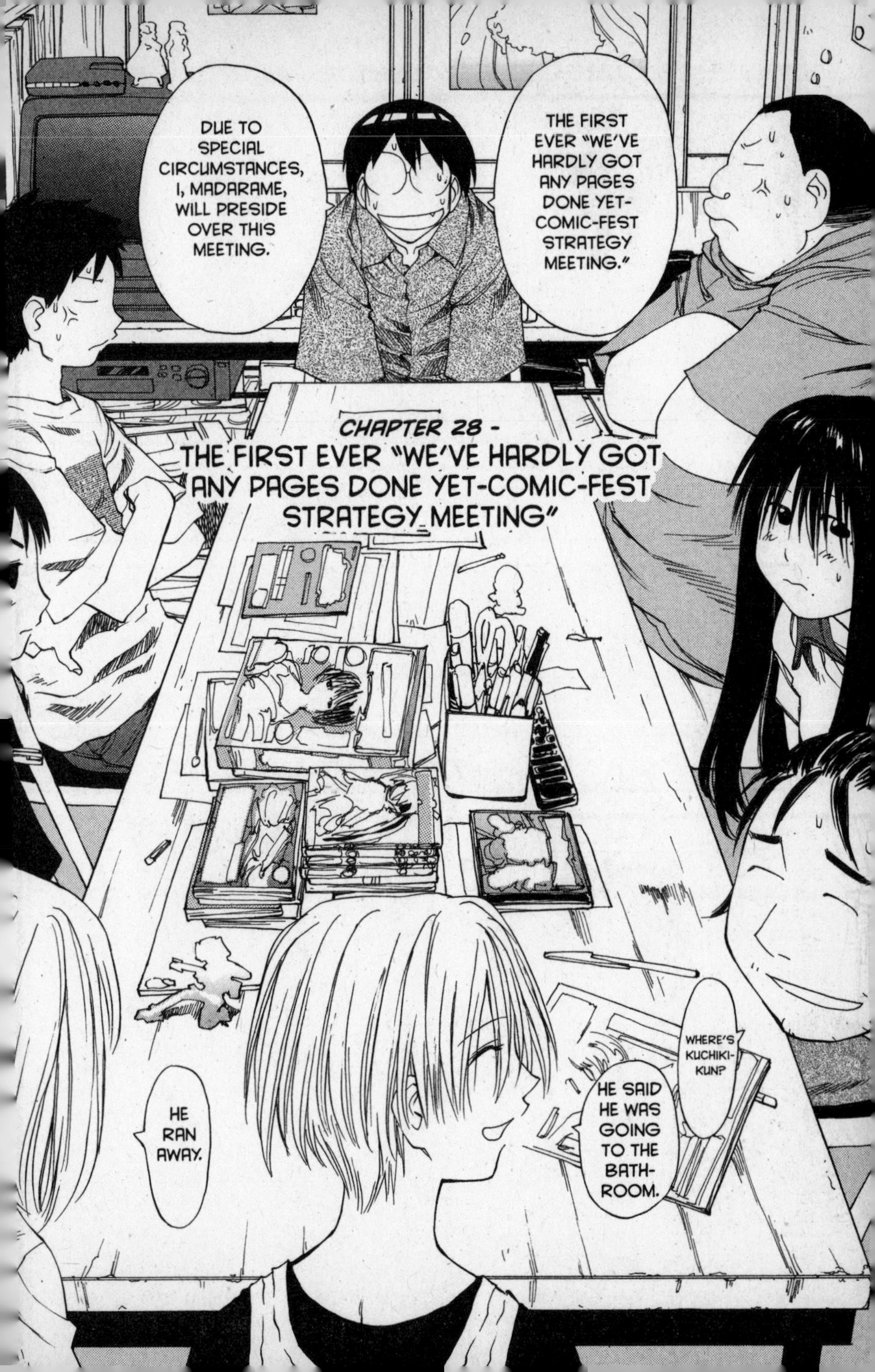
THE FIRST EVER "WE'VE HARDLY GOT ANY PAGES DONE YET-COMIC-FEST STRATEGY MEETING."
DUE TO SPECIAL CIRCUMSTANCES, I, MADARAME, WILL PRESIDE OVER THIS MEETING.
CHAPTER 28 -
THE FIRST EVER "WE'VE HARDLY GOT ANY PAGES DONE YET-COMIC-FEST STRATEGY MEETING"
WHERE'S KUCHIKI-KUN?
HE SAID HE WAS GOING TO THE BATH-ROOM.
HE RAN AWAY.

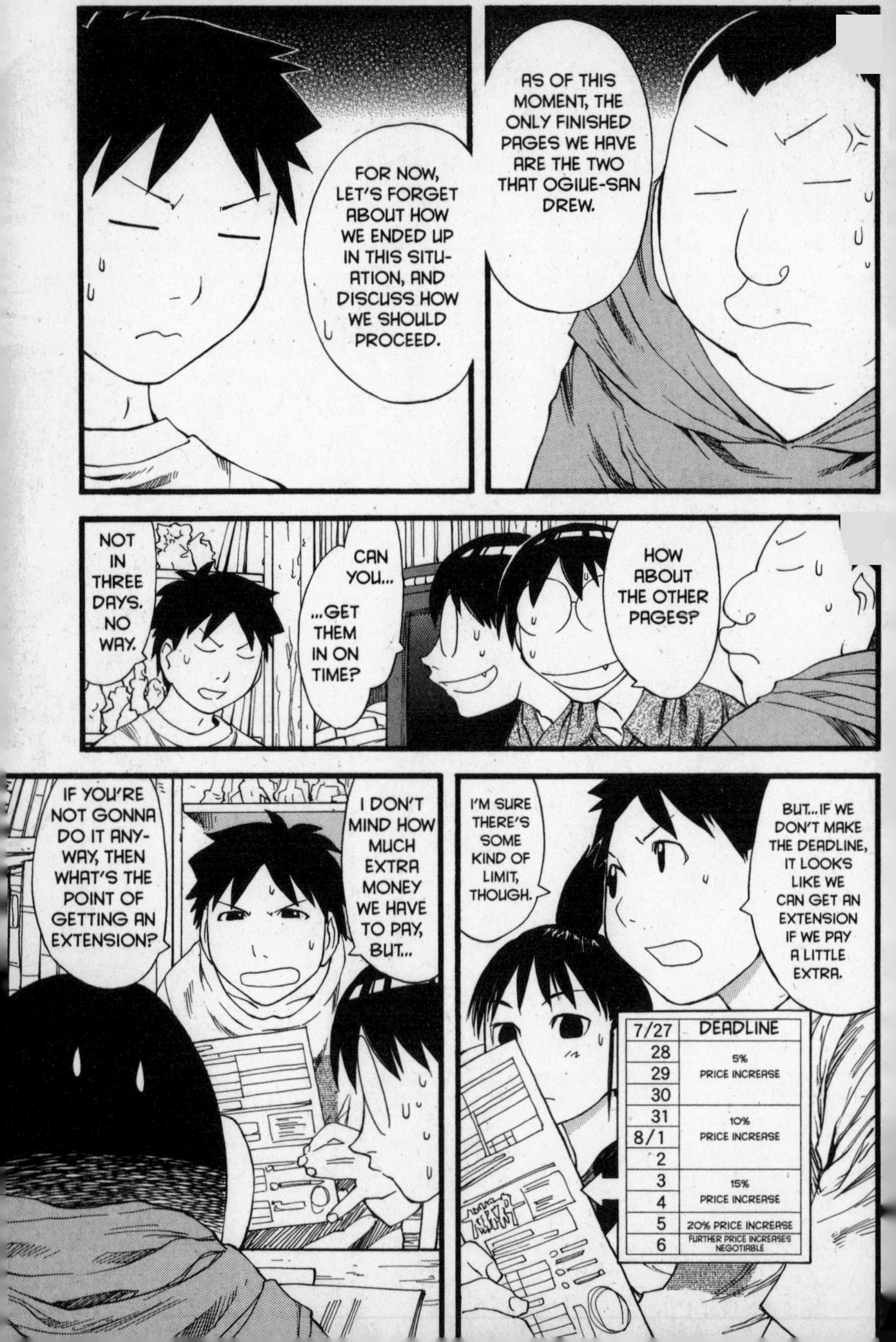
AS OF THIS MOMENT, THE ONLY FINISHED PAGES WE HAVE ARE THE TWO THAT OGIUE-SAN DREW.
FOR NOW, LET'S FORGET ABOUT HOW WE ENDED UP IN THIS SITU-ATION, AND DISCUSS HOW WE SHOULD PROCEED.
HOW ABOUT THE OTHER PAGES?
CAN YOU...
...GET THEM IN ON TIME?
NOT IN THREE DAYS. NO WAY.
BUT...IF WE DON'T MAKE THE DEADLINE, IT LOOKS LIKE WE CAN GET AN EXTENSION IF WE PAY A LITTLE EXTRA.
7/27 DEADLINE
28
29 5% PRICE INCREASE
30
31
8/1 10% PRICE INCREASE
2
3 15% PRICE INCREASE
4
5 20% PRICE INCREASE
6 FURTHER PRICE INCREASES NEGOTIABLE
I'M SURE THERE'S SOME KIND OF LIMIT, THOUGH.
I DON'T MIND HOW MUCH EXTRA MONEY WE HAVE TO PAY, BUT...
IF YOU'RE NOT GONNA DO IT ANY-WAY, THEN WHAT'S THE POINT OF GETTING AN EXTENSION?

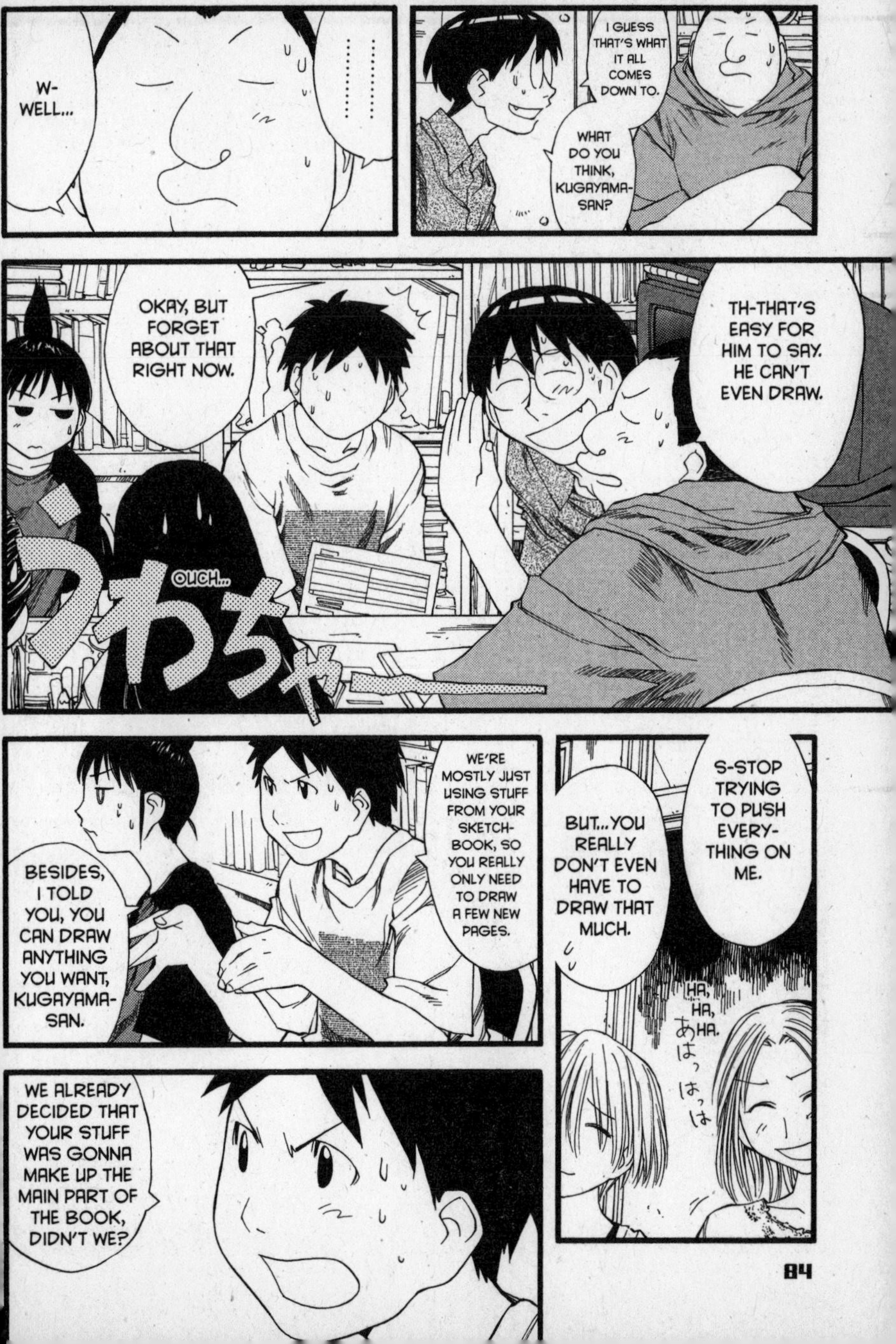
I GUESS THAT'S WHAT IT ALL COMES DOWN TO.
WHAT DO YOU THINK, KUGAYAMA-SAN?
......
W-WELL...
TH-THAT'S EASY FOR HIM TO SAY. HE CAN'T EVEN DRAW.
OKAY, BUT FORGET ABOUT THAT RIGHT NOW.
OUCH...
うわちゃー
S-STOP TRYING TO PUSH EVERY-THING ON ME.
BUT...YOU REALLY DON'T EVEN HAVE TO DRAW THAT MUCH.
HA, HA, HA.
あはっはっは
WE'RE MOSTLY JUST USING STUFF FROM YOUR SKETCH-BOOK, SO YOU REALLY ONLY NEED TO DRAW A FEW NEW PAGES.
BESIDES, I TOLD YOU, YOU CAN DRAW ANYTHING YOU WANT, KUGAYAMA-SAN.
WE ALREADY DECIDED THAT YOUR STUFF WAS GONNA MAKE UP THE MAIN PART OF THE BOOK, DIDN'T WE?

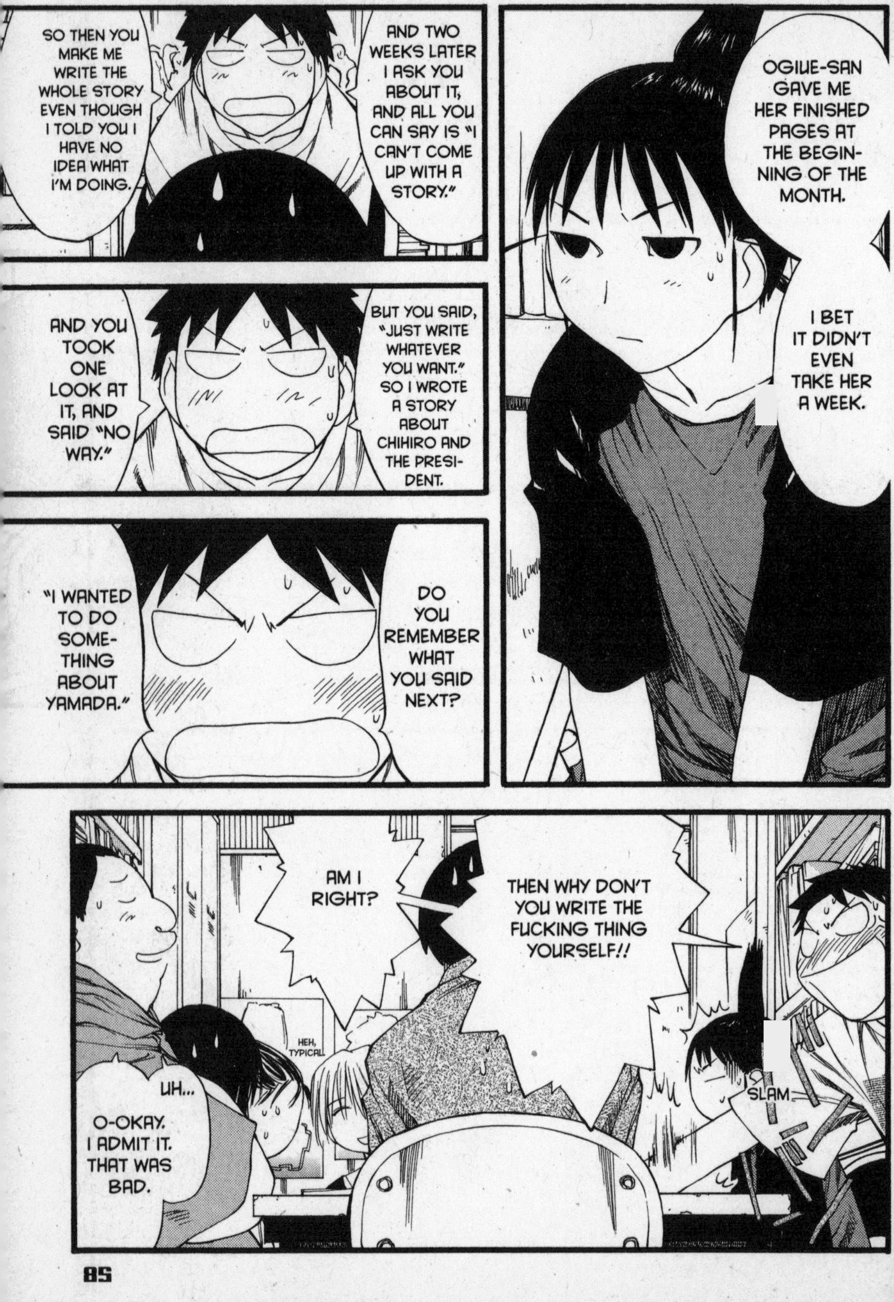
OGIUE-SAN GAVE ME HER FINISHED PAGES AT THE BEGIN- NING OF THE MONTH.
I BET IT DIDN'T EVEN TAKE HER A WEEK.
AND TWO WEEKS LATER I ASK YOU ABOUT IT, AND ALL YOU CAN SAY IS "I CAN'T COME UP WITH A STORY."
SO THEN YOU MAKE ME WRITE THE WHOLE STORY EVEN THOUGH I TOLD YOU I HAVE NO IDEA WHAT I'M DOING.
BUT YOU SAID, "JUST WRITE WHATEVER YOU WANT." SO I WROTE A STORY ABOUT CHIHIRO AND THE PRESI- DENT.
AND YOU TOOK ONE LOOK AT IT, AND SAID "NO WAY."
DO YOU REMEMBER WHAT YOU SAID NEXT?
"I WANTED TO DO SOME- THING ABOUT YAMADA."
AM I RIGHT?
THEN WHY DON'T YOU WRITE THE FUCKING THING YOURSELF!!
SLAM
HEH, TYPICAL
UH...
O-OKAY. I ADMIT IT. THAT WAS BAD.

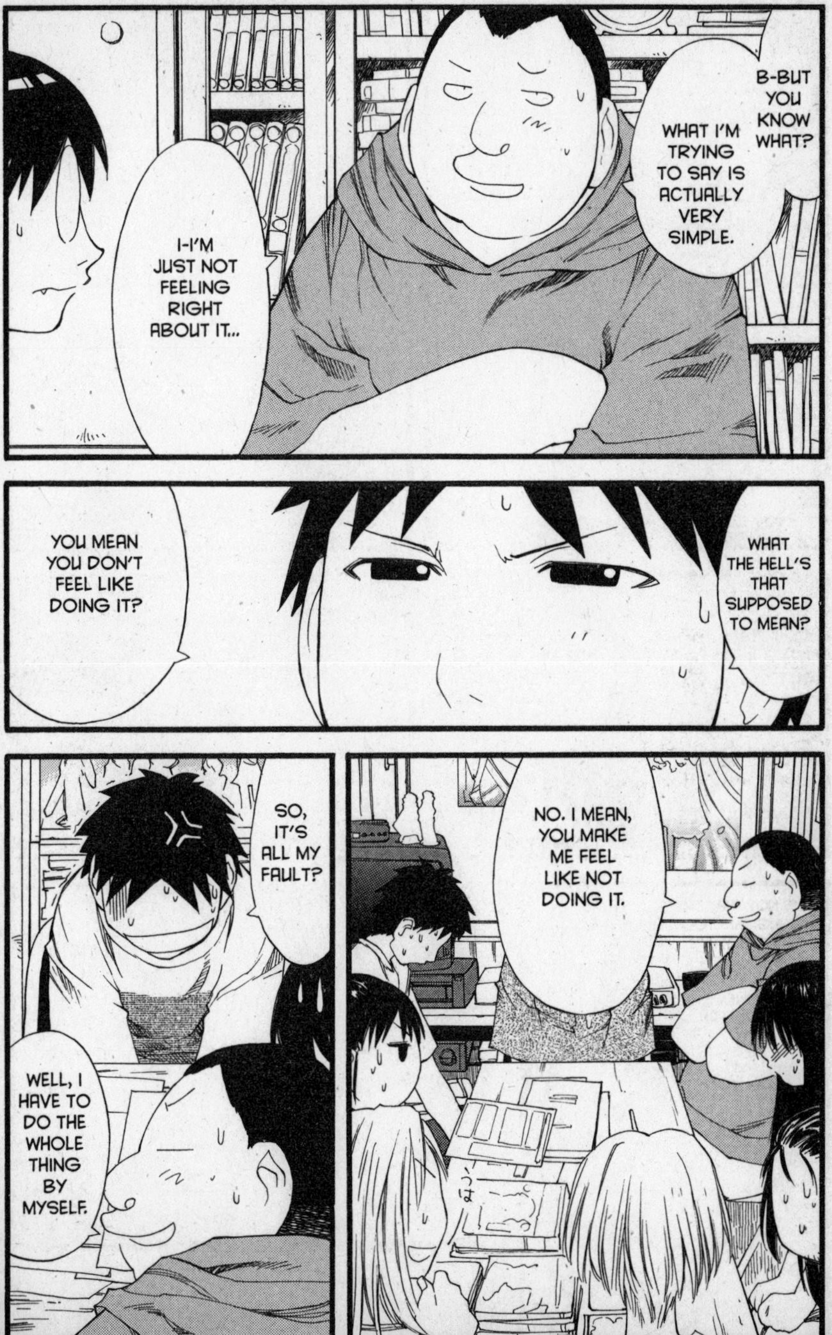
B-BUT YOU KNOW WHAT?
WHAT I'M TRYING TO SAY IS ACTUALLY VERY SIMPLE.
I-I'M JUST NOT FEELING RIGHT ABOUT IT...
WHAT THE HELL'S THAT SUPPOSED TO MEAN?
YOU MEAN YOU DON'T FEEL LIKE DOING IT?
NO. I MEAN, YOU MAKE ME FEEL LIKE NOT DOING IT.
SO, IT'S ALL MY FAULT?
WELL, I HAVE TO DO THE WHOLE THING BY MYSELF.

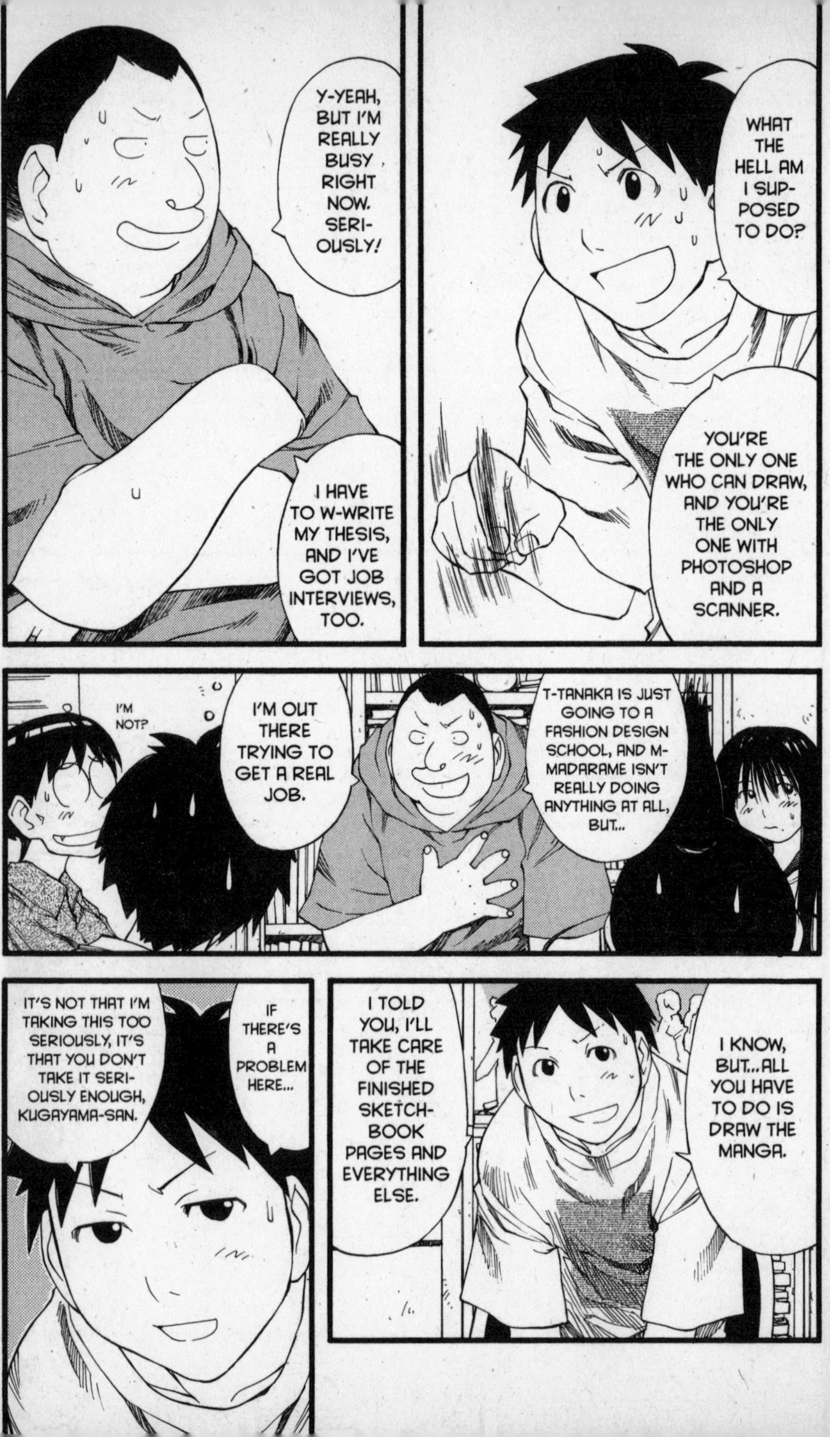
WHAT THE HELL AM I SUPPOSED TO DO?
YOU'RE THE ONLY ONE WHO CAN DRAW, AND YOU'RE THE ONLY ONE WITH PHOTOSHOP AND A SCANNER.
Y-YEAH, BUT I'M REALLY BUSY RIGHT NOW. SERIOUSLY!
I HAVE TO W-WRITE MY THESIS, AND I'VE GOT JOB INTERVIEWS, TOO.
T-TANAKA IS JUST GOING TO A FASHION DESIGN SCHOOL, AND M-MADARAME ISN'T REALLY DOING ANYTHING AT ALL, BUT...
I'M OUT THERE TRYING TO GET A REAL JOB.
I'M NOT?
I KNOW, BUT...ALL YOU HAVE TO DO IS DRAW THE MANGA.
I TOLD YOU, I'LL TAKE CARE OF THE FINISHED SKETCHBOOK PAGES AND EVERYTHING ELSE.
IF THERE'S A PROBLEM HERE...
IT'S NOT THAT I'M TAKING THIS TOO SERIOUSLY, IT'S THAT YOU DON'T TAKE IT SERIOUSLY ENOUGH, KUGAYAMA-SAN.

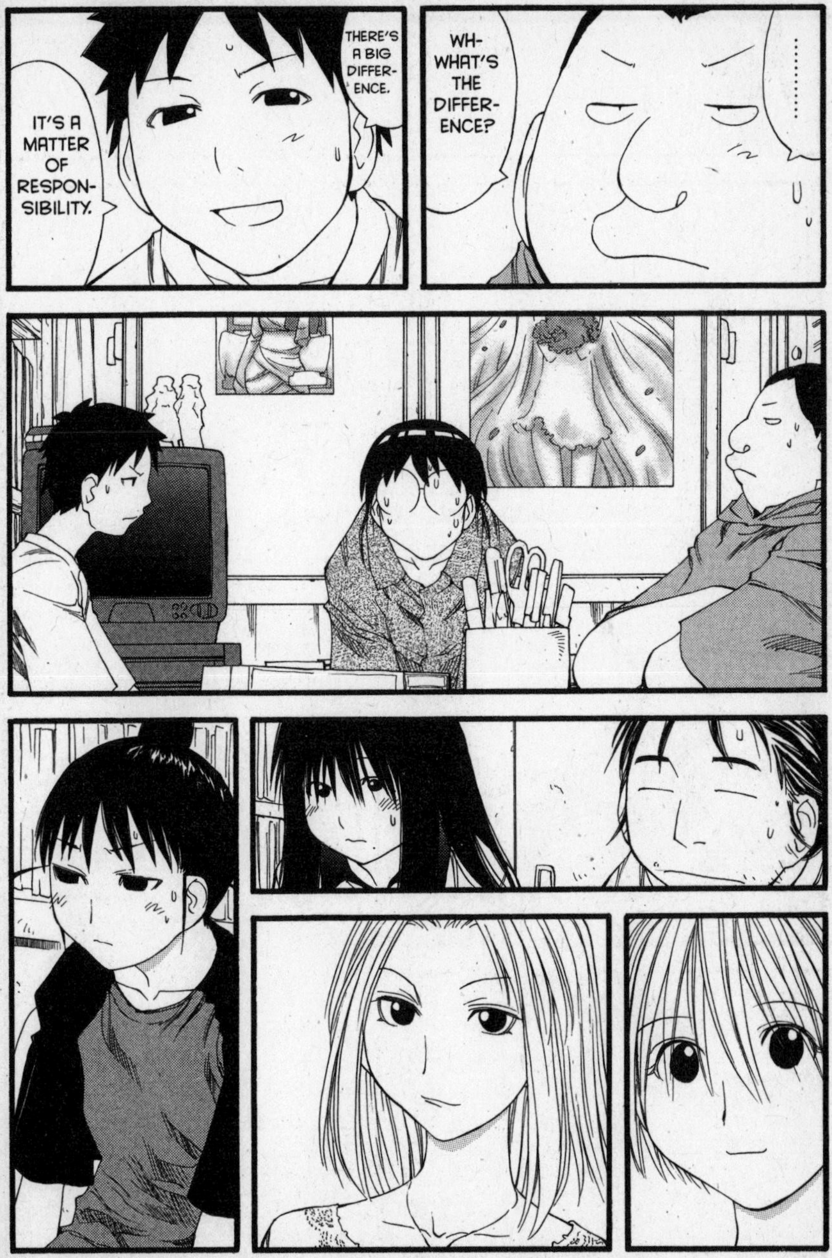
......
WH-WHAT'S THE DIFFERENCE?
THERE'S A BIG DIFFERENCE.
IT'S A MATTER OF RESPONSIBILITY.

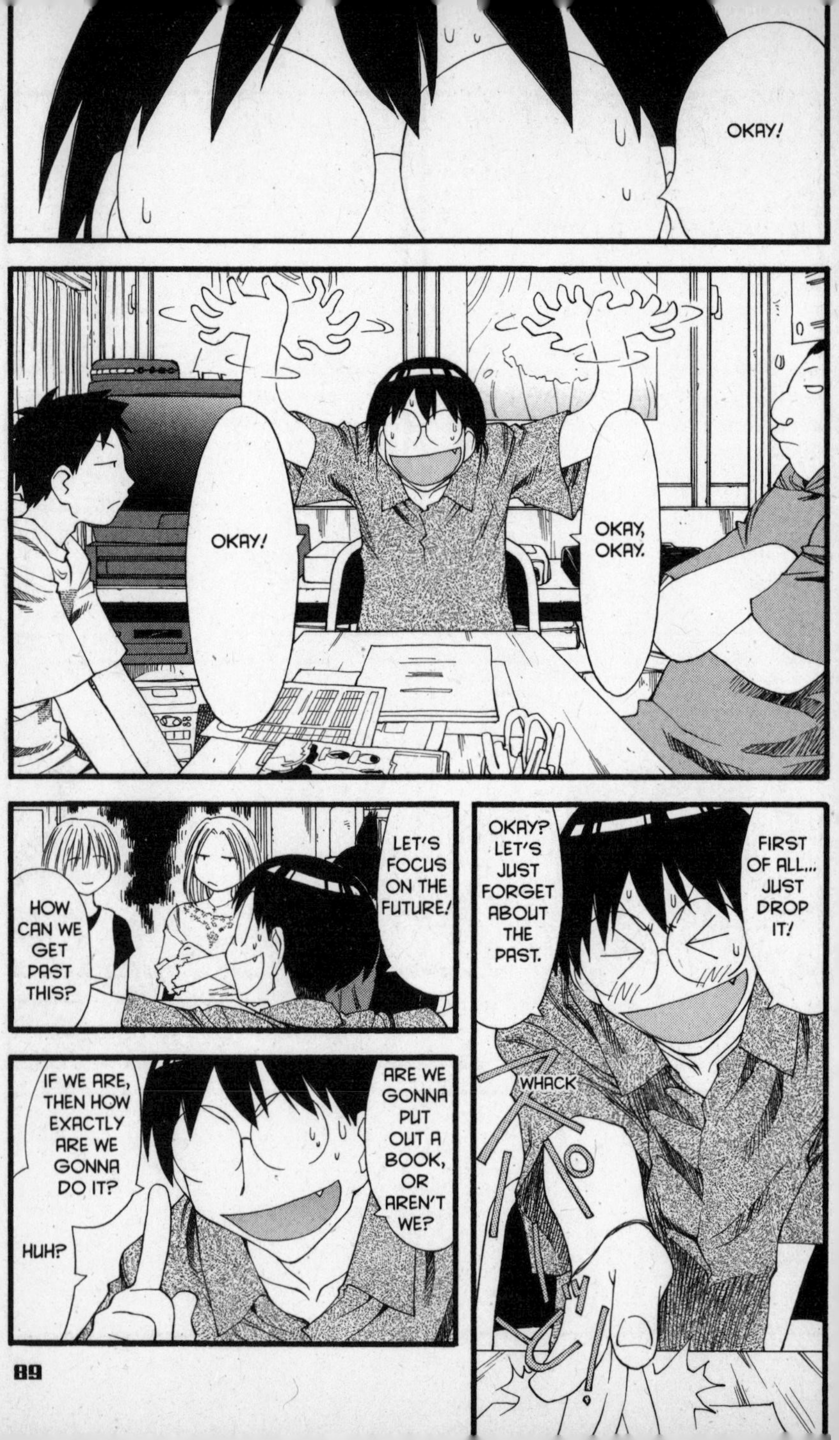
OKAY!
OKAY, OKAY.
OKAY!
FIRST OF ALL... JUST DROP IT!
OKAY? LET'S JUST FORGET ABOUT THE PAST.
WHACK
LET'S FOCUS ON THE FUTURE!
HOW CAN WE GET PAST THIS?
ARE WE GONNA PUT OUT A BOOK, OR AREN'T WE?
IF WE ARE, THEN HOW EXACTLY ARE WE GONNA DO IT?
HUH?

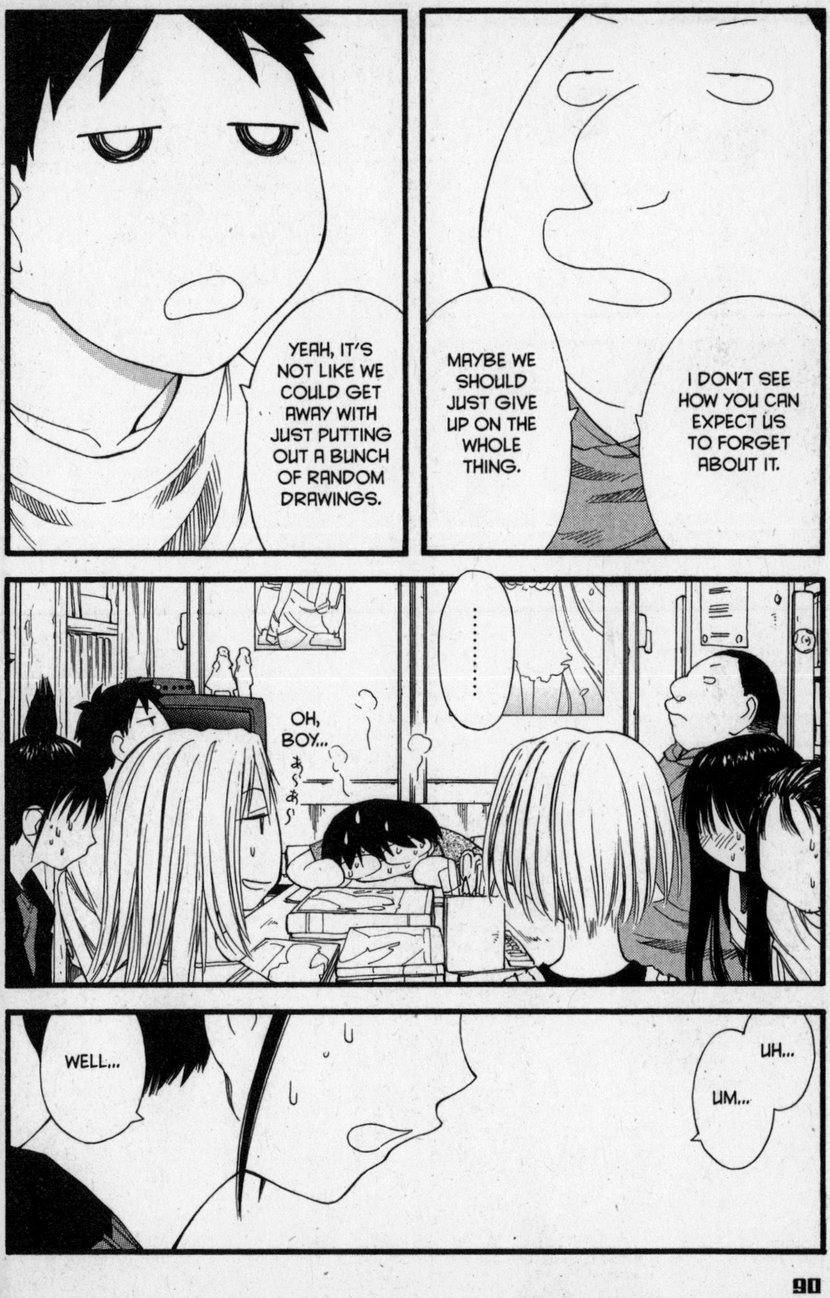
I DON'T SEE HOW YOU CAN EXPECT US TO FORGET ABOUT IT.
MAYBE WE SHOULD JUST GIVE UP ON THE WHOLE THING.
YEAH, IT'S NOT LIKE WE COULD GET AWAY WITH JUST PUTTING OUT A BUNCH OF RANDOM DRAWINGS.
......
OH, BOY...
UH...
UM...
WELL...

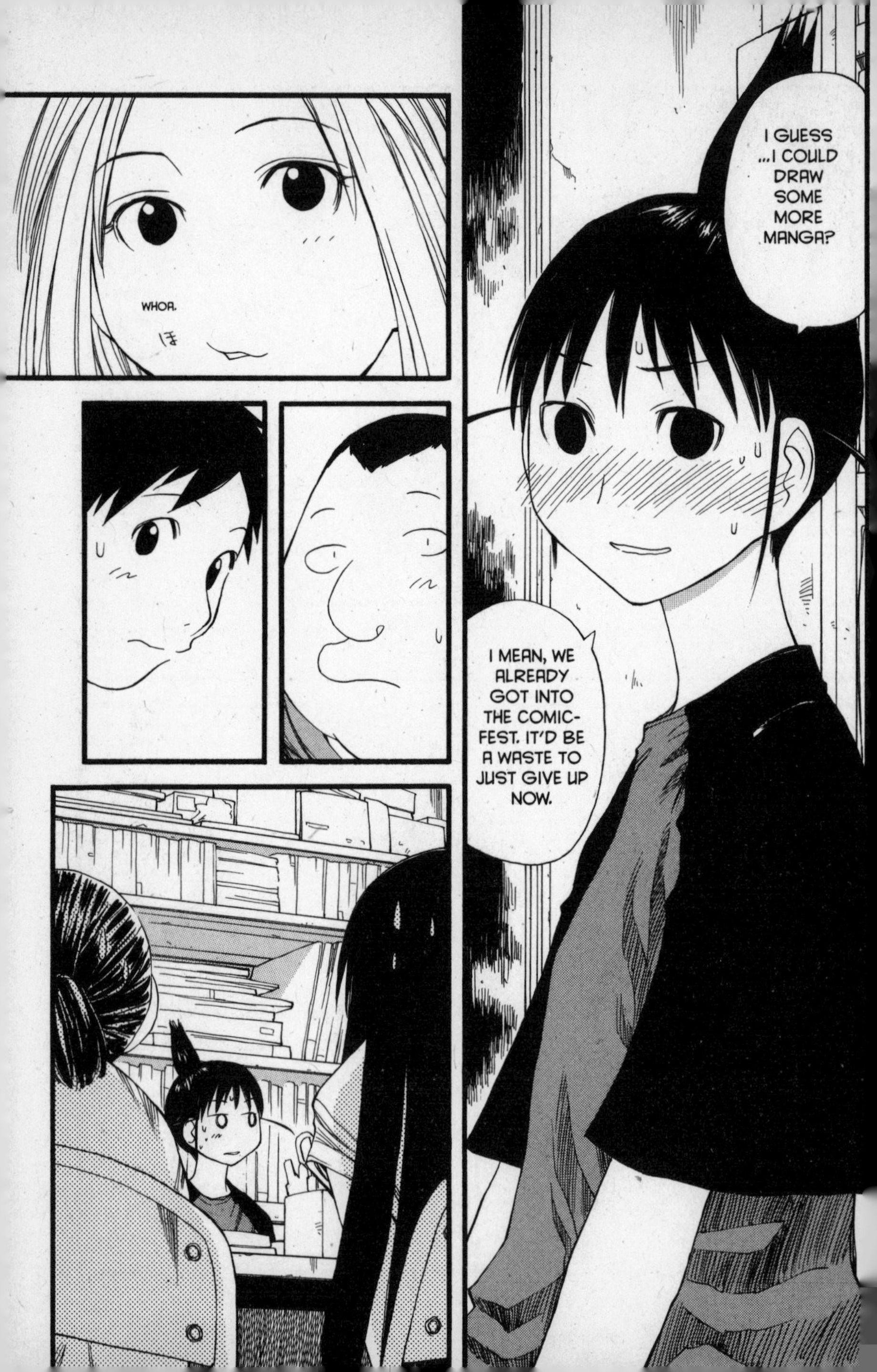
I GUESS ...I COULD DRAW SOME MORE MANGA?
I MEAN, WE ALREADY GOT INTO THE COMIC-FEST. IT'D BE A WASTE TO JUST GIVE UP NOW.
WHOA.
ほ

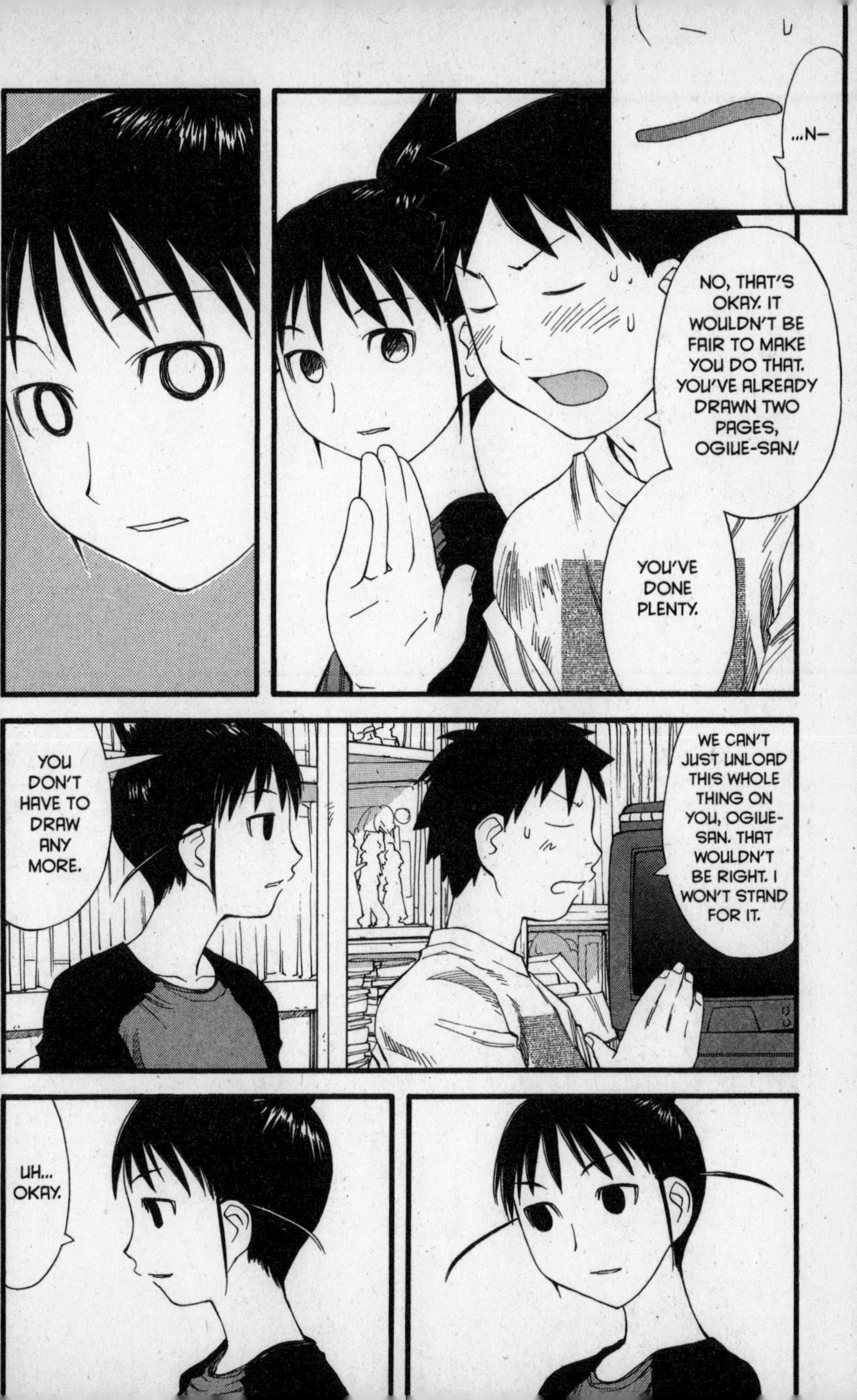
...N—
NO, THAT'S OKAY. IT WOULDN'T BE FAIR TO MAKE YOU DO THAT. YOU'VE ALREADY DRAWN TWO PAGES, OGIUE-SAN!
YOU'VE DONE PLENTY.
WE CAN'T JUST UNLOAD THIS WHOLE THING ON YOU, OGIUE-SAN. THAT WOULDN'T BE RIGHT. I WON'T STAND FOR IT.
YOU DON'T HAVE TO DRAW ANY MORE.
UH... OKAY.

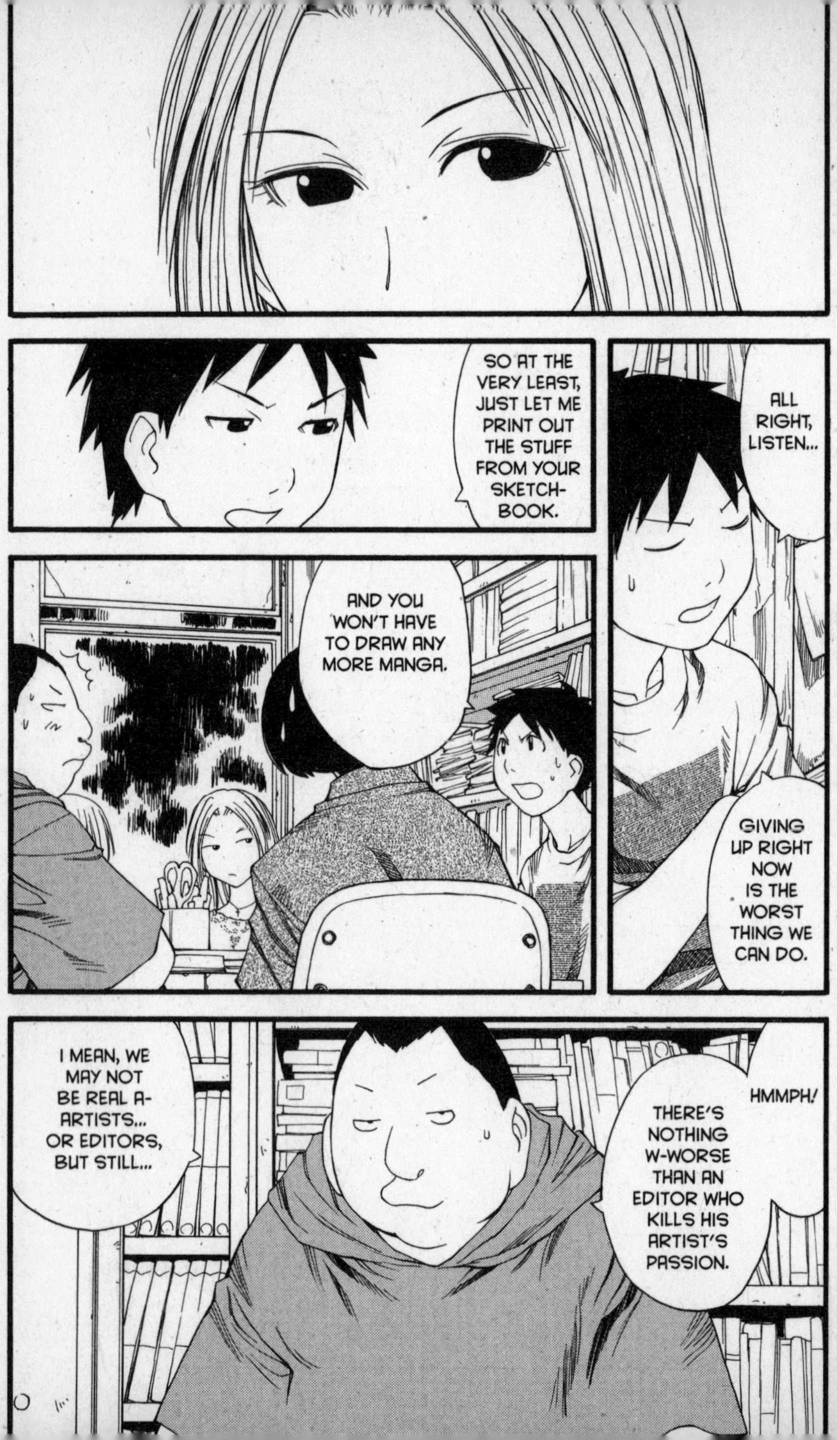
ALL RIGHT, LISTEN...
GIVING UP RIGHT NOW IS THE WORST THING WE CAN DO.
SO AT THE VERY LEAST, JUST LET ME PRINT OUT THE STUFF FROM YOUR SKETCH-BOOK.
AND YOU WON'T HAVE TO DRAW ANY MORE MANGA.
HMMPH!
THERE'S NOTHING W-WORSE THAN AN EDITOR WHO KILLS HIS ARTIST'S PASSION.
I MEAN, WE MAY NOT BE REAL A-ARTISTS... OR EDITORS, BUT STILL...

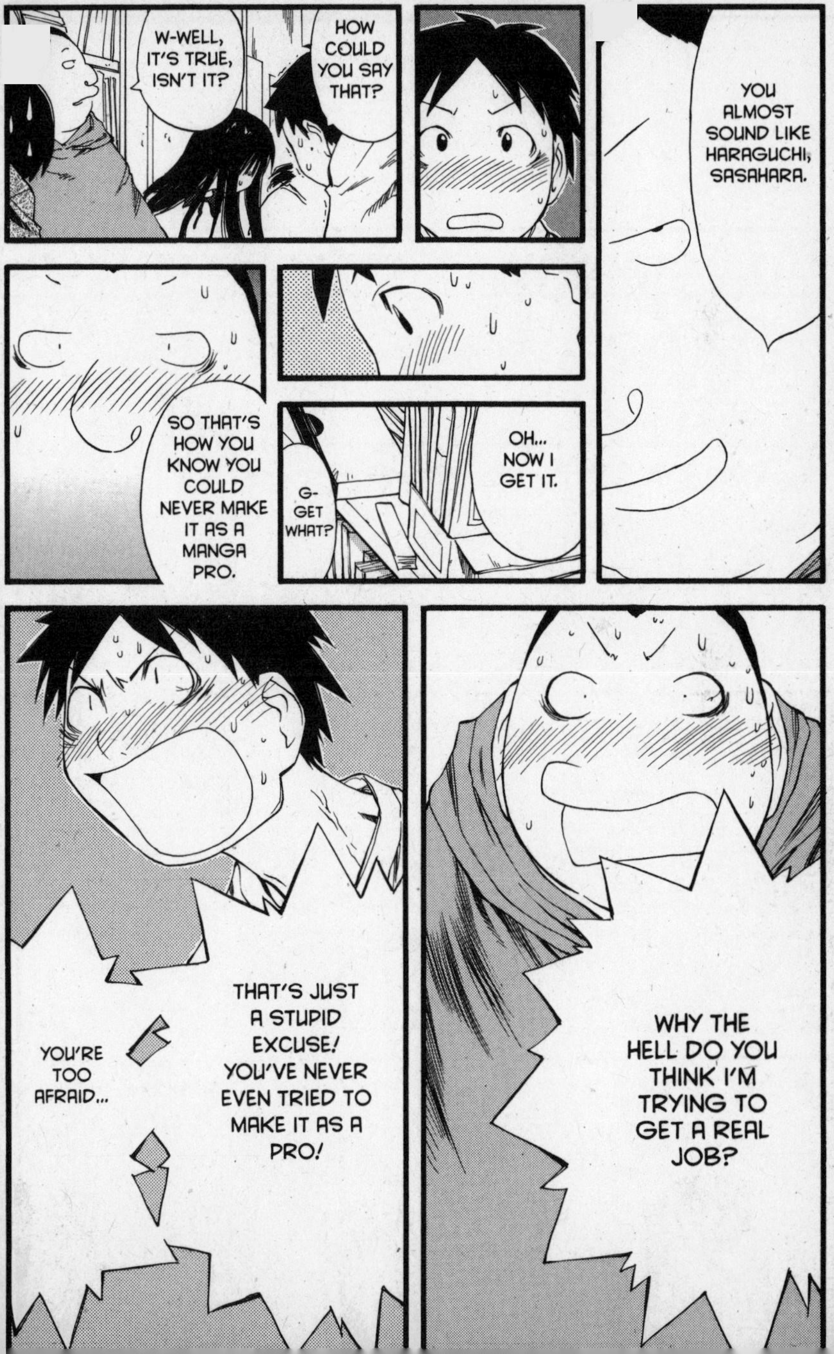
YOU ALMOST SOUND LIKE HARAGUCHI, SASAHARA.
HOW COULD YOU SAY THAT?
W-WELL, IT'S TRUE, ISN'T IT?
OH... NOW I GET IT.
G-GET WHAT?
SO THAT'S HOW YOU KNOW YOU COULD NEVER MAKE IT AS A MANGA PRO.
WHY THE HELL DO YOU THINK I'M TRYING TO GET A REAL JOB?
THAT'S JUST A STUPID EXCUSE! YOU'VE NEVER EVEN TRIED TO MAKE IT AS A PRO!
YOU'RE TOO AFRAID...

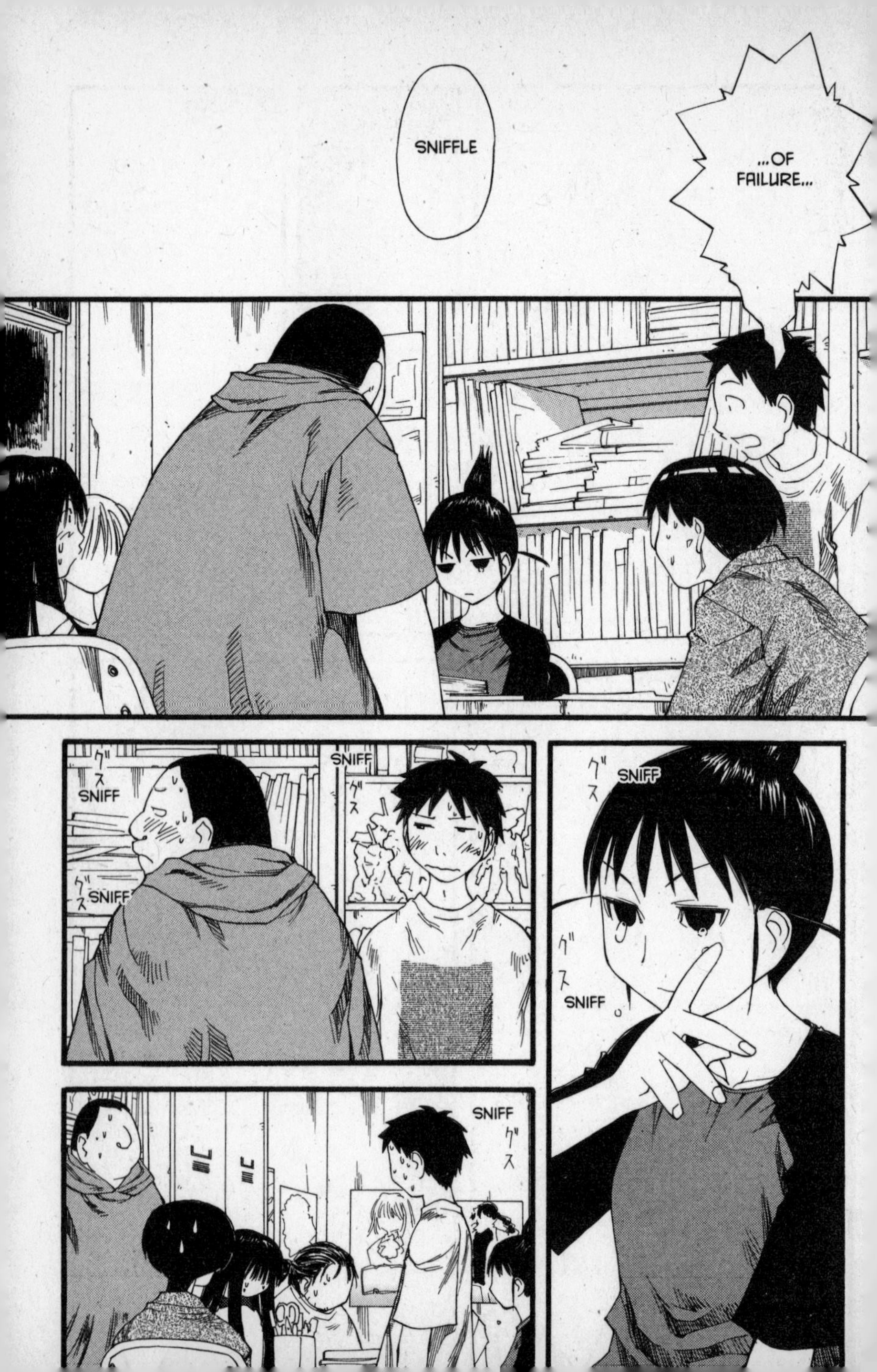
...OF FAILURE...
SNIFFLE
グス
SNIFF
グス
SNIFF
SNIFF
グス
グス
SNIFF
グス
SNIFF
SNIFF
グス

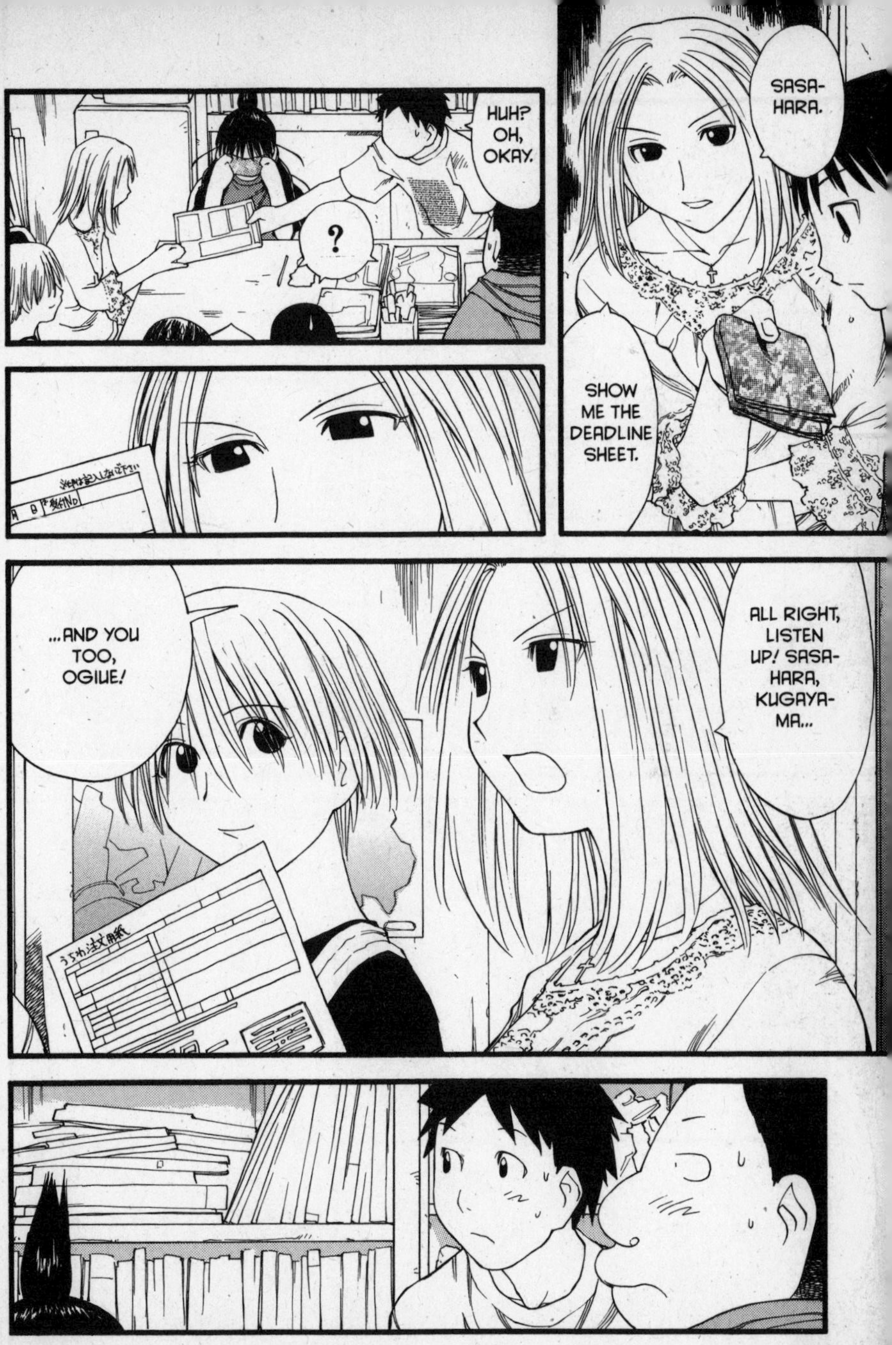
SASA-HARA.
SHOW ME THE DEADLINE SHEET.
HUH? OH, OKAY.
?
ALL RIGHT, LISTEN UP! SASA-HARA, KUGAYA-MA...
...AND YOU TOO, OGIUE!

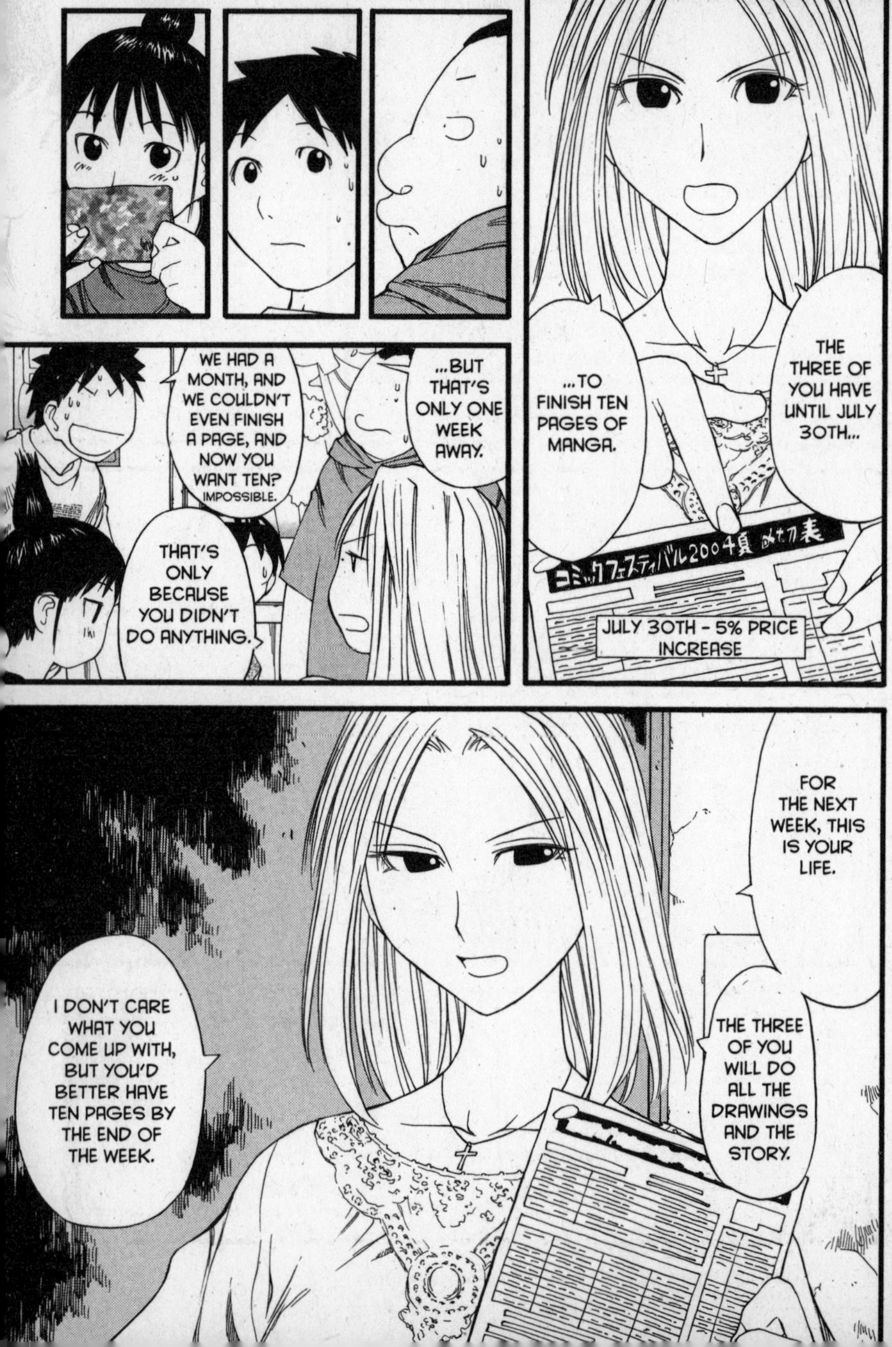
THE THREE OF YOU HAVE UNTIL JULY 30TH...
...TO FINISH TEN PAGES OF MANGA.
JULY 30TH - 5% PRICE INCREASE
...BUT THAT'S ONLY ONE WEEK AWAY.
WE HAD A MONTH, AND WE COULDN'T EVEN FINISH A PAGE, AND NOW YOU WANT TEN? IMPOSSIBLE.
THAT'S ONLY BECAUSE YOU DIDN'T DO ANYTHING.
FOR THE NEXT WEEK, THIS IS YOUR LIFE.
THE THREE OF YOU WILL DO ALL THE DRAWINGS AND THE STORY.
I DON'T CARE WHAT YOU COME UP WITH, BUT YOU'D BETTER HAVE TEN PAGES BY THE END OF THE WEEK.

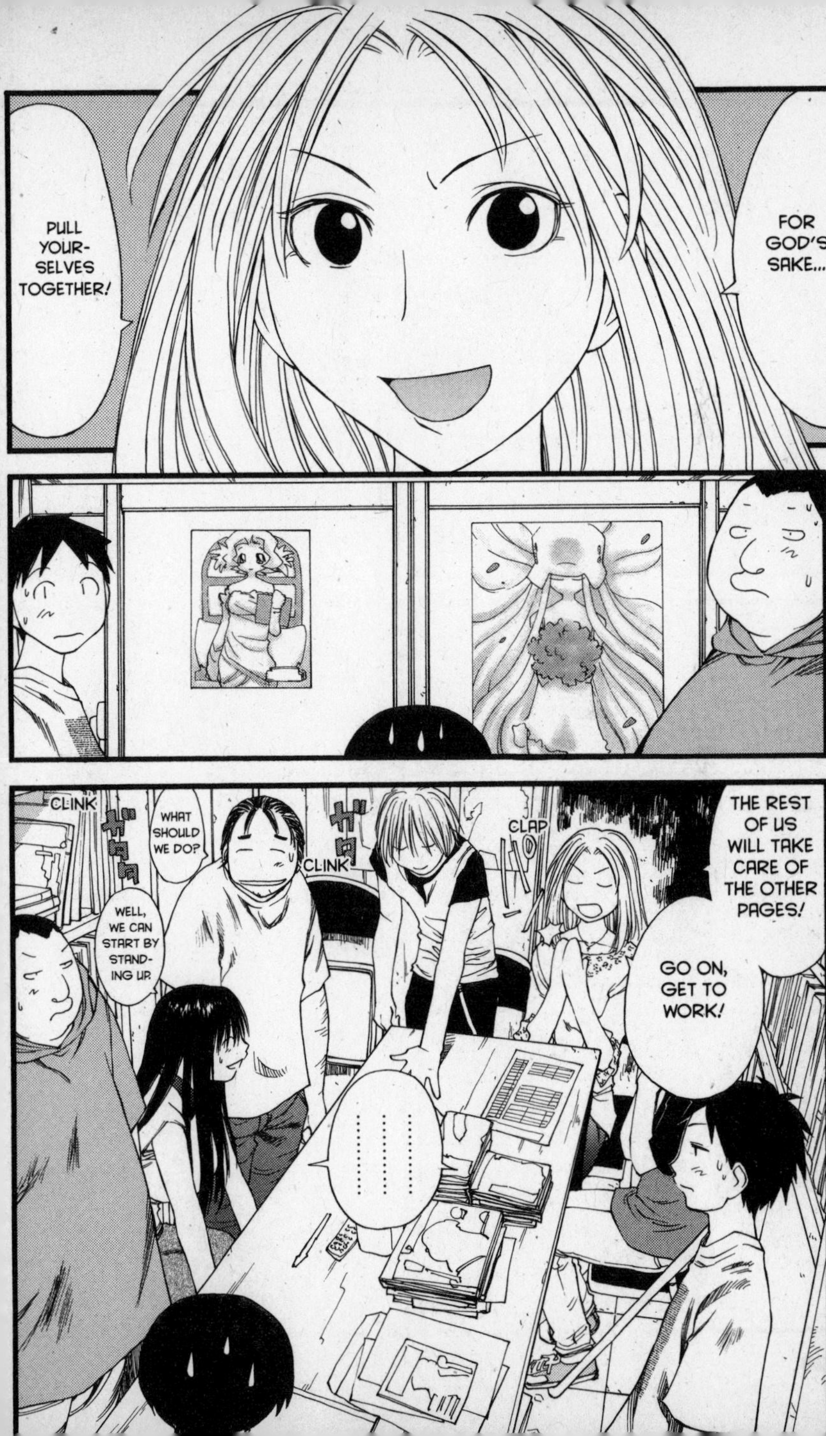
FOR GOD'S SAKE...
PULL YOUR-SELVES TOGETHER!
THE REST OF US WILL TAKE CARE OF THE OTHER PAGES!
GO ON, GET TO WORK!
CLAP
......
CLINK
WHAT SHOULD WE DO?
WELL, WE CAN START BY STAND-ING UP.
CLINK

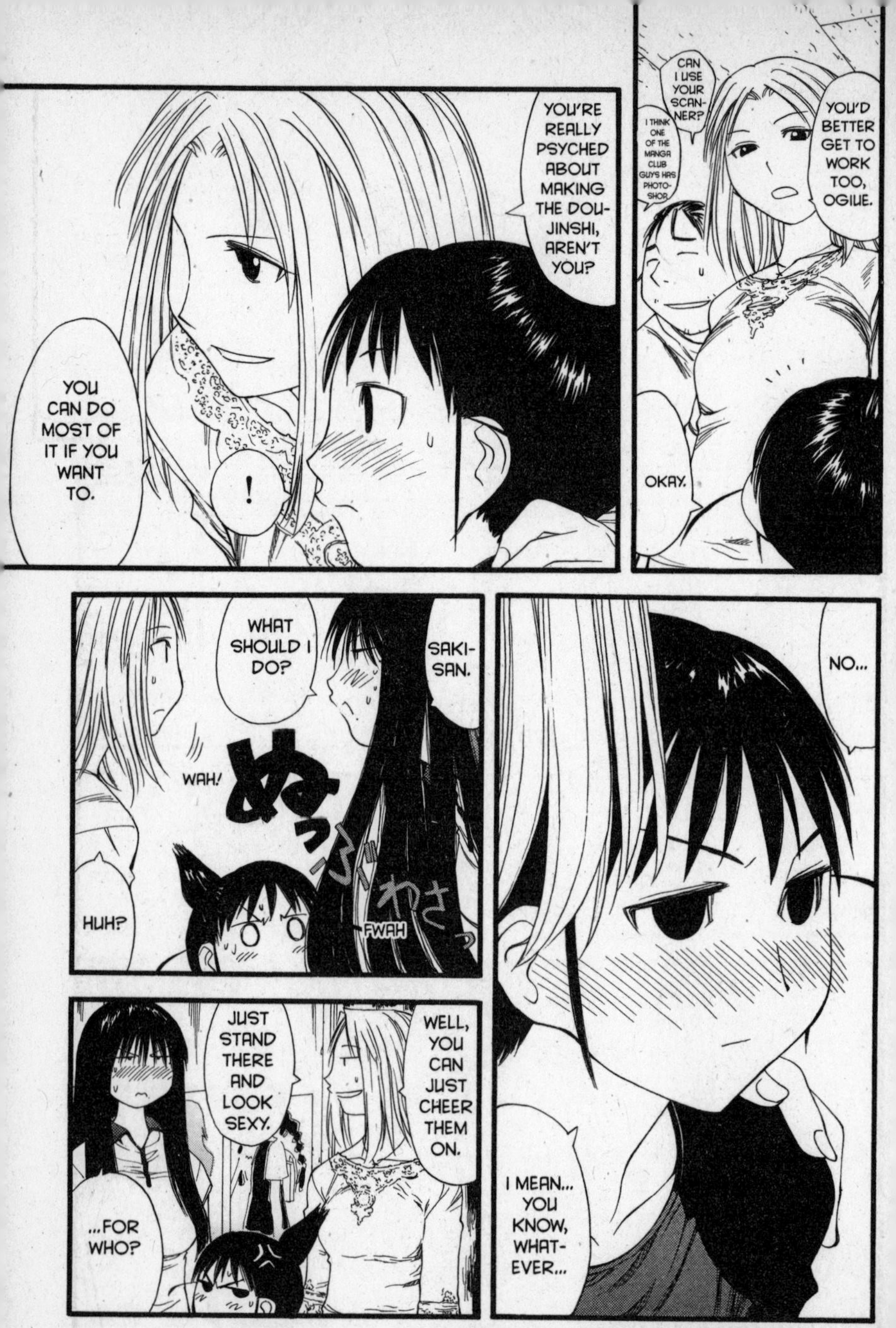
YOU'D BETTER GET TO WORK TOO, OGIUE.
CAN I USE YOUR SCANNER?
I THINK ONE OF THE MANGA CLUB GUYS HAS PHOTOSHOP.
OKAY.
YOU'RE REALLY PSYCHED ABOUT MAKING THE DOUJINSHI, AREN'T YOU?
!
YOU CAN DO MOST OF IT IF YOU WANT TO.
NO...
I MEAN... YOU KNOW, WHATEVER...
SAKI-SAN.
WHAT SHOULD I DO?
WAH!
FWAH
HUH?
WELL, YOU CAN JUST CHEER THEM ON.
JUST STAND THERE AND LOOK SEXY.
...FOR WHO?

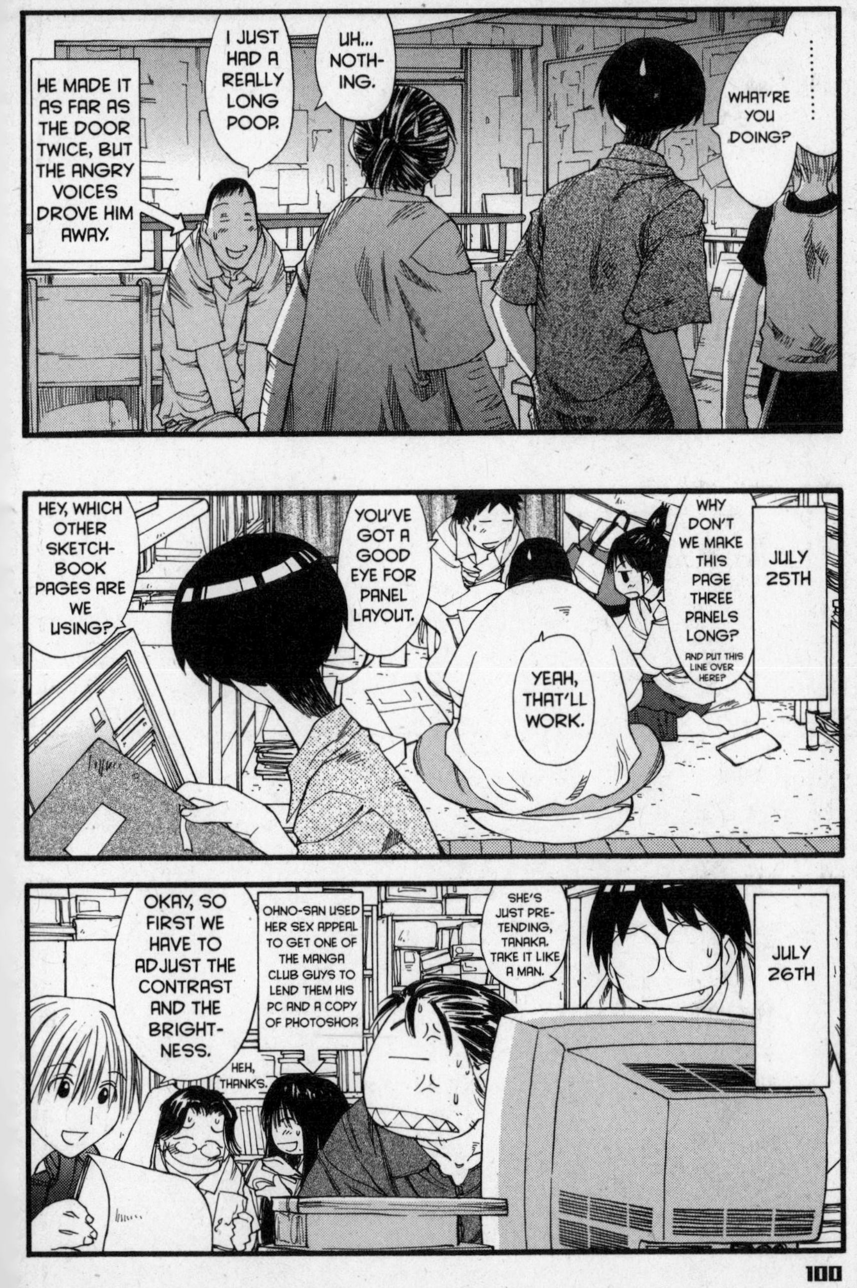
......
WHAT'RE YOU DOING?
UH... NOTHING.
I JUST HAD A REALLY LONG POOP.
HE MADE IT AS FAR AS THE DOOR TWICE, BUT THE ANGRY VOICES DROVE HIM AWAY.
JULY 25TH
WHY DON'T WE MAKE THIS PAGE THREE PANELS LONG?
AND PUT THIS LINE OVER HERE?
YEAH, THAT'LL WORK.
YOU'VE GOT A GOOD EYE FOR PANEL LAYOUT.
HEY, WHICH OTHER SKETCHBOOK PAGES ARE WE USING?
JULY 26TH
SHE'S JUST PRETENDING, TANAKA. TAKE IT LIKE A MAN.
OHNO-SAN USED HER SEX APPEAL TO GET ONE OF THE MANGA CLUB GUYS TO LEND THEM HIS PC AND A COPY OF PHOTOSHOP.
OKAY, SO FIRST WE HAVE TO ADJUST THE CONTRAST AND THE BRIGHTNESS.
HEH, THANKS.

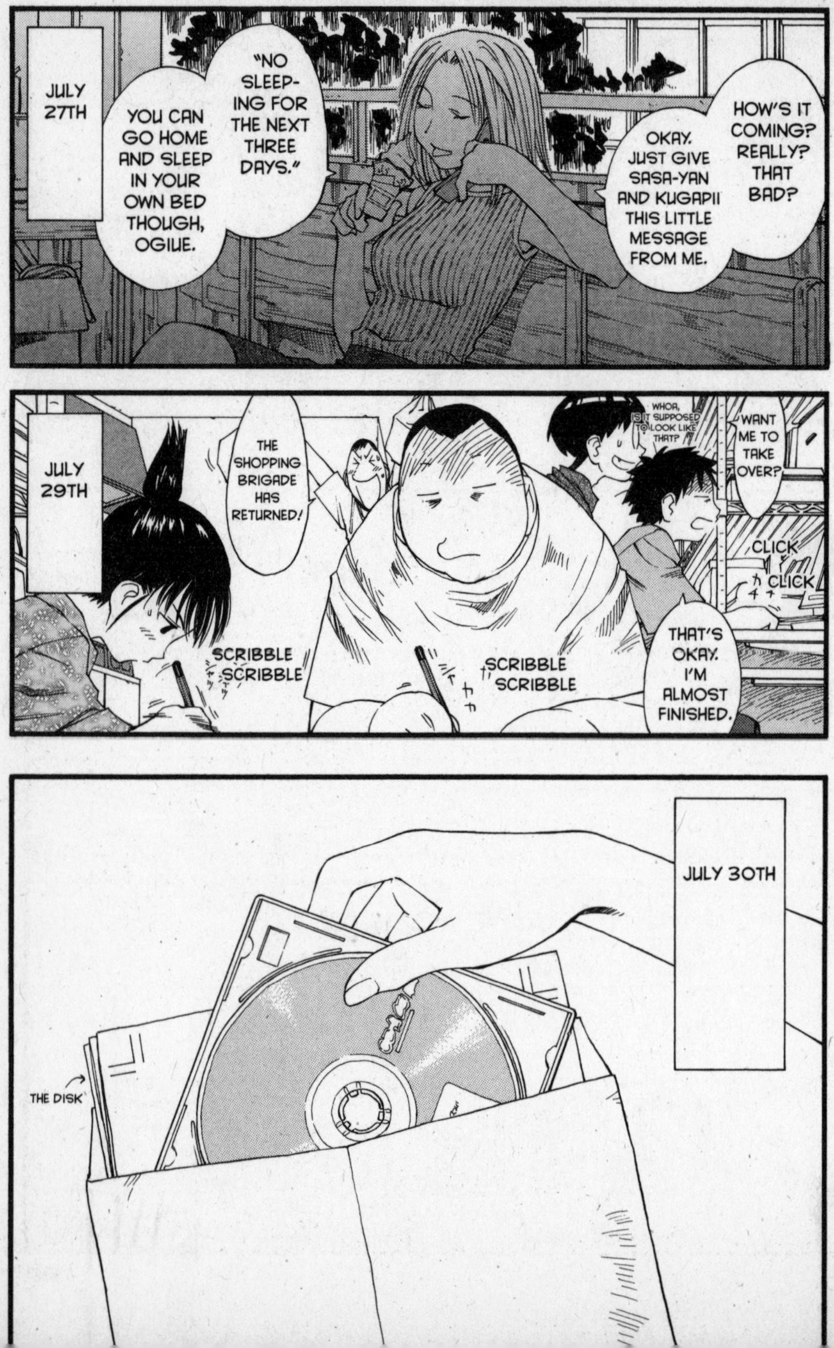
HOW'S IT COMING? REALLY? THAT BAD?
OKAY. JUST GIVE SASA-YAN AND KUGAPII THIS LITTLE MESSAGE FROM ME.
"NO SLEEP-ING FOR THE NEXT THREE DAYS."
YOU CAN GO HOME AND SLEEP IN YOUR OWN BED THOUGH, OGIUE.
JULY 27TH
WANT ME TO TAKE OVER?
WHOA, IS IT SUPPOSED TO LOOK LIKE THAT?
CLICK
CLICK
THAT'S OKAY. I'M ALMOST FINISHED.
THE SHOPPING BRIGADE HAS RETURNED!
SCRIBBLE SCRIBBLE
SCRIBBLE SCRIBBLE
JULY 29TH
JULY 30TH
THE DISK

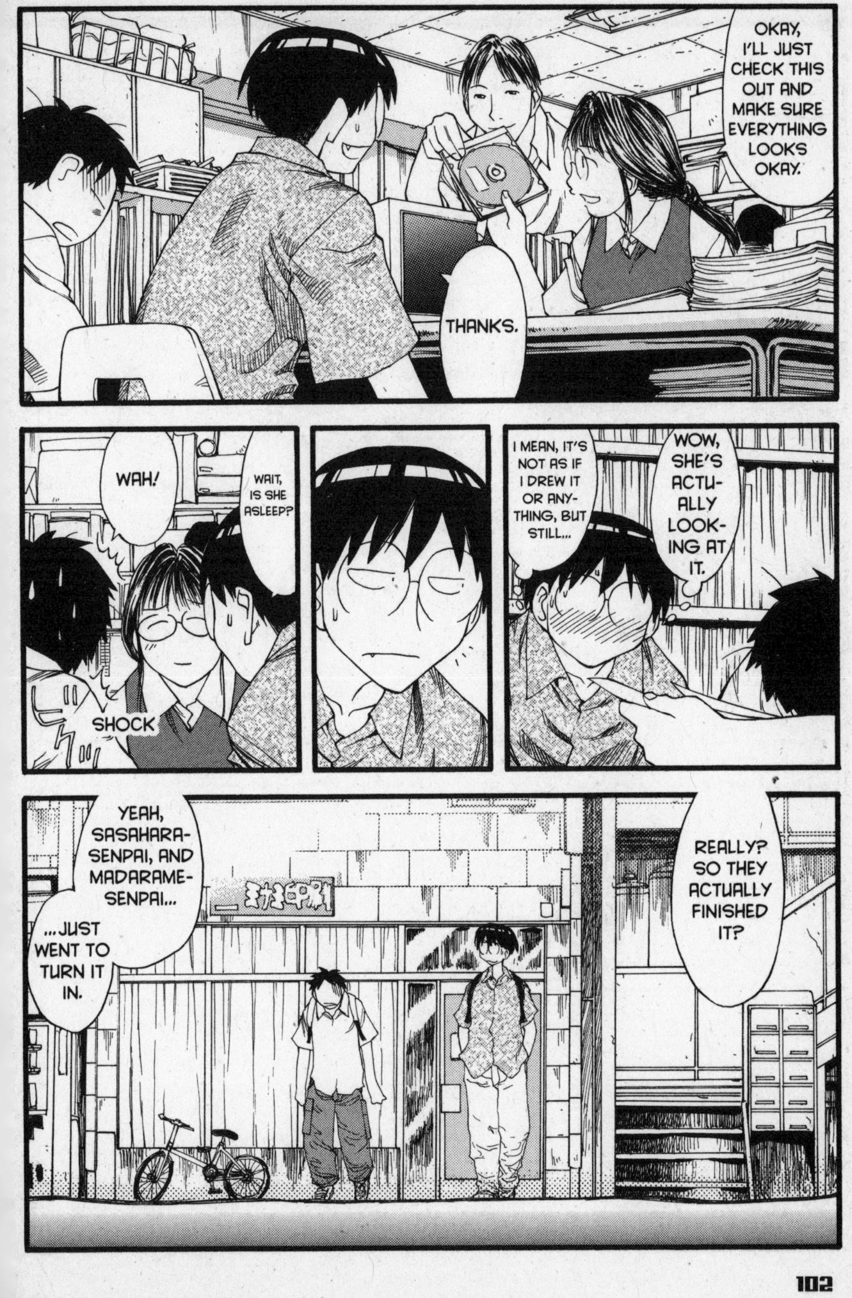
OKAY, I'LL JUST CHECK THIS OUT AND MAKE SURE EVERYTHING LOOKS OKAY.
THANKS.
WOW, SHE'S ACTU-ALLY LOOK-ING AT IT.
I MEAN, IT'S NOT AS IF I DREW IT OR ANY-THING, BUT STILL...
WAIT, IS SHE ASLEEP?
WAH!
SHOCK
REALLY? SO THEY ACTUALLY FINISHED IT?
YEAH, SASAHARA-SENPAI, AND MADARAME-SENPAI...
...JUST WENT TO TURN IT IN.

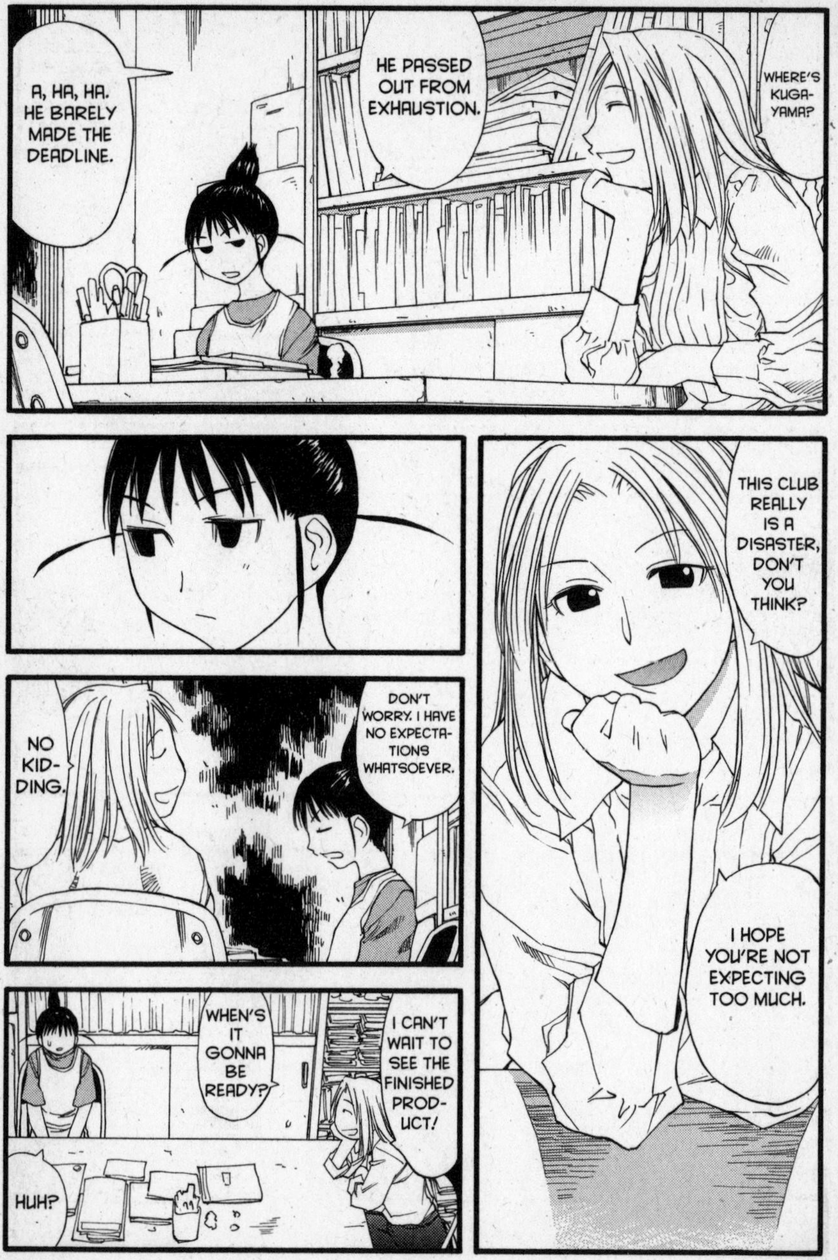
WHERE'S KUGA-YAMA?
HE PASSED OUT FROM EXHAUSTION.
A, HA, HA. HE BARELY MADE THE DEADLINE.
THIS CLUB REALLY IS A DISASTER, DON'T YOU THINK?
I HOPE YOU'RE NOT EXPECTING TOO MUCH.
DON'T WORRY. I HAVE NO EXPECTATIONS WHATSOEVER.
NO KID-DING.
I CAN'T WAIT TO SEE THE FINISHED PROD-UCT!
WHEN'S IT GONNA BE READY?
HUH?

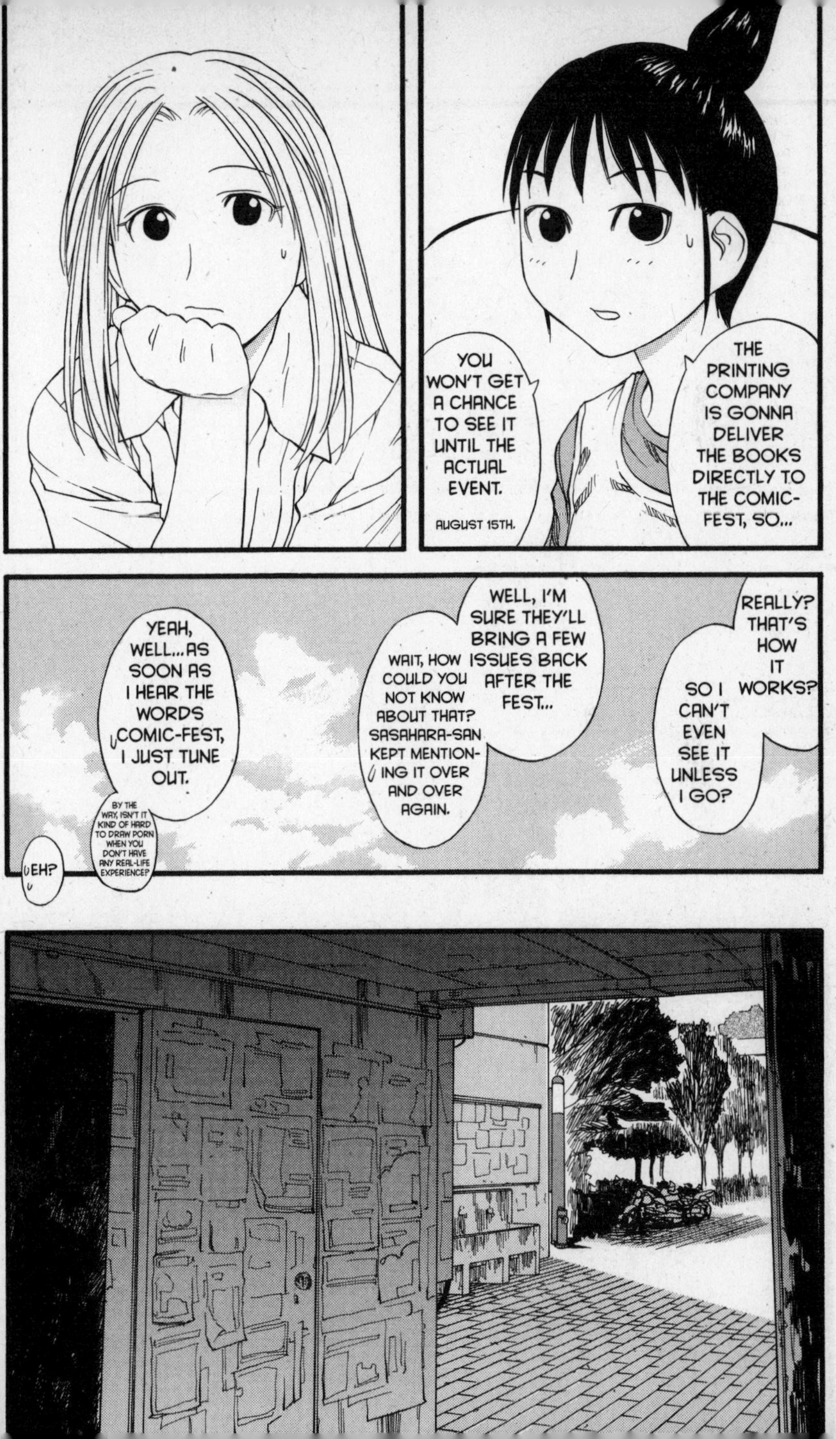
THE PRINTING COMPANY IS GONNA DELIVER THE BOOKS DIRECTLY TO THE COMIC-FEST, SO...
YOU WON'T GET A CHANCE TO SEE IT UNTIL THE ACTUAL EVENT.
AUGUST 15TH.
REALLY? THAT'S HOW IT WORKS?
SO I CAN'T EVEN SEE IT UNLESS I GO?
WELL, I'M SURE THEY'LL BRING A FEW ISSUES BACK AFTER THE FEST...
WAIT, HOW COULD YOU NOT KNOW ABOUT THAT? SASAHARA-SAN KEPT MENTIONING IT OVER AND OVER AGAIN.
YEAH, WELL...AS SOON AS I HEAR THE WORDS COMIC-FEST, I JUST TUNE OUT.
BY THE WAY, ISN'T IT KIND OF HARD TO DRAW PORN WHEN YOU DON'T HAVE ANY REAL-LIFE EXPERIENCE?
EH?

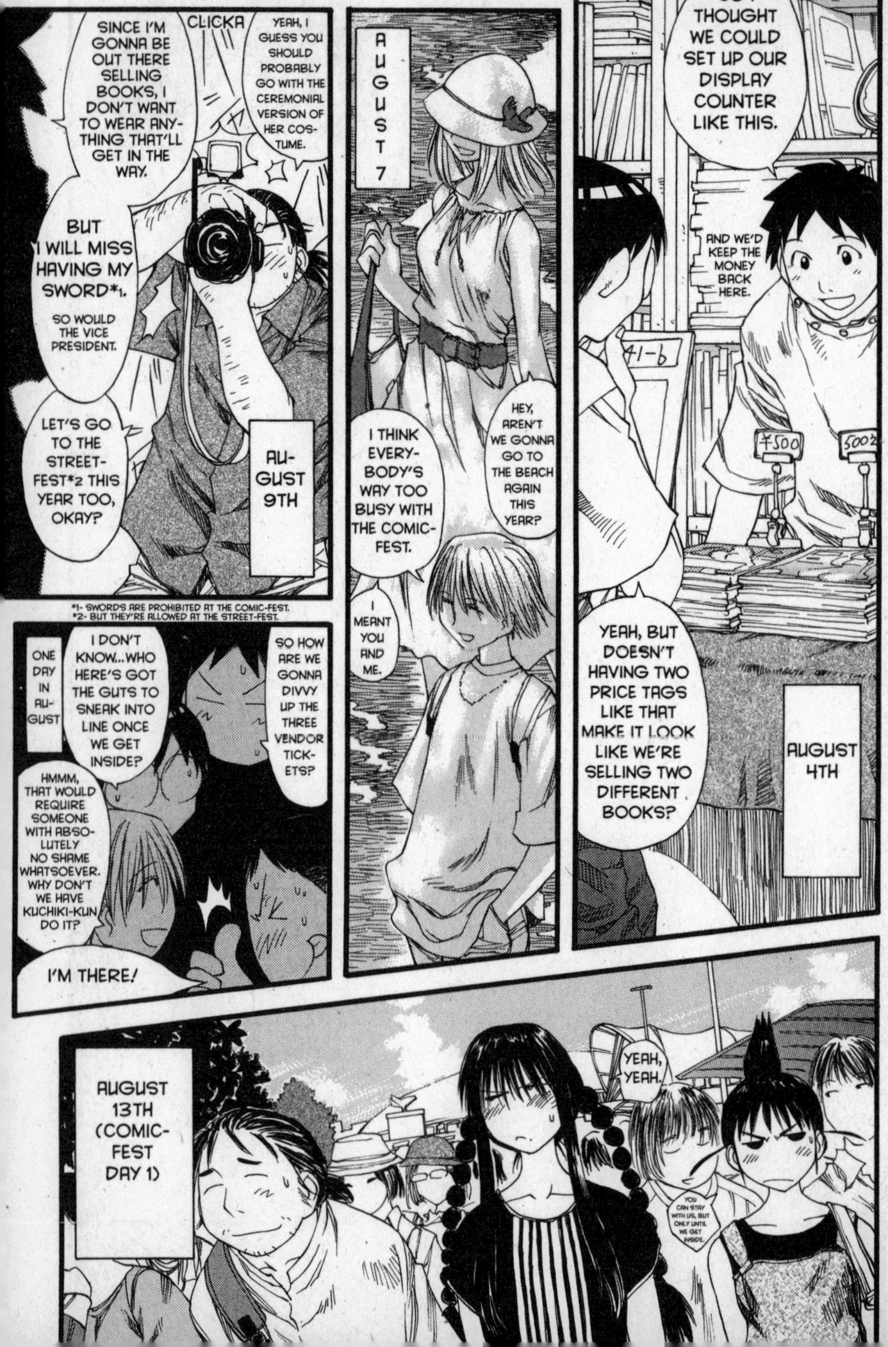
AUGUST 4TH
SO I THOUGHT WE COULD SET UP OUR DISPLAY COUNTER LIKE THIS.
AND WE'D KEEP THE MONEY BACK HERE.
YEAH, BUT DOESN'T HAVING TWO PRICE TAGS LIKE THAT MAKE IT LOOK LIKE WE'RE SELLING TWO DIFFERENT BOOKS?
AUGUST 7
HEY, AREN'T WE GONNA GO TO THE BEACH AGAIN THIS YEAR?
I THINK EVERYBODY'S WAY TOO BUSY WITH THE COMIC-FEST.
I MEANT YOU AND ME.
YEAH, I GUESS YOU SHOULD PROBABLY GO WITH THE CEREMONIAL VERSION OF HER COSTUME.
CLICKA
SINCE I'M GONNA BE OUT THERE SELLING BOOKS, I DON'T WANT TO WEAR ANYTHING THAT'LL GET IN THE WAY.
BUT I WILL MISS HAVING MY SWORD*1.
SO WOULD THE VICE PRESIDENT.
AUGUST 9TH
LET'S GO TO THE STREET-FEST*2 THIS YEAR TOO, OKAY?
*1- SWORDS ARE PROHIBITED AT THE COMIC-FEST.
*2- BUT THEY'RE ALLOWED AT THE STREET-FEST.
SO HOW ARE WE GONNA DIVVY UP THE THREE VENDOR TICKETS?
I DON'T KNOW...WHO HERE'S GOT THE GUTS TO SNEAK INTO LINE ONCE WE GET INSIDE?
ONE DAY IN AUGUST
HMMM, THAT WOULD REQUIRE SOMEONE WITH ABSOLUTELY NO SHAME WHATSOEVER. WHY DON'T WE HAVE KUCHIKI-KUN DO IT?
I'M THERE!
YEAH, YEAH.
YOU CAN STAY WITH US, BUT ONLY UNTIL WE GET INSIDE.
AUGUST 13TH (COMIC-FEST DAY 1)

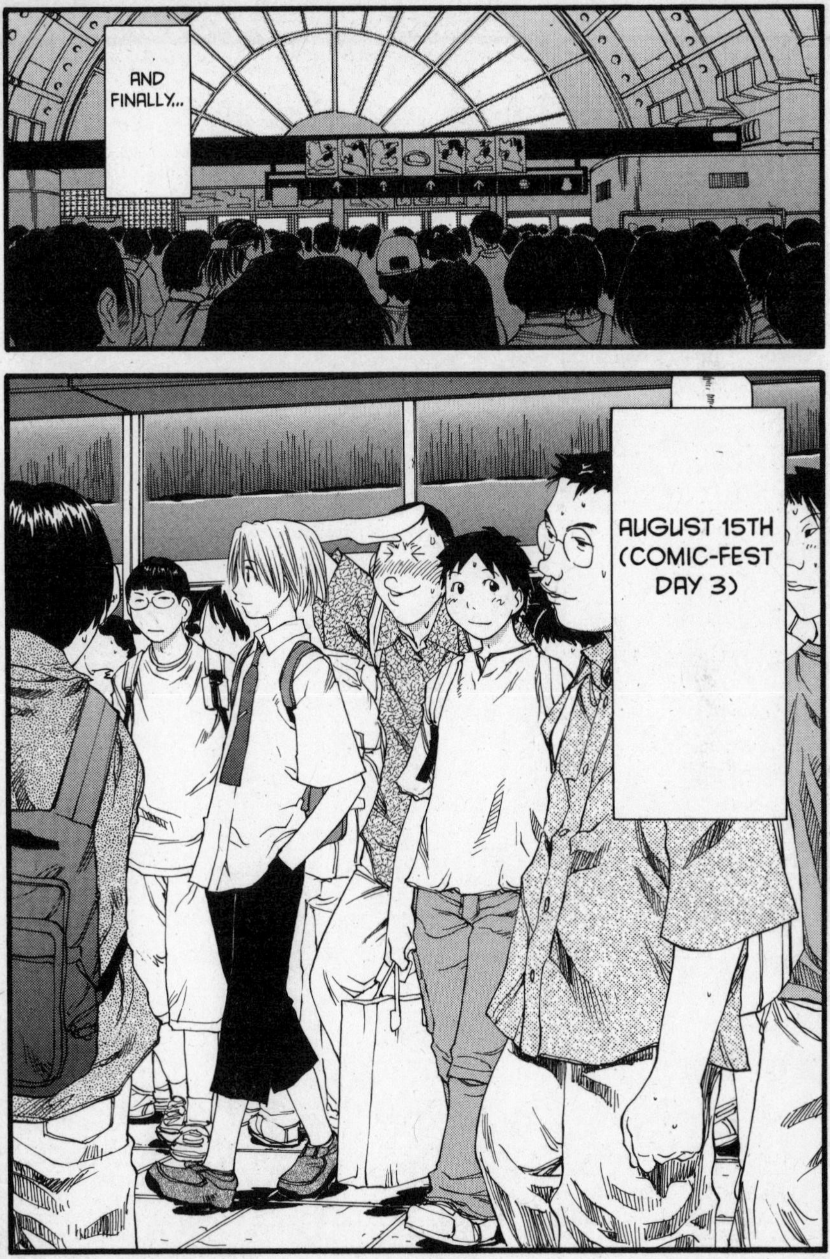
AND FINALLY...
AUGUST 15TH (COMIC-FEST DAY 3)

END OF CHAPTER 28

THE RETURN OF MY FAVORITE SCENES FROM KUJI-UN - PART 4

BY KODAMA

I'VE GATHERED UP A FEW OF THE SCENES WHERE YAMADA GETS ATTACKED (BY KAMISHAKUJII, OF COURSE). [LAUGHS] IT WAS SO COOL TO HEAR YAMADA'S VOICE IN THE ANIME. THE FIRST TIME I HEARD IT, I WAS LIKE, "HUH?" BUT NOW I HEAR THAT VOICE IN MY HEAD EVERY TIME I READ THE MANGA. I ESPECIALLY LOVE TO HEAR HER VOICE WHEN SHE'S GETTING HER BUTT KICKED. [LAUGHS] I HEAR THAT WHEN OONITA-SAN WAS IN THE RECORDING BOOTH, SHE SAID SOMETHING LIKE, "I BET YAMADA'S THE TYPE OF GIRL WHO FEELS NO PAIN." AND THAT'S EXACTLY HOW OONITA-SAN PLAYED THE CHARACTER. THANKS TO HER STRONG CHOICE, EVEN THE MOST PAINFUL SCENES ARE REALLY FUN TO WATCH. I WENT AHEAD AND WROTE OUT HER DIALOGUE BELOW THE SCENES I CHOSE, BUT YOU REALLY HAVE TO HEAR IT TO FULLY APPRECIATE IT. IT'LL DEFINITELY BRING A SMILE TO YOUR FACE.

...UNFORTUNATELY, THE ANIME DIDN'T REALLY EXPLORE YAMADA'S LOVE OF "YAOI." WELL, I GUESS IT IS A DIFFICULT SUBJECT TO DEAL WITH. [LAUGHS] BUT THE RADIO SHOW REALLY GETS INTO IT...ALMOST TO THE POINT WHERE IT'S TOO MUCH. THE CHIHIRO VS MUGI OTOKO EPISODE, AND THE TOKINO VS RENKO EPISODE ARE SAID TO BE THE GREATEST EXAMPLES OF RADIO DRAMA EVER MADE (?). IN THE EPISODE WHERE KAMISHAKUJII GETS LOST IN THE COMIC-FEST CONVENTION HALL, SHE COMES ACROSS YAMADA WORKING WITH ONE OF THE MORE FAMOUS CIRCLES. HER PEN NAME WAS KAORUKO KAKYOUIN—IT'S KIND OF SAD THAT SHE USED PART OF HER REAL NAME. SHE PROBABLY WON'T EVER REVEAL HER FULL NAME. [K]

EPISODE 1 "AN UNBALANCED ENCOUNTER"

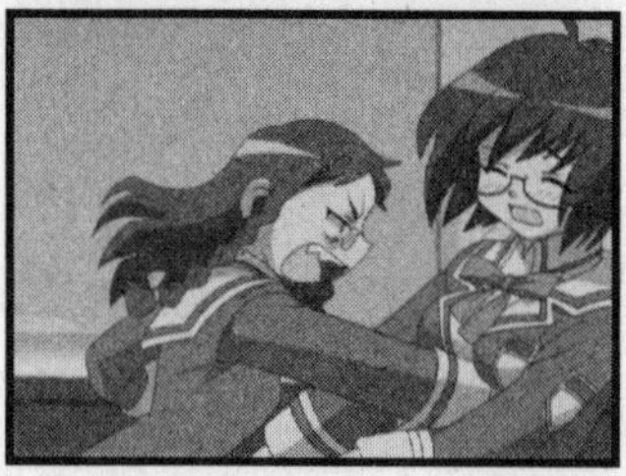

▲ "AAHHH!"

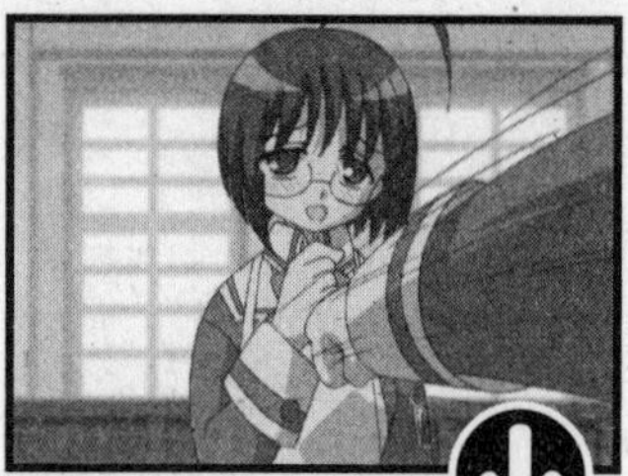

▲ KAMISHAKUJII'S DEADLY FISTS

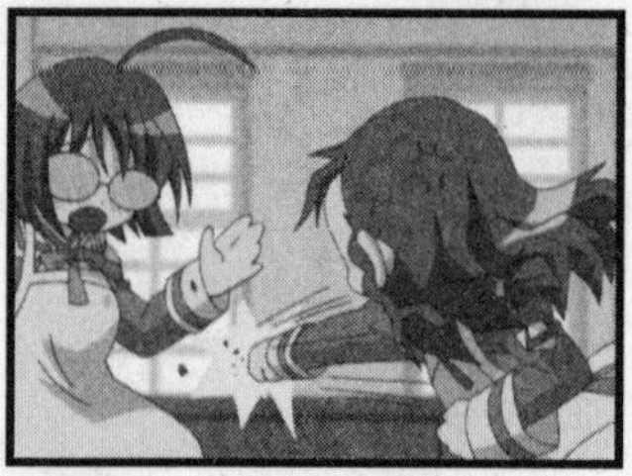

▲ "WAHH! "

EPISODE 25 "KUJIBIKI FOREVER"

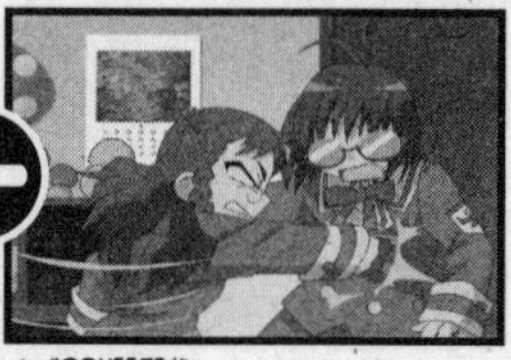

▲ "SQUEEZE!"

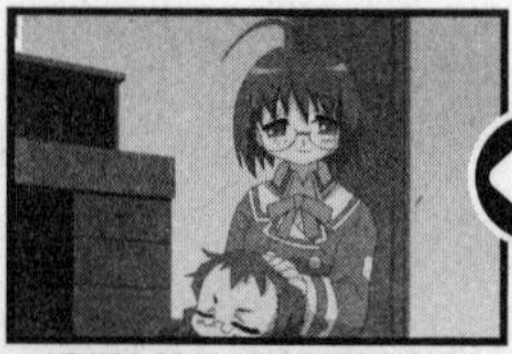

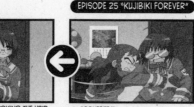

▲ YAMADA GENTLY STROKING THE HAIR OF THE UNCONSCIOUS RENKO...HOW SWEET. EVEN AFTER ALL THAT ABUSE. [LAUGHS] WHAT A TURN-ON.

I JUST LOVE SEEING YAMADA GET ATTACKED. [LAUGHS] THAT SHY VOICE OF HERS...SHE'S GOT THAT GIRLISH LITTLE FACE, BUT HER BODY IS ABSOLUTELY DYNAMITE. OF COURSE HER BOOBS CAN'T HOLD A CANDLE TO THE PRESIDENT'S, BUT WHEN IT COMES TO CURVES AND PROPORTIONS, THERE'S NO BEATING YAMADA. SHE'S GOT THE BODY OF A MODEL. SUPER SEXY... ALMOST TO THE POINT WHERE IT PISSES ME OFF. [LAUGHS] I GUESS THAT'S WHY I LIKE TO SEE HER GETTING BEAT UP. [PIT VIPER]

THE TREE OF KNOWLEDGE

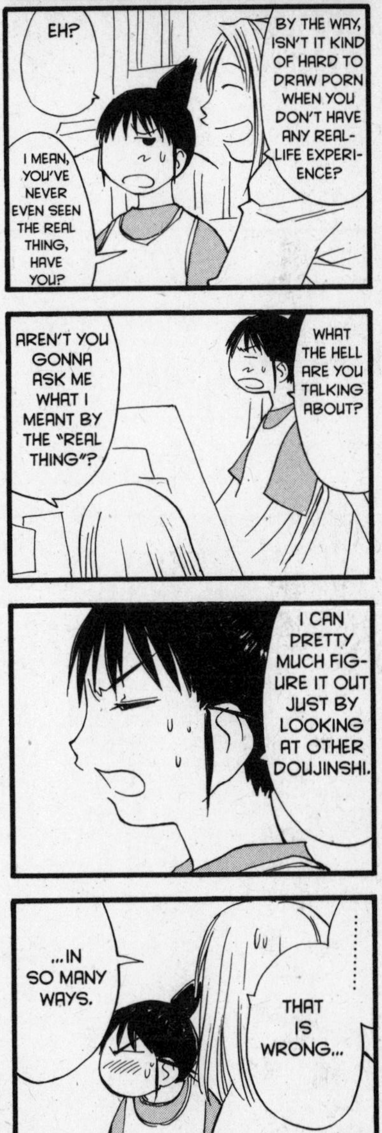
BY THE WAY, ISN'T IT KIND OF HARD TO DRAW PORN WHEN YOU DON'T HAVE ANY REAL-LIFE EXPERIENCE?
EH?
I MEAN, YOU'VE NEVER EVEN SEEN THE REAL THING, HAVE YOU?
WHAT THE HELL ARE YOU TALKING ABOUT?
AREN'T YOU GONNA ASK ME WHAT I MEANT BY THE "REAL THING"?
I CAN PRETTY MUCH FIGURE IT OUT JUST BY LOOKING AT OTHER DOUJINSHI.
......
THAT IS WRONG...
...IN SO MANY WAYS.

IN HIS OWN WAY...

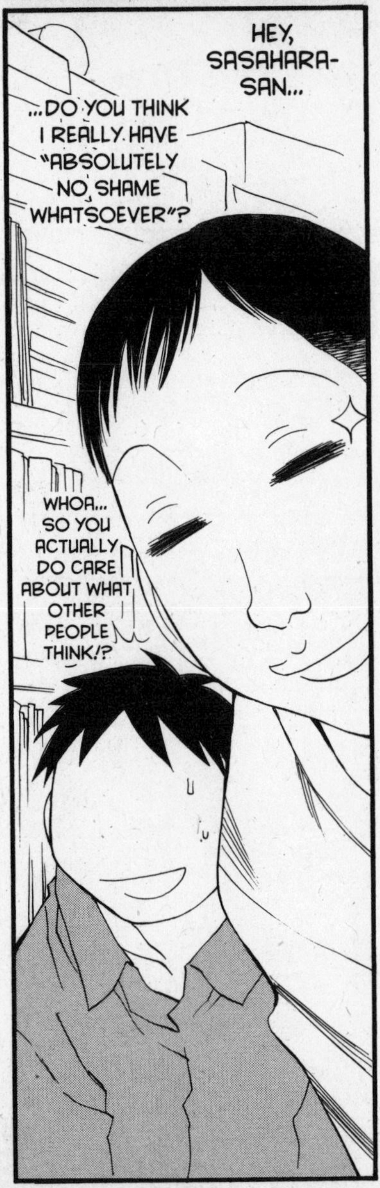
HEY, SASAHARA-SAN...
...DO YOU THINK I REALLY HAVE "ABSOLUTELY NO SHAME WHATSOEVER"?
WHOA... SO YOU ACTUALLY DO CARE ABOUT WHAT OTHER PEOPLE THINK!?

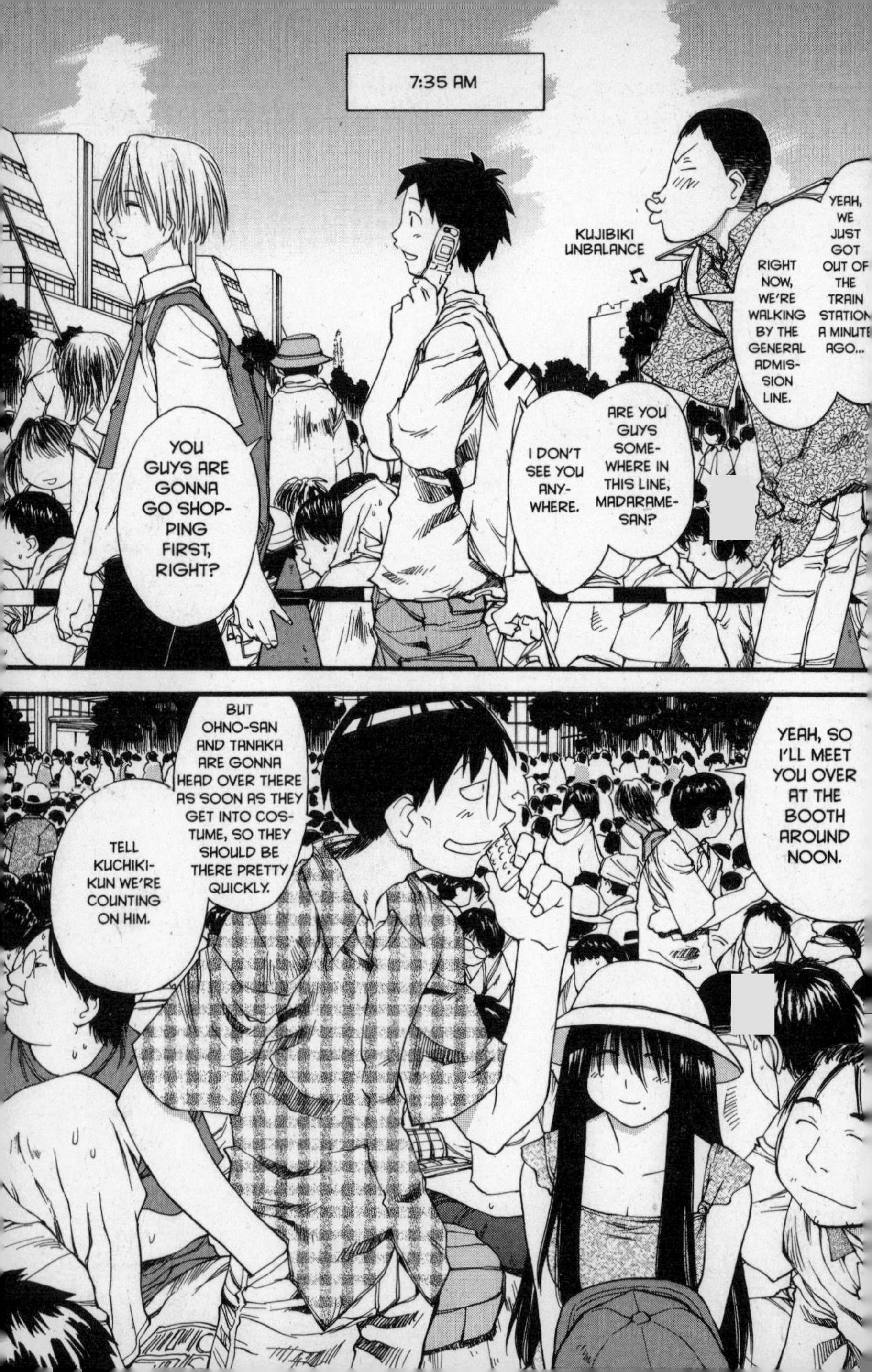
7:35 AM
YEAH, WE JUST GOT OUT OF THE TRAIN STATION A MINUTE AGO...
RIGHT NOW, WE'RE WALKING BY THE GENERAL ADMISSION LINE.
KUJIBIKI UNBALANCE ♪
ARE YOU GUYS SOMEWHERE IN THIS LINE, MADARAME-SAN?
I DON'T SEE YOU ANYWHERE.
YOU GUYS ARE GONNA GO SHOPPING FIRST, RIGHT?
YEAH, SO I'LL MEET YOU OVER AT THE BOOTH AROUND NOON.
BUT OHNO-SAN AND TANAKA ARE GONNA HEAD OVER THERE AS SOON AS THEY GET INTO COSTUME, SO THEY SHOULD BE THERE PRETTY QUICKLY.
TELL KUCHIKI-KUN WE'RE COUNTING ON HIM.

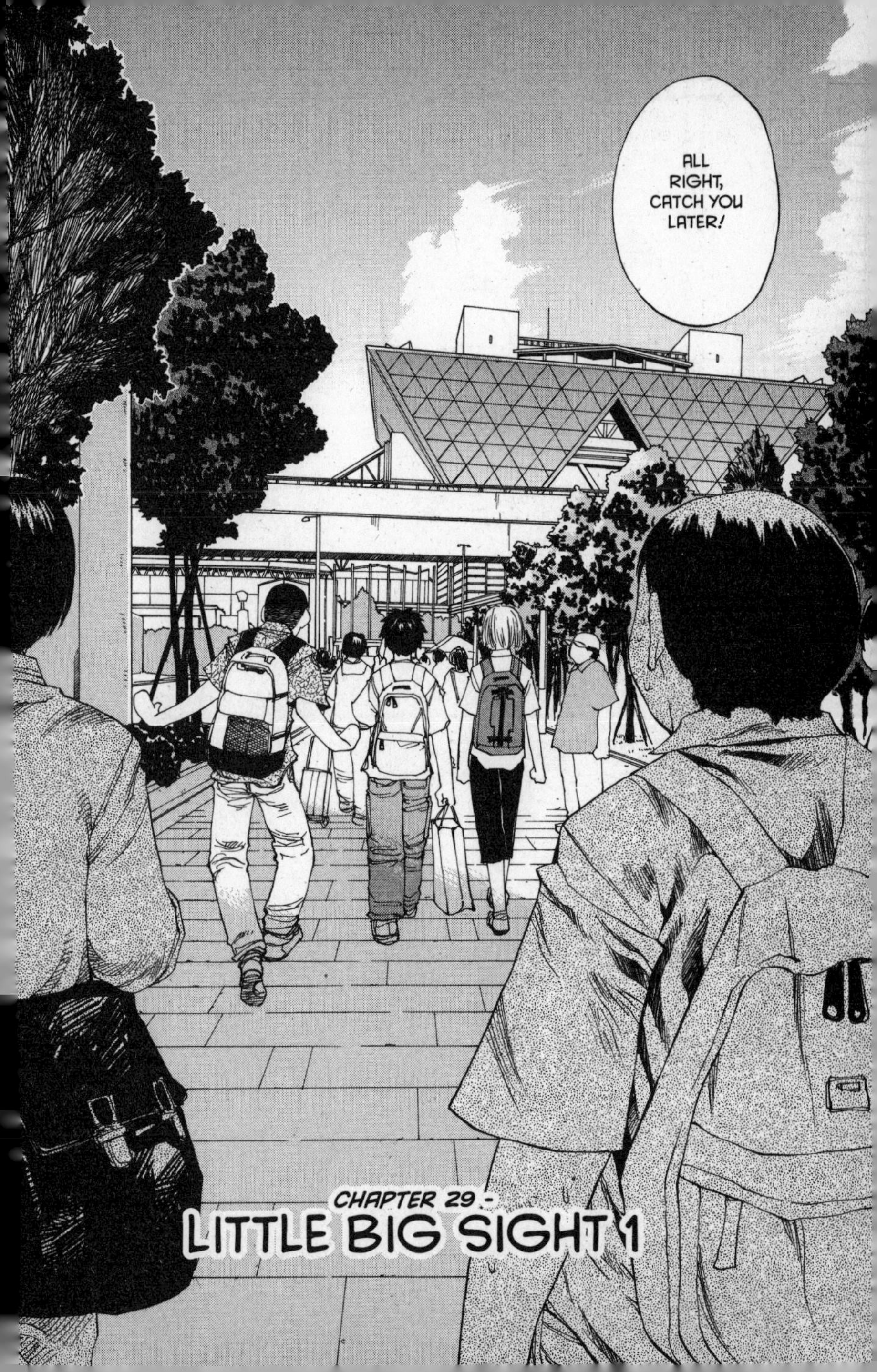
ALL RIGHT, CATCH YOU LATER!
CHAPTER 29 -
LITTLE BIG SIGHT 1

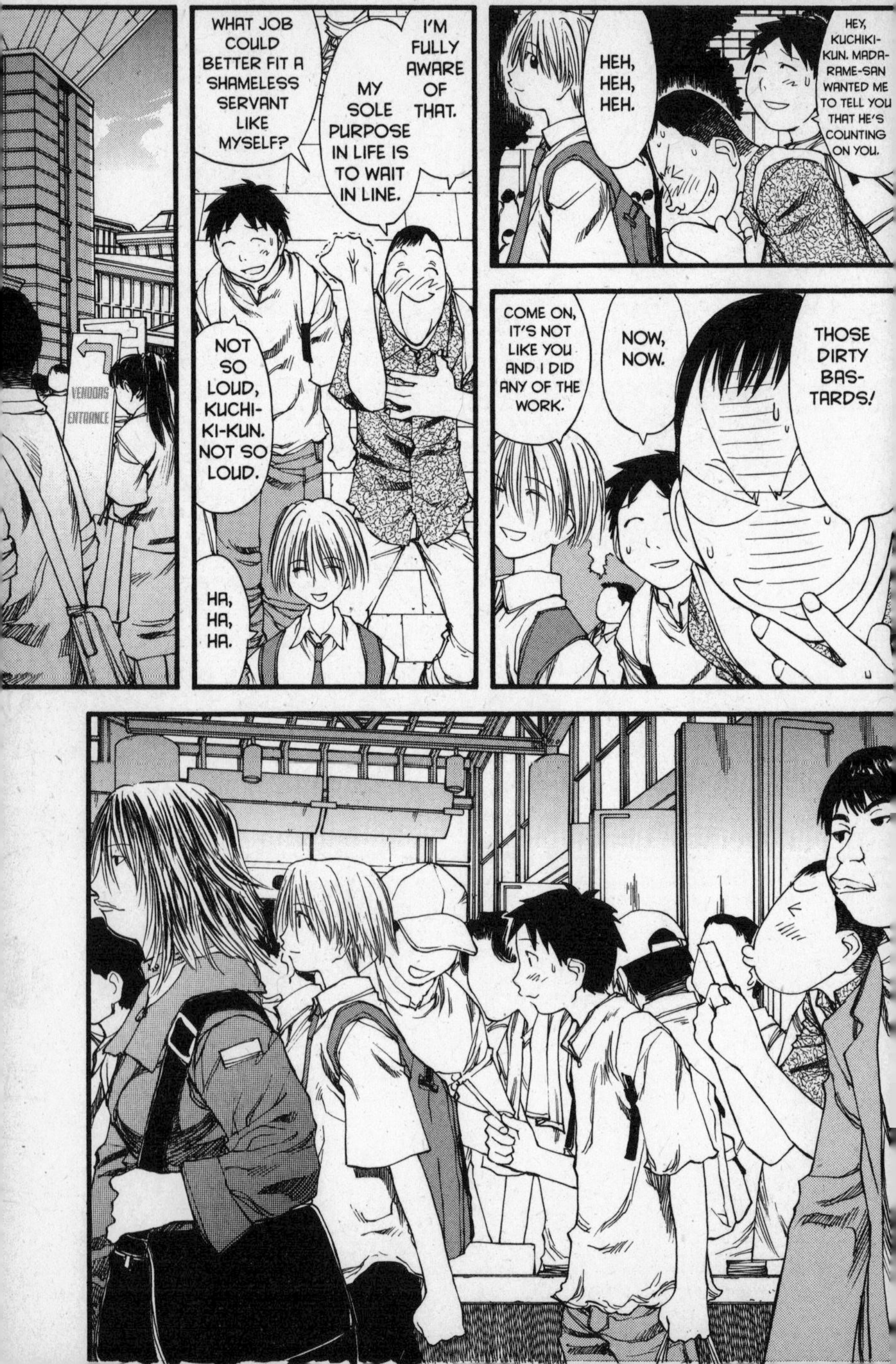
HEY, KUCHIKI-KUN. MADARAME-SAN WANTED ME TO TELL YOU THAT HE'S COUNTING ON YOU.
HEH, HEH, HEH.
THOSE DIRTY BASTARDS!
NOW, NOW.
COME ON, IT'S NOT LIKE YOU AND I DID ANY OF THE WORK.
I'M FULLY AWARE OF THAT.
MY SOLE PURPOSE IN LIFE IS TO WAIT IN LINE.
WHAT JOB COULD BETTER FIT A SHAMELESS SERVANT LIKE MYSELF?
NOT SO LOUD, KUCHIKI-KUN. NOT SO LOUD.
HA, HA, HA.
VENDORS ENTRANCE

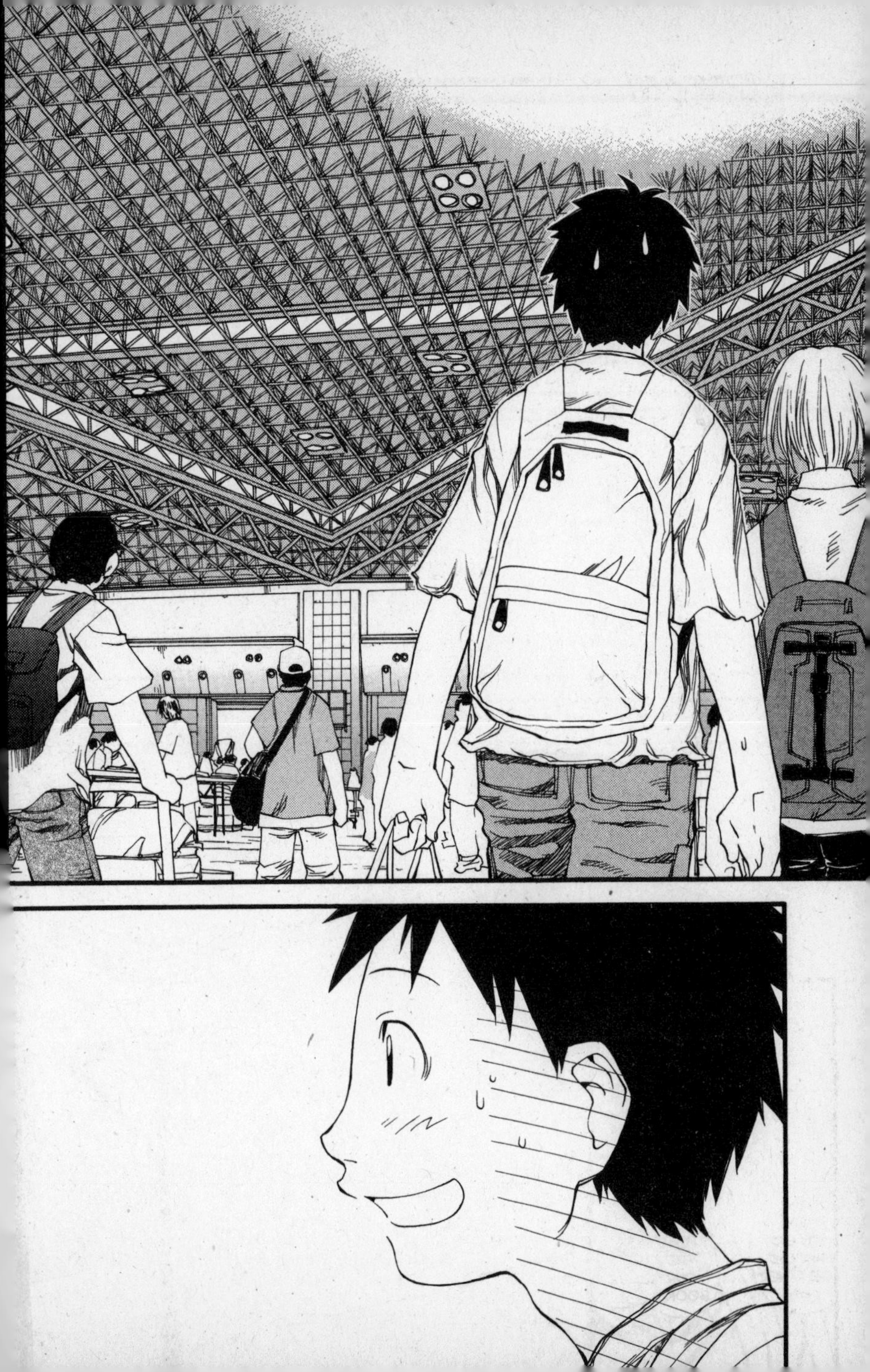

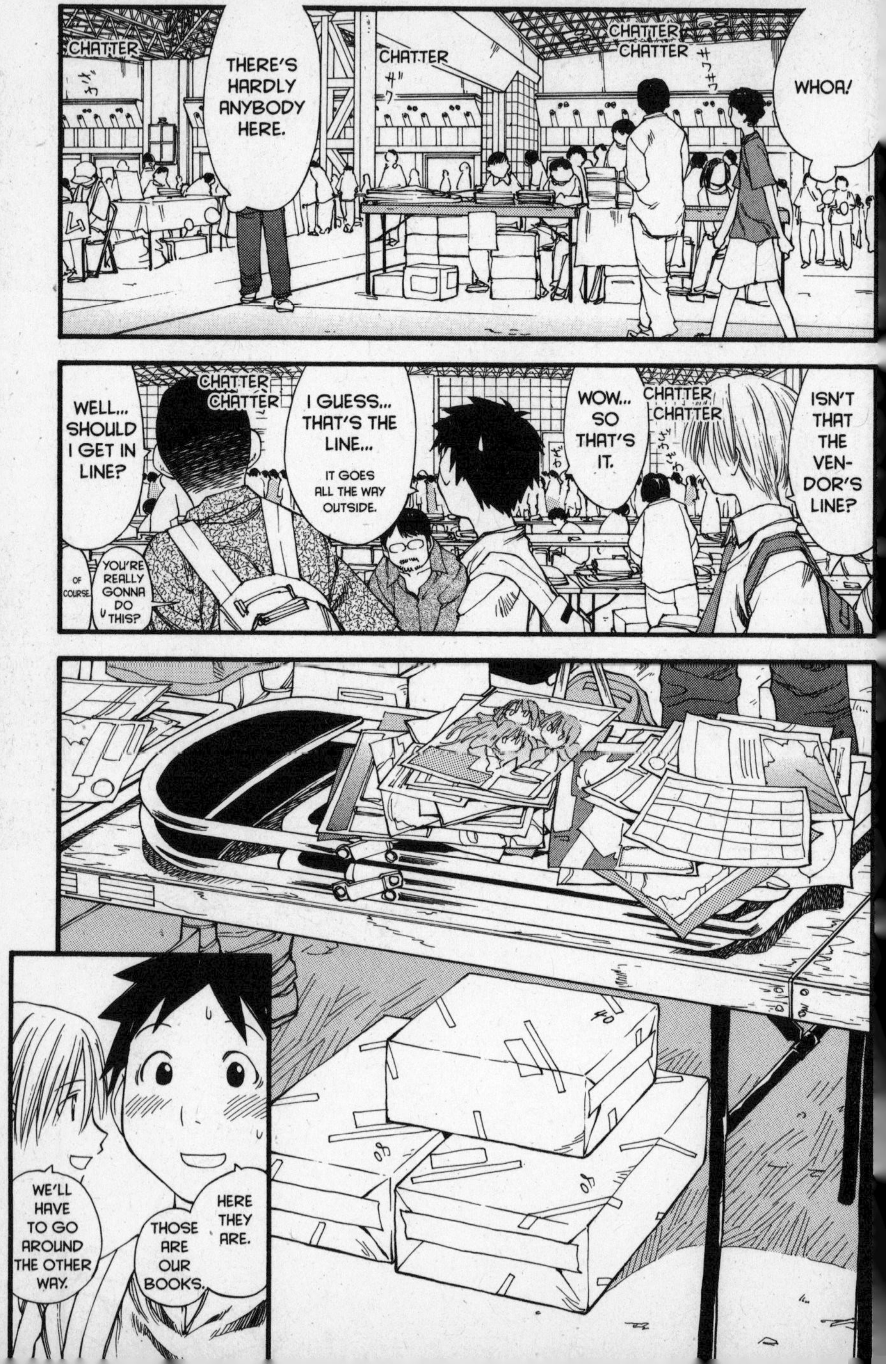
WHOA!
CHATTER CHATTER
CHATTER
THERE'S HARDLY ANYBODY HERE.
CHATTER
ISN'T THAT THE VEN-DOR'S LINE?
CHATTER CHATTER
WOW... SO THAT'S IT.
I GUESS... THAT'S THE LINE...
IT GOES ALL THE WAY OUTSIDE.
CHATTER CHATTER
WELL... SHOULD I GET IN LINE?
YOU'RE REALLY GONNA DO THIS?
OF COURSE.
HERE THEY ARE.
THOSE ARE OUR BOOKS.
WE'LL HAVE TO GO AROUND THE OTHER WAY.

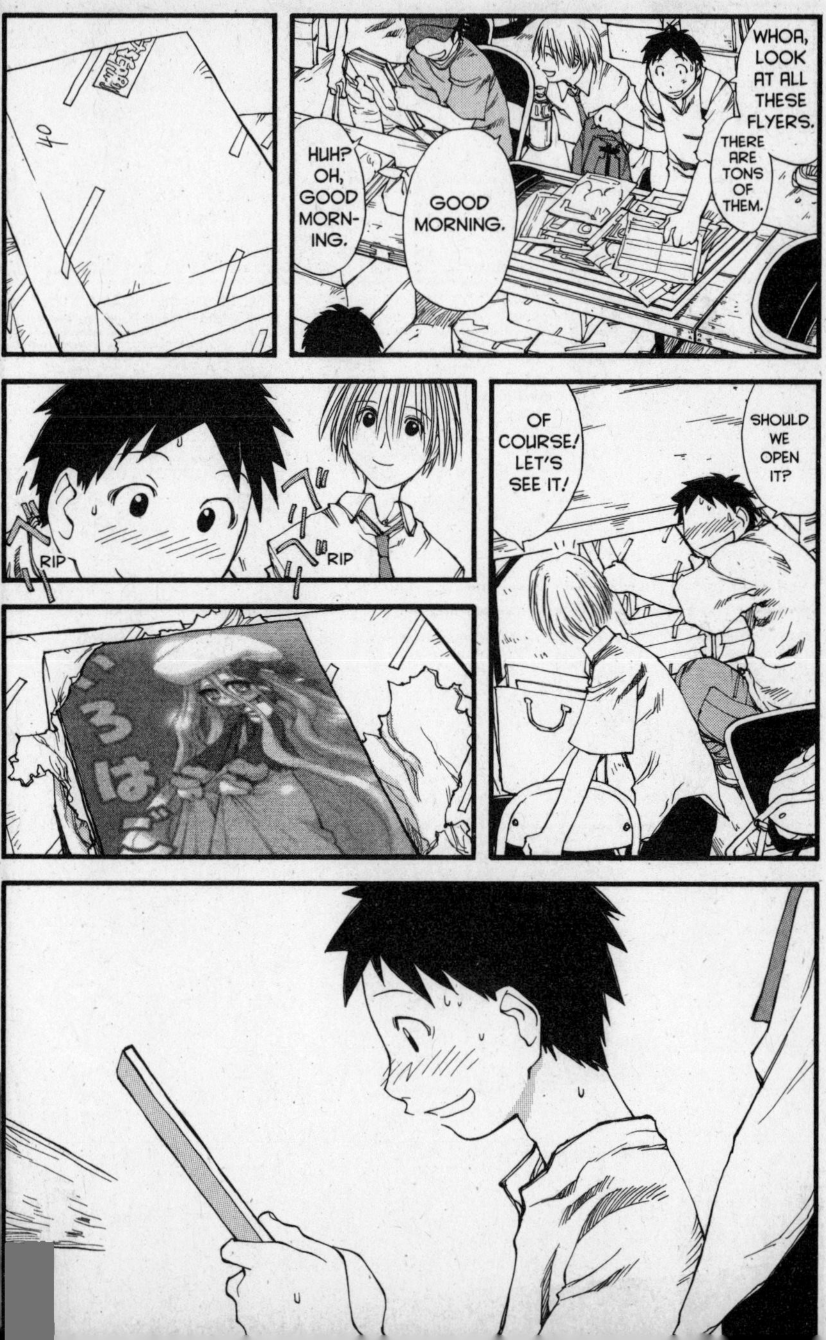
WHOA, LOOK AT ALL THESE FLYERS.
THERE ARE TONS OF THEM.
GOOD MORNING.
HUH? OH, GOOD MORNING.
SHOULD WE OPEN IT?
OF COURSE! LET'S SEE IT!
RIP
RIP

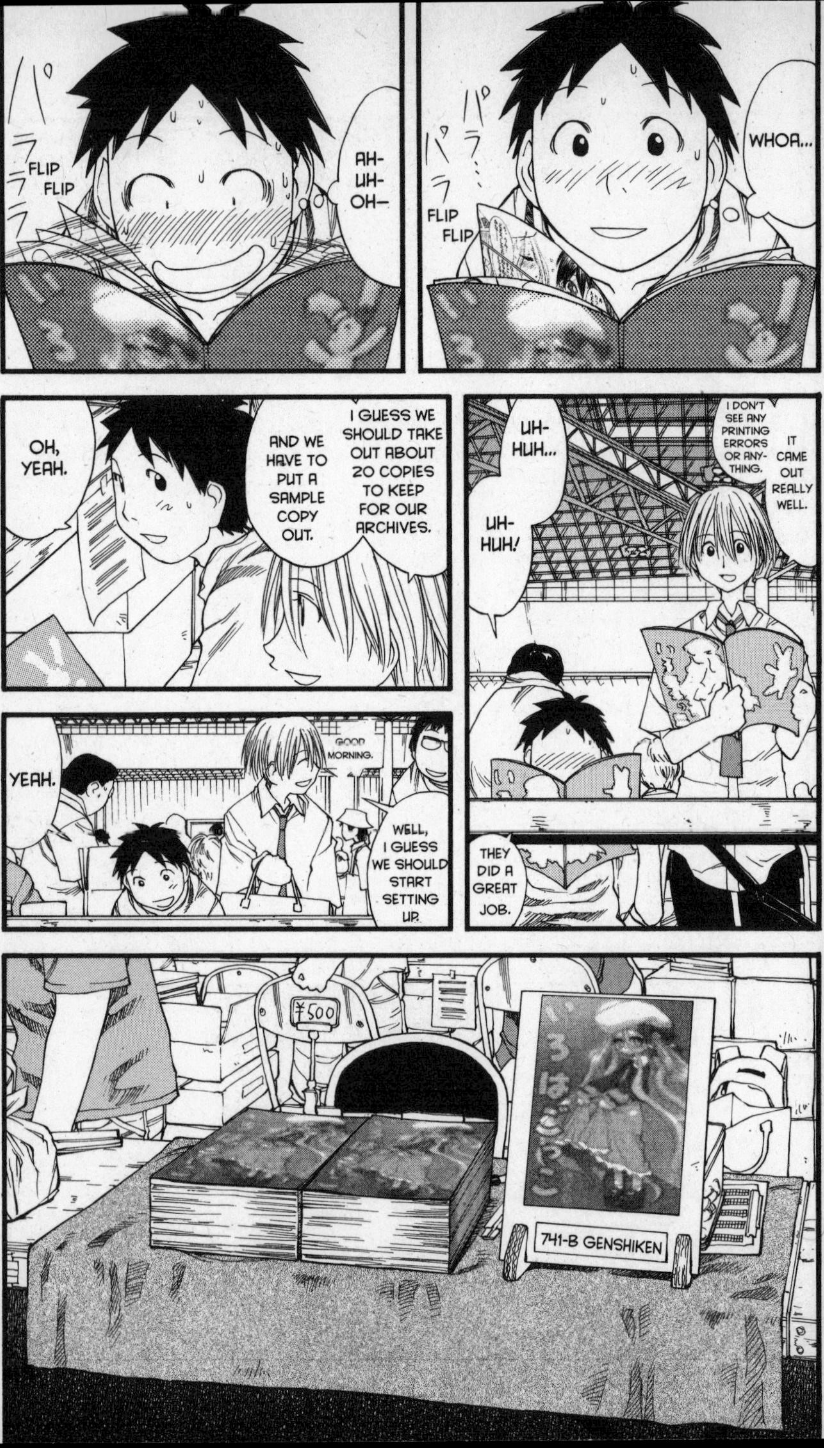
WHOA...
パラ パラ
FLIP FLIP
パラララ
FLIP FLIP
AH- UH- OH—
I DON'T SEE ANY PRINTING ERRORS OR ANY- THING.
IT CAME OUT REALLY WELL.
UH- HUH...
UH- HUH!
I GUESS WE SHOULD TAKE OUT ABOUT 20 COPIES TO KEEP FOR OUR ARCHIVES.
AND WE HAVE TO PUT A SAMPLE COPY OUT.
OH, YEAH.
THEY DID A GREAT JOB.
GOOD MORNING.
WELL, I GUESS WE SHOULD START SETTING UP.
YEAH.
¥500
741-B GENSHIKEN

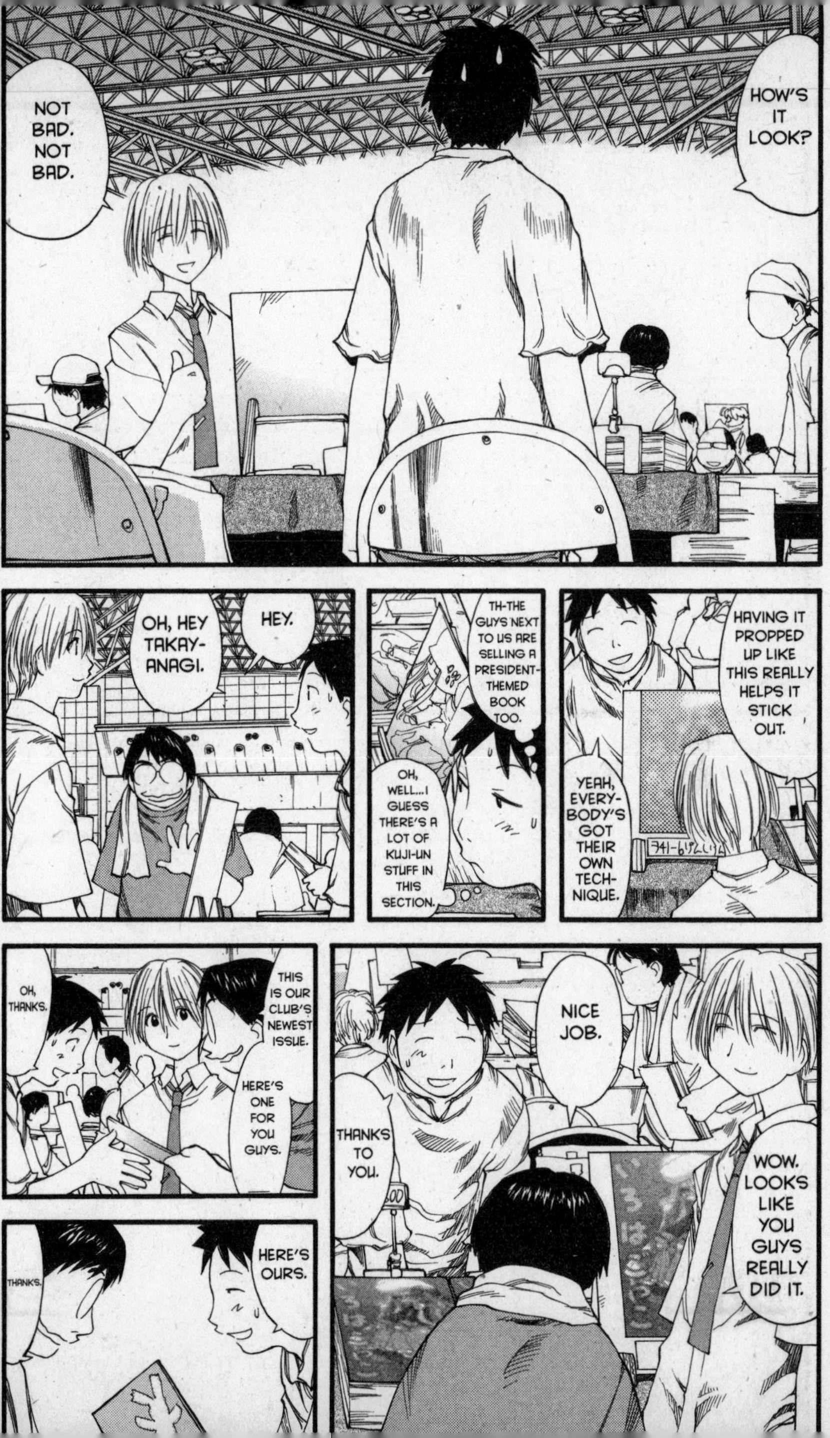
HOW'S IT LOOK?
NOT BAD. NOT BAD.
HAVING IT PROPPED UP LIKE THIS REALLY HELPS IT STICK OUT.
YEAH, EVERYBODY'S GOT THEIR OWN TECHNIQUE.
TH-THE GUYS NEXT TO US ARE SELLING A PRESIDENT-THEMED BOOK TOO.
OH, WELL...I GUESS THERE'S A LOT OF KUJI-UN STUFF IN THIS SECTION.
HEY.
OH, HEY TAKAY-ANAGI.
NICE JOB.
THANKS TO YOU.
WOW. LOOKS LIKE YOU GUYS REALLY DID IT.
THIS IS OUR CLUB'S NEWEST ISSUE.
HERE'S ONE FOR YOU GUYS.
OH, THANKS.
HERE'S OURS.
THANKS.

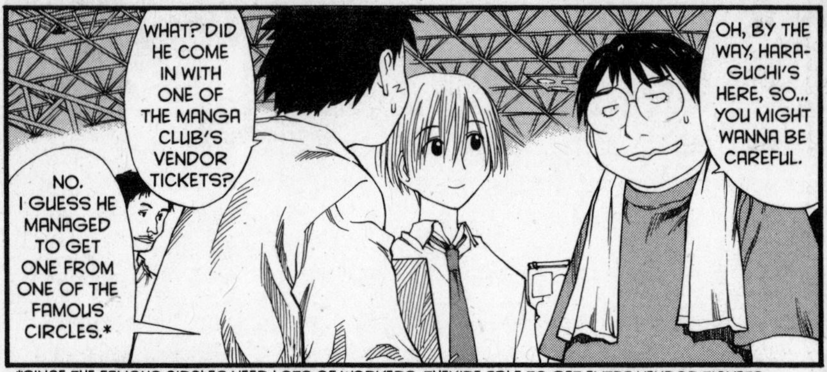
OH, BY THE WAY, HARA-GUCHI'S HERE, SO... YOU MIGHT WANNA BE CAREFUL.
WHAT? DID HE COME IN WITH ONE OF THE MANGA CLUB'S VENDOR TICKETS?
NO. I GUESS HE MANAGED TO GET ONE FROM ONE OF THE FAMOUS CIRCLES.*

*SINCE THE FAMOUS CIRCLES NEED LOTS OF WORKERS, THEY'RE ABLE TO GET EXTRA VENDOR TICKETS.

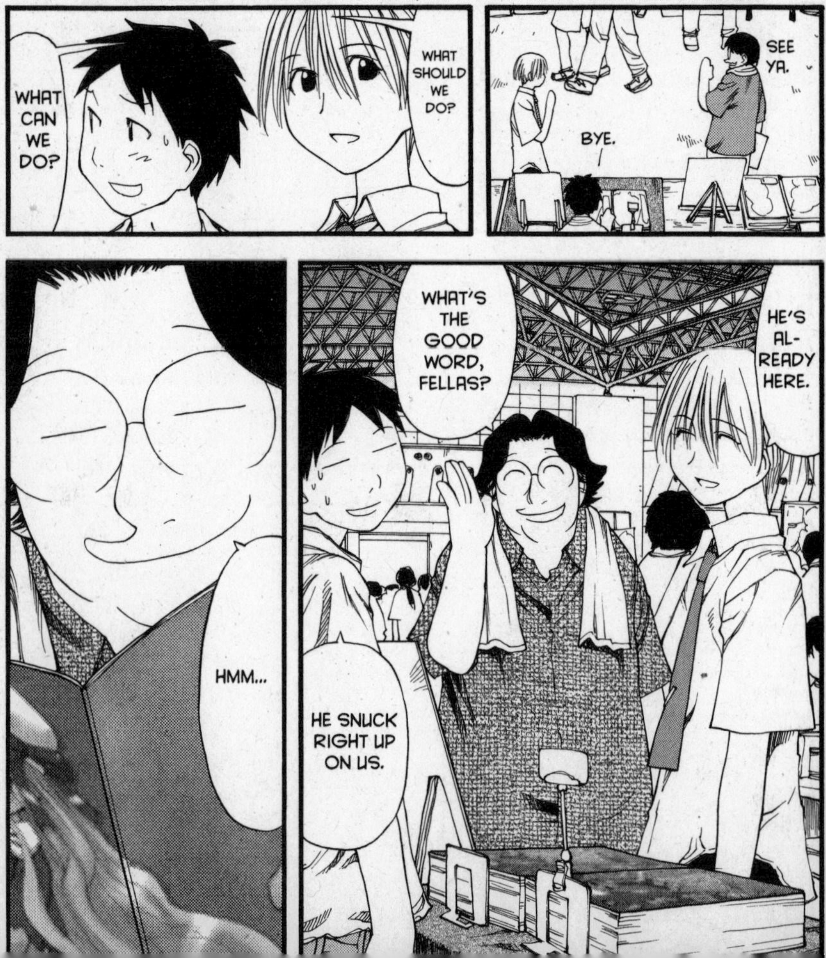
SEE YA.
BYE.
WHAT SHOULD WE DO?
WHAT CAN WE DO?
HE'S AL-READY HERE.
WHAT'S THE GOOD WORD, FELLAS?
HE SNUCK RIGHT UP ON US.
HMM...

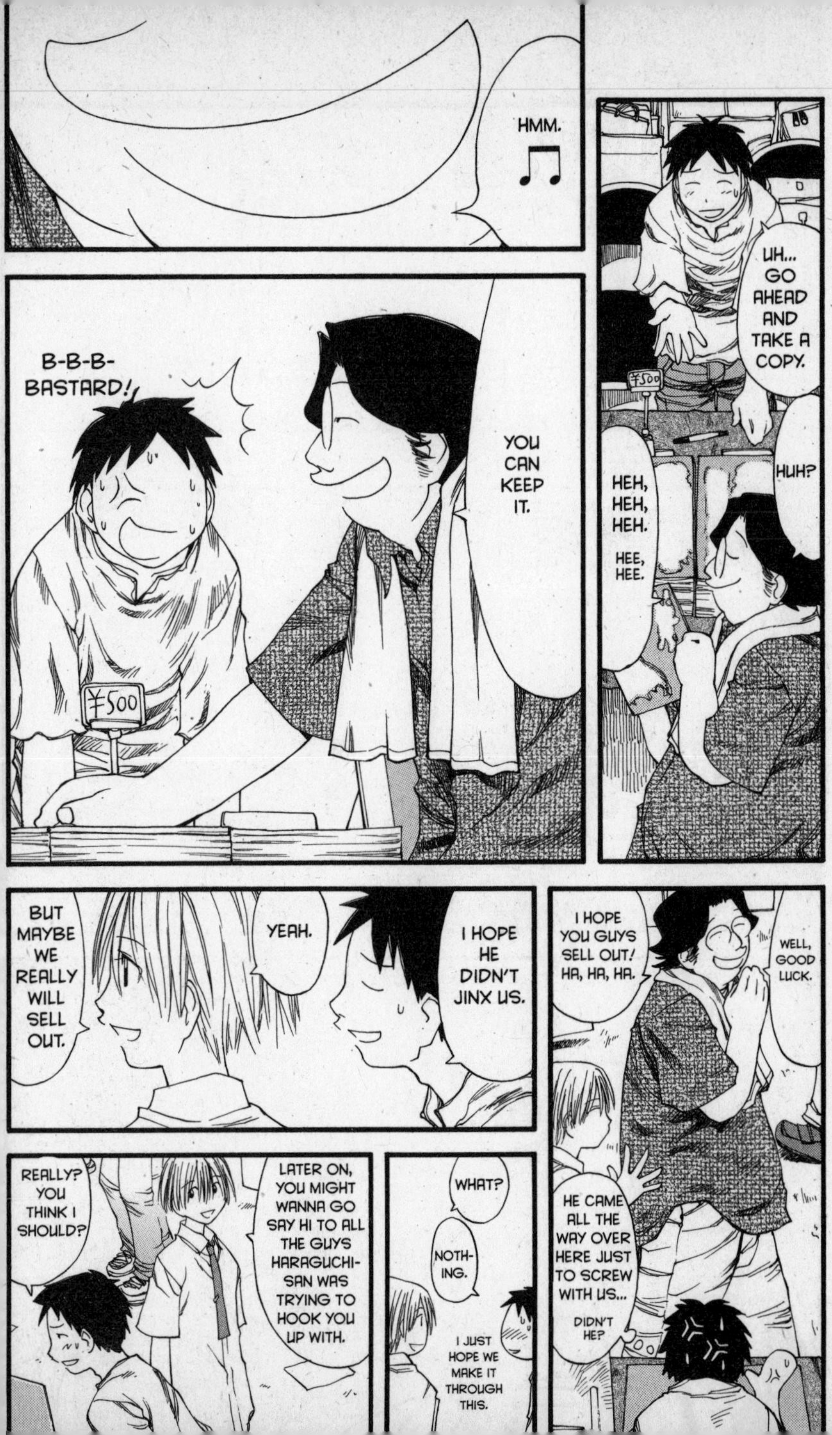
HMM.
♫
UH... GO AHEAD AND TAKE A COPY.
HUH?
HEH, HEH, HEH.
HEE, HEE.
YOU CAN KEEP IT.
B-B-B-BASTARD!
WELL, GOOD LUCK.
I HOPE YOU GUYS SELL OUT! HA, HA, HA.
HE CAME ALL THE WAY OVER HERE JUST TO SCREW WITH US...
DIDN'T HE?
I HOPE HE DIDN'T JINX US.
YEAH.
BUT MAYBE WE REALLY WILL SELL OUT.
WHAT?
NOTH-ING.
I JUST HOPE WE MAKE IT THROUGH THIS.
LATER ON, YOU MIGHT WANNA GO SAY HI TO ALL THE GUYS HARAGUCHI-SAN WAS TRYING TO HOOK YOU UP WITH.
REALLY? YOU THINK I SHOULD?

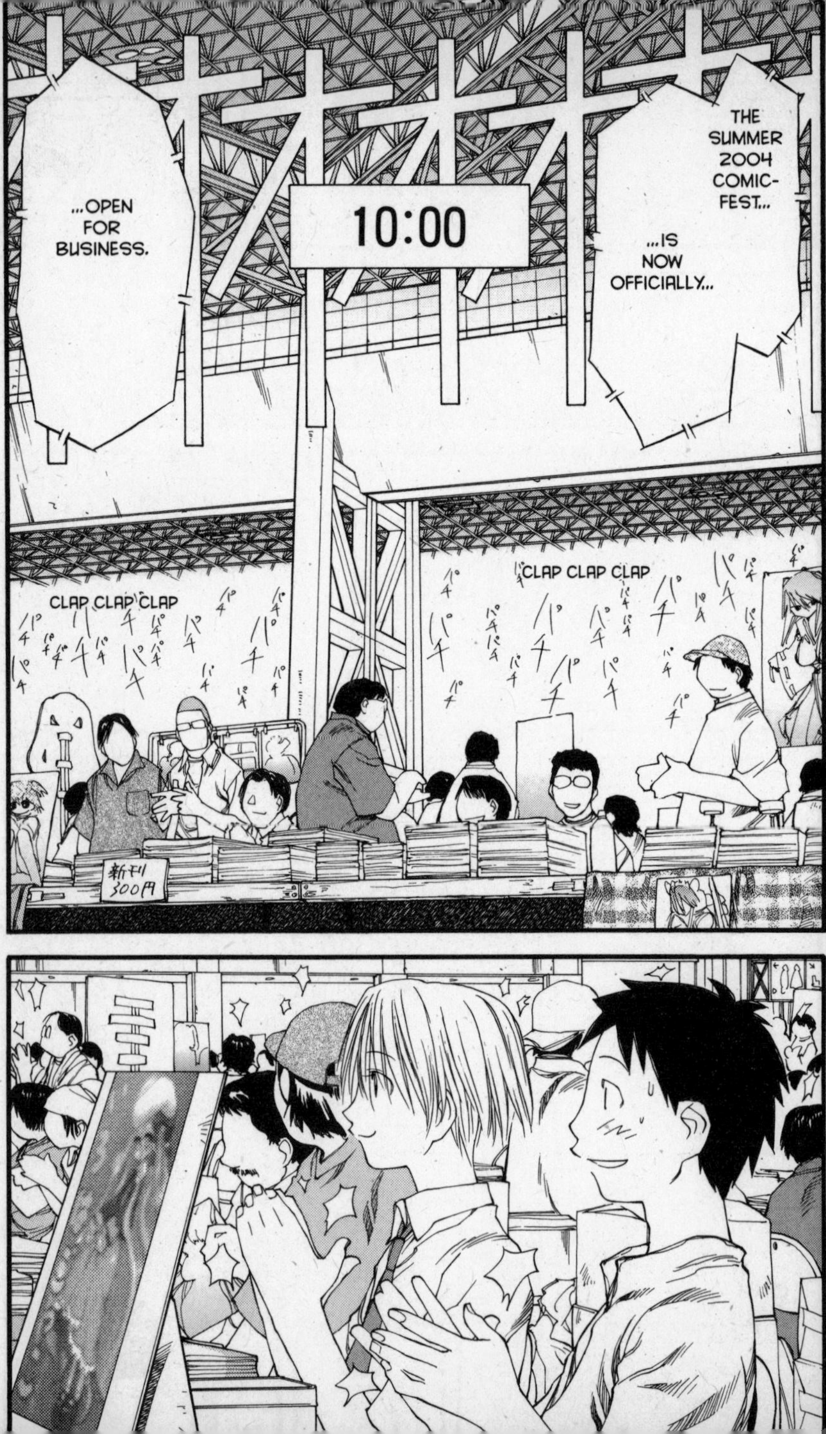
10:00
THE SUMMER 2004 COMIC-FEST...
...IS NOW OFFICIALLY...
...OPEN FOR BUSINESS.
CLAP CLAP CLAP
CLAP CLAP CLAP

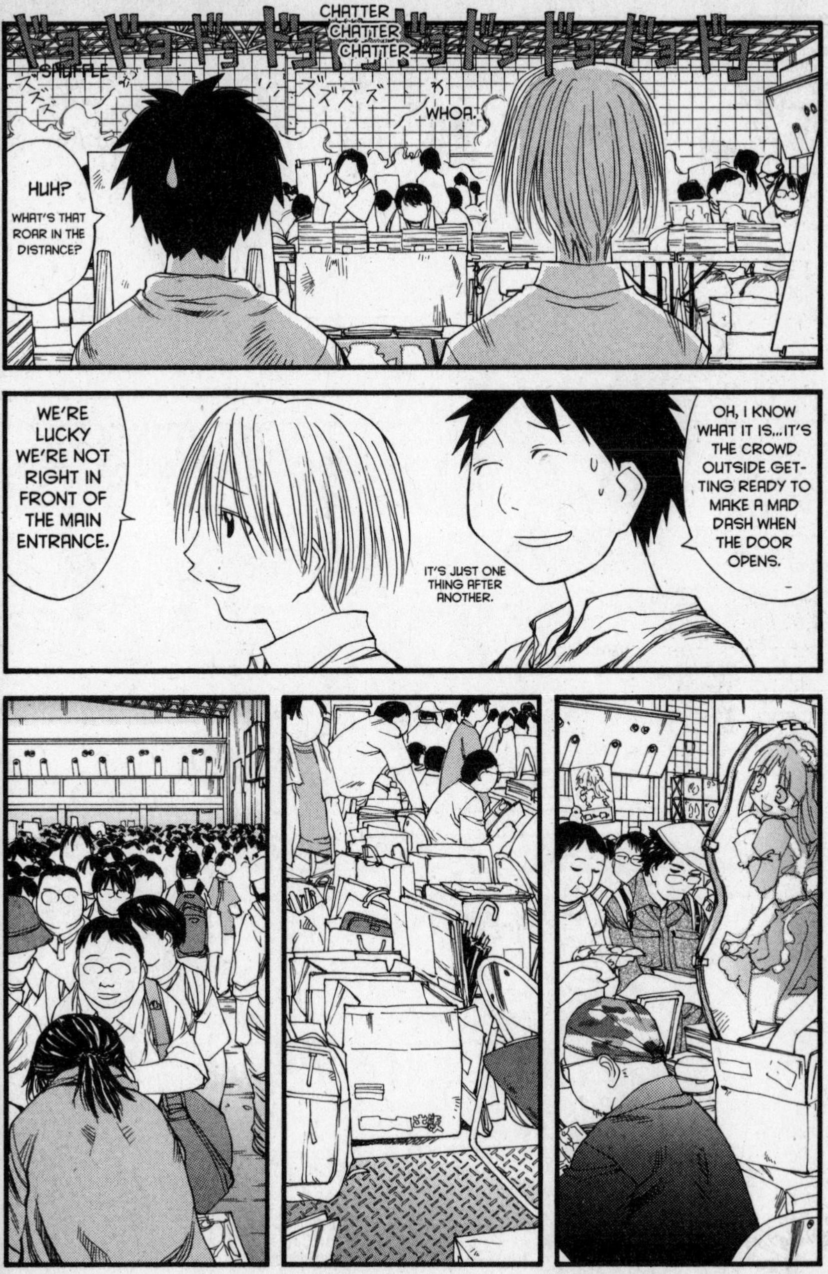
CHATTER CHATTER CHATTER
WHOA.
SHUFFLE
HUH?
WHAT'S THAT ROAR IN THE DISTANCE?
OH, I KNOW WHAT IT IS...IT'S THE CROWD OUTSIDE GETTING READY TO MAKE A MAD DASH WHEN THE DOOR OPENS.
IT'S JUST ONE THING AFTER ANOTHER.
WE'RE LUCKY WE'RE NOT RIGHT IN FRONT OF THE MAIN ENTRANCE.

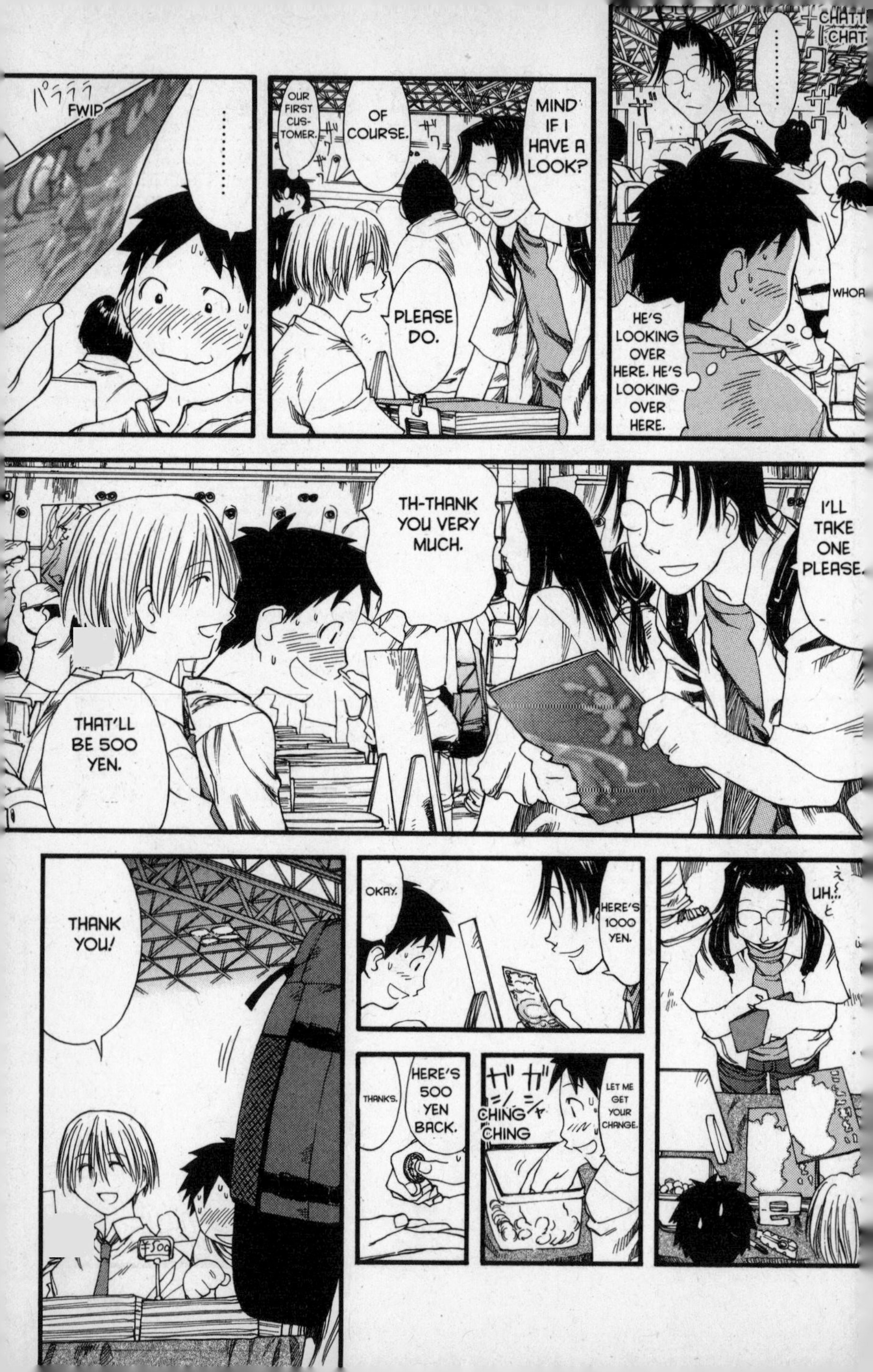

......
CHATT CHAT
HE'S LOOKING OVER HERE. HE'S LOOKING OVER HERE.
WHOA
MIND IF I HAVE A LOOK?
OF COURSE.
OUR FIRST CUS-TOMER.
PLEASE DO.
パラララ
FWIP
......
I'LL TAKE ONE PLEASE.
TH-THANK YOU VERY MUCH.
THAT'LL BE 500 YEN.
え…と
UH...
HERE'S 1000 YEN.
OKAY.
LET ME GET YOUR CHANGE.
ガガ
CHING CHING
HERE'S 500 YEN BACK.
THANKS.
THANK YOU!

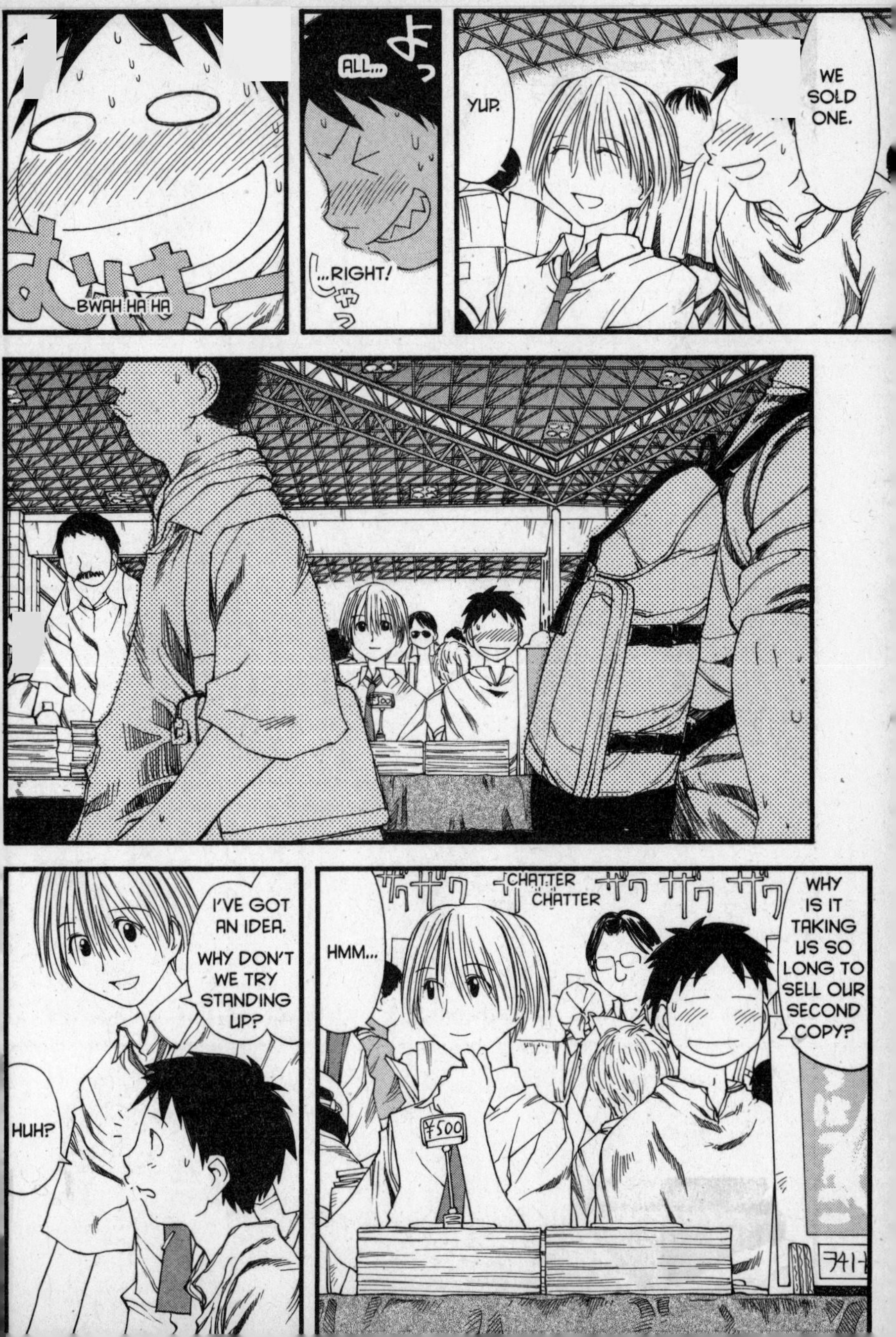
WE SOLD ONE.
YUP.
ALL...
よっ
...RIGHT!
BWAH HA HA
WHY IS IT TAKING US SO LONG TO SELL OUR SECOND COPY?
CHATTER CHATTER
HMM...
¥500
I'VE GOT AN IDEA.
WHY DON'T WE TRY STANDING UP?
HUH?

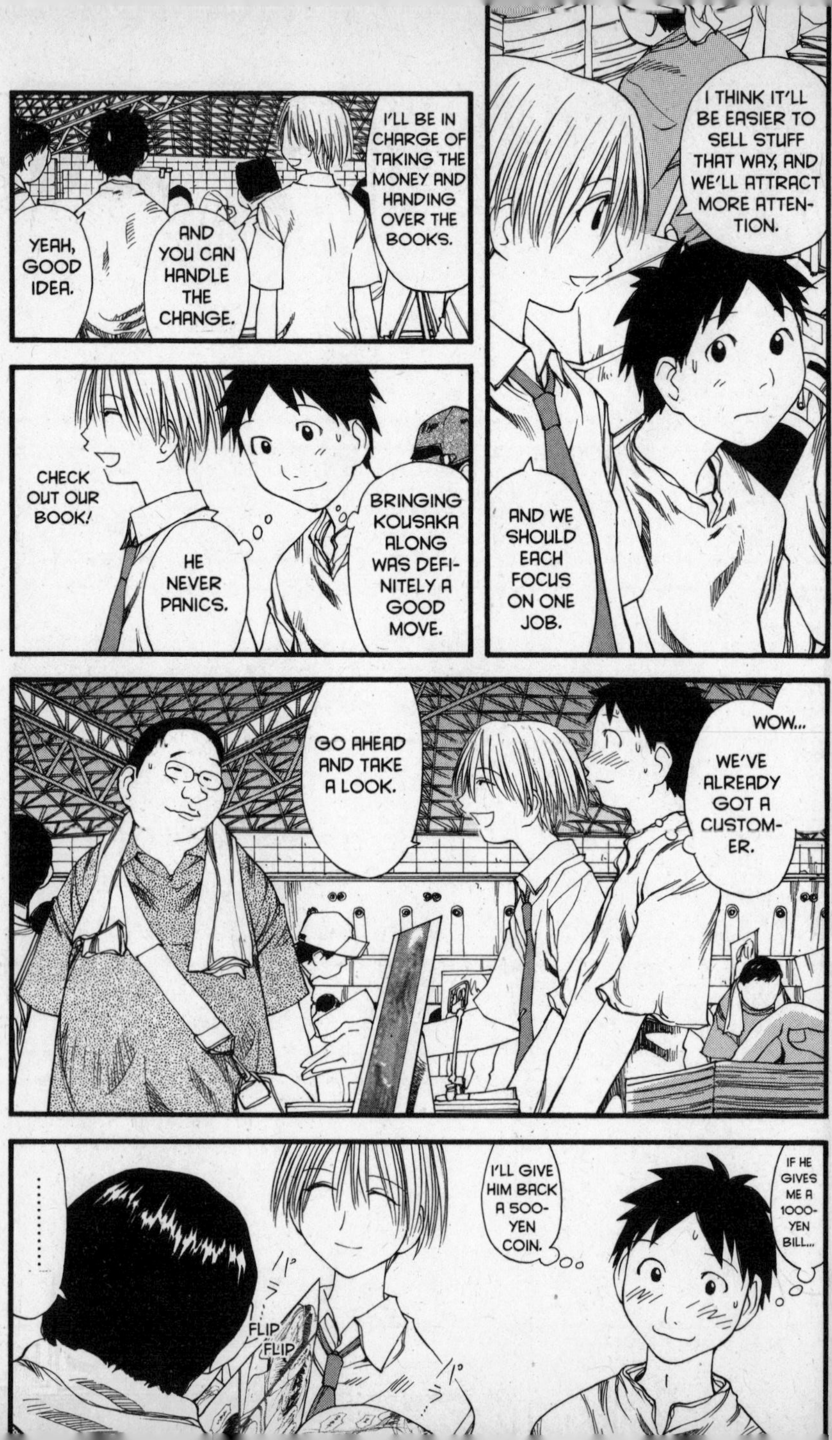
I THINK IT'LL BE EASIER TO SELL STUFF THAT WAY, AND WE'LL ATTRACT MORE ATTEN-TION.
AND WE SHOULD EACH FOCUS ON ONE JOB.
I'LL BE IN CHARGE OF TAKING THE MONEY AND HANDING OVER THE BOOKS.
AND YOU CAN HANDLE THE CHANGE.
YEAH, GOOD IDEA.
BRINGING KOUSAKA ALONG WAS DEFI-NITELY A GOOD MOVE.
HE NEVER PANICS.
CHECK OUT OUR BOOK!
WOW... WE'VE ALREADY GOT A CUSTOM-ER.
GO AHEAD AND TAKE A LOOK.
IF HE GIVES ME A 1000-YEN BILL...
I'LL GIVE HIM BACK A 500-YEN COIN.
FLIP FLIP
....

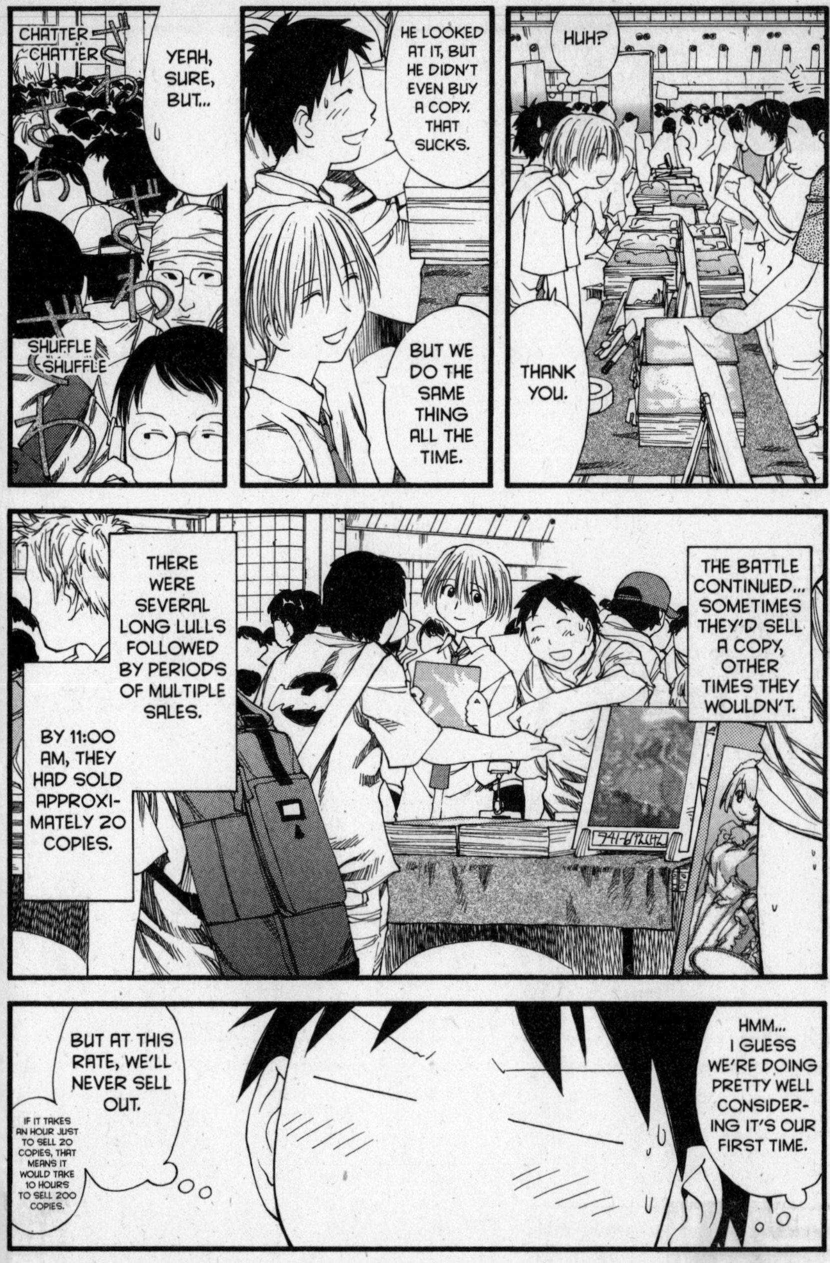
HUH?
THANK YOU.
HE LOOKED AT IT, BUT HE DIDN'T EVEN BUY A COPY. THAT SUCKS.
BUT WE DO THE SAME THING ALL THE TIME.
YEAH, SURE, BUT...
CHATTER CHATTER
SHUFFLE SHUFFLE
THE BATTLE CONTINUED... SOMETIMES THEY'D SELL A COPY, OTHER TIMES THEY WOULDN'T.
THERE WERE SEVERAL LONG LULLS FOLLOWED BY PERIODS OF MULTIPLE SALES.
BY 11:00 AM, THEY HAD SOLD APPROXIMATELY 20 COPIES.
HMM... I GUESS WE'RE DOING PRETTY WELL CONSIDERING IT'S OUR FIRST TIME.
BUT AT THIS RATE, WE'LL NEVER SELL OUT.
IF IT TAKES AN HOUR JUST TO SELL 20 COPIES, THAT MEANS IT WOULD TAKE 10 HOURS TO SELL 200 COPIES.

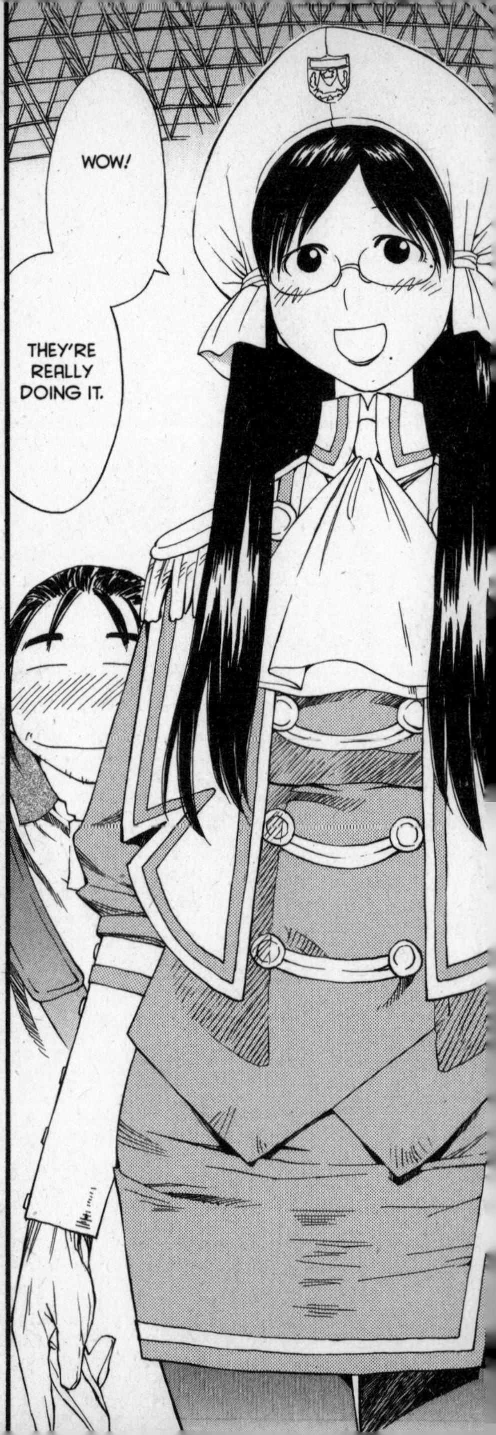
WOW!
THEY'RE REALLY DOING IT.

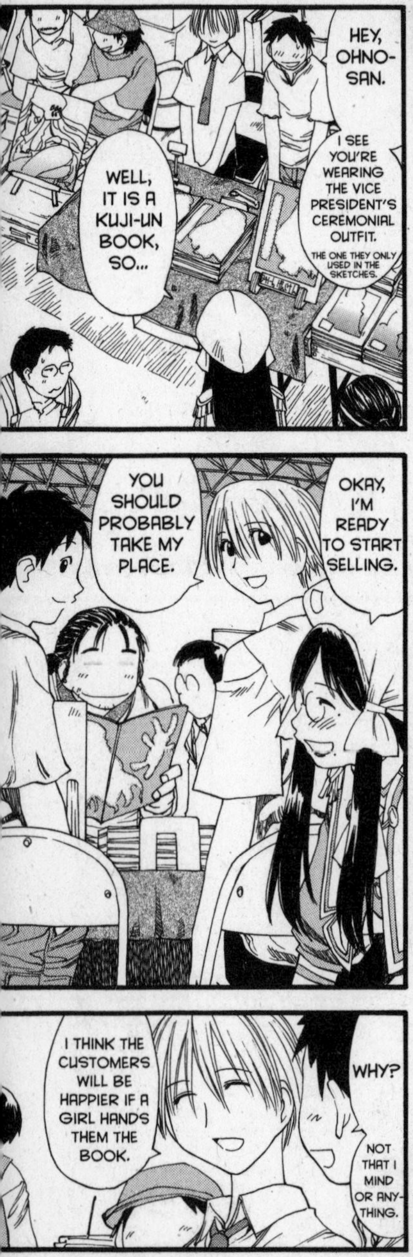
HEY, OHNO-SAN.
I SEE YOU'RE WEARING THE VICE PRESIDENT'S CEREMONIAL OUTFIT.
THE ONE THEY ONLY USED IN THE SKETCHES.
WELL, IT IS A KUJI-UN BOOK, SO...
OKAY, I'M READY TO START SELLING.
YOU SHOULD PROBABLY TAKE MY PLACE.
WHY?
NOT THAT I MIND OR ANY-THING.
I THINK THE CUSTOMERS WILL BE HAPPIER IF A GIRL HANDS THEM THE BOOK.

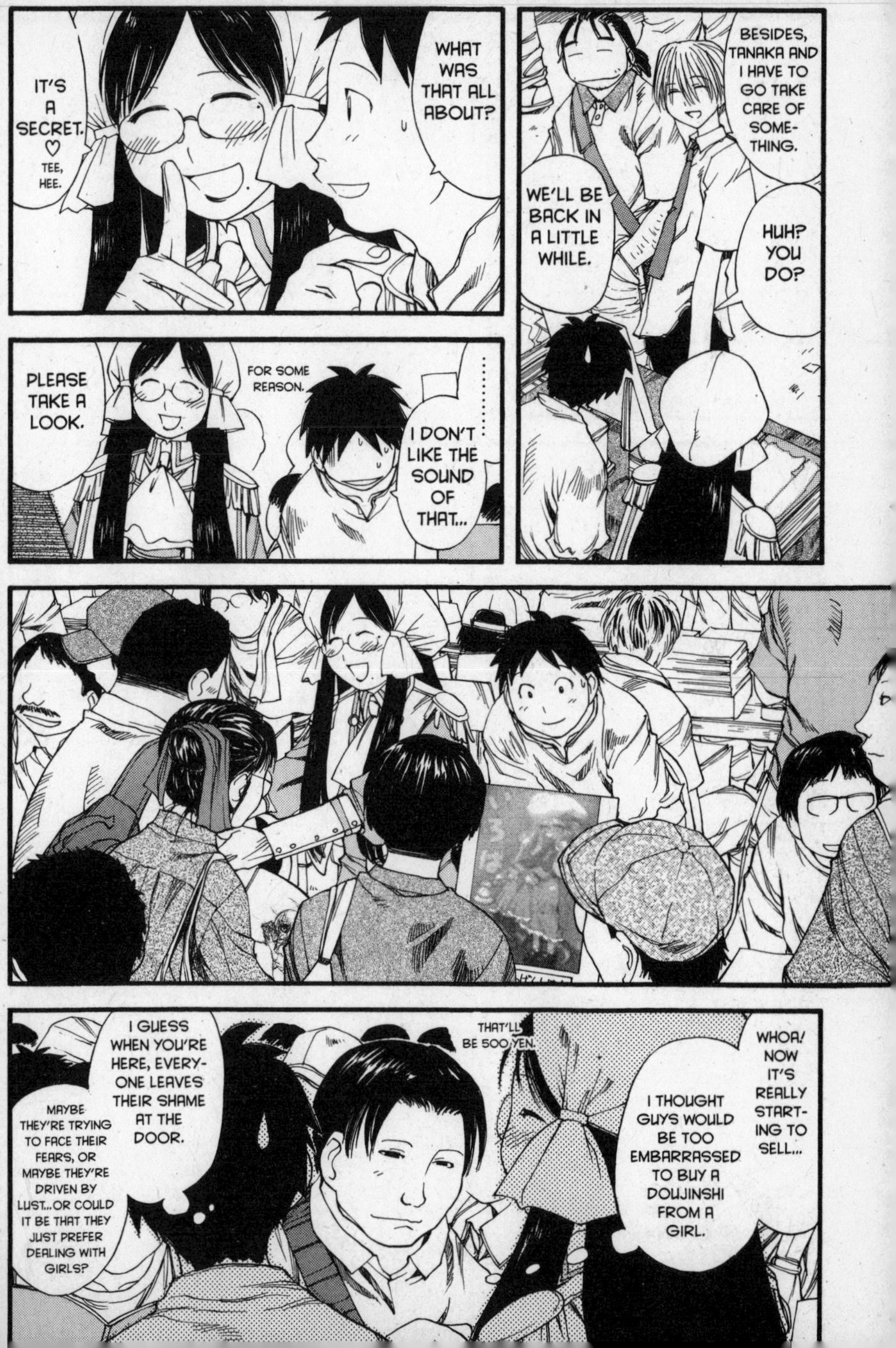
BESIDES, TANAKA AND I HAVE TO GO TAKE CARE OF SOMETHING.
WE'LL BE BACK IN A LITTLE WHILE.
HUH? YOU DO?
WHAT WAS THAT ALL ABOUT?
IT'S A SECRET. ♡
TEE, HEE.
......
I DON'T LIKE THE SOUND OF THAT...
FOR SOME REASON.
PLEASE TAKE A LOOK.
WHOA! NOW IT'S REALLY STARTING TO SELL...
THAT'LL BE 500 YEN.
I THOUGHT GUYS WOULD BE TOO EMBARRASSED TO BUY A DOUJINSHI FROM A GIRL.
I GUESS WHEN YOU'RE HERE, EVERYONE LEAVES THEIR SHAME AT THE DOOR.
MAYBE THEY'RE TRYING TO FACE THEIR FEARS, OR MAYBE THEY'RE DRIVEN BY LUST...OR COULD IT BE THAT THEY JUST PREFER DEALING WITH GIRLS?

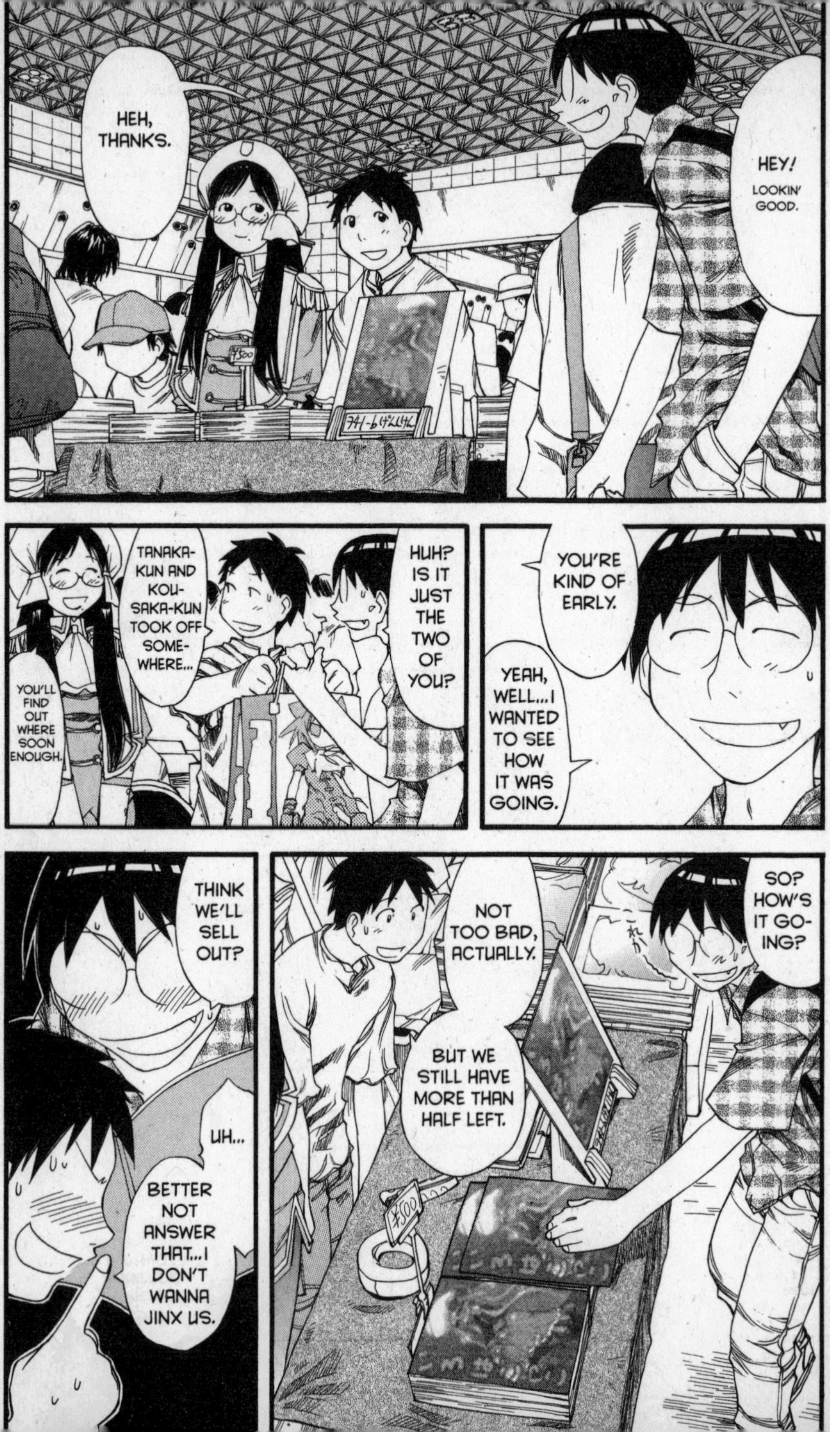
HEY! LOOKIN' GOOD.
HEH, THANKS.
YOU'RE KIND OF EARLY.
YEAH, WELL...I WANTED TO SEE HOW IT WAS GOING.
HUH? IS IT JUST THE TWO OF YOU?
TANAKA-KUN AND KOU-SAKA-KUN TOOK OFF SOME-WHERE...
YOU'LL FIND OUT WHERE SOON ENOUGH.
SO? HOW'S IT GOING?
NOT TOO BAD, ACTUALLY.
BUT WE STILL HAVE MORE THAN HALF LEFT.
THINK WE'LL SELL OUT?
UH...
BETTER NOT ANSWER THAT...I DON'T WANNA JINX US.

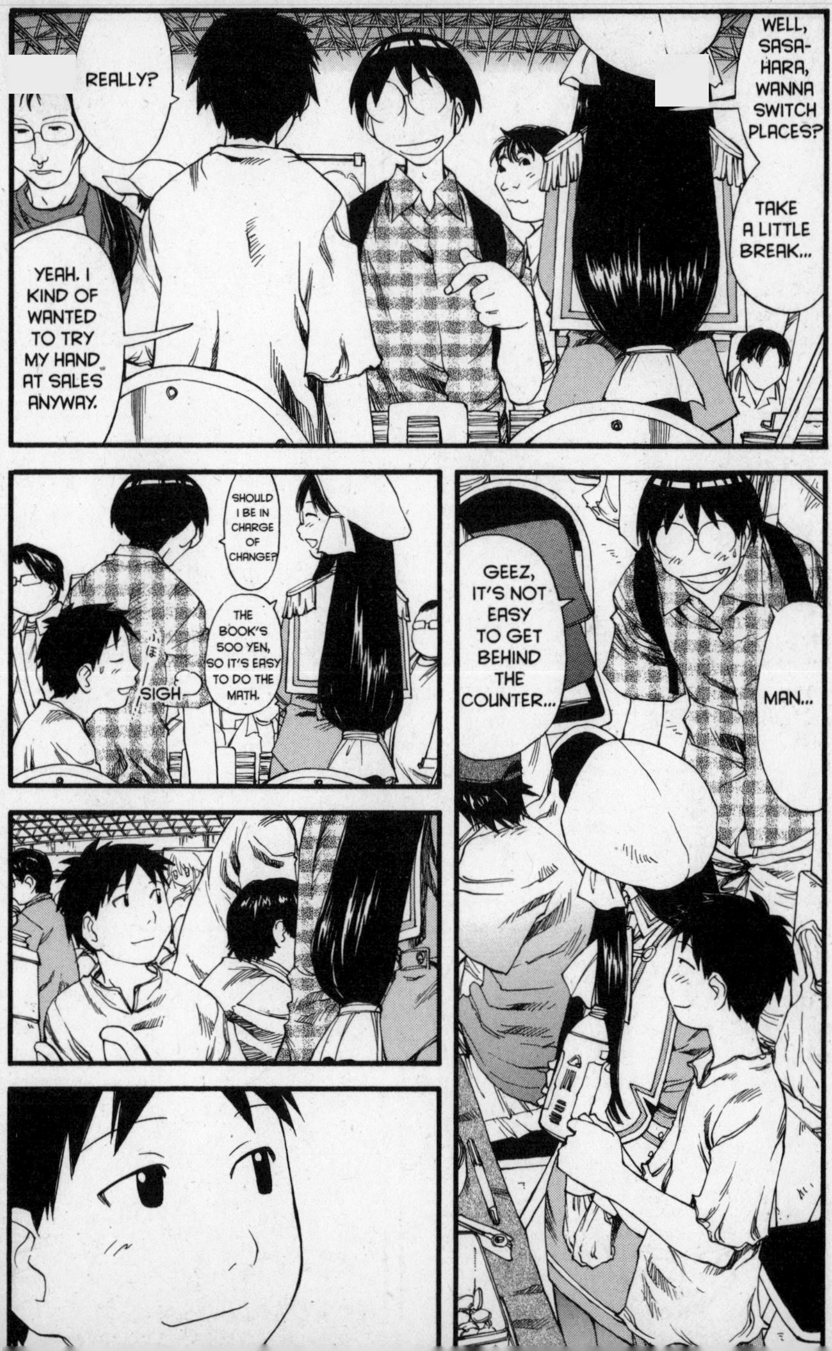
WELL, SASA-HARA, WANNA SWITCH PLACES?
TAKE A LITTLE BREAK...
REALLY?
YEAH. I KIND OF WANTED TO TRY MY HAND AT SALES ANYWAY.
MAN...
GEEZ, IT'S NOT EASY TO GET BEHIND THE COUNTER...
SHOULD I BE IN CHARGE OF CHANGE?
THE BOOK'S 500 YEN, SO IT'S EASY TO DO THE MATH.
SIGH

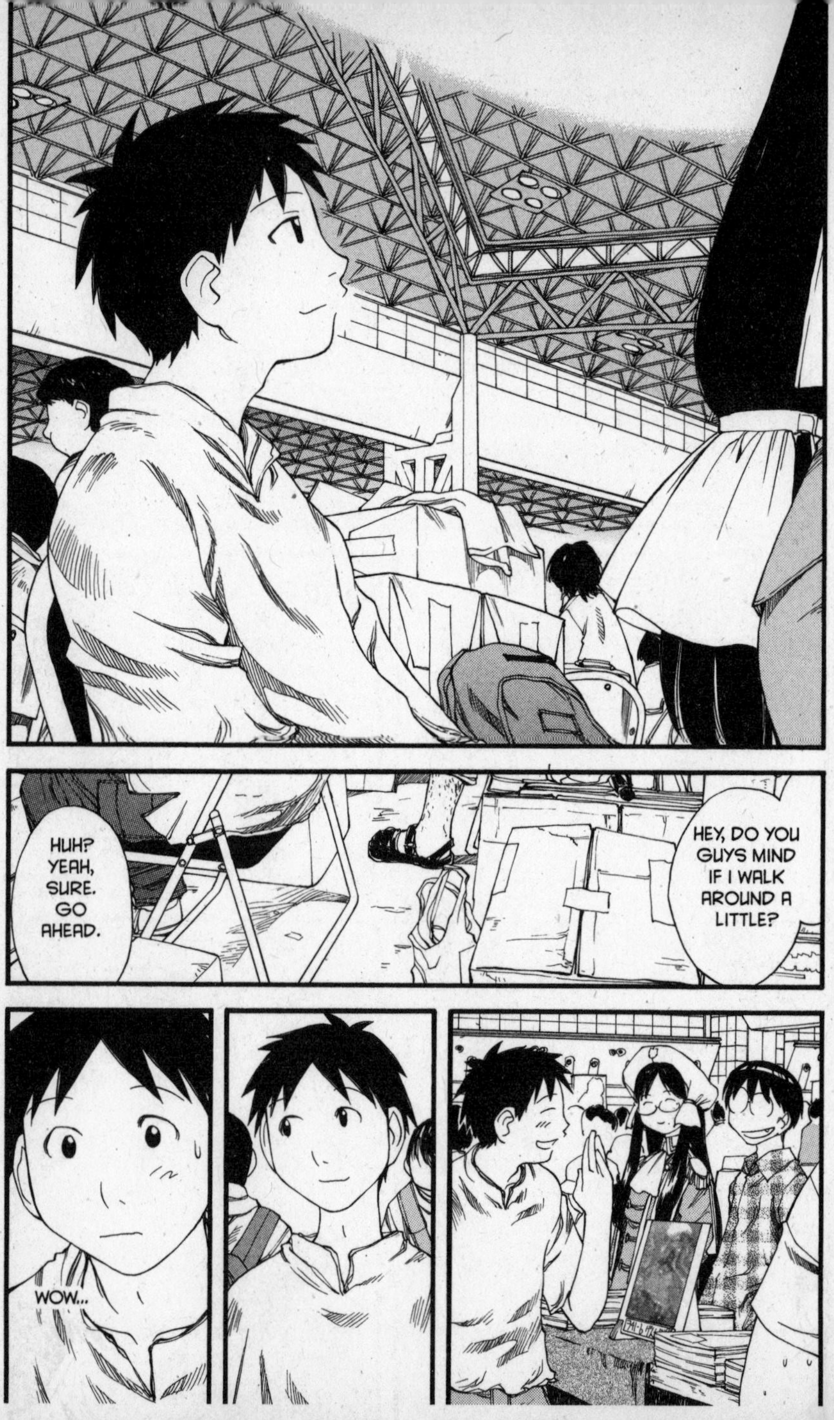
HEY, DO YOU GUYS MIND IF I WALK AROUND A LITTLE?
HUH? YEAH, SURE. GO AHEAD.
WOW...

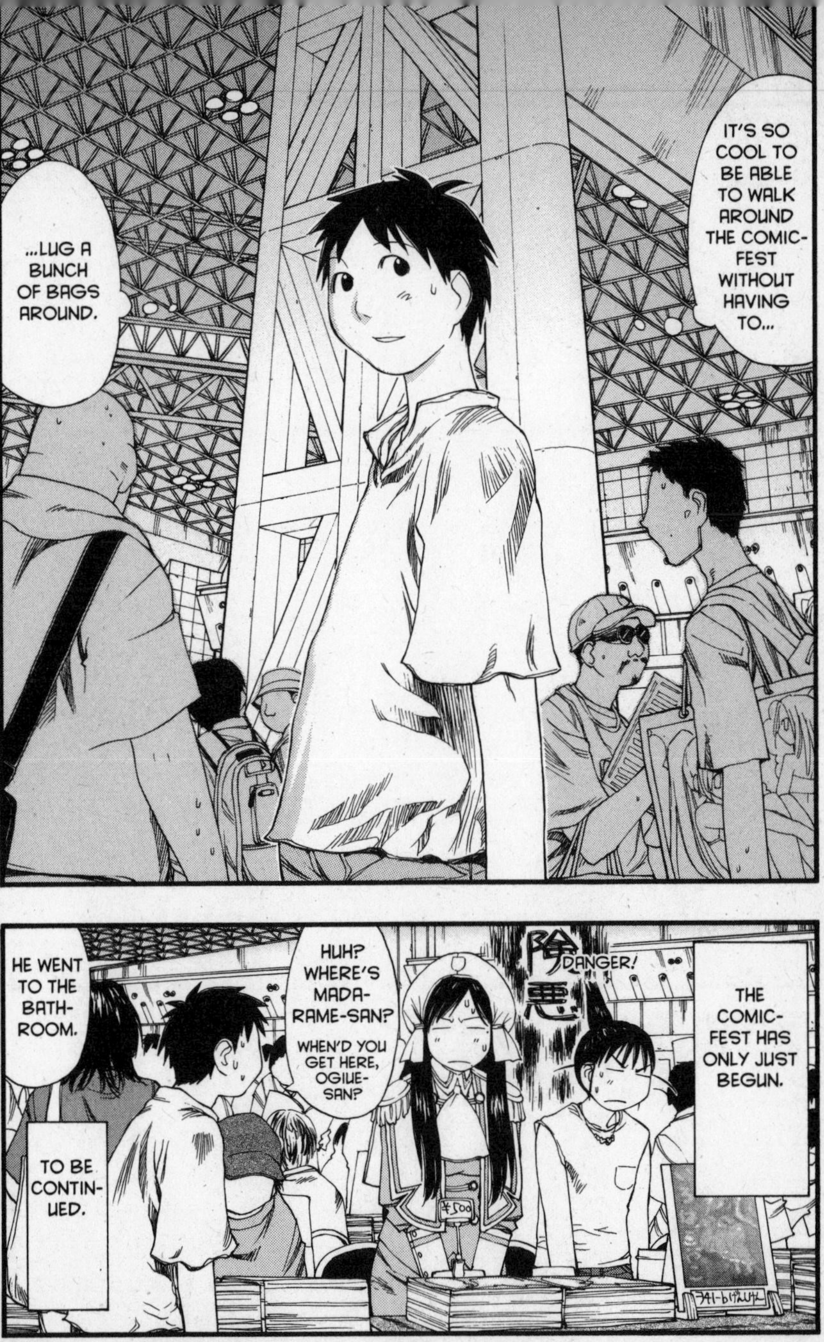
IT'S SO COOL TO BE ABLE TO WALK AROUND THE COMIC-FEST WITHOUT HAVING TO...
...LUG A BUNCH OF BAGS AROUND.
THE COMIC-FEST HAS ONLY JUST BEGUN.
険悪
DANGER!
HUH? WHERE'S MADARAME-SAN?
WHEN'D YOU GET HERE, OGIUE-SAN?
HE WENT TO THE BATHROOM.
TO BE CONTINUED.
¥500

END OF CHAPTER 29

THE RETURN OF MY FAVORITE SCENES FROM KUJI-UN - PART 5

BY TOSHIZO

EPISODE 14 "THE SICKLY ALIEN"

I CHOSE EPISODE 14. IT'S AN ORIGINAL STORY THAT DIDN'T APPEAR IN THE MANGA. IT'S DIRECTED BY MIZUTORI, AND IT'S DEFINITELY VERY MIZUTORI-ESQUE.
APPARENTLY, WHEN HE MET WITH YUU KUROKI FOR THE FIRST TIME (BACK WHEN THE SERIES WAS STILL IN DEVELOPMENT), HE SUPPOSEDLY ASKED HER, "CAN YOU DO ALIEN VOICES?" I GUESS HE'D BEEN HOPING TO DO SOMETHING LIKE THAT FOR A WHILE (LAUGHS). [TOSHIZO]

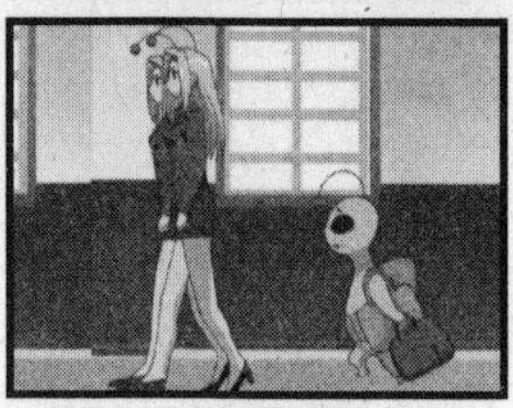

▲ ERUDO THE ALIEN HAS AN IQ OF 1300 AND THE STRENGTH TO MATCH. KOMAKI UNCOVERS HIS ONE WEAKNESS...

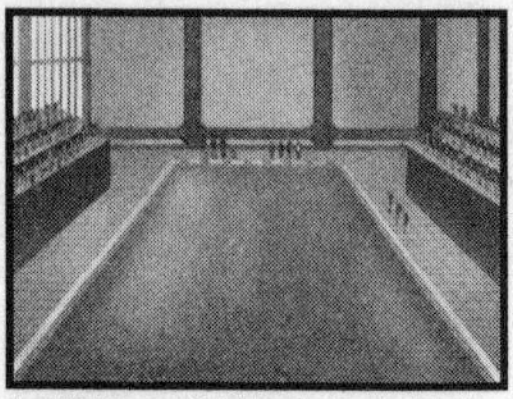

▲ HE HAS A WEAK STOMACH. SHE CHALLENGES HIM TO A 400-METER SWIM RELAY.

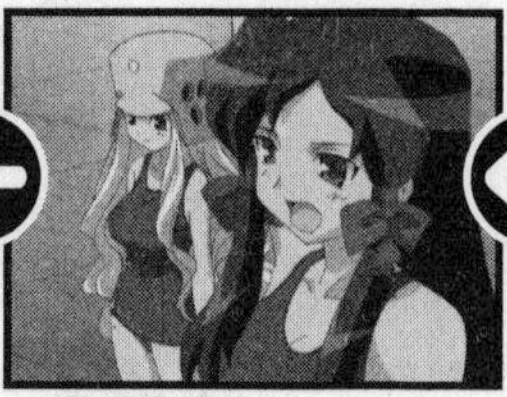

▲ "ON YOUR MARK..."

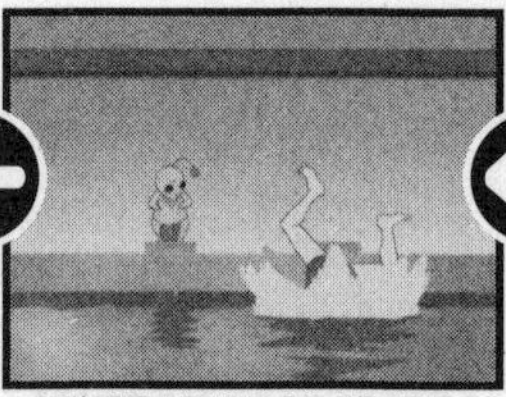

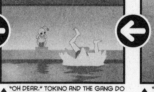

▲ "OH DEAR." TOKINO AND THE GANG DO THEIR BEST TO BUY TIME.

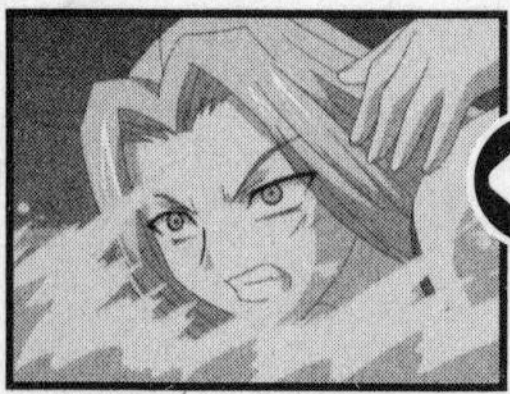

▲ THE ALIEN SWIMS WITH ALL HIS HEART.

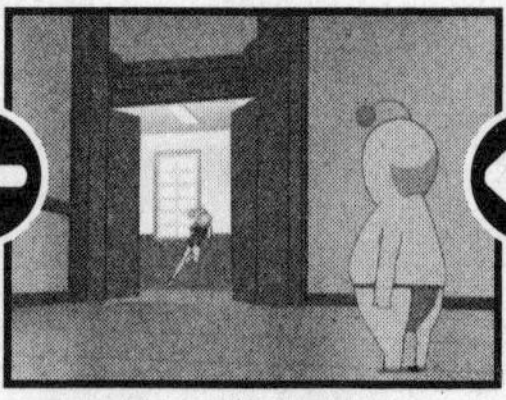

▲ AFTER THE ALIEN WAS DONE SWIMMING, IT RAN STRAIGHT TO THE BATHROOM.

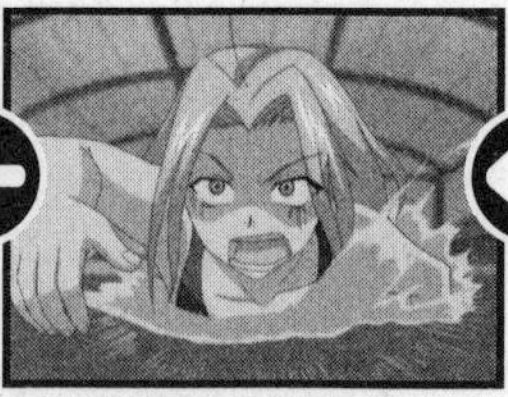

▲ THE TEAM'S ANCHOR. HER STOMACH IS ABOUT TO BURST...JUST LOOK AT THAT EXPRESSION ON HER FACE.

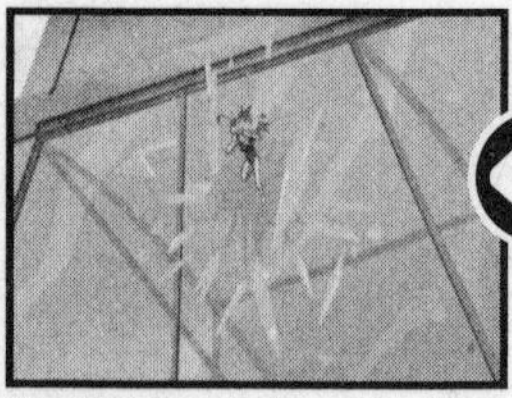

▲ WHEN THE ALIEN COULD NO LONGER TAKE ANY MORE, IT JUMPED OFF COURSE, AND FLEW OUTSIDE.

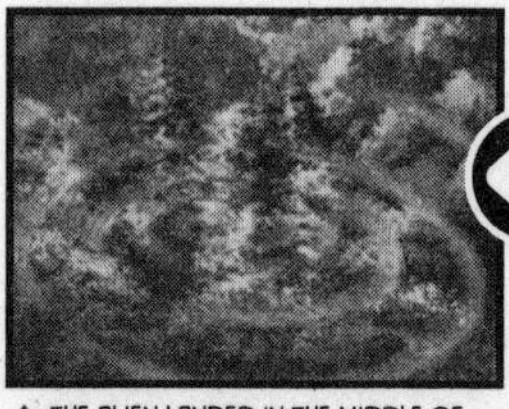

▲ THE ALIEN LANDED IN THE MIDDLE OF THE FOREST, AND RUMORS STARTED TO SPREAD.

SPECIAL BONUS - FROM THE OPENING SCENE

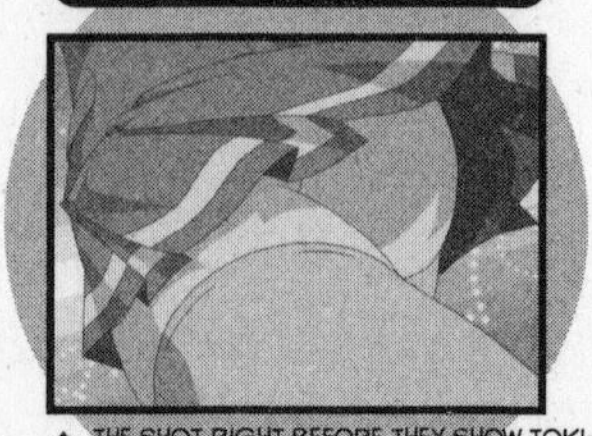

▲ THE SHOT RIGHT BEFORE THEY SHOW TOKINO'S UNDERWEAR. DOESN'T IT LOOK LIKE SHE'S NOT WEARING ANY PANTIES?

AH!...AFTER THAT IT GETS CRAZIER AND CRAZIER. IT IS REALLY COOL, THOUGH. YOU EITHER LOVE THIS EPISODE OR YOU HATE IT...YUP.

OH, YEAH...AND WHAT'S WITH YOUR "SPECIAL BONUS SCENE"? WHY DIDN'T YOU JUST CHOOSE THE ACTUAL PANTY SCENE?...BUT I GUESS I DO KNOW HOW YOU FEEL. [PIT VIPER]

THE SEARCH FOR OGI! LEVEL 3

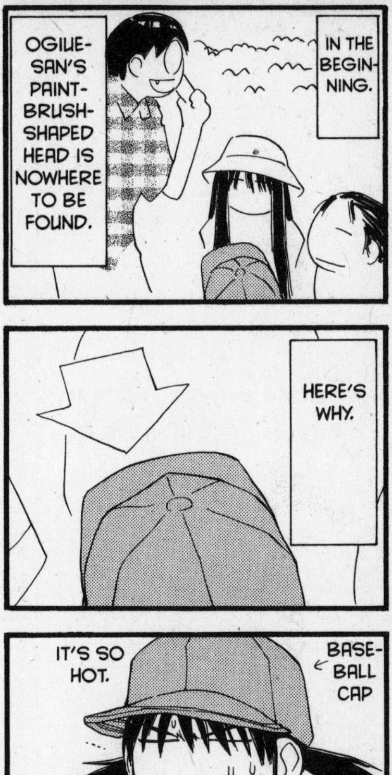
IN THE BEGIN-NING.
OGIUE-SAN'S PAINT-BRUSH-SHAPED HEAD IS NOWHERE TO BE FOUND.
HERE'S WHY.
BASE-BALL CAP
IT'S SO HOT.
PIG TAILS
APPAR-ENTLY, SHE SWITCHED BACK TO HER USUAL HAIRSTYLE A FEW MIN-UTES AFTER SHE GOT INSIDE.
SORRY, BUT THAT JUST LOOKED WAY TOO OTAKU FOR ME.
AND THIS HAIR-STYLE DOESN'T?

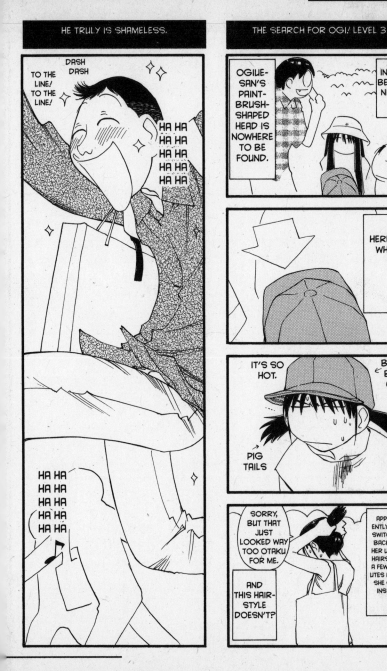

HE TRULY IS SHAMELESS.

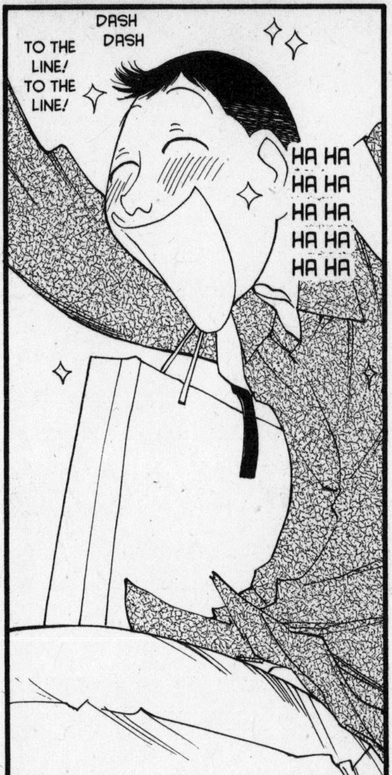
DASH DASH
TO THE LINE! TO THE LINE!
HA HA HA HA HA HA HA HA HA HA
HA HA HA HA HA HA HA HA HA HA

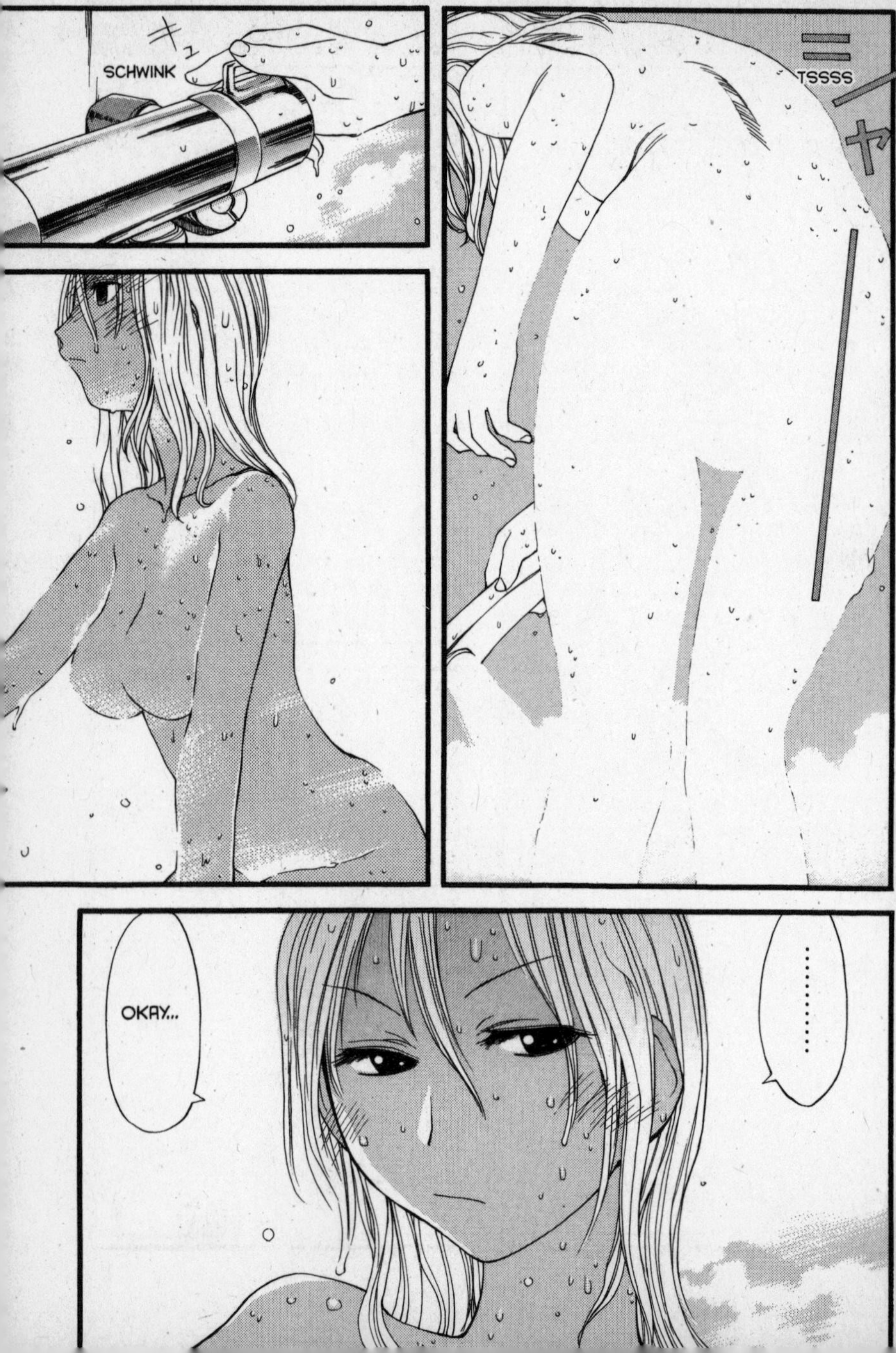
TSSSS
SCHWINK
......
OKAY...

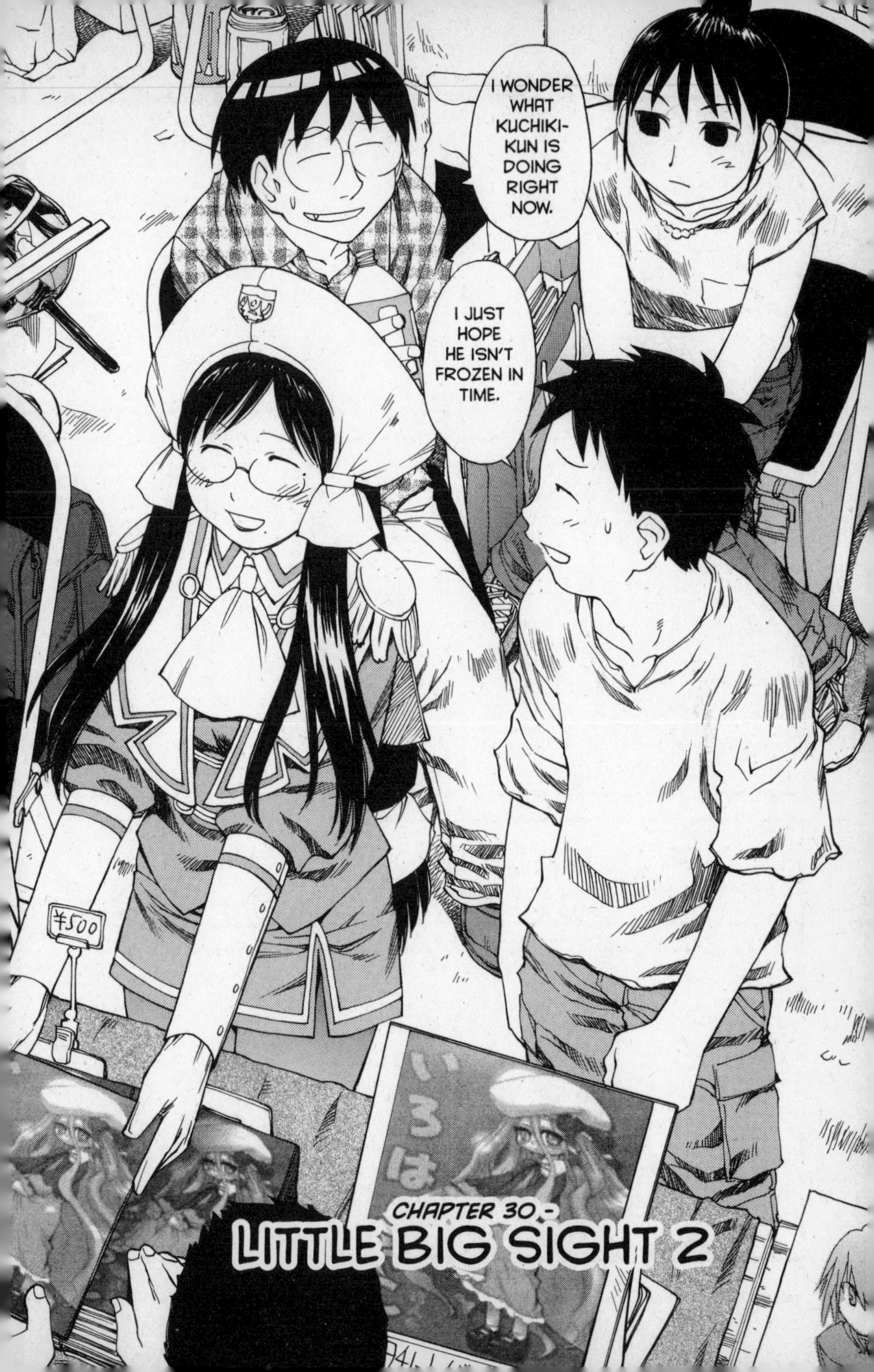
I WONDER WHAT KUCHIKI-KUN IS DOING RIGHT NOW.
I JUST HOPE HE ISN'T FROZEN IN TIME.
¥500
CHAPTER 30 -
LITTLE BIG SIGHT 2

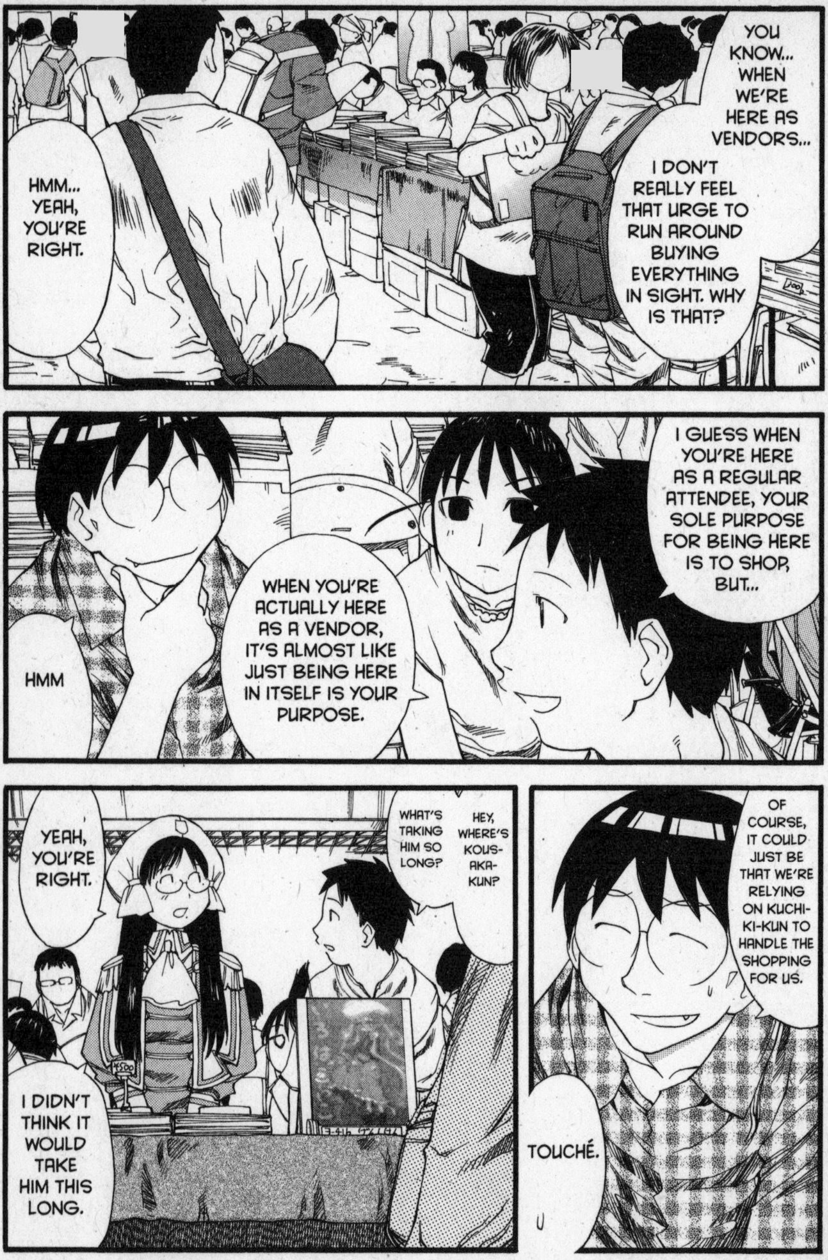

YOU KNOW... WHEN WE'RE HERE AS VENDORS...
I DON'T REALLY FEEL THAT URGE TO RUN AROUND BUYING EVERYTHING IN SIGHT. WHY IS THAT?
HMM... YEAH, YOU'RE RIGHT.
I GUESS WHEN YOU'RE HERE AS A REGULAR ATTENDEE, YOUR SOLE PURPOSE FOR BEING HERE IS TO SHOP, BUT...
WHEN YOU'RE ACTUALLY HERE AS A VENDOR, IT'S ALMOST LIKE JUST BEING HERE IN ITSELF IS YOUR PURPOSE.
HMM
OF COURSE, IT COULD JUST BE THAT WE'RE RELYING ON KUCHIKI-KUN TO HANDLE THE SHOPPING FOR US.
TOUCHÉ.
HEY, WHERE'S KOUSAKA-KUN?
WHAT'S TAKING HIM SO LONG?
YEAH, YOU'RE RIGHT.
I DIDN'T THINK IT WOULD TAKE HIM THIS LONG.

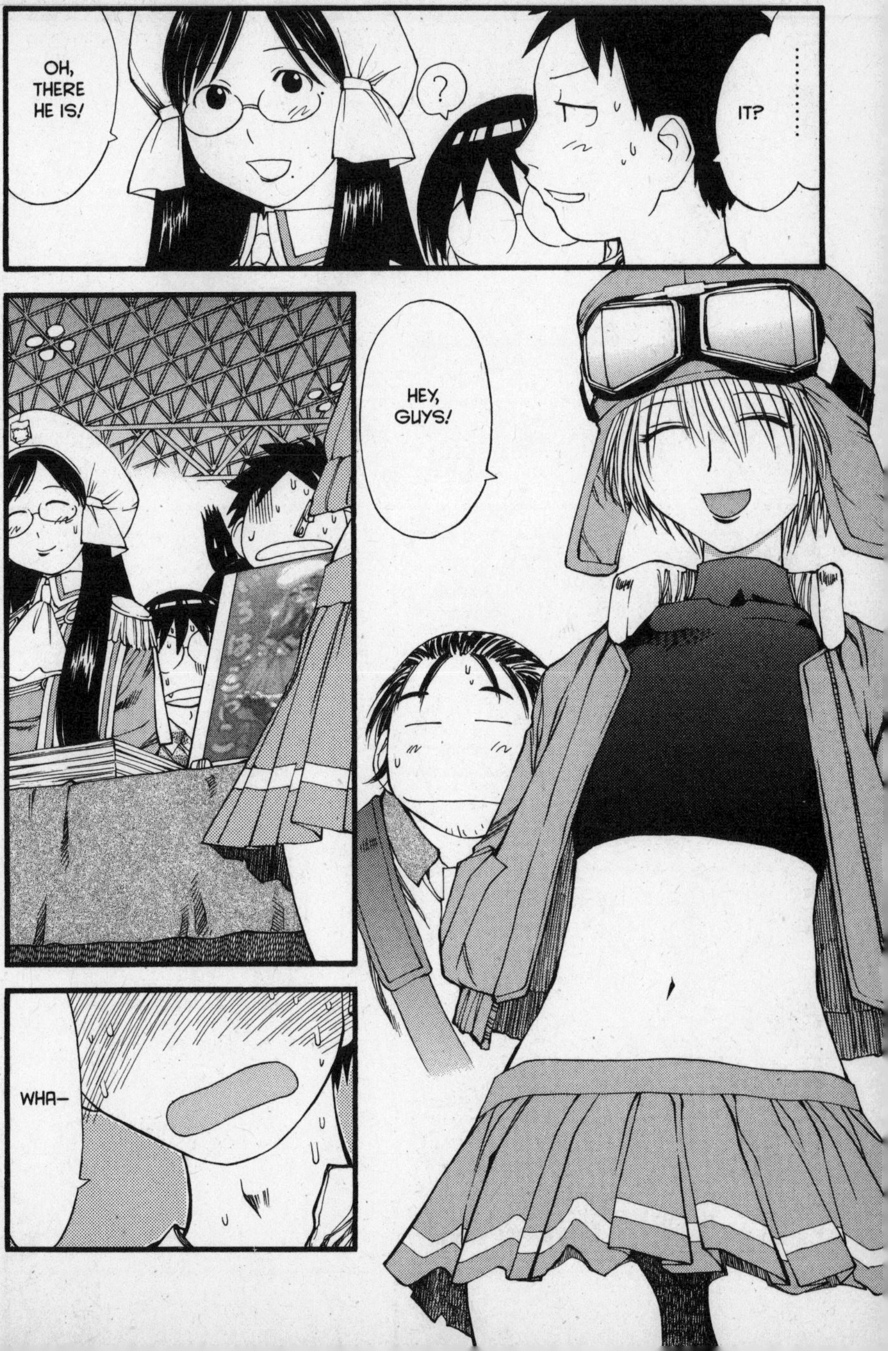
......IT?
?
OH, THERE HE IS!
HEY, GUYS!
WHA–

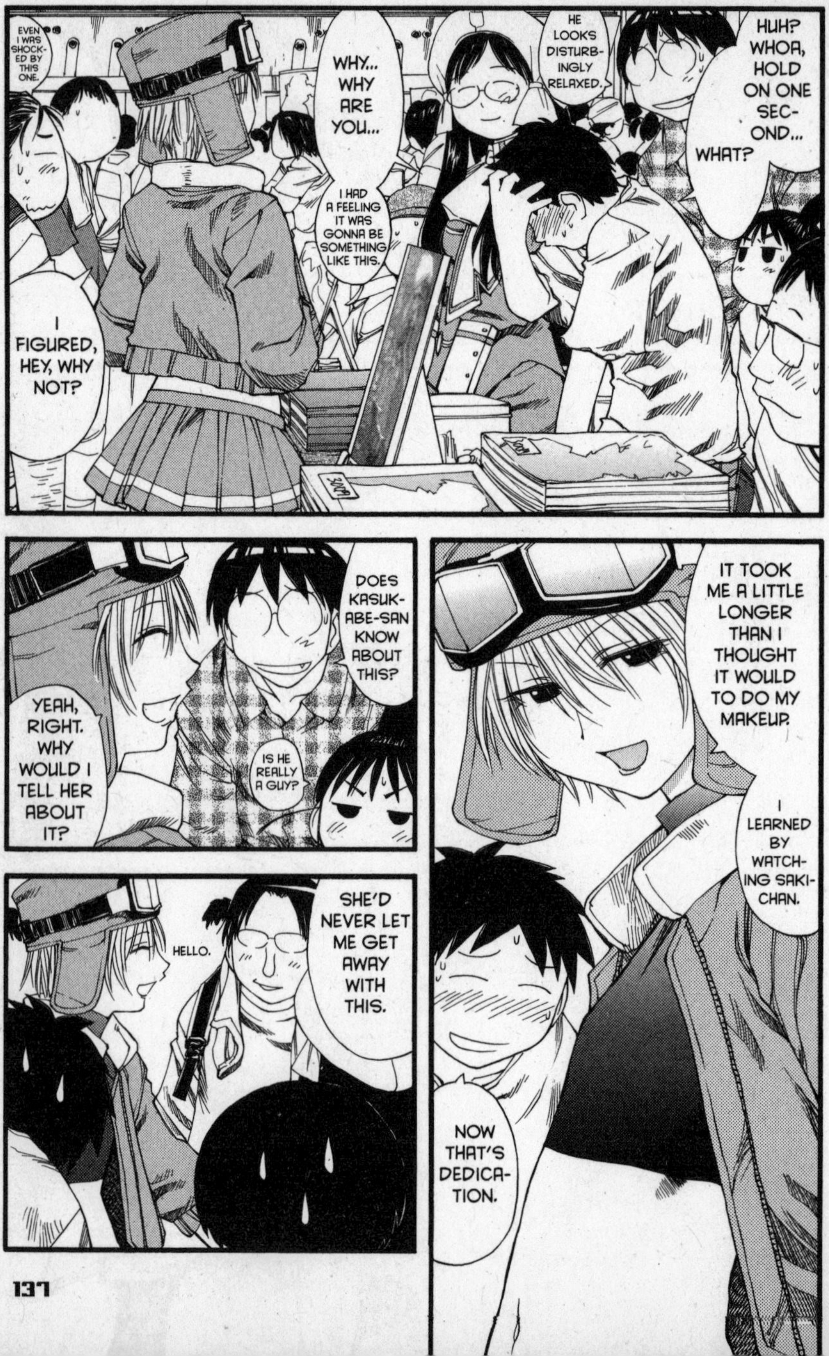
HUH? WHOA, HOLD ON ONE SECOND... WHAT?
HE LOOKS DISTURBINGLY RELAXED.
WHY... WHY ARE YOU...
I HAD A FEELING IT WAS GONNA BE SOMETHING LIKE THIS.
EVEN I WAS SHOCKED BY THIS ONE.
I FIGURED, HEY, WHY NOT?
IT TOOK ME A LITTLE LONGER THAN I THOUGHT IT WOULD TO DO MY MAKEUP.
I LEARNED BY WATCHING SAKI-CHAN.
NOW THAT'S DEDICATION.
DOES KASUKABE-SAN KNOW ABOUT THIS?
YEAH, RIGHT. WHY WOULD I TELL HER ABOUT IT?
IS HE REALLY A GUY?
SHE'D NEVER LET ME GET AWAY WITH THIS.
HELLO.

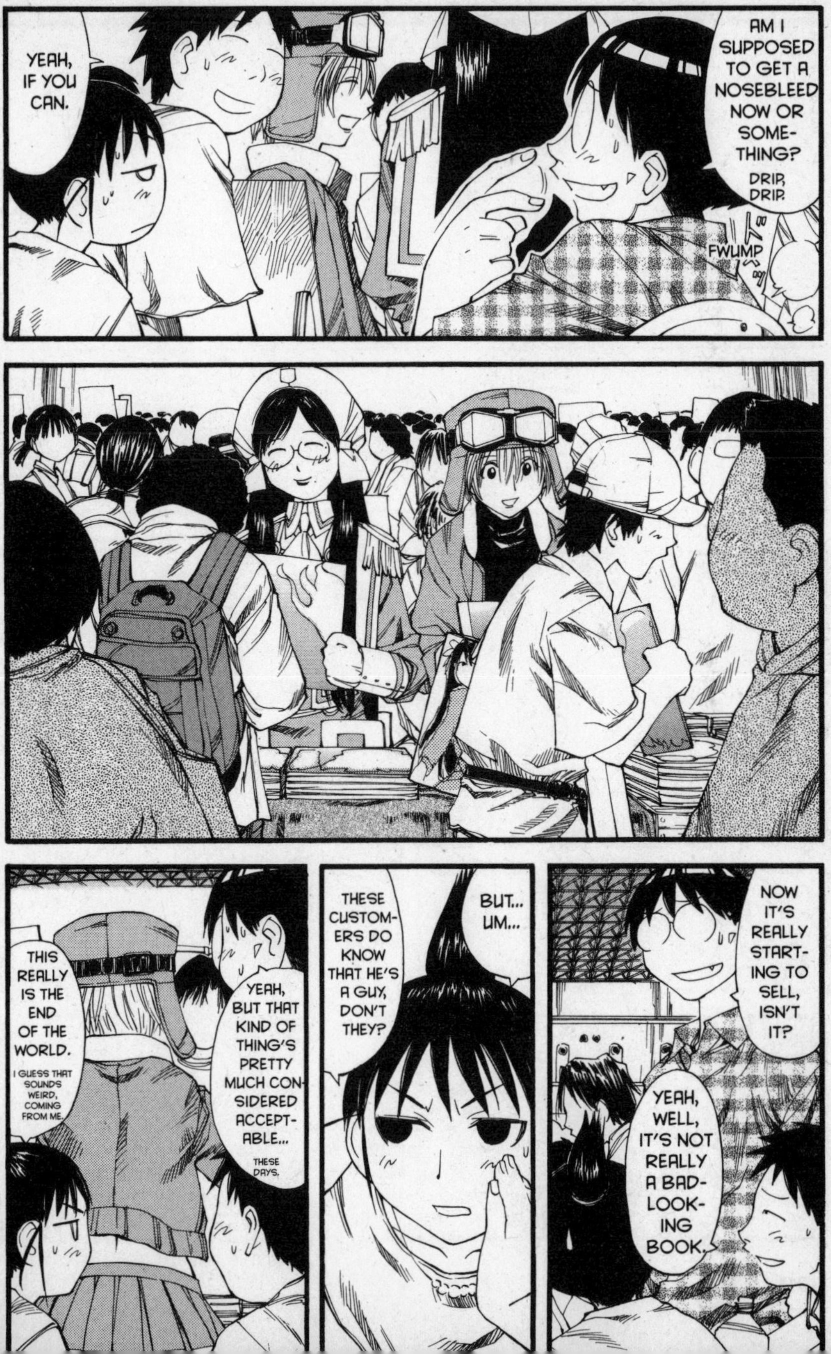
AM I SUPPOSED TO GET A NOSEBLEED NOW OR SOMETHING?
DRIP, DRIP.
FWUMP
YEAH, IF YOU CAN.
NOW IT'S REALLY STARTING TO SELL, ISN'T IT?
YEAH, WELL, IT'S NOT REALLY A BAD-LOOKING BOOK.
BUT... UM...
THESE CUSTOMERS DO KNOW THAT HE'S A GUY, DON'T THEY?
YEAH, BUT THAT KIND OF THING'S PRETTY MUCH CONSIDERED ACCEPTABLE...
THESE DAYS.
THIS REALLY IS THE END OF THE WORLD.
I GUESS THAT SOUNDS WEIRD, COMING FROM ME.

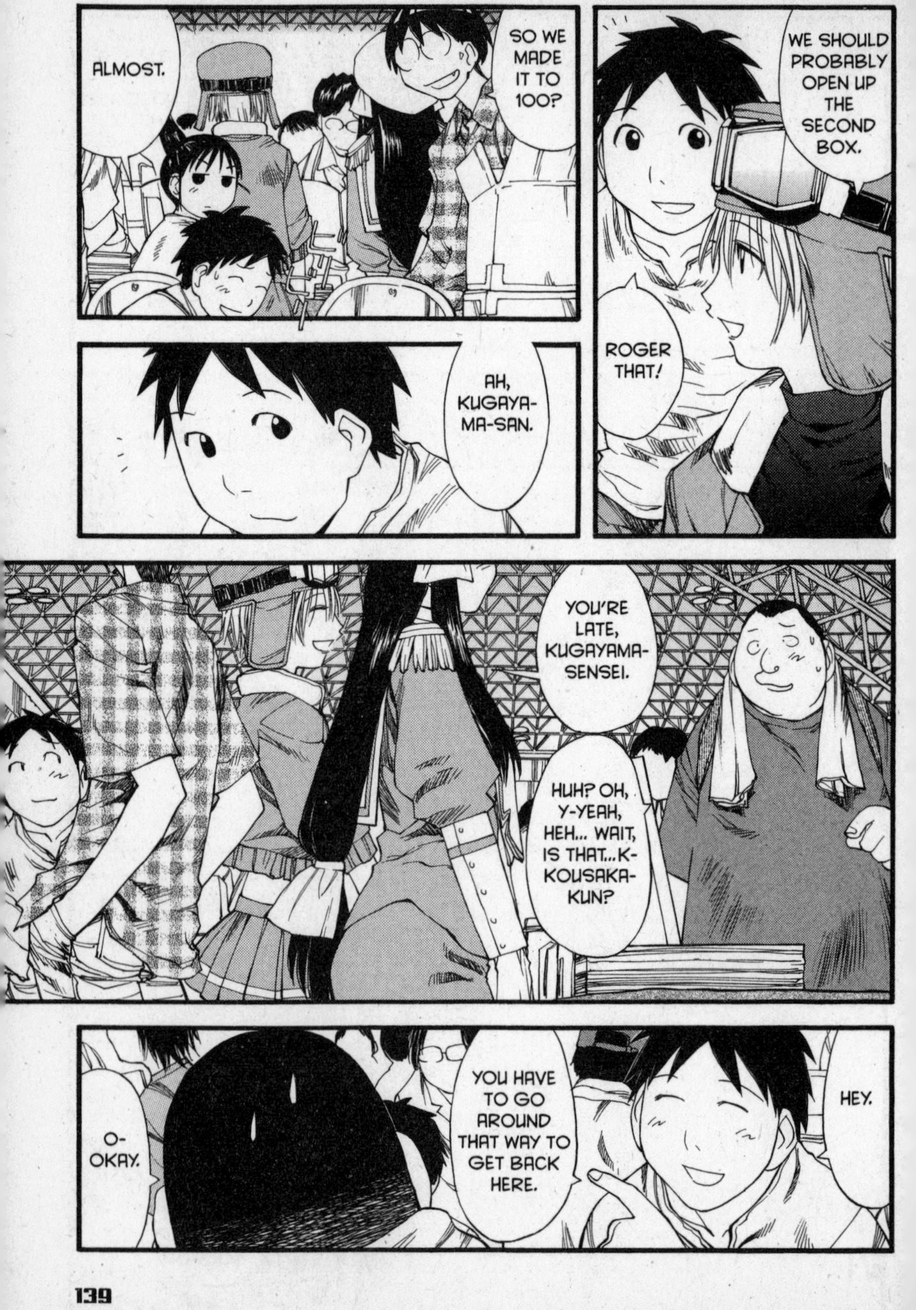
WE SHOULD PROBABLY OPEN UP THE SECOND BOX.
ROGER THAT!
SO WE MADE IT TO 100?
ALMOST.
AH, KUGAYA-MA-SAN.
YOU'RE LATE, KUGAYAMA-SENSEI.
HUH? OH, Y-YEAH, HEH... WAIT, IS THAT...K-KOUSAKA-KUN?
HEY.
YOU HAVE TO GO AROUND THAT WAY TO GET BACK HERE.
O-OKAY.

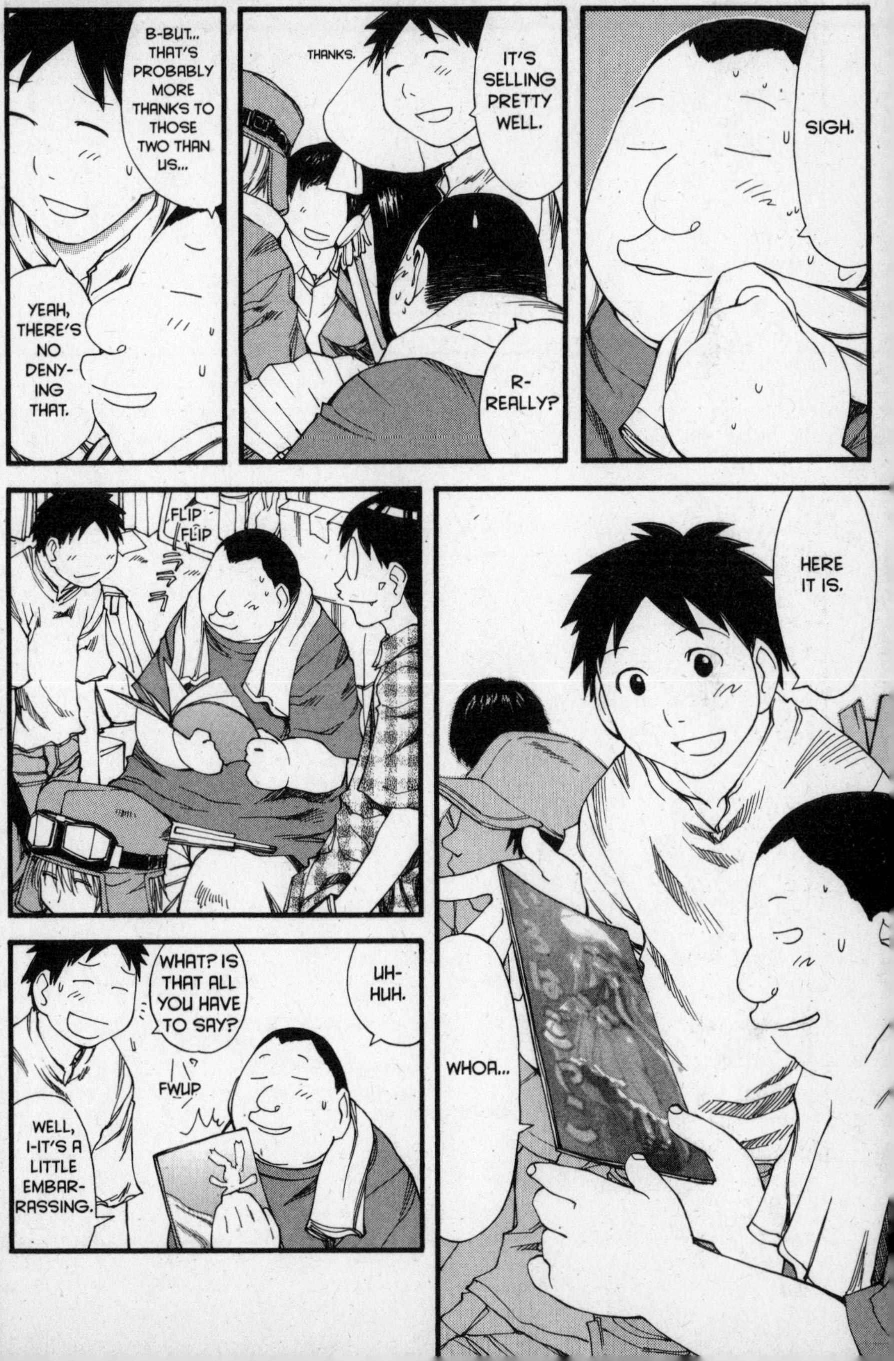
SIGH.
IT'S SELLING PRETTY WELL.
THANKS.
R- REALLY?
B-BUT... THAT'S PROBABLY MORE THANKS TO THOSE TWO THAN US...
YEAH, THERE'S NO DENY- ING THAT.
HERE IT IS.
WHOA...
FLIP FLIP
UH- HUH.
WHAT? IS THAT ALL YOU HAVE TO SAY?
FWUP
WELL, I-IT'S A LITTLE EMBAR- RASSING.

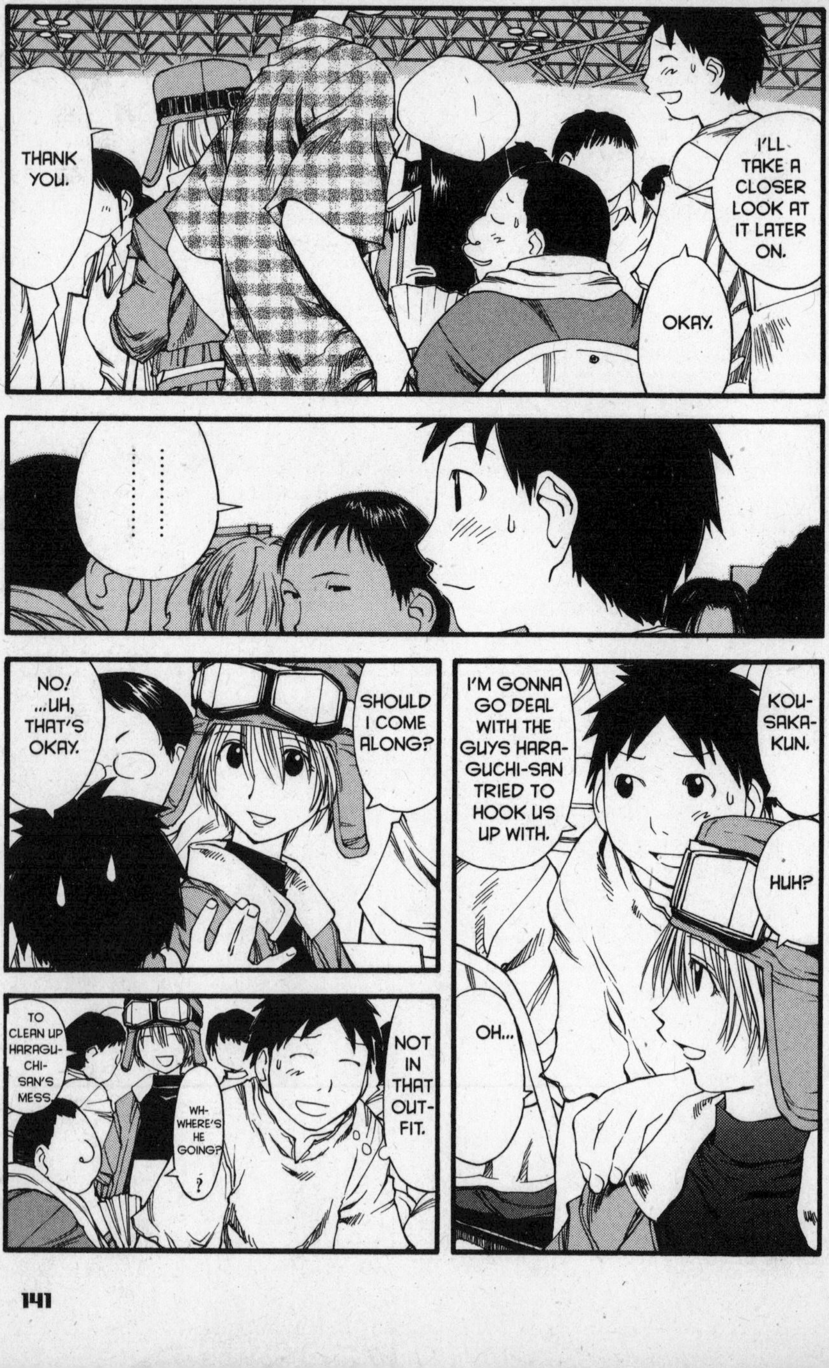
I'LL TAKE A CLOSER LOOK AT IT LATER ON.
OKAY.
THANK YOU.
......
KOU-SAKA-KUN.
I'M GONNA GO DEAL WITH THE GUYS HARA-GUCHI-SAN TRIED TO HOOK US UP WITH.
HUH?
OH...
SHOULD I COME ALONG?
NO! ...UH, THAT'S OKAY.
NOT IN THAT OUT-FIT.
WH-WHERE'S HE GOING?
?
TO CLEAN UP HARAGU-CHI-SAN'S MESS.

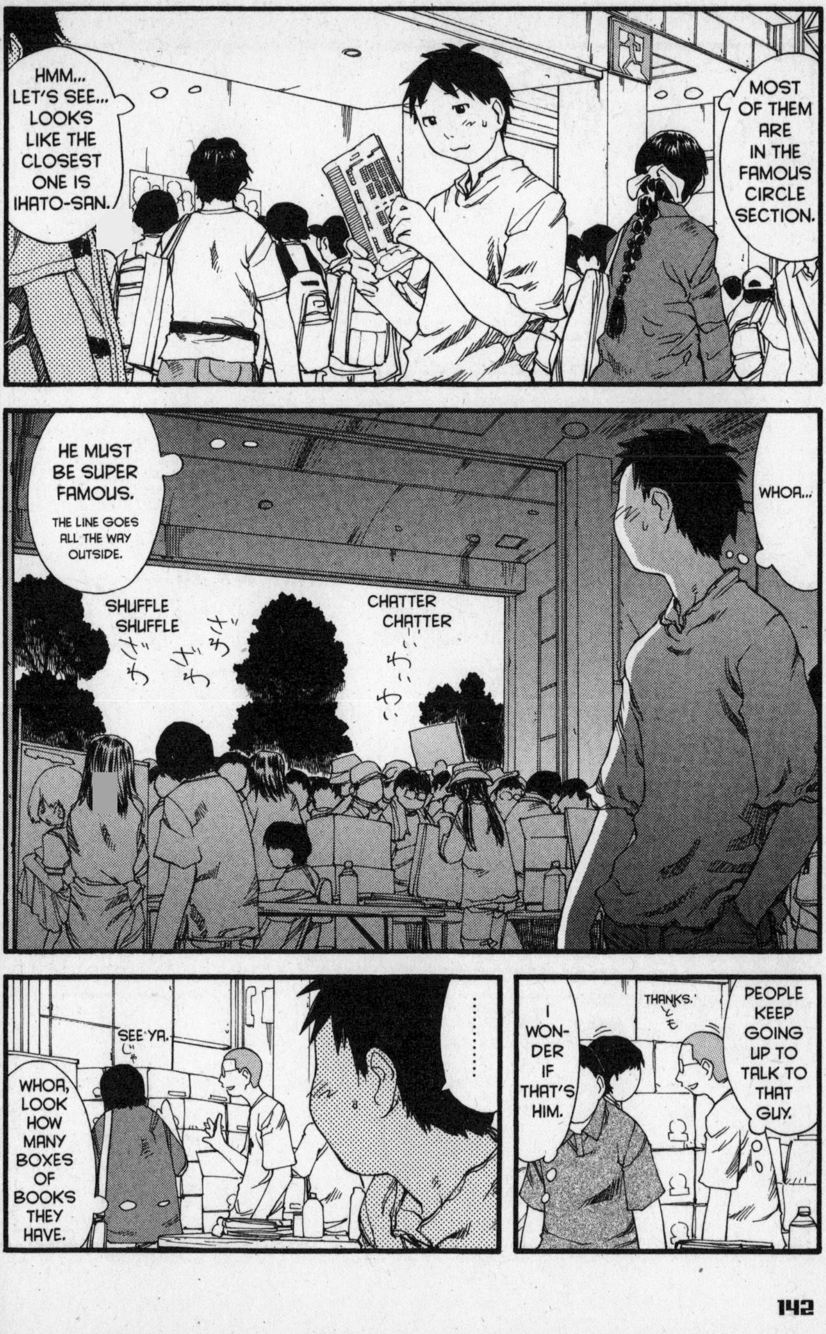
MOST OF THEM ARE IN THE FAMOUS CIRCLE SECTION.
HMM... LET'S SEE... LOOKS LIKE THE CLOSEST ONE IS IHATO-SAN.
WHOA...
HE MUST BE SUPER FAMOUS.
THE LINE GOES ALL THE WAY OUTSIDE.
CHATTER CHATTER
わいわい
SHUFFLE SHUFFLE
ざわざわ
PEOPLE KEEP GOING UP TO TALK TO THAT GUY.
THANKS.
ども
I WONDER IF THAT'S HIM.
......
SEE YA.
じゃ
WHOA, LOOK HOW MANY BOXES OF BOOKS THEY HAVE.

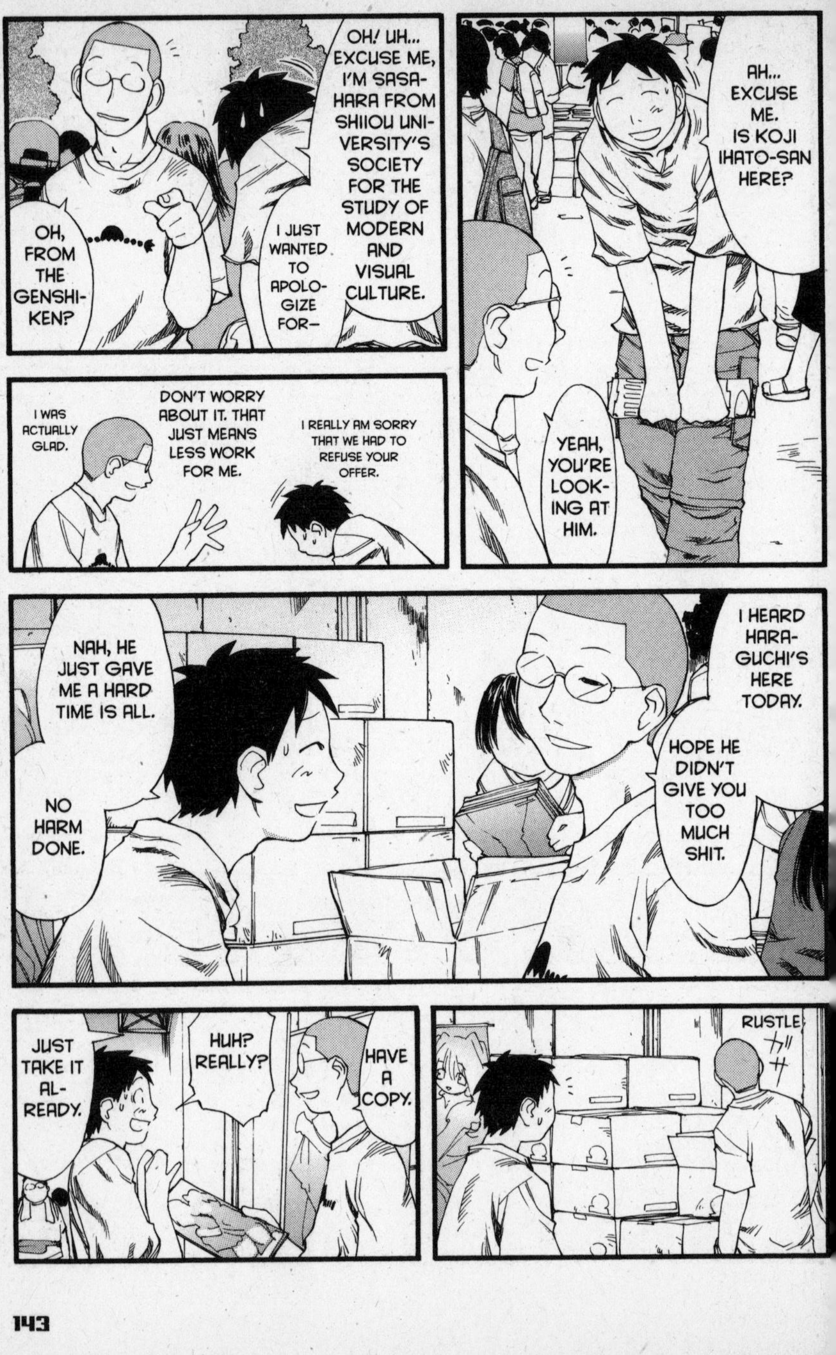
AH... EXCUSE ME. IS KOJI IHATO-SAN HERE?
YEAH, YOU'RE LOOKING AT HIM.
OH! UH... EXCUSE ME, I'M SASAHARA FROM SHIIOU UNIVERSITY'S SOCIETY FOR THE STUDY OF MODERN AND VISUAL CULTURE.
I JUST WANTED TO APOLOGIZE FOR—
OH, FROM THE GENSHIKEN?
I REALLY AM SORRY THAT WE HAD TO REFUSE YOUR OFFER.
DON'T WORRY ABOUT IT. THAT JUST MEANS LESS WORK FOR ME.
I WAS ACTUALLY GLAD.
I HEARD HARAGUCHI'S HERE TODAY.
HOPE HE DIDN'T GIVE YOU TOO MUCH SHIT.
NAH, HE JUST GAVE ME A HARD TIME IS ALL.
NO HARM DONE.
RUSTLE
HAVE A COPY.
HUH? REALLY?
JUST TAKE IT ALREADY.

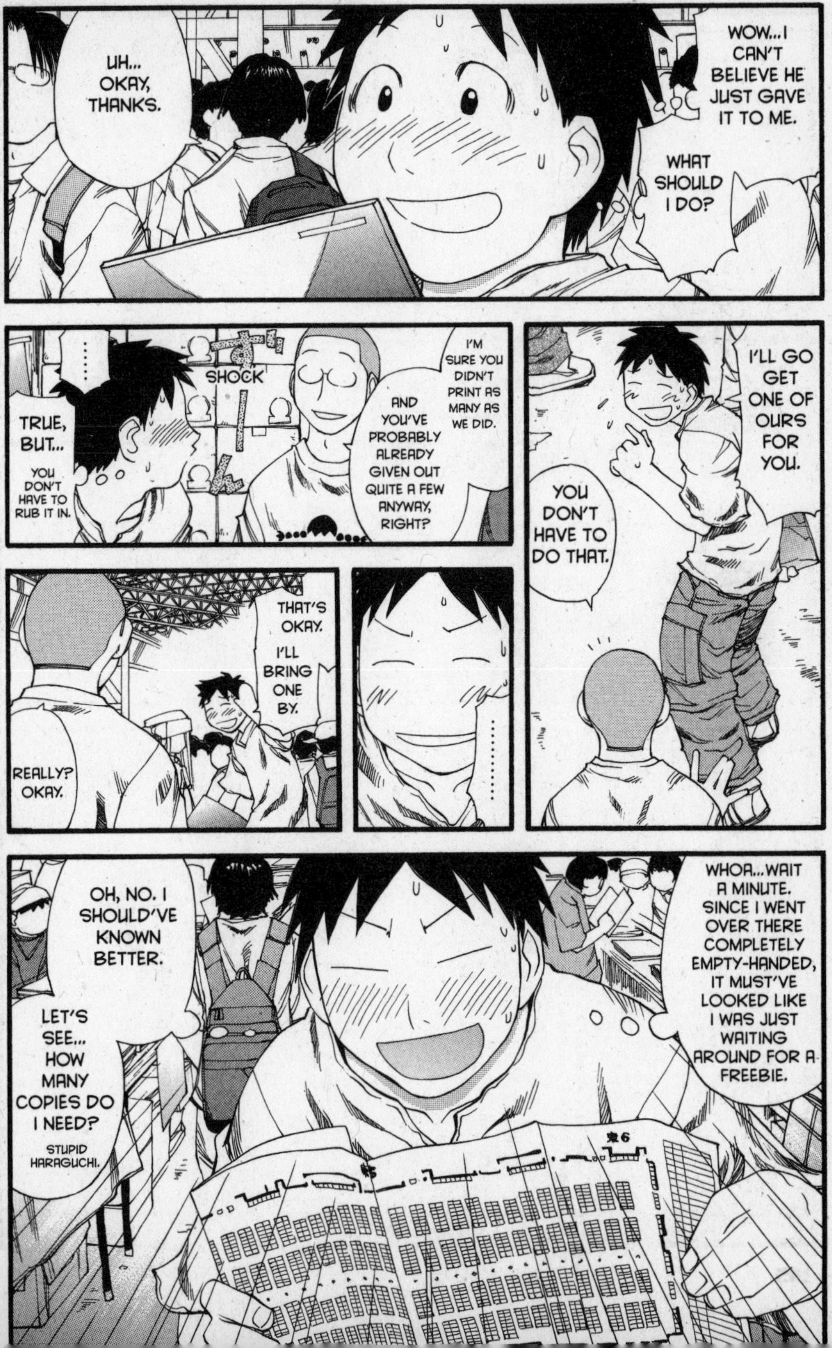
WOW...I CAN'T BELIEVE HE JUST GAVE IT TO ME.
WHAT SHOULD I DO?
UH... OKAY, THANKS.
I'LL GO GET ONE OF OURS FOR YOU.
YOU DON'T HAVE TO DO THAT.
I'M SURE YOU DIDN'T PRINT AS MANY AS WE DID.
AND YOU'VE PROBABLY ALREADY GIVEN OUT QUITE A FEW ANYWAY, RIGHT?
SHOCK
......
TRUE, BUT...
YOU DON'T HAVE TO RUB IT IN.
......
THAT'S OKAY.
I'LL BRING ONE BY.
REALLY? OKAY.
WHOA...WAIT A MINUTE. SINCE I WENT OVER THERE COMPLETELY EMPTY-HANDED, IT MUST'VE LOOKED LIKE I WAS JUST WAITING AROUND FOR A FREEBIE.
OH, NO. I SHOULD'VE KNOWN BETTER.
LET'S SEE... HOW MANY COPIES DO I NEED?
STUPID HARAGUCHI.

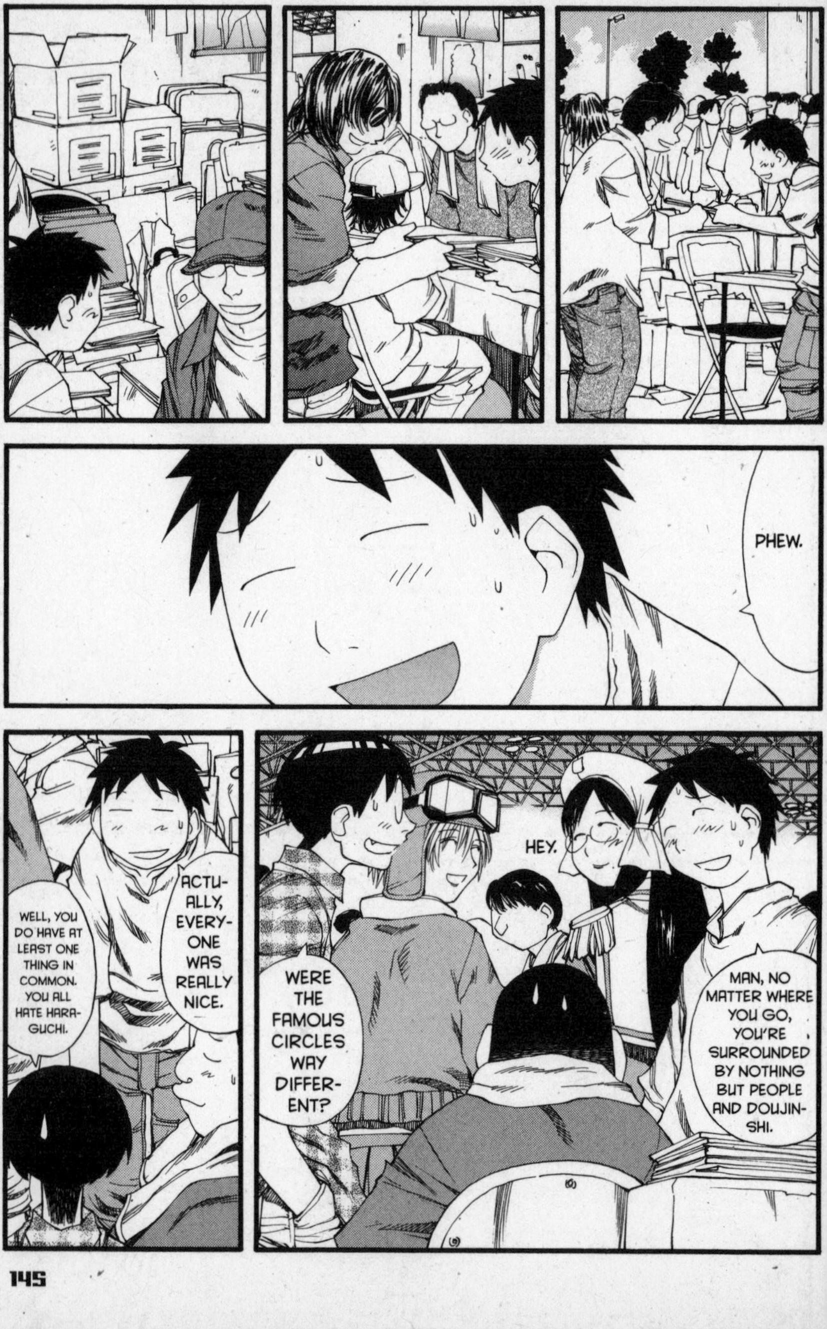
PHEW.
HEY.
MAN, NO MATTER WHERE YOU GO, YOU'RE SURROUNDED BY NOTHING BUT PEOPLE AND DOUJIN-SHI.
WERE THE FAMOUS CIRCLES WAY DIFFER-ENT?
ACTU-ALLY, EVERY-ONE WAS REALLY NICE.
WELL, YOU DO HAVE AT LEAST ONE THING IN COMMON. YOU ALL HATE HARA-GUCHI.

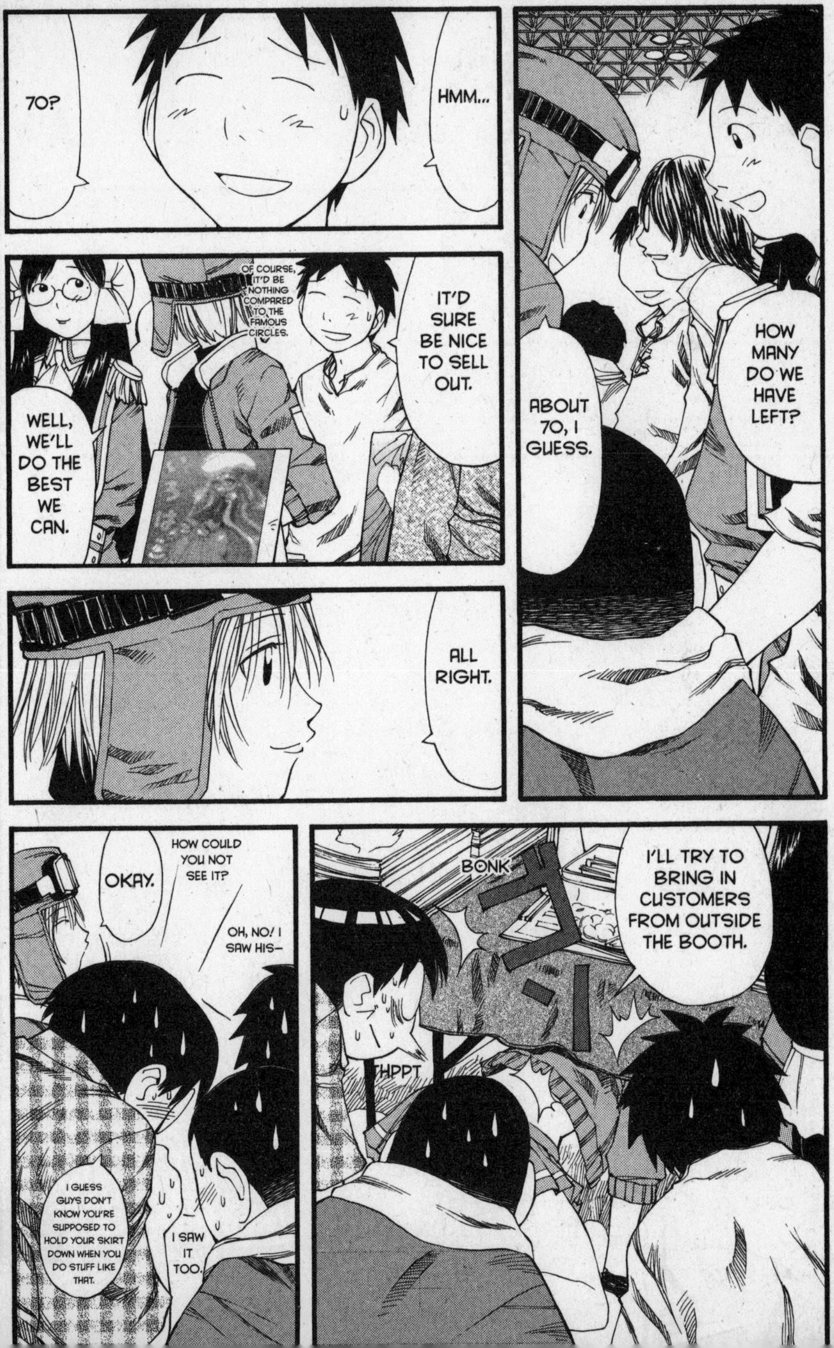
HOW MANY DO WE HAVE LEFT?
ABOUT 70, I GUESS.
HMM...
70?
IT'D SURE BE NICE TO SELL OUT.
OF COURSE, IT'D BE NOTHING COMPARED TO THE FAMOUS CIRCLES.
WELL, WE'LL DO THE BEST WE CAN.
ALL RIGHT.
I'LL TRY TO BRING IN CUSTOMERS FROM OUTSIDE THE BOOTH.
BONK
THPPT
OKAY.
HOW COULD YOU NOT SEE IT?
OH, NO! I SAW HIS—
I SAW IT TOO.
I GUESS GUYS DON'T KNOW YOU'RE SUPPOSED TO HOLD YOUR SKIRT DOWN WHEN YOU DO STUFF LIKE THAT.

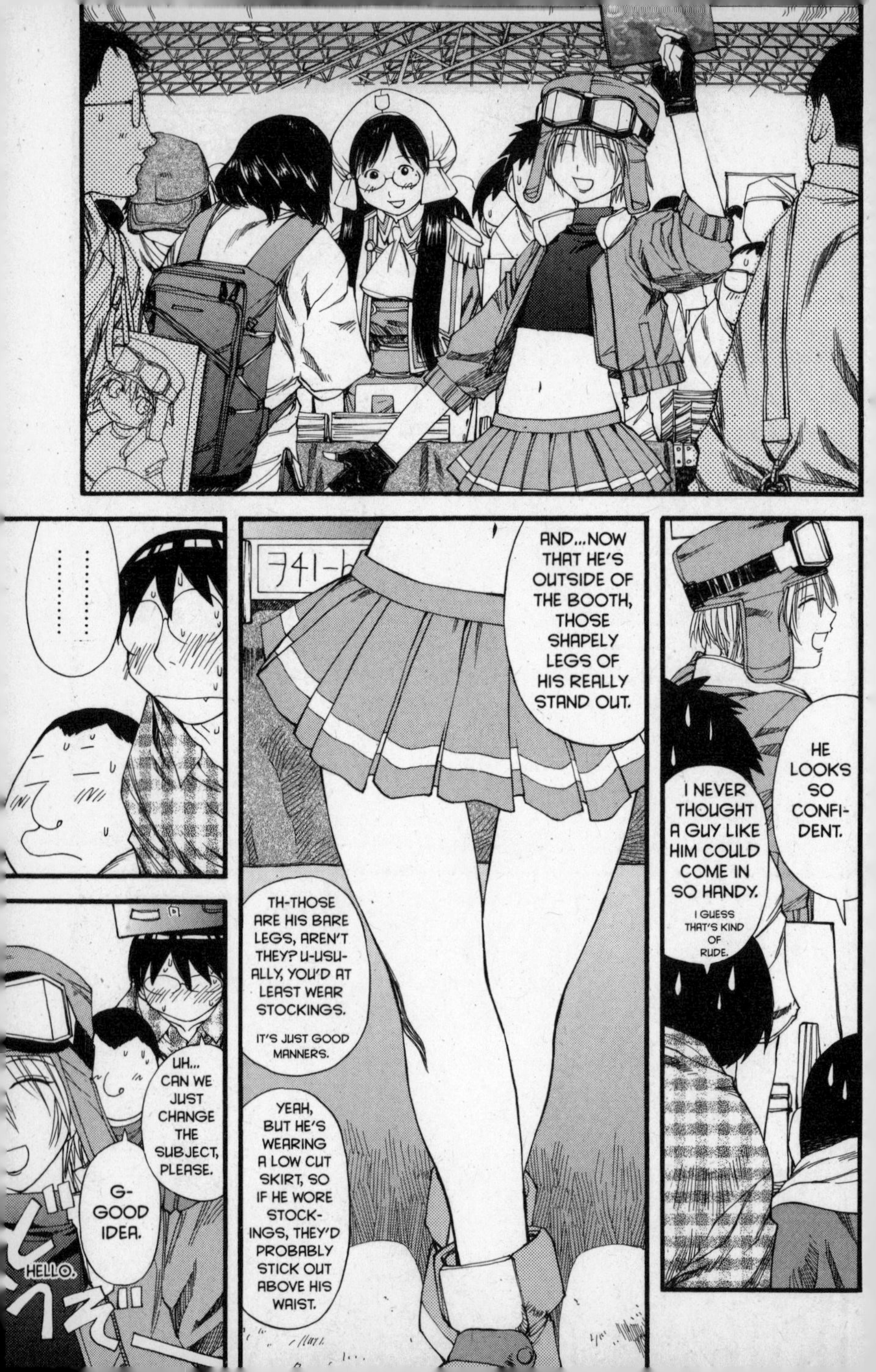
HE LOOKS SO CONFI-DENT.
I NEVER THOUGHT A GUY LIKE HIM COULD COME IN SO HANDY.
I GUESS THAT'S KIND OF RUDE.
AND...NOW THAT HE'S OUTSIDE OF THE BOOTH, THOSE SHAPELY LEGS OF HIS REALLY STAND OUT.
TH-THOSE ARE HIS BARE LEGS, AREN'T THEY? U-USU-ALLY, YOU'D AT LEAST WEAR STOCKINGS.
IT'S JUST GOOD MANNERS.
YEAH, BUT HE'S WEARING A LOW CUT SKIRT, SO IF HE WORE STOCK-INGS, THEY'D PROBABLY STICK OUT ABOVE HIS WAIST.
......
......
UH... CAN WE JUST CHANGE THE SUBJECT, PLEASE.
G-GOOD IDEA.
HELLO.

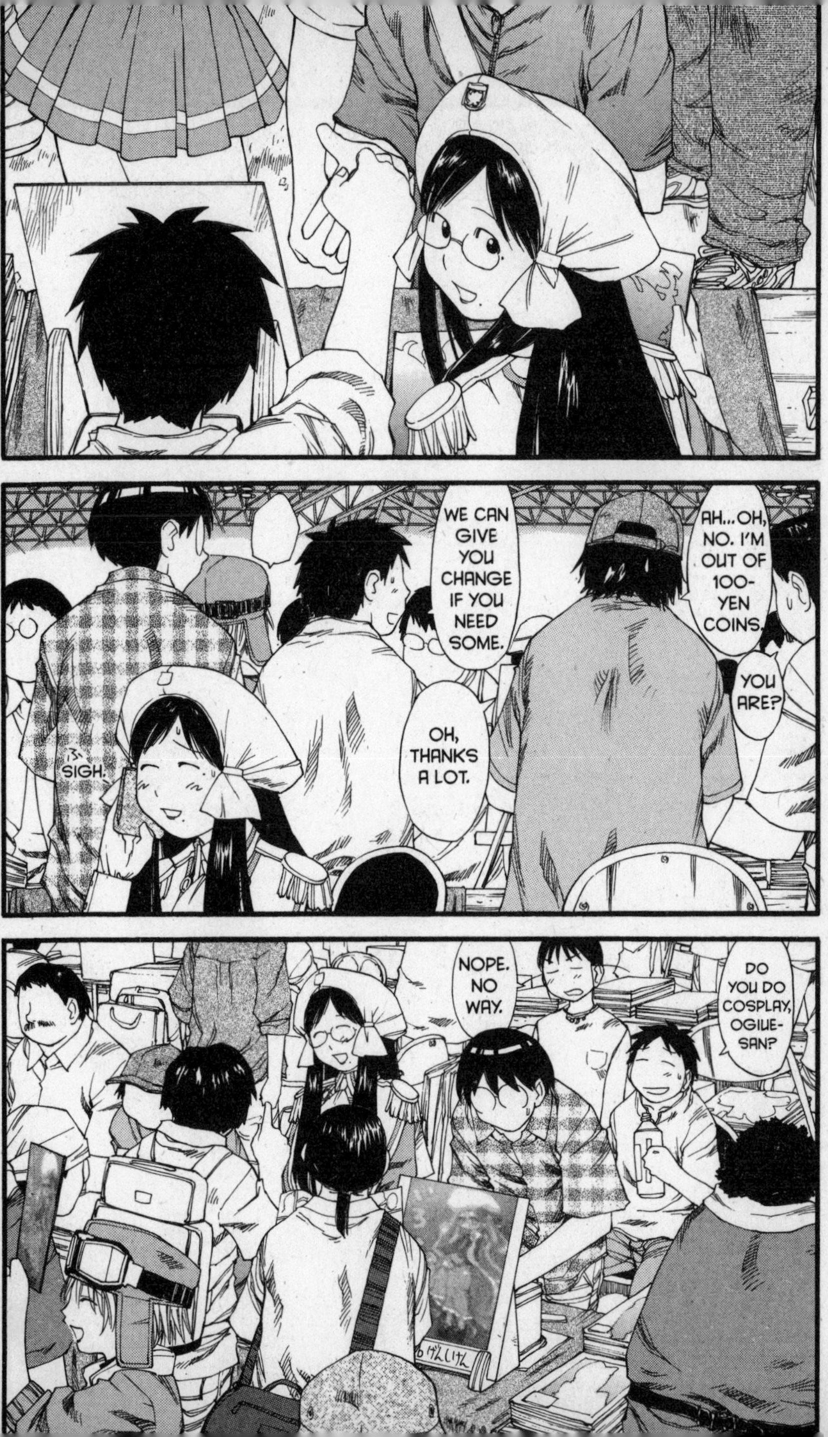
AH...OH, NO. I'M OUT OF 100-YEN COINS.
YOU ARE?
WE CAN GIVE YOU CHANGE IF YOU NEED SOME.
OH, THANKS A LOT.
ふ SIGH.
DO YOU DO COSPLAY, OGIUE-SAN?
NOPE. NO WAY.
げんしけん

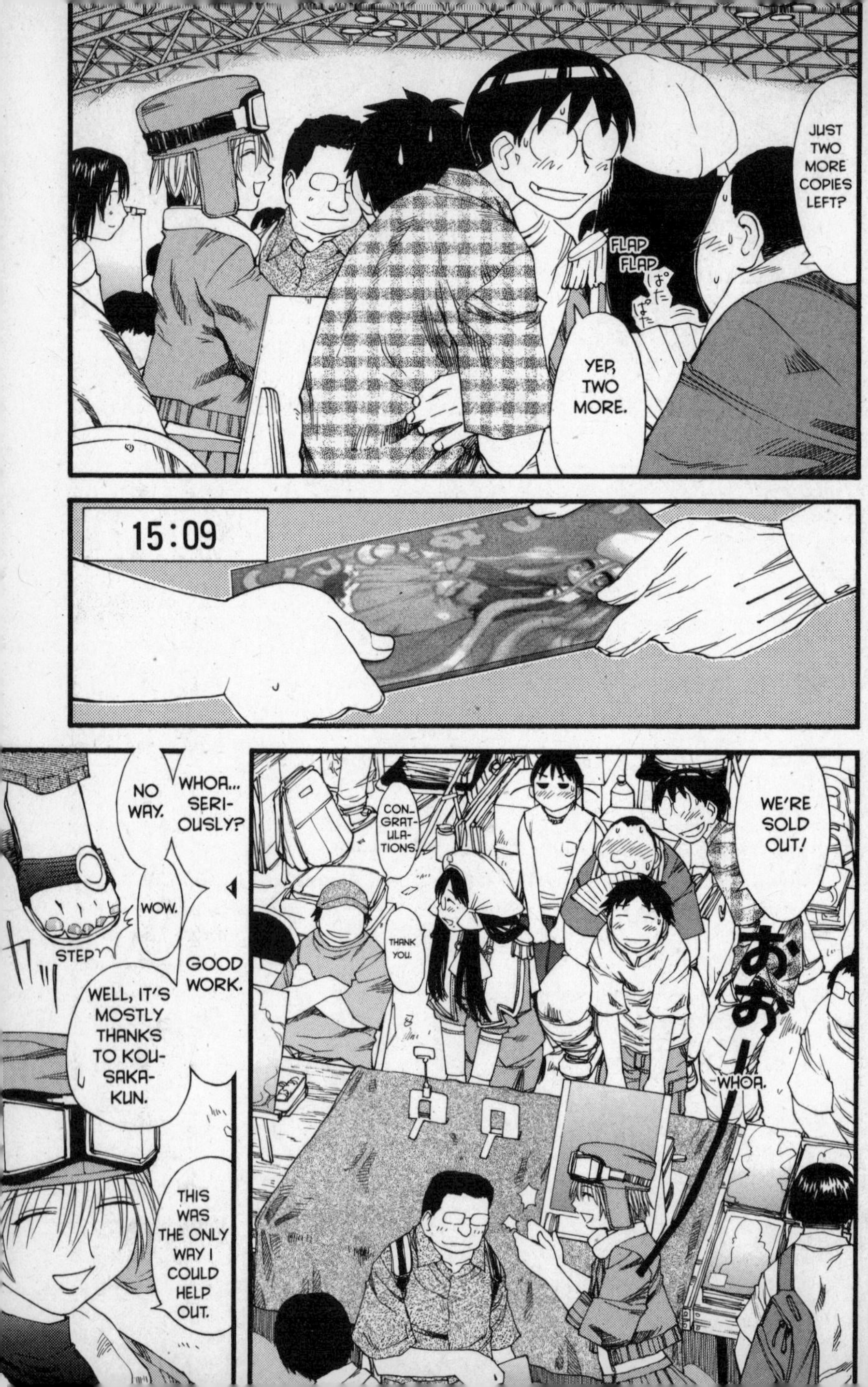
JUST TWO MORE COPIES LEFT?
FLAP FLAP
ぱたぱた
YEP, TWO MORE.
15:09
WE'RE SOLD OUT!
おおー
-WHOA.
CONGRATULATIONS.
THANK YOU.
WHOA... SERIOUSLY?
NO WAY.
WOW.
GOOD WORK.
STEP
WELL, IT'S MOSTLY THANKS TO KOUSAKA-KUN.
THIS WAS THE ONLY WAY I COULD HELP OUT.

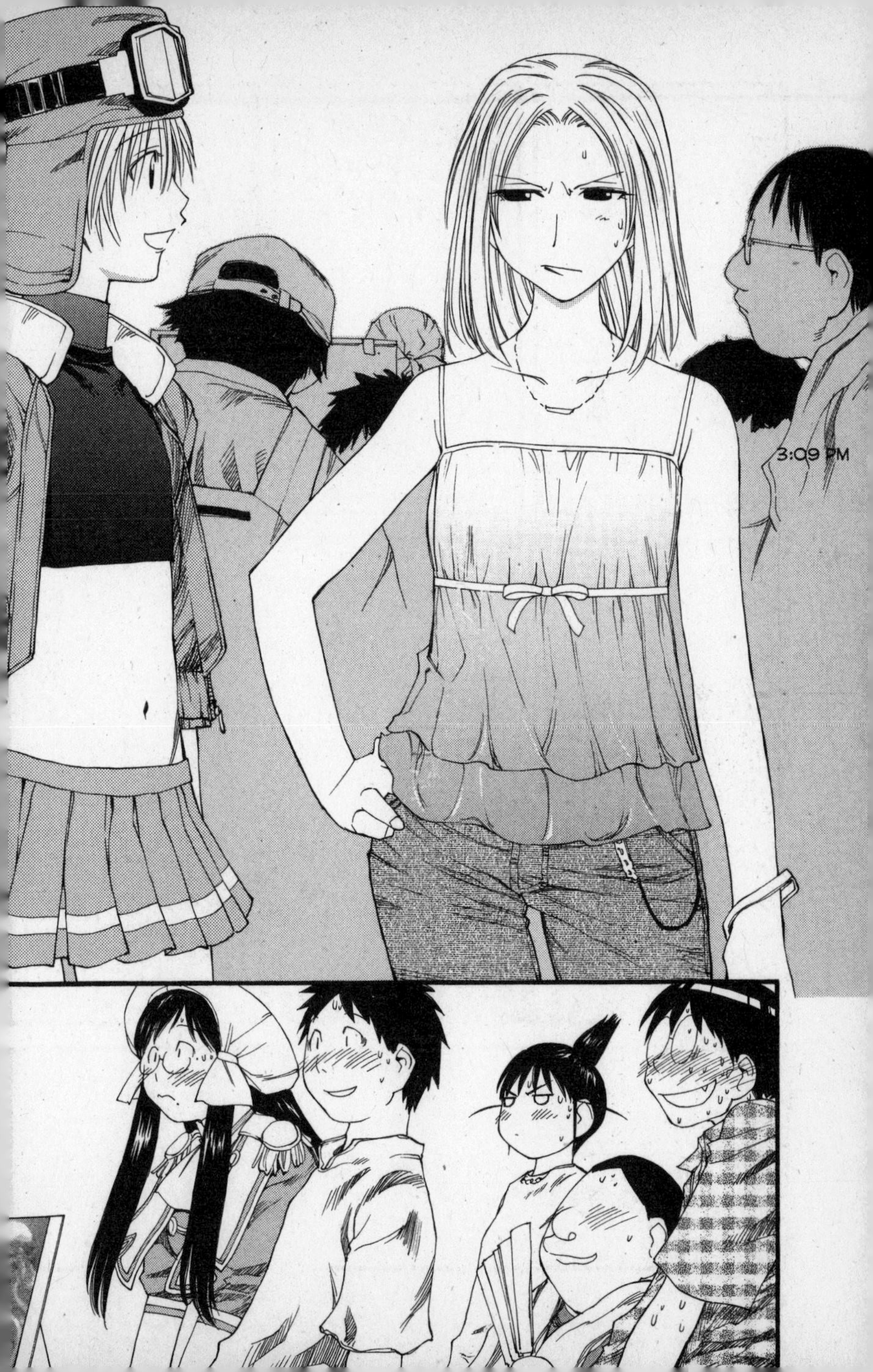
3:09 PM

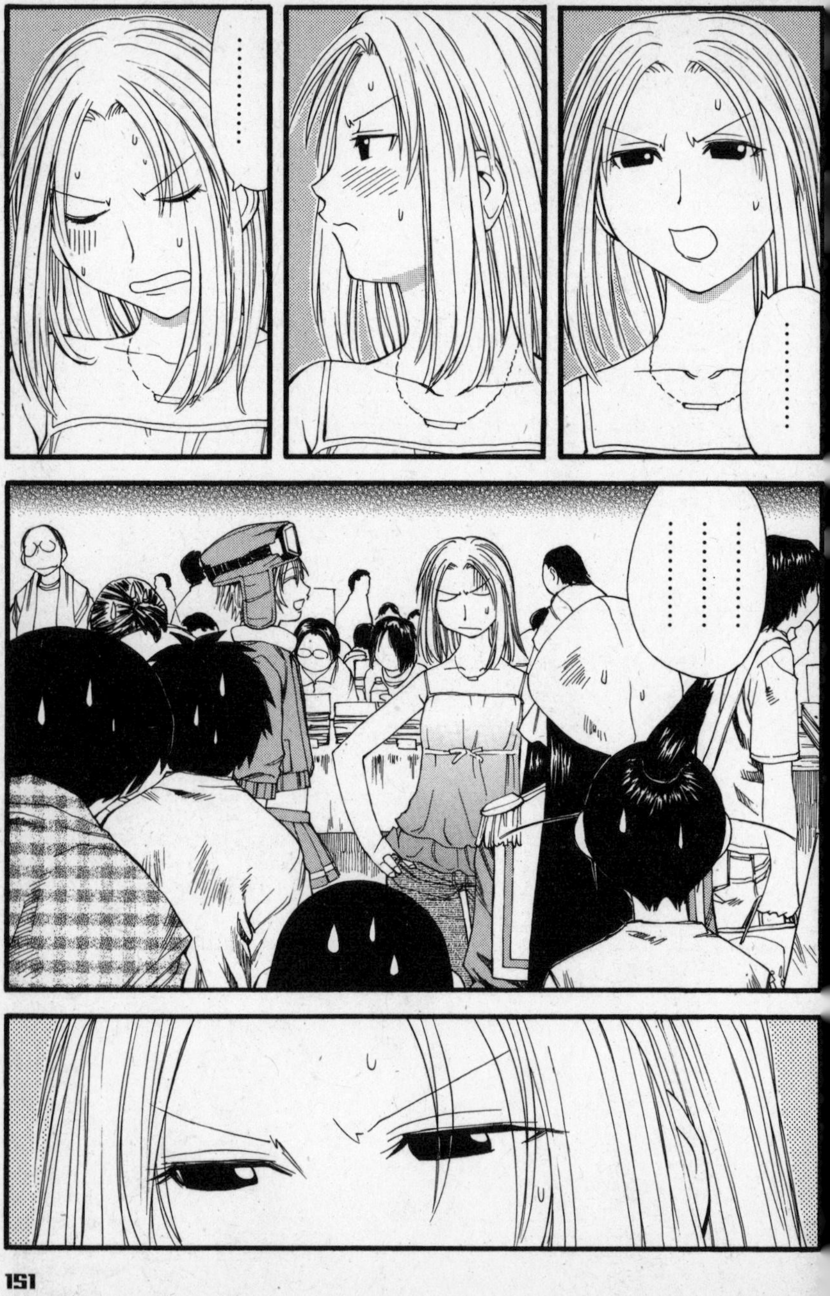
……
……
………

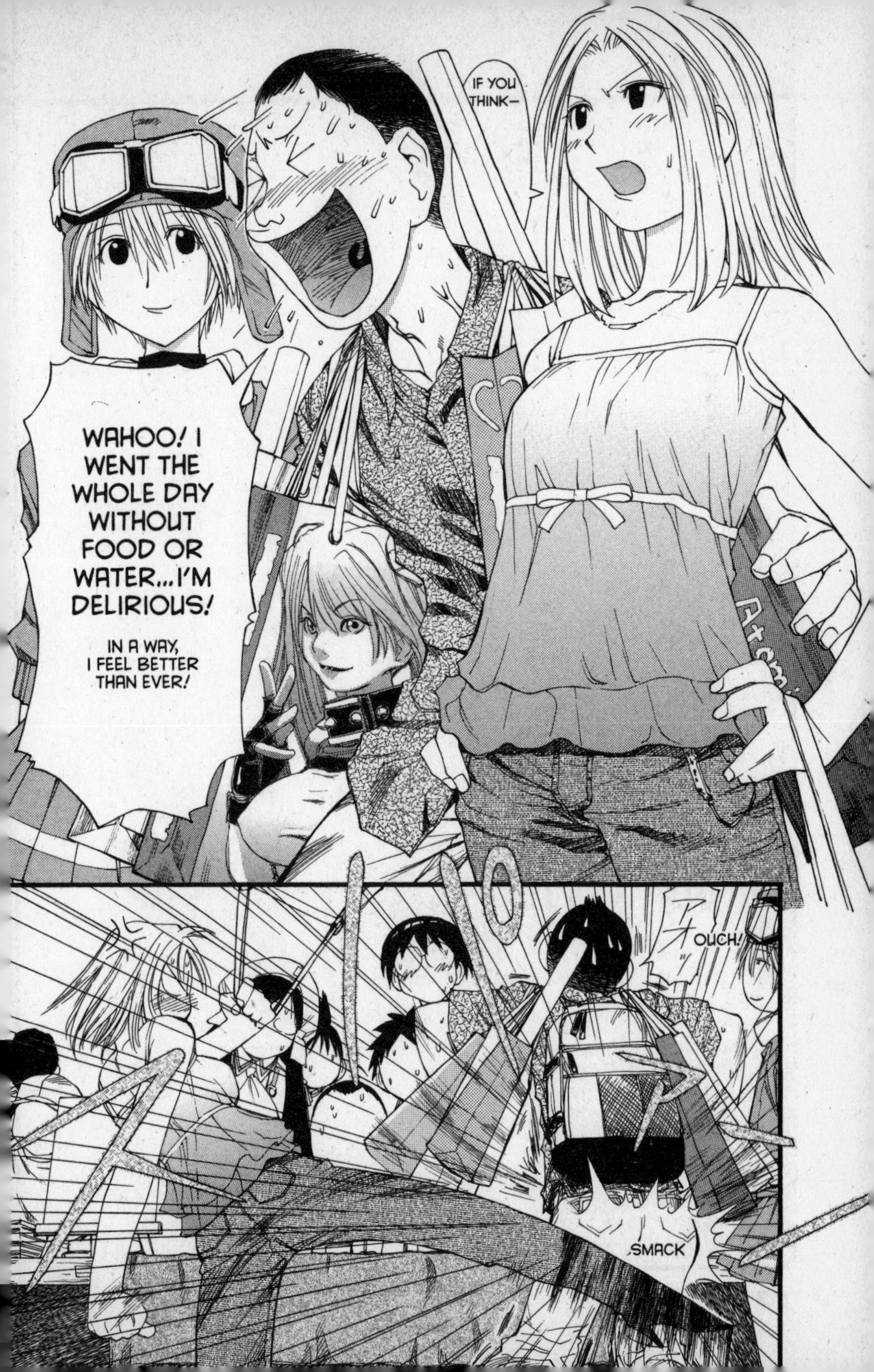
IF YOU THINK—
WAHOO! I WENT THE WHOLE DAY WITHOUT FOOD OR WATER...I'M DELIRIOUS!
IN A WAY, I FEEL BETTER THAN EVER!
OUCH!
SMACK

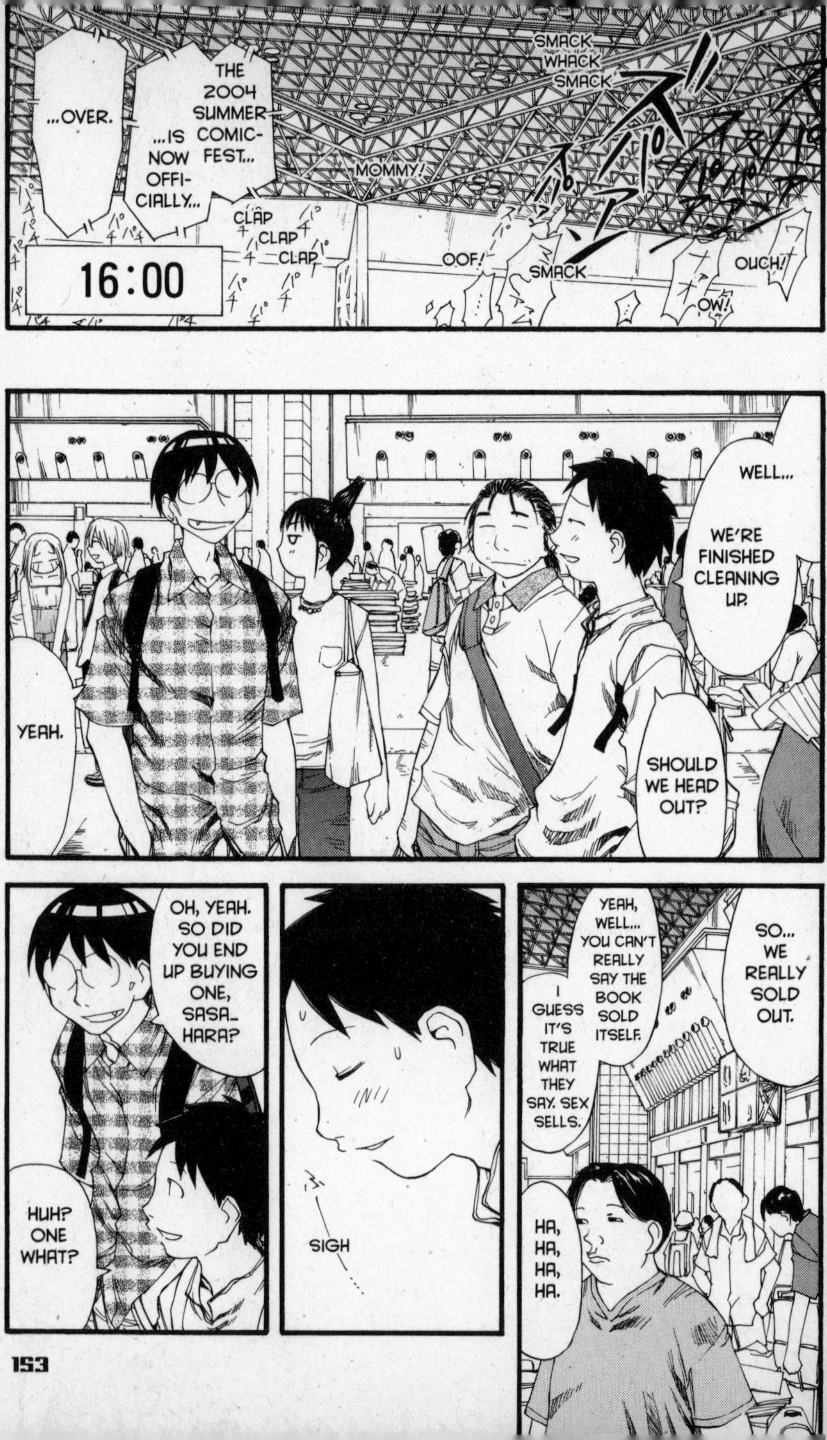
16:00
OUCH!
OW!
SMACK
OOF!
SMACK WHACK SMACK
MOMMY!
CLAP CLAP CLAP
THE 2004 SUMMER COMIC-FEST...
...IS NOW OFFICIALLY...
...OVER.
WELL... WE'RE FINISHED CLEANING UP.
SHOULD WE HEAD OUT?
YEAH.
SO... WE REALLY SOLD OUT.
YEAH, WELL... YOU CAN'T REALLY SAY THE BOOK SOLD ITSELF.
I GUESS IT'S TRUE WHAT THEY SAY. SEX SELLS.
HA, HA, HA, HA.
SIGH
OH, YEAH. SO DID YOU END UP BUYING ONE, SASAHARA?
HUH? ONE WHAT?

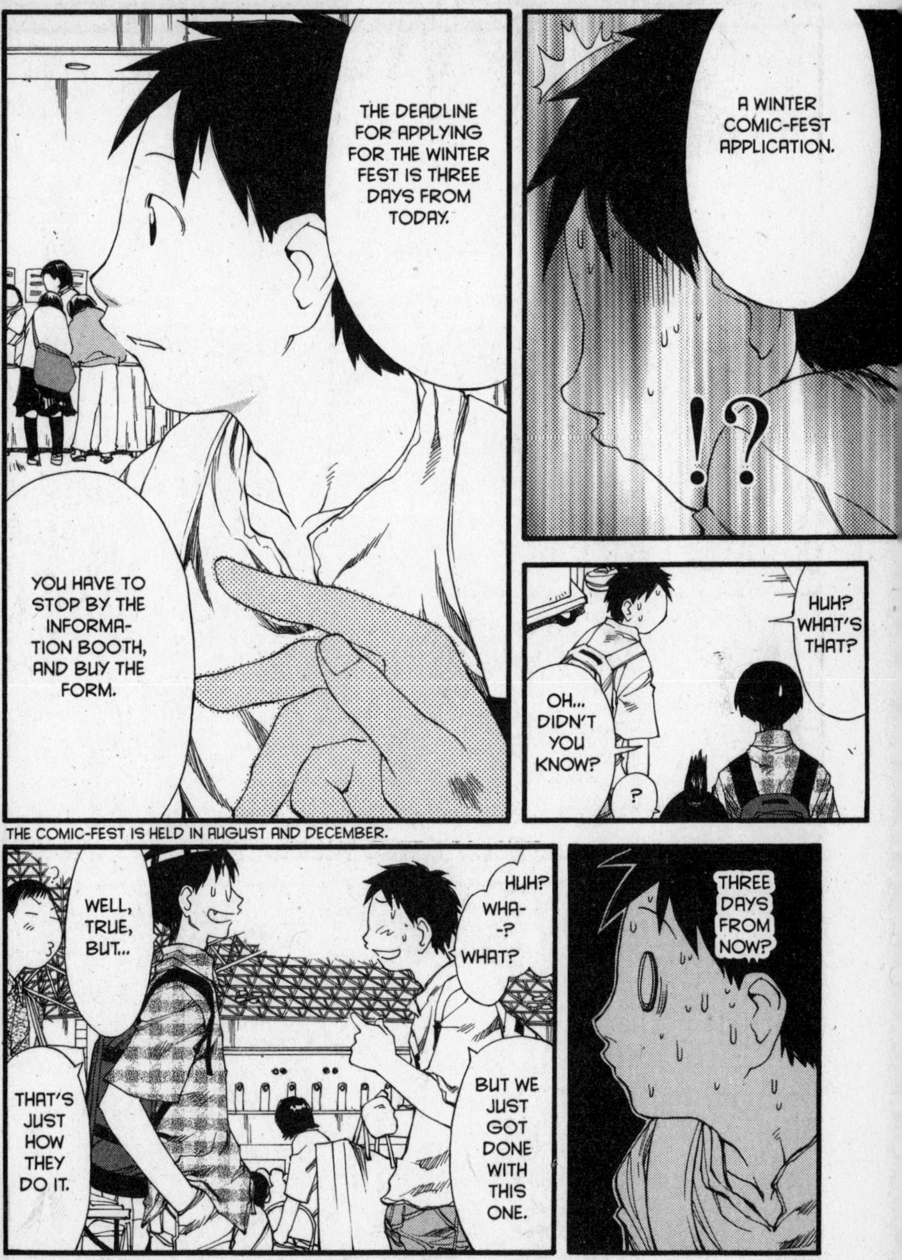
A WINTER COMIC-FEST APPLICATION.
!?
HUH? WHAT'S THAT?
OH... DIDN'T YOU KNOW?
?
THE DEADLINE FOR APPLYING FOR THE WINTER FEST IS THREE DAYS FROM TODAY.
YOU HAVE TO STOP BY THE INFORMA-TION BOOTH, AND BUY THE FORM.
THE COMIC-FEST IS HELD IN AUGUST AND DECEMBER.
THREE DAYS FROM NOW?
HUH? WHA- -? WHAT?
BUT WE JUST GOT DONE WITH THIS ONE.
WELL, TRUE, BUT...
THAT'S JUST HOW THEY DO IT.

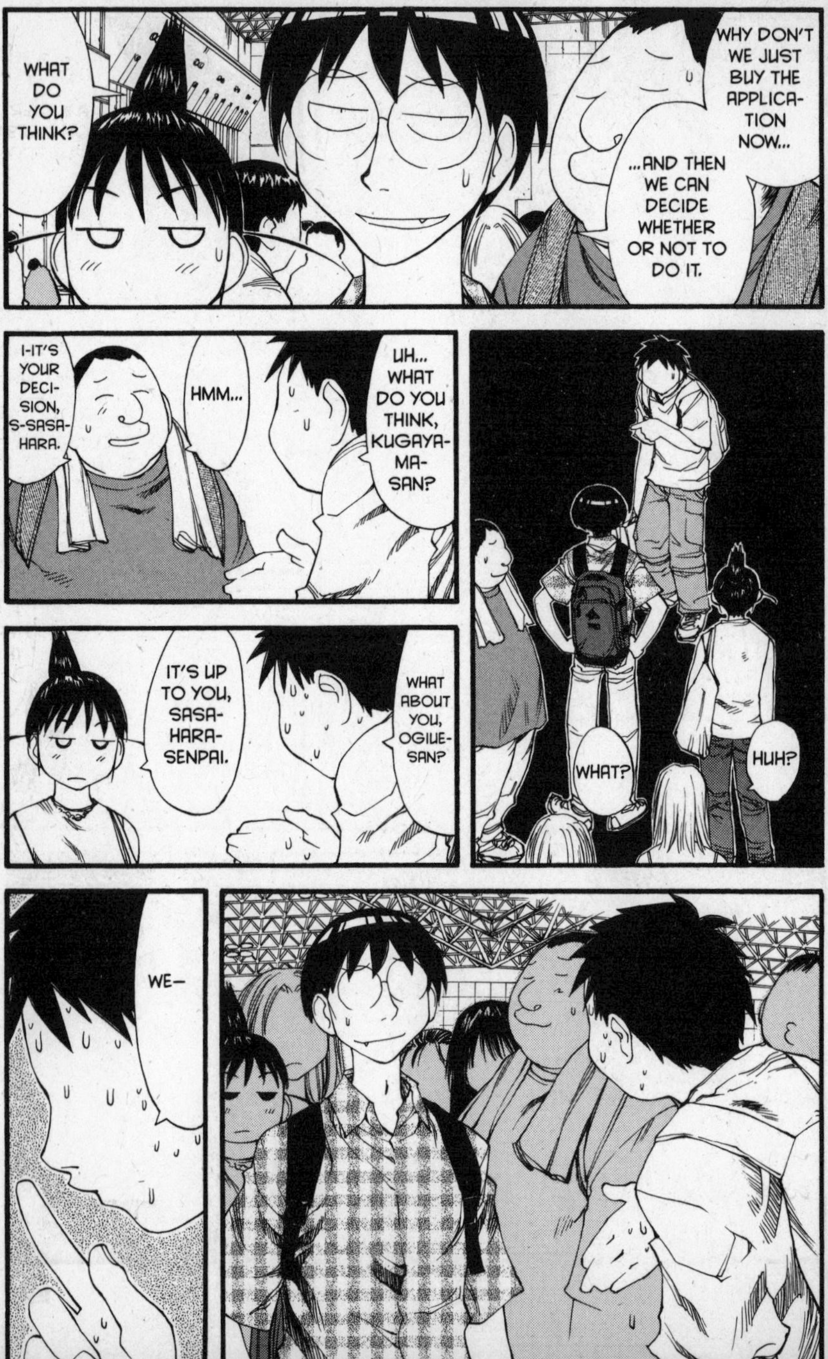
WHY DON'T WE JUST BUY THE APPLICATION NOW...
...AND THEN WE CAN DECIDE WHETHER OR NOT TO DO IT.
WHAT DO YOU THINK?
HUH?
WHAT?
UH... WHAT DO YOU THINK, KUGAYAMA-SAN?
HMM...
I-IT'S YOUR DECISION, S-SASAHARA.
WHAT ABOUT YOU, OGIUE-SAN?
IT'S UP TO YOU, SASAHARA-SENPAI.
WE—

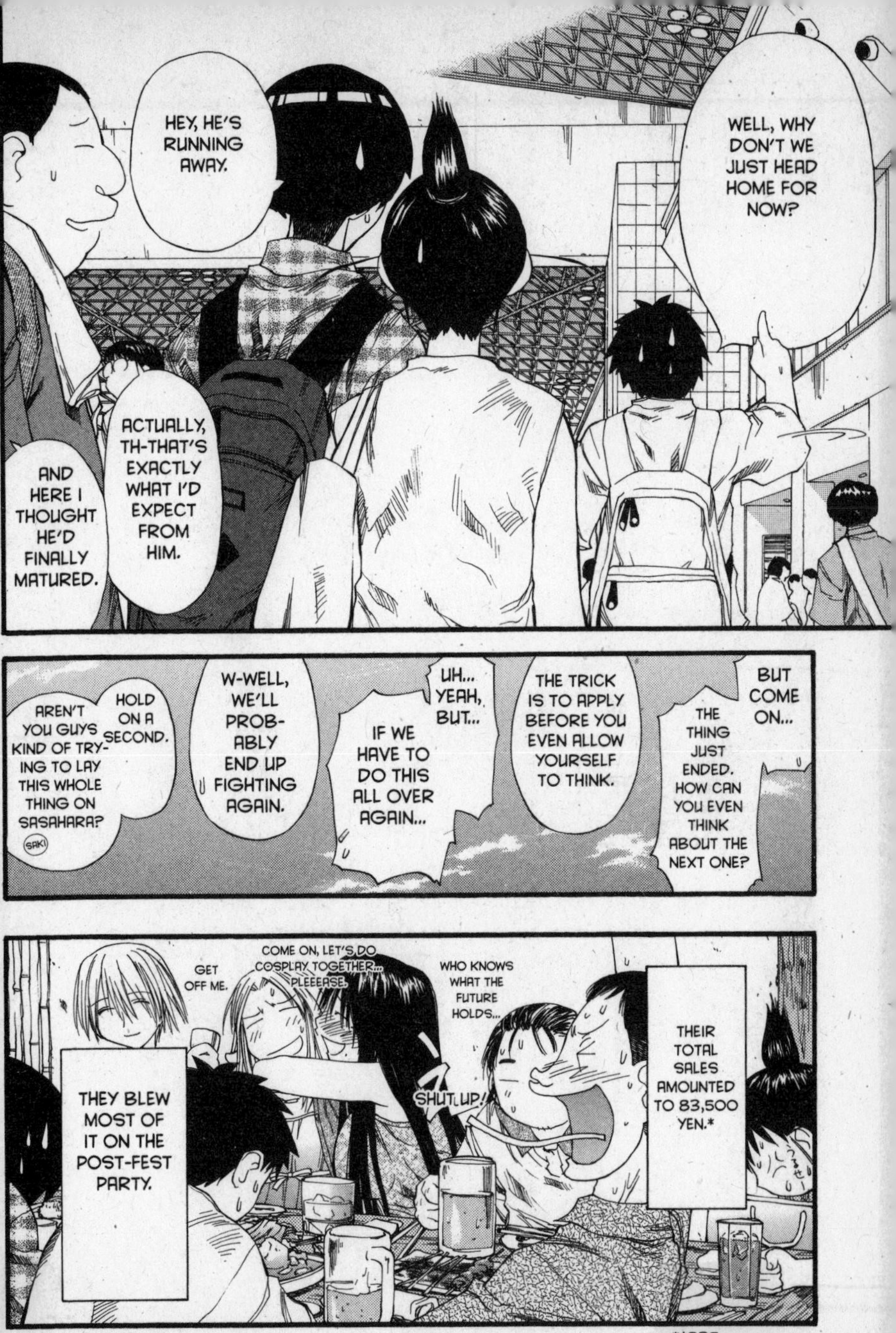
WELL, WHY DON'T WE JUST HEAD HOME FOR NOW?
HEY, HE'S RUNNING AWAY.
ACTUALLY, TH-THAT'S EXACTLY WHAT I'D EXPECT FROM HIM.
AND HERE I THOUGHT HE'D FINALLY MATURED.
BUT COME ON...
THE THING JUST ENDED. HOW CAN YOU EVEN THINK ABOUT THE NEXT ONE?
THE TRICK IS TO APPLY BEFORE YOU EVEN ALLOW YOURSELF TO THINK.
UH... YEAH, BUT...
IF WE HAVE TO DO THIS ALL OVER AGAIN...
W-WELL, WE'LL PROBABLY END UP FIGHTING AGAIN.
HOLD ON A SECOND.
AREN'T YOU GUYS KIND OF TRYING TO LAY THIS WHOLE THING ON SASAHARA?
SAKI
THEIR TOTAL SALES AMOUNTED TO 83,500 YEN.*
WHO KNOWS WHAT THE FUTURE HOLDS...
SHUT UP!
COME ON, LET'S DO COSPLAY TOGETHER... PLEEEASE.
GET OFF ME.
THEY BLEW MOST OF IT ON THE POST-FEST PARTY.

END OF CHAPTER 30

*$835

BY YOKO KANNAZUKI

THEY'RE ATTACHED! THEY'RE ATTACHED! [YOKO]

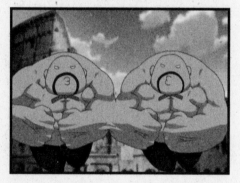

COME ON, ARE YOU JUST TOO DAMN LAZY TO WRITE SOMETHING? [LAUGHS] THERE ARE TONS OF HERNANDEZ SCENES THAT ARE WAY BETTER THAN THIS ONE, LIKE EPISODE TEN. THERE'S THAT STORY WHERE HERNANDEZ REMINISCES ABOUT HIS PAST...ALTHOUGH IT'S ACTUALLY MORE OF A STORY ABOUT THE VICE PRESIDENT GROWING UP. HUH? BUT MAYBE YOU CHOSE THIS ONE BECAUSE IT HAS HERNANDEZ AND ISHIMATSU. YOU'RE SO PICKY. [PIT VIPER]

ARE YOU TRULY HAPPY?

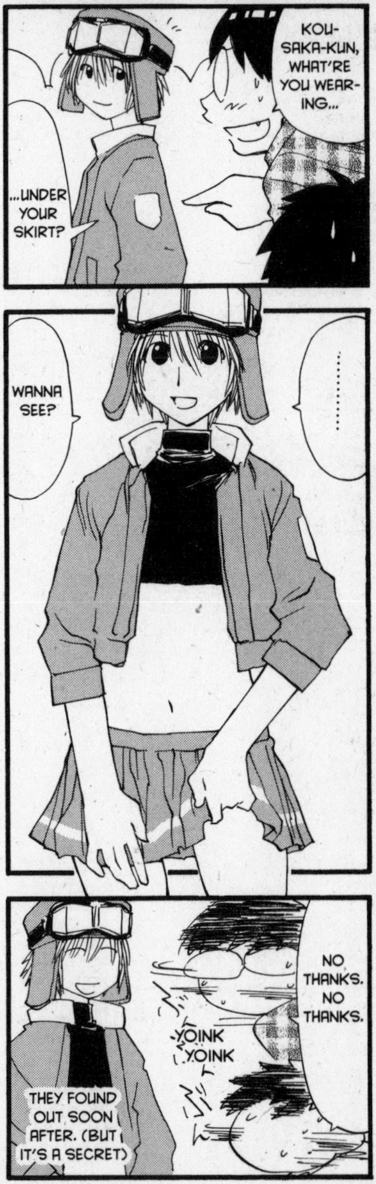
KOU-SAKA-KUN, WHAT'RE YOU WEARING...
...UNDER YOUR SKIRT?
......
WANNA SEE?
NO THANKS. NO THANKS.
YOINK YOINK
THEY FOUND OUT SOON AFTER. (BUT IT'S A SECRET)

OHNO-SAN CAN HOLD HER LIQUOR

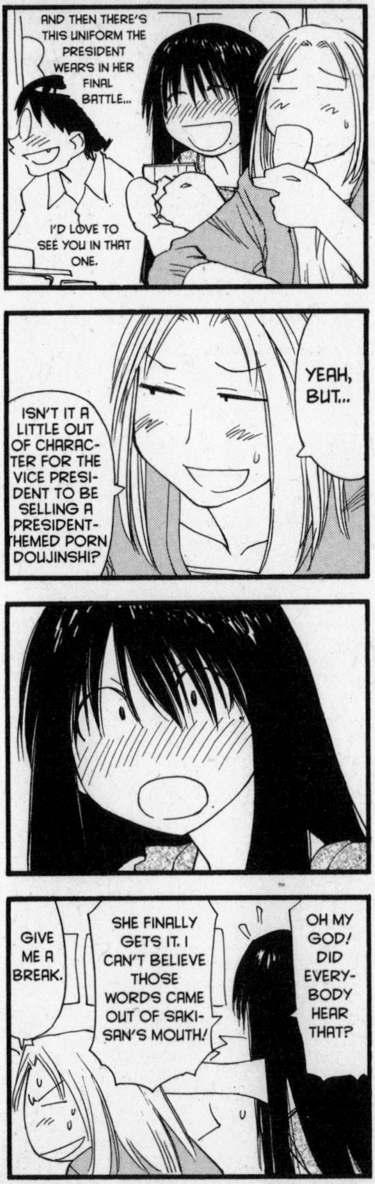
AND THEN THERE'S THIS UNIFORM THE PRESIDENT WEARS IN HER FINAL BATTLE...
I'D LOVE TO SEE YOU IN THAT ONE.
YEAH, BUT...
ISN'T IT A LITTLE OUT OF CHARACTER FOR THE VICE PRESIDENT TO BE SELLING A PRESIDENT-THEMED PORN DOUJINSHI?
OH MY GOD! DID EVERYBODY HEAR THAT?
SHE FINALLY GETS IT. I CAN'T BELIEVE THOSE WORDS CAME OUT OF SAKI-SAN'S MOUTH!
GIVE ME A BREAK.

PLEASE TURN THE BOOK ON ITS SIDE.

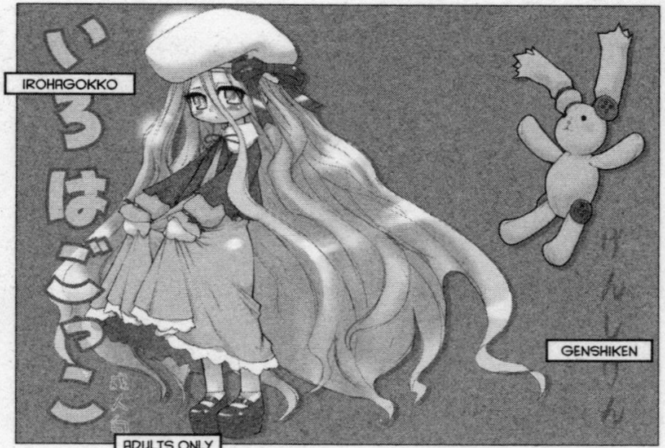
いろはごっこ
IROHAGOKKO
ADULTS ONLY
GENSHIKEN

SPECIAL BONUS

IROHAGOKKO

*DUE TO THE GRAPHIC NATURE OF THIS BOOK, WE WERE FORCED TO BLACK OUT LARGE PORTIONS OF THESE BONUS PAGES. WE WOULD LIKE TO APOLOGIZE TO THE BOOK'S CREATORS. PLEASE FORGIVE US. WE HOPE THE READERS WILL NOT FIND THE FOLLOWING MATERIAL OFFENSIVE. [EDITORIAL DEPARTMENT]

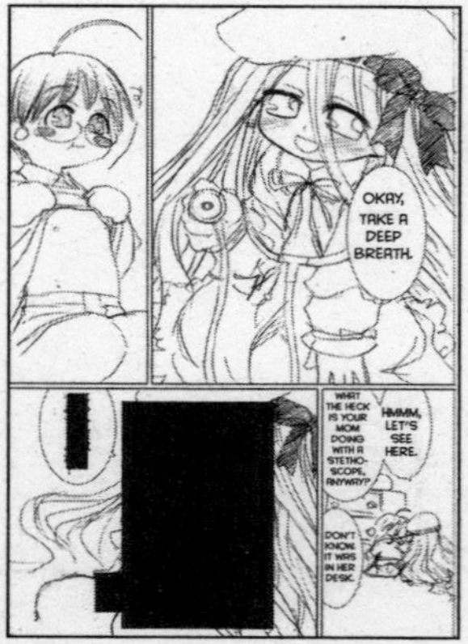
OKAY, TAKE A DEEP BREATH.
HMMM, LET'S SEE HERE.
WHAT THE HECK IS YOUR MOM DOING WITH A STETHOSCOPE, ANYWAY?
DON'T KNOW. IT WAS IN HER DESK.

1

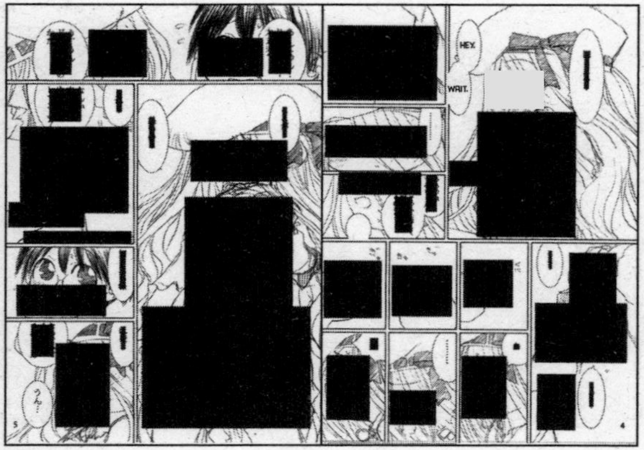
HEY.
WAIT.

2

3

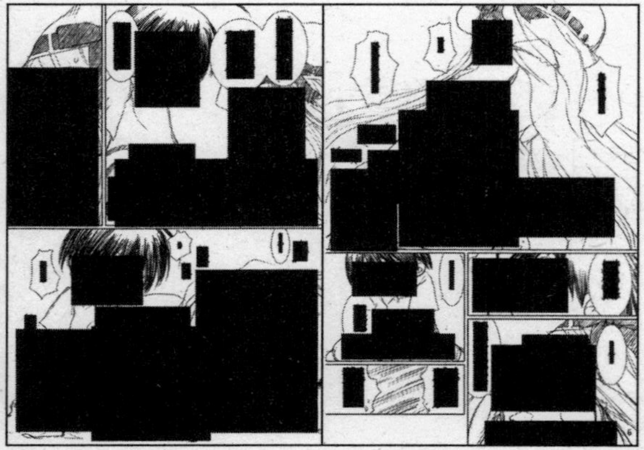

4

5

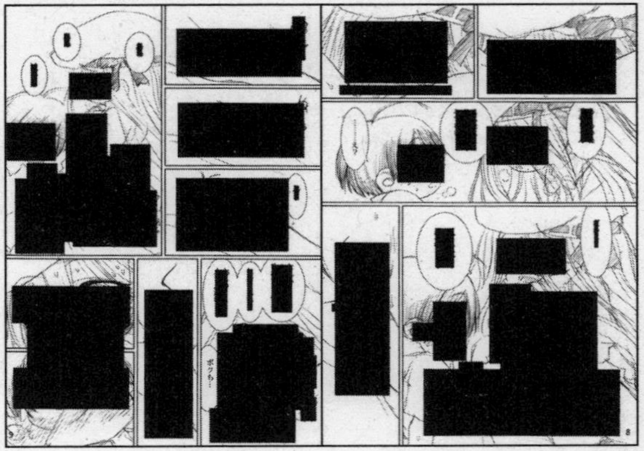
ボクも…
[redacted]

6

7

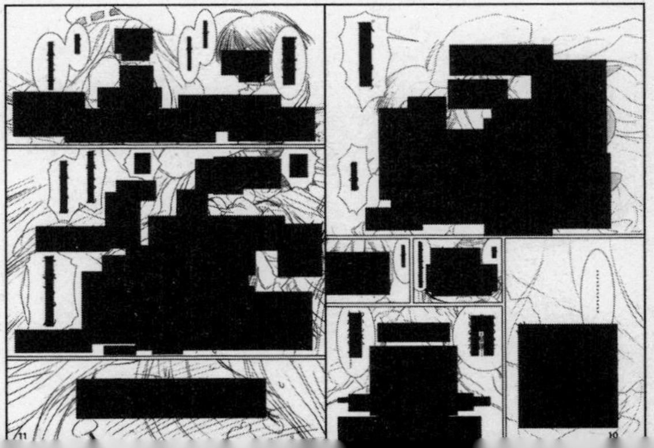
[redacted]

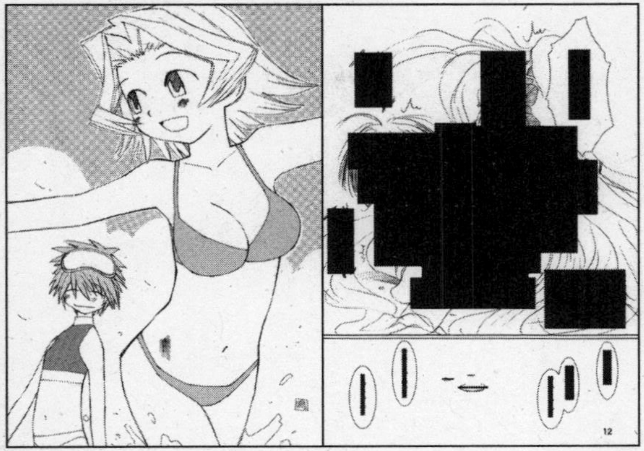
[redacted]

10

11

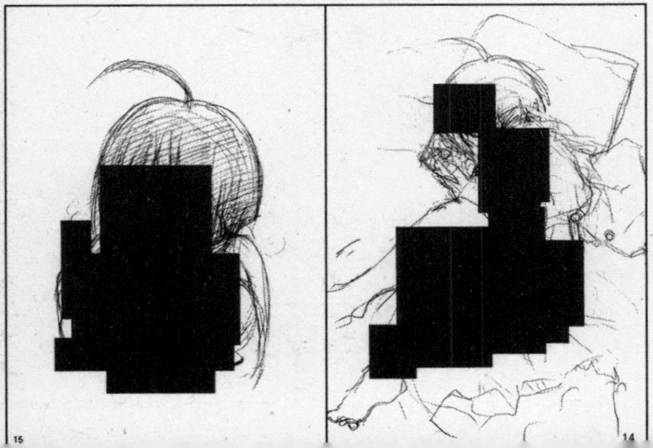
[redacted]

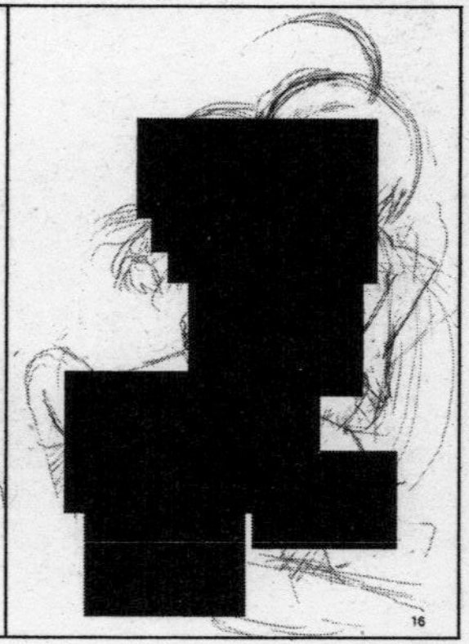

14

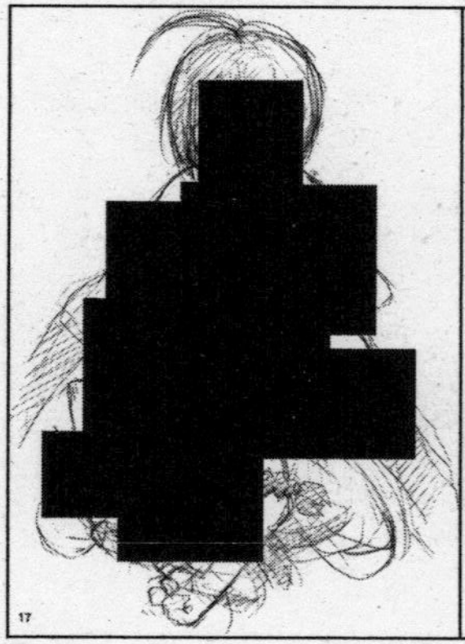

15

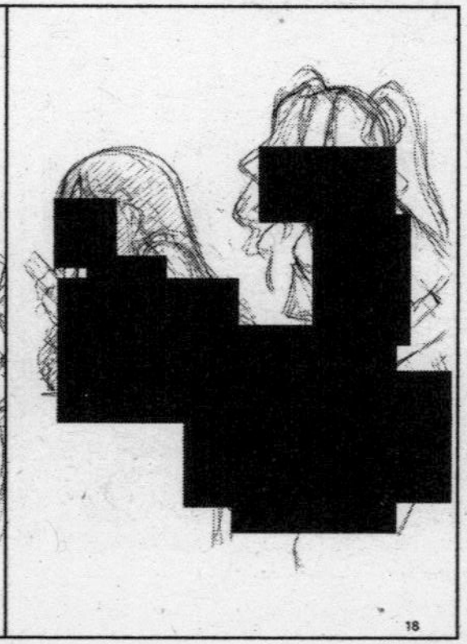

16

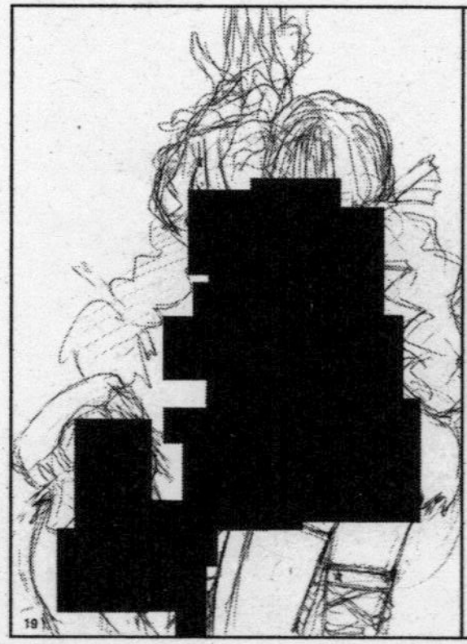

17

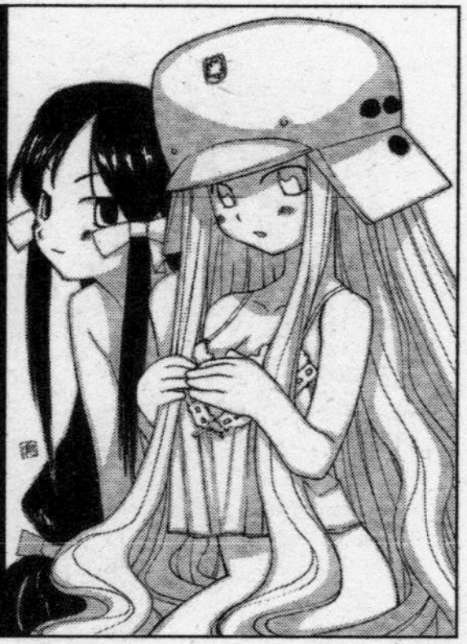

18

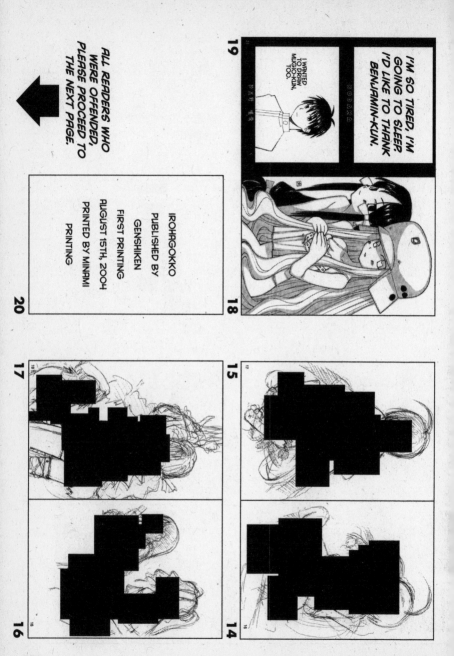

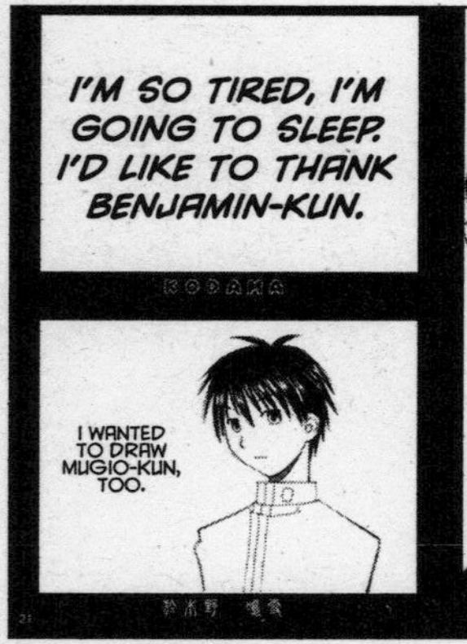
I'M SO TIRED, I'M GOING TO SLEEP. I'D LIKE TO THANK BENJAMIN-KUN.
I WANTED TO DRAW MUGIO-KUN, TOO.

19

IROHAGOKKO
PUBLISHED BY
GENSHIKEN
FIRST PRINTING
AUGUST 15TH, 2004
PRINTED BY MINAMI
PRINTING

20

ALL READERS WHO WERE OFFENDED, PLEASE PROCEED TO THE NEXT PAGE.

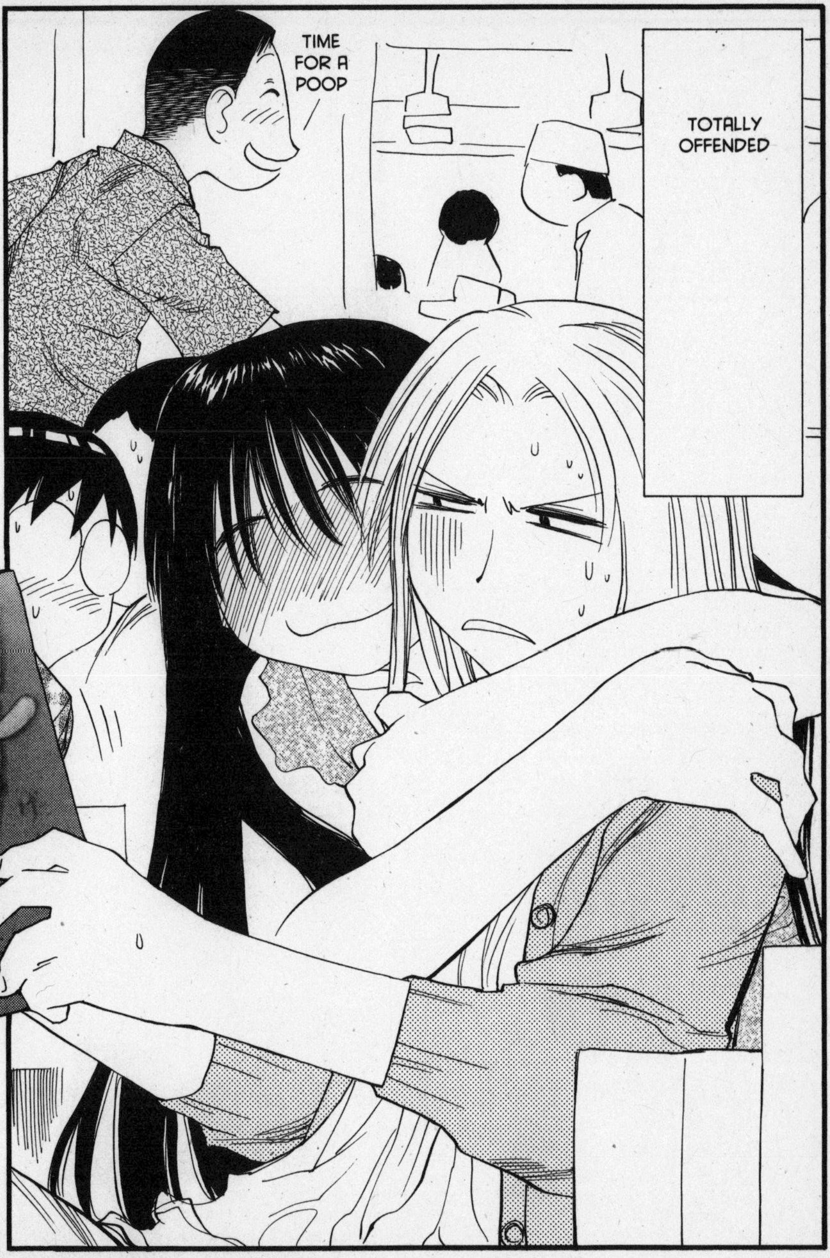
TOTALLY OFFENDED
TIME FOR A POOP

END OF GENSHIKEN BOOK 5

About the Author

Kio Shimoku was born in 1974.
In 1994 his debut work, *Ten No Ryoiki*, received
second place in the "Afternoon Shiki Prize"
contest. Other past works include *Kageriybikii*,
Yonensei, and *Gonensei*, all of which
appeared in *Afternoon* magazine.
He has been working on Genshiken
since 2002.

Translation Notes

Japanese is a tricky language for most Westerners, and translation is often more art than science. For your edification and reading pleasure, here are notes on some of the places where we could have gone in a different direction in our translation of the work, or where a Japanese cultural reference is used.

Yaoi Manga, page 19

Yaoi manga are gay-themed shojo manga that are generally drawn by women for a female audience.

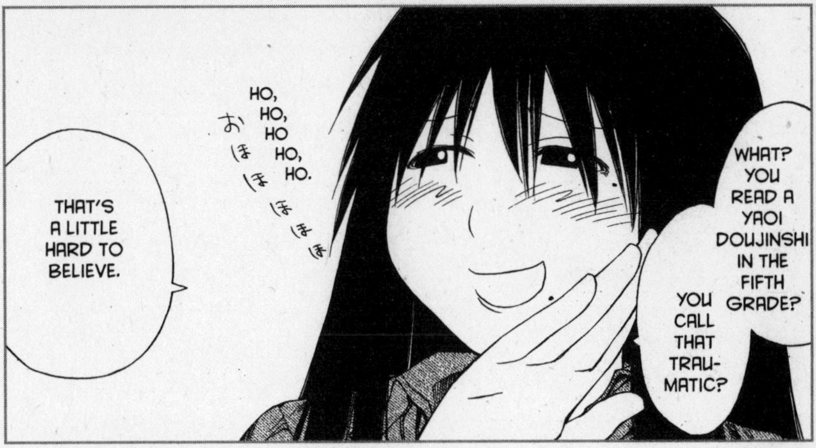
WHAT? YOU READ A YAOI DOUJINSHI IN THE FIFTH GRADE?
YOU CALL THAT TRAU-MATIC?
HO, HO, HO HO, HO.
おほほほほほ
THAT'S A LITTLE HARD TO BELIEVE.

Ogi-chin, page 22

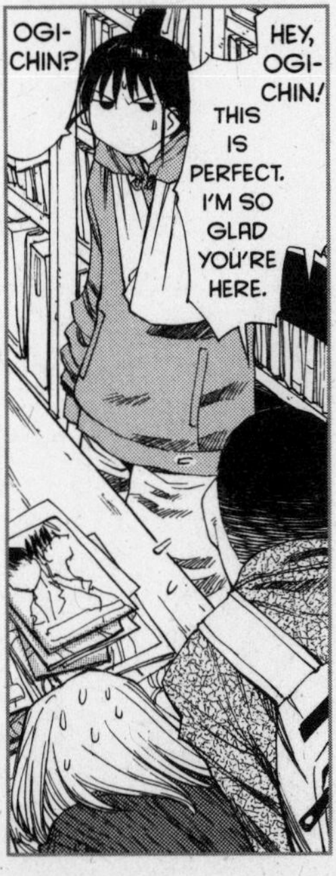
HEY, OGI-CHIN!
THIS IS PERFECT. I'M SO GLAD YOU'RE HERE.
OGI-CHIN?

"Chin" is a nickname-ish variation of the honorific "-chan." It is generally used only by young people.

Scram Dunk!, page 22

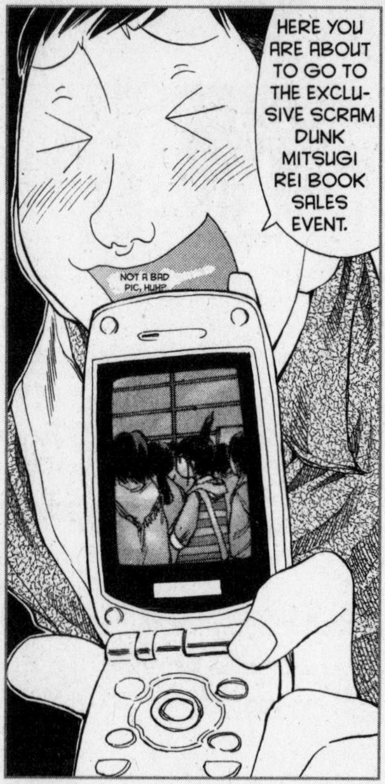
HERE YOU ARE ABOUT TO GO TO THE EXCLUSIVE SCRAM DUNK MITSUGI REI BOOK SALES EVENT.
NOT A BAD PIC, HUH?

A play on the name of the popular basketball manga, *Slam Dunk*.

Tohoku Dialect, page 25

A regional dialect spoken in northern Japan.

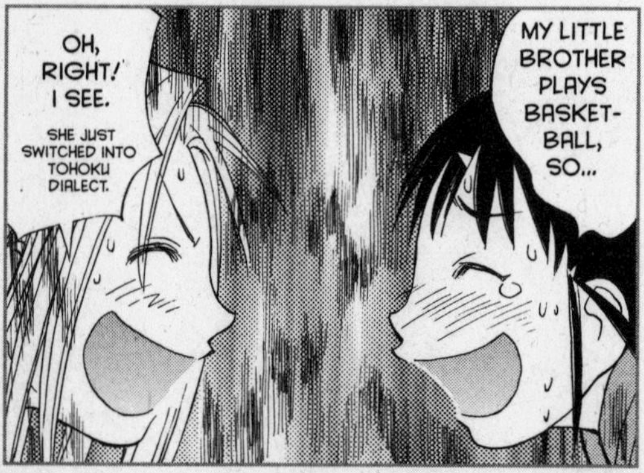
MY LITTLE BROTHER PLAYS BASKETBALL, SO...
OH, RIGHT! I SEE.
SHE JUST SWITCHED INTO TOHOKU DIALECT.

Name That Mag, page 28

*J*mp* is a reference to the weekly manga title, *Shonen Jump.*

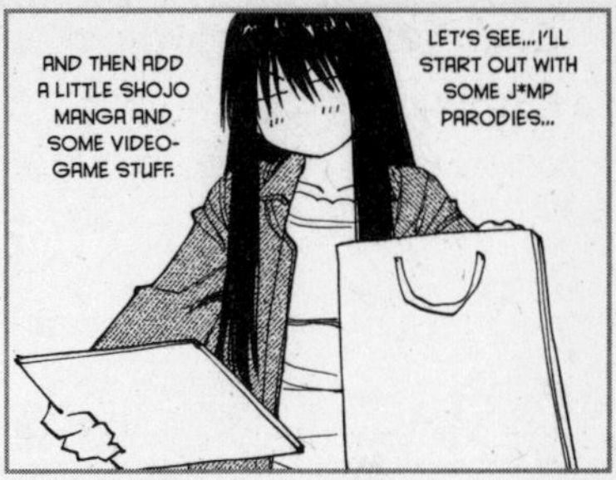
LET'S SEE...I'LL START OUT WITH SOME J*MP PARODIES...
AND THEN ADD A LITTLE SHOJO MANGA AND SOME VIDEO-GAME STUFF.

Uniglow and Jean Mates, page 39

Uniglow is a play on the name Uniqlo, a discount clothing chain. Jean Mates is a play on the name of a clothing store called Jean's Mate.

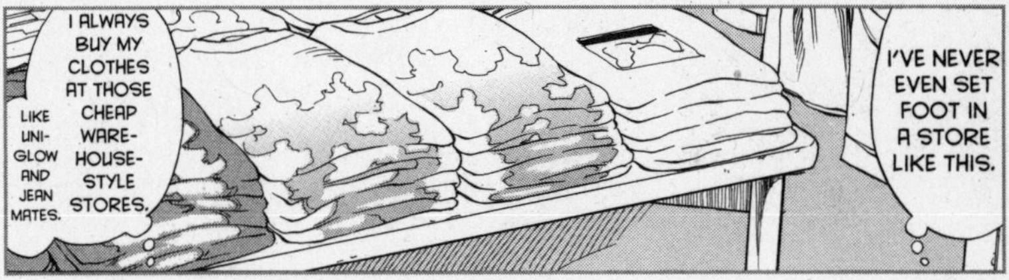
I'VE NEVER EVEN SET FOOT IN A STORE LIKE THIS.
I ALWAYS BUY MY CLOTHES AT THOSE CHEAP WARE-HOUSE-STYLE STORES.
LIKE UNI-GLOW AND JEAN MATES.

Famous Circles, page 117

On-campus groups such as the Genshiken are called "circles" in Japanese. Certain well-known (notorious?) circles get special treatment at the Comic-Fest.

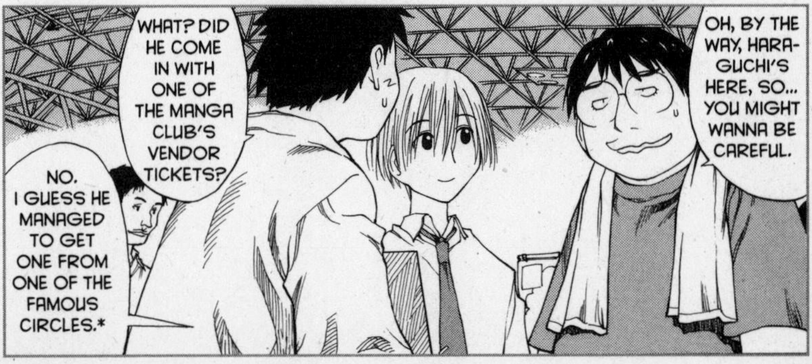
OH, BY THE WAY, HARA-GUCHI'S HERE, SO... YOU MIGHT WANNA BE CAREFUL.
WHAT? DID HE COME IN WITH ONE OF THE MANGA CLUB'S VENDOR TICKETS?
NO. I GUESS HE MANAGED TO GET ONE FROM ONE OF THE FAMOUS CIRCLES.*

Sensei, page 139

Ohno-san uses the honorific "sensei" because Kugayama is now a manga artist. While most Americans think of the term "sensei" as meaning *teacher*, it actually has various usages. "Sensei" is generally used when referring to any type of respected artist. It is also used for doctors.

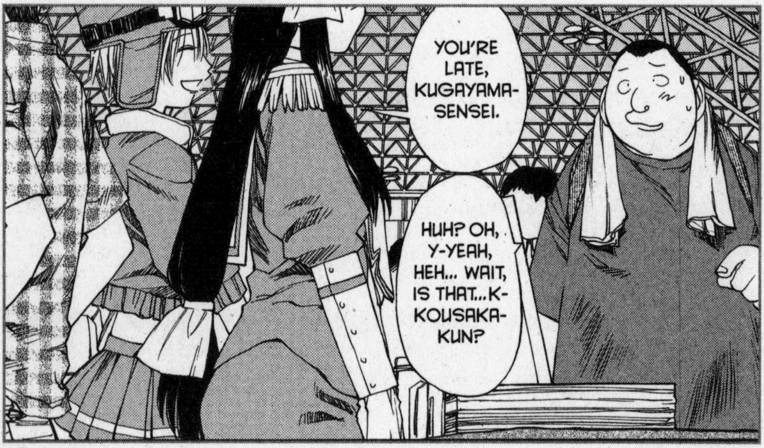
YOU'RE LATE, KUGAYAMA-SENSEI.
HUH? OH, Y-YEAH, HEH... WAIT, IS THAT...K-KOUSAKA-KUN?

A Note from the Editor

The next installment of Genshiken (Volume 6, on sale July 25, 2006) will contain a special attraction—more than twenty pages of Genshiken "doujinshi" created by professional manga artists who are fans of Kio Shimoku's series! It's pretty funny to see how other creators view the characters and situations appearing in this series. You'll enjoy it!

This photo was taken by Genshiken translator David Ury at the Akihabara subway station in Tokyo. It's a Kodansha promotional poster for the series—but it looks just like a subway directional sign. So cool!

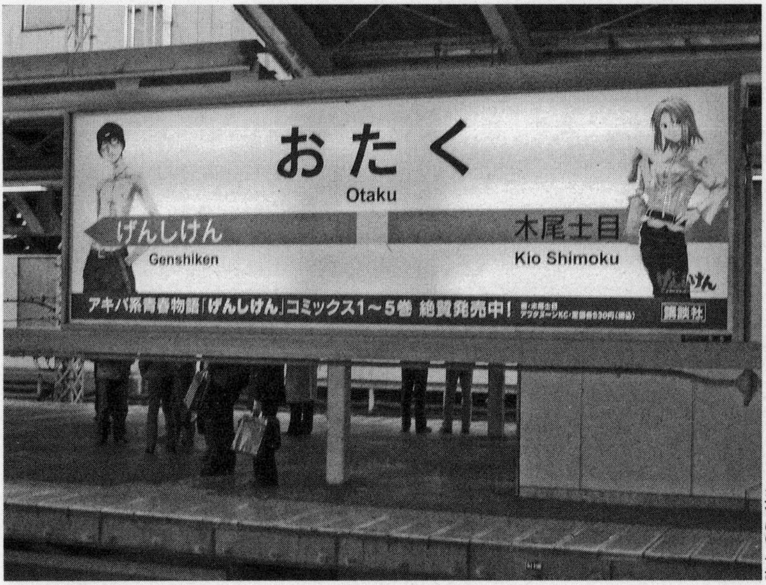
おたく
Otaku
げんしけん
Genshiken
木尾士目
Kio Shimoku
アキバ系青春物語「げんしけん」コミックス1～5巻 絶賛発売中!
講談社

Photo © David Ury

On the two pages that follow, we present the black-and-white art that appeared on the cover of this volume of Genshiken in the Kodansha edition. Most Japanese manga are published with a "dust jacket" of full-color art wrapped around an inside cover that is printed on heavy paper stock. Why don't U.S. publishers do the same, you may ask? Because having two covers is very expensive. That's why you'll see dust jackets confined almost entirely to hardcover books over here.

Until next time,

Your friendly Del Rey editor.

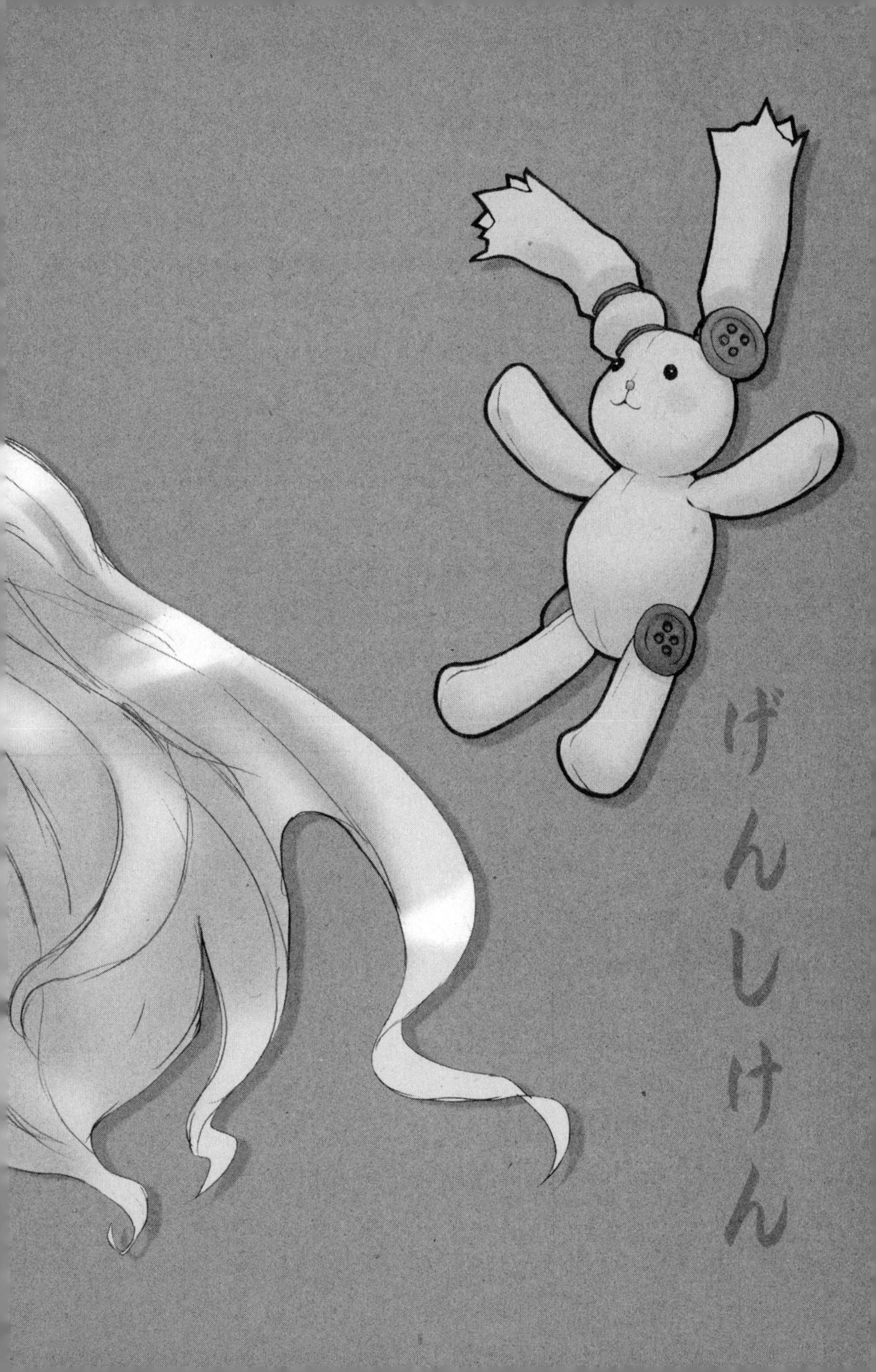
げんしけん

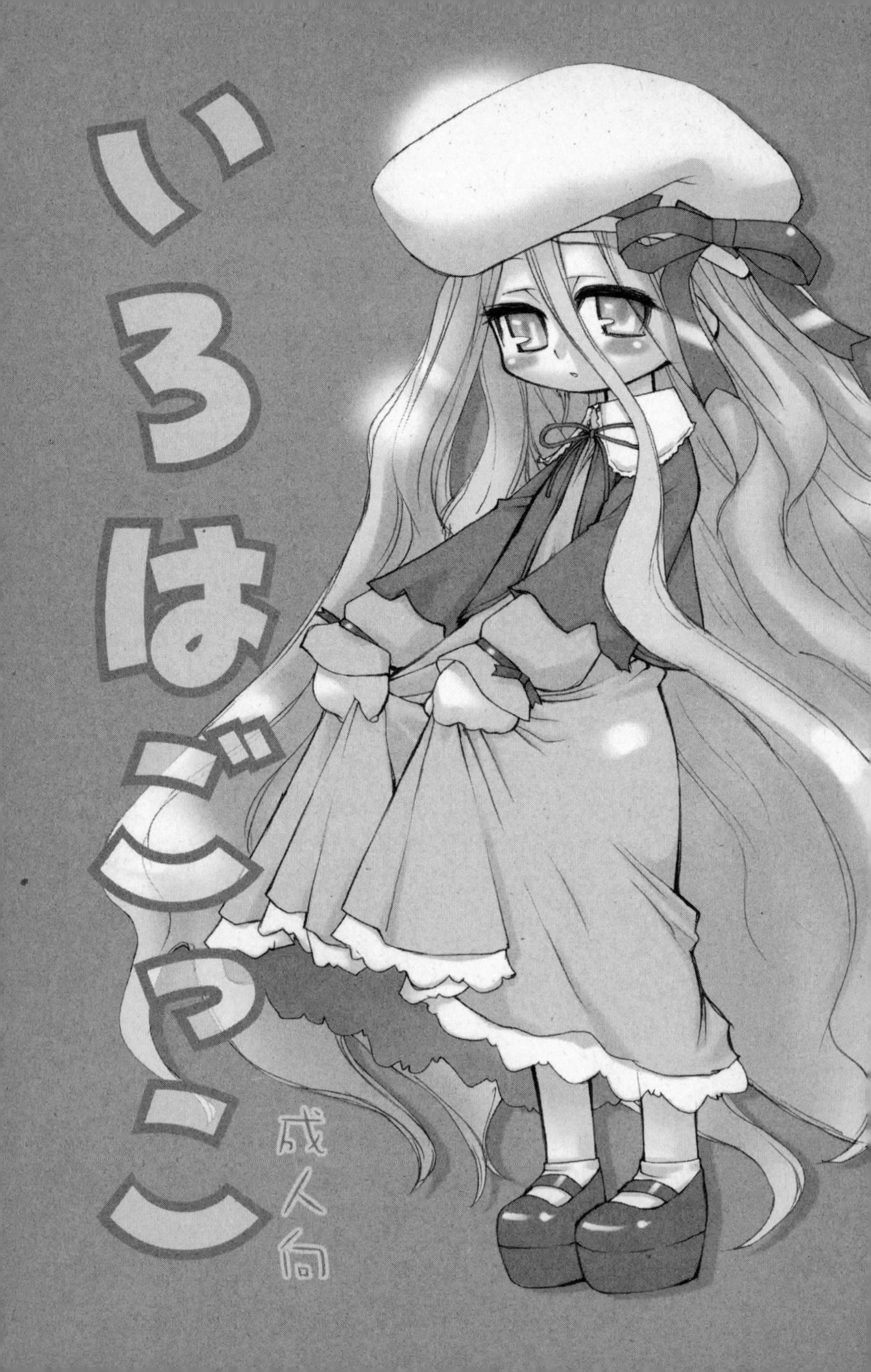
いろはぢっこ
成人向

Preview of Volume 6

We're pleased to present you a preview from Volume 6.
This volume will be available on July 25, 2006.

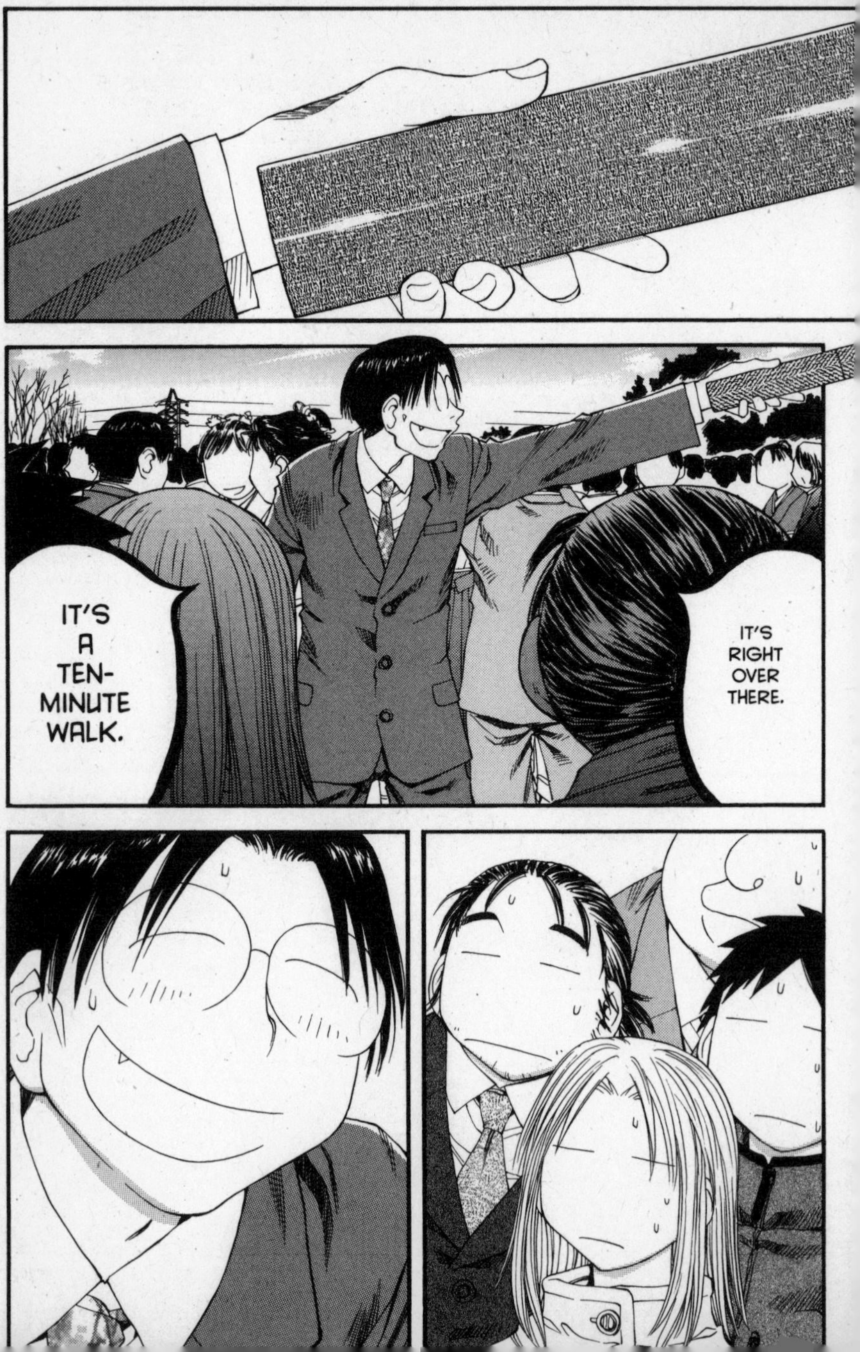
IT'S RIGHT OVER THERE.
IT'S A TEN-MINUTE WALK.

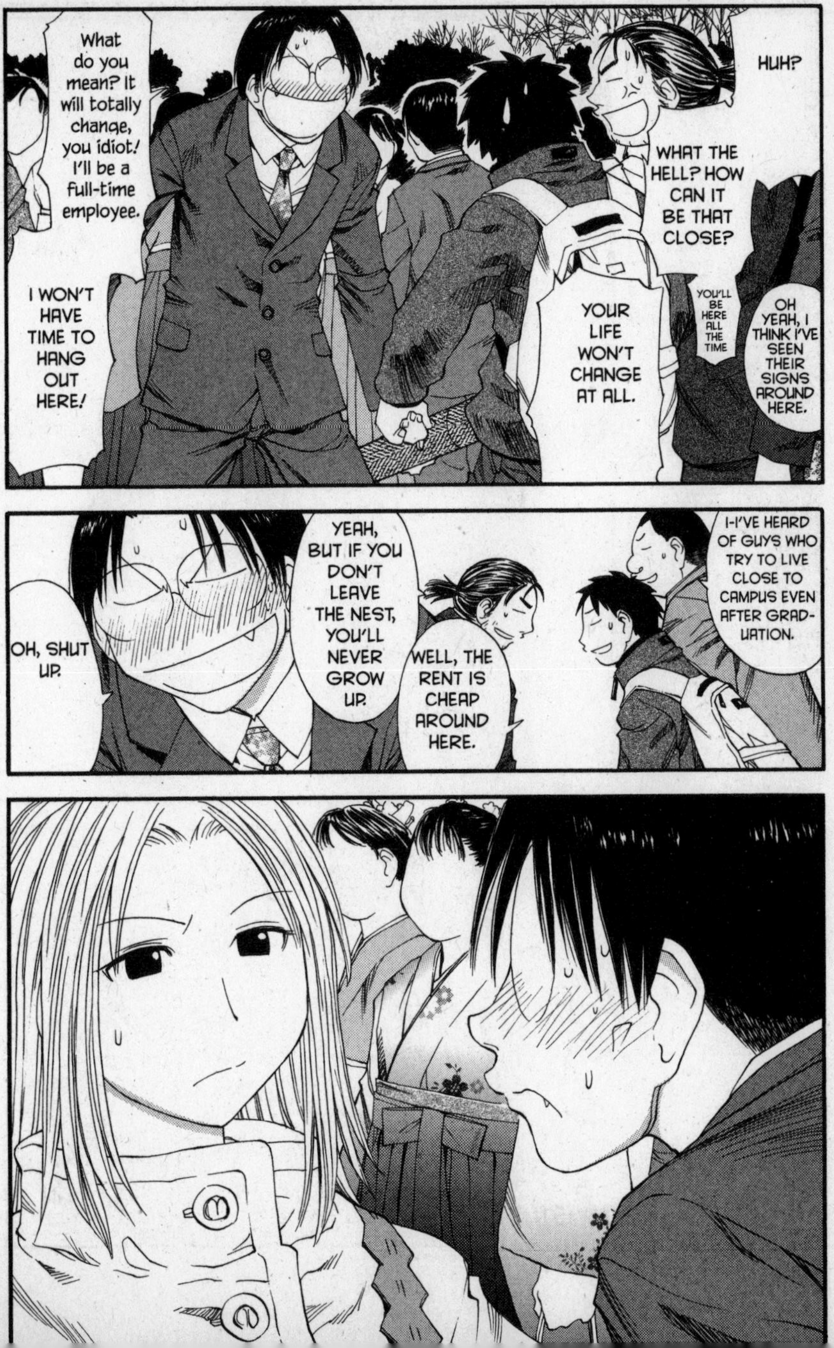
HUH?
WHAT THE HELL? HOW CAN IT BE THAT CLOSE?
OH YEAH, I THINK I'VE SEEN THEIR SIGNS AROUND HERE.
YOU'LL BE HERE ALL THE TIME
YOUR LIFE WON'T CHANGE AT ALL.
What do you mean? It will totally change, you idiot! I'll be a full-time employee.
I WON'T HAVE TIME TO HANG OUT HERE!
I-I'VE HEARD OF GUYS WHO TRY TO LIVE CLOSE TO CAMPUS EVEN AFTER GRAD-UATION.
WELL, THE RENT IS CHEAP AROUND HERE.
YEAH, BUT IF YOU DON'T LEAVE THE NEST, YOU'LL NEVER GROW UP.
OH, SHUT UP.

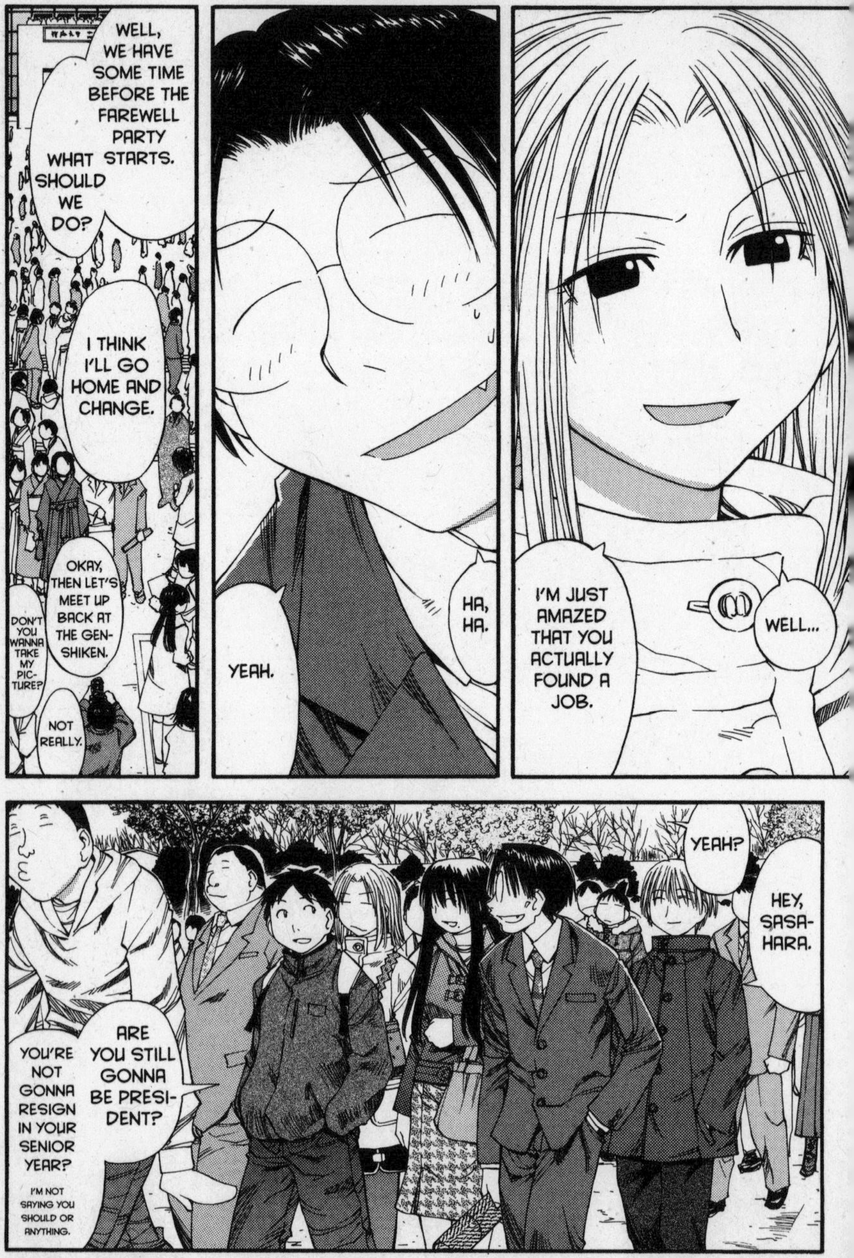
WELL...
I'M JUST AMAZED THAT YOU ACTUALLY FOUND A JOB.
HA, HA.
YEAH.
WELL, WE HAVE SOME TIME BEFORE THE FAREWELL PARTY STARTS.
WHAT SHOULD WE DO?
I THINK I'LL GO HOME AND CHANGE.
OKAY, THEN LET'S MEET UP BACK AT THE GEN-SHIKEN.
DON'T YOU WANNA TAKE MY PIC-TURE?
NOT REALLY.
HEY, SASA-HARA.
YEAH?
ARE YOU STILL GONNA BE PRESI-DENT?
YOU'RE NOT GONNA RESIGN IN YOUR SENIOR YEAR?
I'M NOT SAYING YOU SHOULD OR ANYTHING.

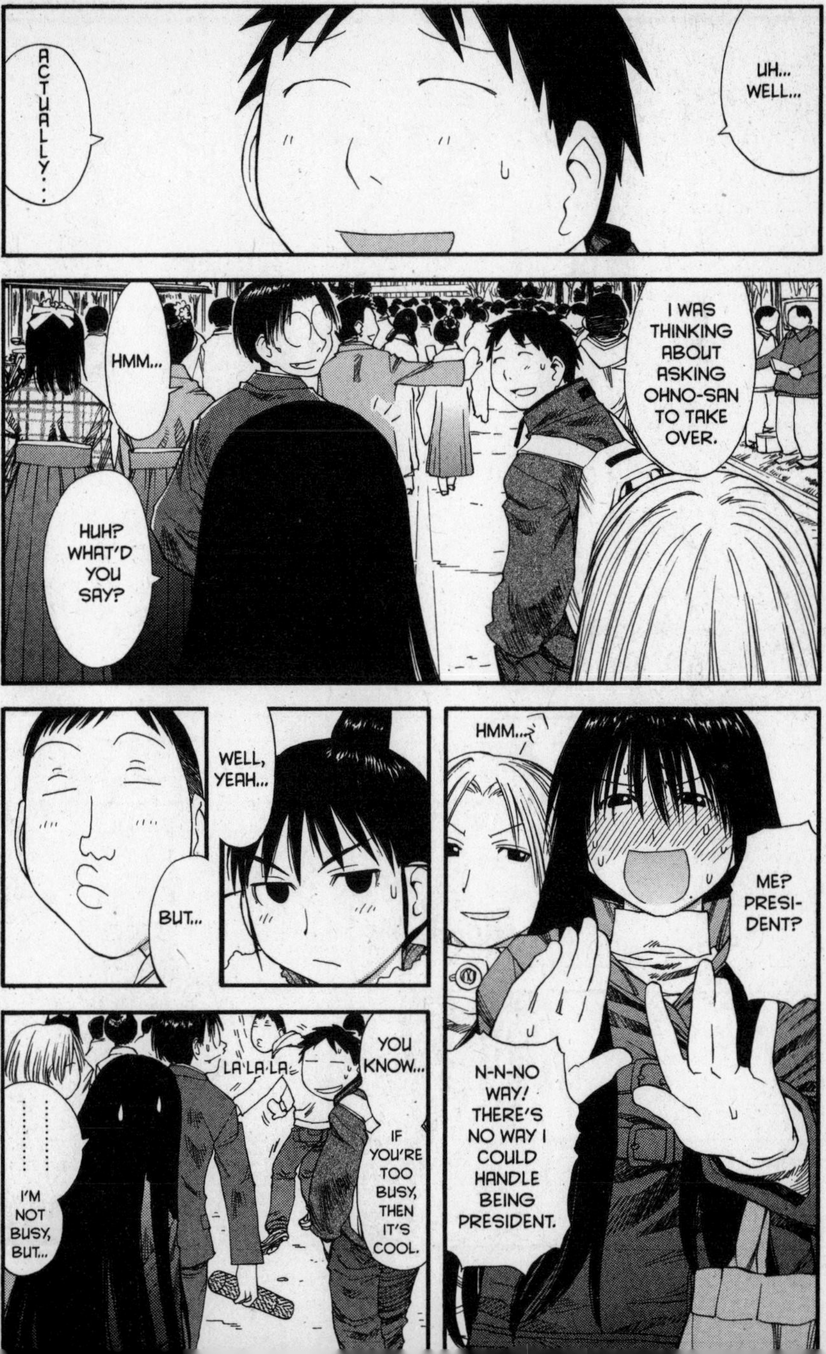
UH... WELL...
ACTUALLY...
I WAS THINKING ABOUT ASKING OHNO-SAN TO TAKE OVER.
HMM...
HUH? WHAT'D YOU SAY?
HMM...
ME? PRESIDENT?
N-N-NO WAY! THERE'S NO WAY I COULD HANDLE BEING PRESIDENT.
WELL, YEAH...
BUT...
YOU KNOW...
IF YOU'RE TOO BUSY, THEN IT'S COOL.
LA LA LA
......
I'M NOT BUSY, BUT...

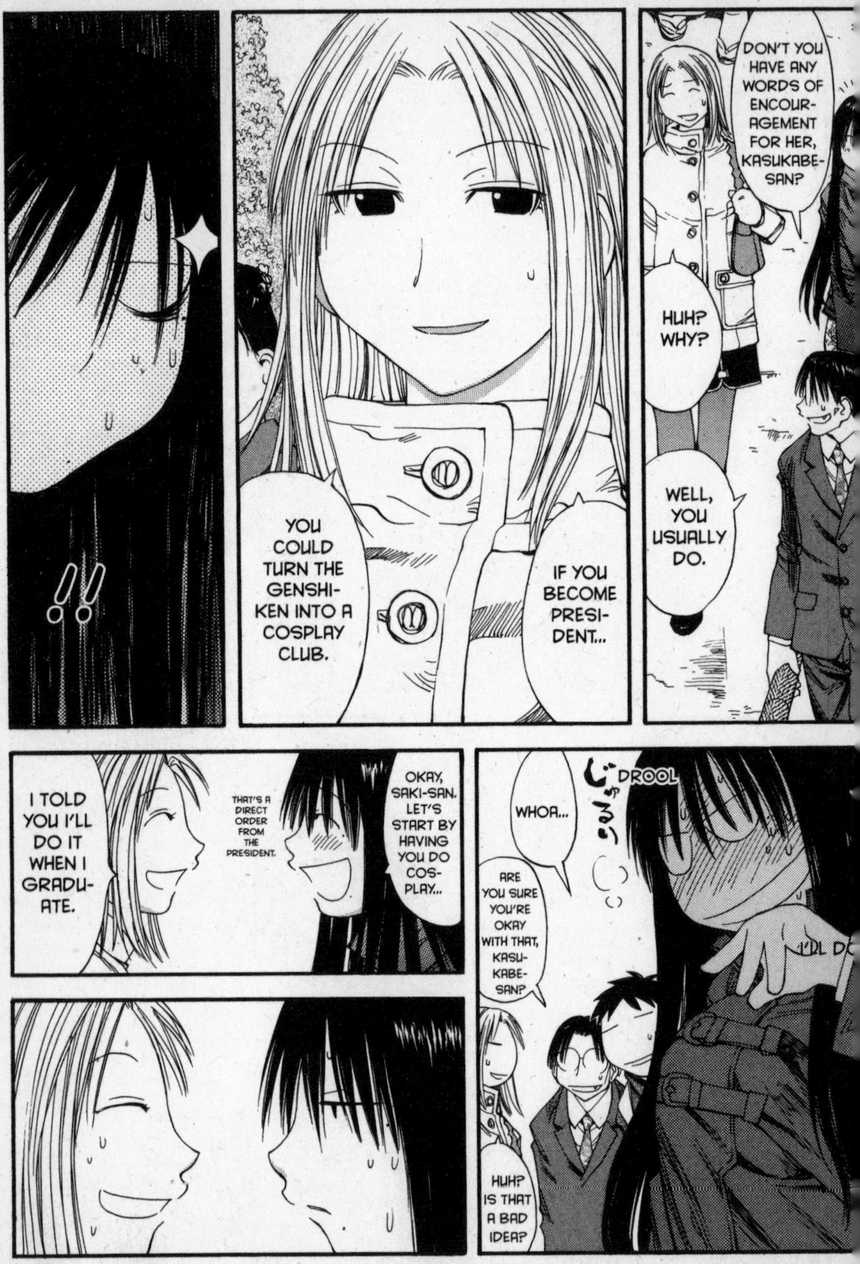
DON'T YOU HAVE ANY WORDS OF ENCOUR-AGEMENT FOR HER, KASUKABE-SAN?
HUH? WHY?
WELL, YOU USUALLY DO.
IF YOU BECOME PRESI-DENT...
YOU COULD TURN THE GENSHI-KEN INTO A COSPLAY CLUB.
!!
DROOL
I'LL DO
WHOA...
ARE YOU SURE YOU'RE OKAY WITH THAT, KASU-KABE-SAN?
HUH? IS THAT A BAD IDEA?
OKAY, SAKI-SAN. LET'S START BY HAVING YOU DO COS-PLAY...
THAT'S A DIRECT ORDER FROM THE PRESIDENT.
I TOLD YOU I'LL DO IT WHEN I GRADU-ATE.

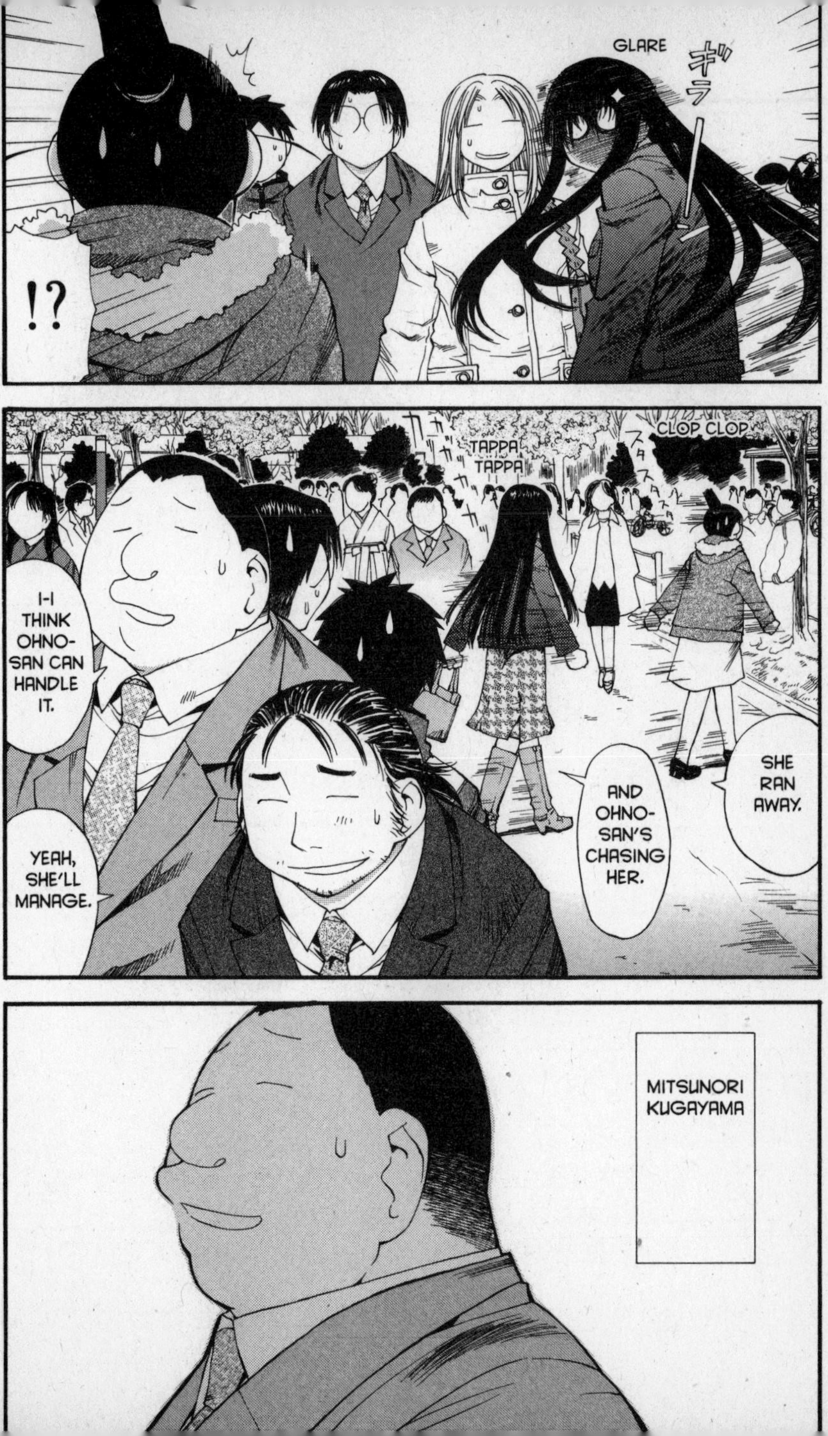
GLARE
ギラ
!?
CLOP CLOP
TAPPA TAPPA
SHE RAN AWAY.
AND OHNO-SAN'S CHASING HER.
I-I THINK OHNO-SAN CAN HANDLE IT.
YEAH, SHE'LL MANAGE.
MITSUNORI KUGAYAMA

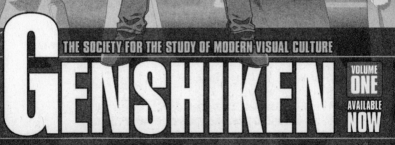

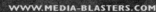

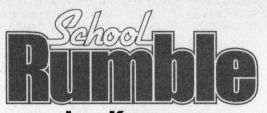
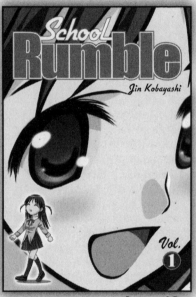

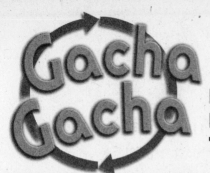

By Hiroyuki Tamakoshi

Kouhei is your typical Japanese high school student—he's usually late, he loves beef bowls, he pals around with his buddies, and he's got his first-ever crush on his childhood friend Kurara. Before he can express his feelings, however, Kurara heads off to Hawaii with her mother for summer vacation. When she returns, she seems like a totally different person . . . and that's because she is! While she was away, Kurara somehow developed an alternate personality: Arisa! And where Kurara has no time for boys, Arisa isn't interested in much else. Now Kouhei must help protect his friend's secret, and make sure that Arisa doesn't do anything Kurara would regret!

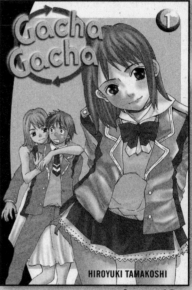

HIROYUKI TAMAKOSHI

Ages: 16+

Special extras in each volume! Read them all!

KAGETORA

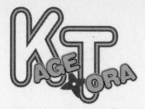

BY AKIRA SEGAMI

MISSION IMPOSSIBLE

The young ninja Kagetora has been given a great honor—to serve a renowned family of skilled martial artists. But on arrival, he's handed a challenging assignment: teach the heir to the dynasty, the charming but clumsy Yuki, the deft moves of self-defense and combat.

Yuki's inability to master the martial arts is not what makes this job so difficult for Kagetora. No, it is Yuki herself. Someday she will lead her family dojo, and for a ninja like Kagetora to fall in love with his master is a betrayal of his duty, the ultimate dishonor, and strictly forbidden. Can Kagetora help Yuki overcome her ungainly nature . . . or will he be overcome by his growing feelings?

1
KAGETORA
AKIRA SEGAMI

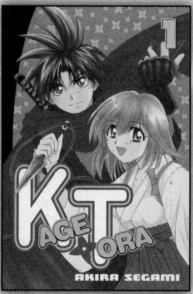

Ages: 13 +

Special extras in each volume! Read them all!

DEL REY

VISIT WWW.DELREYMANGA.COM TO:
- Read sample pages
- View release date calendars for upcoming volumes
- Sign up for Del Rey's free manga e-newsletter
- Find out the latest about new Del Rey Manga series

More Del Rey titles you will enjoy.

PAWN OF PROPHECY
by David Eddings
The Talisman keeping an evil god at bay has been
disturbed—and no one will be safe unless young Garion can
master the magic hidden within him.

TUNNEL IN THE SKY
by Robert A. Heinlein
For Rod Walker and his high school classmates, a simple test
has turned into a life-or-death nightmare.

HAVE SPACE SUIT—WILL TRAVEL
by Robert A. Heinlein
High school student Kip was willing to give up a lot to get
to the moon—but he never expected it to be his life!

ORPHAN STAR
by Alan Dean Foster
One man in the Universe holds the key to the mystery of
Flinx's past—and that man is trying to kill him!

Published by Del Rey
www.delreybooks.com
Available wherever books are sold.

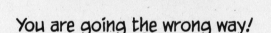

TOMARE!
[STOP!]

You are going the wrong way!

Manga is a completely different
type of reading experience.

To start at the *beginning,* go to the *end!*

That's right! Authentic manga is read the traditional Japanese
way—from right to left. Exactly the *opposite* of how American
books are read. It's easy to follow: Just go to the other end of
the book, and read each page—and each panel—from right side
to left side, starting at the top right. Now you're experiencing
manga as it was meant to be.

-kun: This suffix is used at the end of boys' names to express familiarity or endearment. It is also sometimes used by men among friends, or when addressing someone younger or of a lower station.

-chan: This is used to express endearment, mostly toward girls. It is also used for little boys, pets, and even among lovers. It gives a sense of childish cuteness.

Bozu: This is an informal way to refer to a boy, similar to the English term "kid" or "squirt."

Sempai: This title suggests that the addressee is one's senior in a group or organization. It is most often used in a school setting, where underclassmen refer to their upperclassmen as "sempai." It can also be used in the workplace, such as when a newer employee addresses an employee who has seniority in the company.

Kohai: This is the opposite of "sempai" and is used toward underclassmen in school or newcomers in the workplace. It connotes that the addressee is of a lower station.

Sensei: Literally meaning "one who has come before," this title is used for teachers, doctors, or masters of any profession or art.

[blank]: Usually forgotten in these lists, but perhaps the most significant difference between Japanese and English. The lack of honorific means that the speaker has permission to address the person in a very intimate way. Usually, only family, spouses, or very close friends have this kind of permission. Known as *yobisute,* it can be gratifying when someone who has earned the intimacy starts to call one by one's name without an honorific. But when that intimacy hasn't been earned, it can also be very insulting.

Honorifics

Throughout the Del Rey Manga books, you will find Japanese honorifics left intact in the translations. For those not familiar with how the Japanese use honorifics and, more importantly, how they differ from American honorifics, we present this brief overview.

Politeness has always been a critical facet of Japanese culture. Ever since the feudal era, when Japan was a highly stratified society, use of honorifics—which can be defined as polite speech that indicates relationship or status—has played an essential role in the Japanese language. When addressing someone in Japanese, an honorific usually takes the form of a suffix attached to one's name (example: "Asuna-san"), or as a title at the end of one's name or in place of the name itself (example: "Negi-sensei," or simply "Sensei!").

Honorifics can be expressions of respect or endearment. In the context of manga and anime, honorifics give insight into the nature of the relationship between characters. Many translations into English leave out these important honorifics, and therefore distort the "feel" of the original Japanese. Because Japanese honorifics contain nuances that English honorifics lack, it is our policy at Del Rey not to translate them. Here, instead, is a guide to some of the honorifics you may encounter in Del Rey Manga.

-san: This is the most common honorific and is equivalent to Mr., Miss, Ms., or Mrs. It is the all-purpose honorific and can be used in any situation where politeness is required.

-sama: This is one level higher than "-san" and is used to confer great respect.

-dono: This comes from the word "tono," which means "lord." It is an even higher level than "-sama" and confers utmost respect.

Genshiken, volume 5 is a work of fiction. Names, characters, places, and incidents are the products of the author's imagination or are used fictitiously. Any resemblance to actual events, locales, or persons, living or dead, is entirely coincidental.

A Del Rey Books Trade Paperback Original

Published in the United States by Del Rey Books, an imprint of The Random House Publishing Group, a division of Random House, Inc., New York.

Publication rights arranged through Kodansha Ltd.

First published in Japan in 2004 by Kodansha Ltd., Tokyo

Library of Congress Control Number: 2005922043

ISBN 0-345-49153-X

Printed in the United States of America

www.delreymanga.com

9 8 7 6 5 4 3 2 1

Translated and adapted by David Ury

Lettering—Michaelis/Carpelis Design Associates Inc.

GENSHIKEN

5

KIO SHIMOKU

TRANSLATED AND ADAPTED BY
David Ury

LETTERED BY
Michaelis/Carpelis Design

BALLANTINE BOOKS • NEW YORK